BIG
BROTHER

BIG BROTHER

THE SOVIET UNION AND SOVIET EUROPE

HÉLÈNE CARRÈRE D'ENCAUSSE

TRANSLATED BY GEORGE HOLOCH

HM

HOLMES & MEIER

New York   London

Published in the United States of America 1987 by
Holmes & Meier Publishers, Inc.
30 Irving Place
New York, NY 10003

Great Britain:
1–3 Winton Close
Letchworth, Hertfordshire SG61 1BA
England

The Afterword has been co-translated with Gavin Lewis

Originally published in French as *Le Grand frère*
copyright © Flammarion, 1983

Library of Congress Cataloging-in-Publication Data

Carrère d'Encausse, Hélène.
  Big Brother.

  Translation of : Le grand frère.
  Includes index.
  1. Europe, Eastern—Foreign relations—Soviet Union.
2. Soviet Union—Foreign relations—Europe, Eastern.
I. Title
DJK45.S65C3513 1987·   327.47   86-31885
ISBN 0-8419-1042-1
ISBN 0-8419-1043-X (pbk.)

This book has been printed on acid-free paper.

MANUFACTURED IN THE UNITED STATES OF AMERICA

In memory of Antonín Snejdárek
who believed in the "Prague Spring"

CONTENTS

PART THREE

THE EMPIRE OF THE JANISSARIES

NOTE TO THE READER

The Afterword, which assesses the present relations between Eastern Europe and the Soviet Union, has been written by the author for the English-language edition. This final chapter did not appear in the original French edition (Flammarion, 1983). In addition, the Bibliography has been substantially revised by the author.

INTRODUCTION

In 1871 the publication of a book entitled *Russia and Europe* caused a great stir in Russia. According to its author, Danilevski, the history of human societies was made up of successive periods of dominance by different "historic cultural types." After the periods of Roman and Germanic dominance, he foresaw the imminent approach of Slavic dominance. In the Slavic world, during the historic era of its dominance, the supreme ideal would be Slavism, which would prevail over all human aspirations: freedom, nationalist feelings, education, science, and so on. Slavism would give coherence and meaning to these diverse ideas. The Panslavism that was so brilliantly expounded in the book left one question open: What would be the best form of relations among the peoples of the Slavic world? Would that world be dominated by Russia? Or would it be a world in which all the peoples would be fraternal and equal?

The name of Danilevski has been almost entirely forgotten. But toward the end of our century his book has taken on a strangely prophetic cast. Two world wars and two series of revolutions have given birth to the Slavic dominance that he predicted, even though the idea that unifies that world is foreign to Danilevski's Slavism. The borders of the Slavic world are, however, practically the same as those described by the visionary. Europe is divided in two, cut by a visible line, punctuated by walls, barbed wire, and border posts, running from the Baltic to the Adriatic.

What is this communist Europe, now four decades old, but the modern variant, concealed by the trappings of Marxist ideology, of the dream of dominance of Nicholas I, the "policeman of Europe," or of the political and cultural dream of the disciples of Panslavism? Is it a Russian Empire more extensive than ever before or a fraternal community of an unprecedented variety?

To these questions, the answer of the USSR, the mainspring of this new Europe, is clear; it gives legitimacy to "Europe from the Baltic to the Adriatic." This is a revolutionary legitimacy, since the "European socialist system," following the Russian Revolution, is the second "forward step" of world revolution. This revolutionary Europe has assembled fraternal states held together by adhesion to a single ideology, communism. In this ideological and geographical space lies the reign of peace among men and nations. Beyond it lies the realm of conflict. Within is the kingdom of equality, beyond the kingdom of domination.

The history of the last thirty years has inflicted stinging refutations to these Soviet assertions. On a continent that, for the first time in its history, has known a durable peace, the principal conflicts that have divided nations and the only wars in which they have engaged have been located in the very communist Europe in which, by definition, harmony was supposed to reign. The USSR is or has been in conflict with all the states of the region, with the exception of Bulgaria. In this time of peace, its armies have invaded two fraternal countries, Hungary in 1956 and Czechoslovakia in 1968. For five years it has held a permanent threat of invasion over Poland.

Do these repeated conflicts mean that the USSR has resigned itself to being nothing but an empire whose stability is assured only by violence? And for that very reason, is it not in the short term condemned to the fate of all empires that succumb to the attacks of their subjects? Here, too, the Soviet response contradicts appearances. What is being built in Eastern Europe is not an oppressive empire going against the grain of history, they claim, but a new world whose unity and cohesion increase from one crisis to the next. And the crises are therefore only the final convulsions of a world of nations that has already been condemned.

Which is the true picture, the old empire, or the nascent fraternal world? The answer lies in any event at the heart of the new Europe, in the USSR. Because it is the mainspring of that Europe, its moving force and dominant power, we must begin our investigation with the USSR. What is of first importance are Soviet plans and actions to forge a unified space running from the Baltic to the Adriatic, to confront conflicts, and to impose the ideas and the instrumentalities by which this world is to be integrated. The intent of this book is to follow the USSR step by step in this European adventure of the last four decades. Of course, the countries within its sphere that have participated in the adventure are not absent from the book; but they are only secondary actors, submitting, with some outbursts of opposition, to a fate forged for them elsewhere and largely against their will. This deliberate choice to reconstruct history from the perspective of the USSR is perhaps open to question. But there is no point in denying that it is the thesis of the book. As Danilevski thought and as Marx, with his pathological Russophobia, feared, the USSR now dominates Europe, at least the Europe from the Baltic to the Adriatic. Hence, history is to be deciphered and enacted according to the pattern glimpsed by Danilevski, between the USSR and Europe.

PART ONE

THE EMPIRE: FROM THE BALTIC TO THE ADRIATIC

1

THE PRICE OF VICTORY

Every European statesman has had his own dream of Europe. For General de Gaulle, Europe stretched from the Atlantic to the Urals. The Europe that Stalin snatched from the war and from the men who had been his allies was quite different: "Europe from the Baltic to the Adriatic." Throughout its history as a continental power, Russia has dreamed of an opening to the sea and has battled to reach that goal. It was logical that a war finally allowed it to realize the dream and to define its place in Europe by a line running from one sea to another.

It was in fact the Second World War and a terrible cost—more than twenty million dead, countless casualties, immense destruction—that gave the USSR the power and the European position of which, like the empire of the czars, it had always dreamed. What imperial policy and revolutionary activism had failed to achieve was gained by war, even though Stalin had begun it badly. In 1939, the USSR was confined within the borders of the revolution, a smaller space than that occupied by the empire, and isolated from a Europe that looked on it with suspicion. The Soviet state seemed at the time sufficiently precarious for Hitler to imagine that he could seize its western lands and make it into a rump state definitively exiled from the European continent and turned toward an Asiatic fate that Russia had never wanted. The situation in 1945 was, of course, contrary to Hitler's plans. The USSR had penetrated to the heart of Europe, consolidated its position in the eastern part of the continent, and posed a constant threat to the West. The collective memory of western peoples attributes the division of Europe by Soviet power entirely to the Yalta Conference. For forty years the reigning myth has been that Europe was surrendered to Stalin by Churchill and Roosevelt during their meeting in the Crimean resort. This myth has served as an explanation for the trampled independence of the Eastern European countries, for Soviet domination over a large part of the continent, and for the

3

perpetuation of political systems rejected by populations that had not chosen them.

The real history of Soviet progression in Europe is, however, much more complex than this mythology of cynical division suggests. This reconstituted history allows us to grasp at their origins the causes of Soviet domination over neighboring countries and also the causes of the lasting progress of communism. This history is directly connected to the unfolding of world conflict, to the evolution of Stalin's ambitions, and to the conditions of the alliance against the Axis powers. In the mirror of the war, Yalta was only an episode, a brief act, while the substance of the play had already been enacted at other times and places.

The USSR in 1945

Before changing Europe and the world, the war changed the USSR; in the international realm first, the war caused it to move from the status of a very secondary state to that of a great power, deciding with its partners the future international order. The war also changed it more deeply, by offering to the world a new face that helped to confuse the picture, to modify the certainties of its interlocutors, which affected the future of Europe as a whole.

The first element of this change was Soviet military power, coming after the weaknesses of the beginning of the conflict. Stalin had wanted to keep his country out of the war until 1942, hoping to enter the conflict under conditions chosen by him, confronting a Germany weakened by its efforts on the western front, and at a moment when the negative consequences of the Soviet army purges of 1937–38 would have been rectified.[1] The rapidity of the collapse of the French front, English resistance, and Hitler's impatience to launch the conquest of Russian territory had defeated Stalin's waiting game and in a few days had brought about an unexpected military disaster. The momentary weakness of the USSR fostered both illusions in the West as to the precarious nature of the Soviet system and Stalin's fears about the hidden intentions of his new allies. Thus, he insisted from the outset and persistently that Anglo-American forces open a second front as soon as possible, partly to provide relief for his own troops, but also so that they might, as quickly as possible, reoccupy the lost territories and reestablish Soviet order there before it could be challenged and before anti-Soviet, or even anti-Russian movements could develop.[2] From early 1943, after the Soviet victory at Stalingrad, the course of events shifted decisively, and the military power of the USSR became the dominant element in negotiations, fears, and plans. After liberating Soviet territories, in 1944 the Red Army moved rapidly toward the west and the south. By the beginning of 1945, it had already occupied Bulgaria, Rumania, Poland, Hungary, and part of Yugoslavia, imposed surrender on Finland, and, advancing through Germany, was preparing to take Berlin. Greece appeared to be its next objective in southern Europe, and Great Britain grew alarmed. This apparently irresistible progress of the Red Army contrasted with a certain stagnation among the Allies after the liberation of France. Von Rundstedt's offensive in the Ardennes delayed their plans for a rapid crossing of the Rhine, and the United States had not yet finished with Japan. The USSR, so weak in June 1941, now seemed the most powerful state in the coalition. Its troops were camped over half of Europe and threatened the countries where they were not yet present, and this sudden power cast a new light on inter-Allied relations.

The victorious USSR also presented an unknown face to its allies. In the course of the conflict, the communist state appeared to have given way to a traditional state, attached to the common values of international society: patriotism and the historical tradition of national security. In fact, this mutation had begun to take place even before the war. In the mid-thirties, Stalin had introduced into Soviet ideology and institutions—which until then had rejected the notions of stability of territory and nation in the name of a revolutionary messianism projected toward the future—a stable, statist, national dimension.[3] The USSR seemed to be evolving from internationalism toward a more national vocation. The war precipitated this change. Because communism was not a unanimously accepted and mobilizing system of values, Stalin gradually pushed it into the background. He called on his compatriots to unite to defend the motherland in the name of the solidarity of blood and soil, and no longer that of class. To bring together the living, he invoked the names of the heroes who had made Russia over the centuries. The ideal of the Soviets of ties through work across borders gave way to the ties of a long history lived by men who had come from the same area, spoke the same language, and defended the same interests, the traditional ties of the motherland. The USSR had again become Russia. This change was accompanied by diverse nationalist expressions (Ukrainian, for example) in areas inhabited by non-Russian peoples, who were very numerous in the multi-ethnic Soviet state. But everywhere it was the nation, a community forged over centuries with no regard for social differences, which became Stalin's privileged interlocutor, while social classes—which divided the national community and formed transnational links—were forgotten.[4] We can better measure the evolution of the USSR if we remember that during the First World War Lenin preached defeat as the royal road to revolution and called on the solidarity of the workers of all the belligerent states against the will to defend the nation. If the First World War broke the Russian nation, the Second World War restored it. To consolidate this reborn nation, Stalin multiplied appeals to symbols. The churches—and first of all the Orthodox Church, which in Russia was identified with the nation and the state—were tolerated as early as 1941, after two decades of persecution; then, after Stalingrad, they were reincorporated within the framework of the social institutions granted official recognition in the USSR. All the heroes of the state or the army—from Alexander Nevsky to Suvorov—who had ensured the defense of Russian soil and the development of the empire, became so many emblems of this patriotic renewal and were made into predecessors of the later heroes of the revolution in the collective consciousness. The *Internationale*, whose rhythm and words had accompanied the revolutionary epic and the five-year plans, ceased to be the hymn of the USSR and was replaced by a song better adapted to the tasks of the nation, specific to the USSR and no longer to "the whole human race."

This shift from class to national solidarity, from the universal to the particular, was accentuated by two complementary decisions that reached beyond Soviet borders. These decisions shed light on Stalin's pattern of action as a whole. They were the dissolution of the Comintern and the revival of the idea of Slavic solidarity.

The Comintern, the world party of the revolution, created by Lenin in 1919 to "set the world ablaze with the Russian revolutionary flame," was dissolved on May 15, 1943.[5] The official reason for such a decision, according to the resolution, was that the Comintern had accomplished its historic task and should therefore withdraw in favor of communist parties capable of acting with complete independence. During the war years, when communist parties were often involved in anti-imperialist common fronts, such an insistence on their independence from a common authority in Moscow was no doubt desirable. Moreover, by deciding on the dissolution of the Comintern, the USSR was offering its allies the assurance of a new definition of its plans. From the moment that it no longer set itself up as leader of a world revolutionary movement, it suggested that the goal of that movement—world revolution—had disappeared, or at least had become more distant, and in any event no longer lay at the heart of its action. By placing the Comintern in the prop room of the revolution, the USSR sought to reassure its allies about its future intentions, and it offered them the image of a state like other states, one-dimensional, acting on the international scene with the traditional means of states, that is, power and diplomacy. This apparent abandonment of its revolutionary vocation by the USSR without any doubt bore fruit and partially convinced Stalin's Western allies that the mutation from a revolutionary state to one like the others was, if not complete, at least well under way. For a long time this decision fostered illusions about the nature of the USSR and its ambitions. (Was it an unprecedented system with an international logic, or a traditional political system concealed by remnants of revolutionary phraseology?) Beyond the respectability as a state that the abandonment of the Comintern conferred on it, the USSR revealed through this decision a new perception of the revolution and of its interests. In justifying the dissolution of the world party of the revolution in terms of the "accomplishment of its historic task," Stalin was in fact paying tribute to no accomplishments. In its twenty-four years of existence, the Comintern was noteworthy for its ineptitude in accomplishing its historic task. Throughout its existence, no revolution took place under its aegis. What Stalin, with unquestionable humor, called accomplishment was in reality nonaccomplishment and uselessness. Lenin had created the Comintern to make revolutions. He, and Stalin after him, had later used it to protect the USSR from external threats by mobilizing around it the communist parties of the world whose principal task was no longer to make revolutions but to defend the motherland of the revolution.[6] In 1943, when its rise to power had become patent, the USSR, until then identified with world revolution, decided that it was imperative to make the revolution in other countries, not merely to contribute to it. It also decided that power was a much better protection than the revolutionary illusion.

In this respect, the dissolution of the Comintern was indeed the outcome, if not of the revolutionary movement, at least of institutional and ideological revolution in the Soviet Union. The USSR wished to be an all-powerful state, deriving from its power and from that alone its security and the means to assure the progress of revolution in the world. From besieged citadel and citadel of revolutions, the USSR was being rapidly transformed into the center of a projected socialist camp and the mother of revolutions. The May 15, 1943, decision, which suggested a definitive retreat by the USSR to within its own borders, in fact signified a more dynamic opening to the external world because it was based on a real and growing phenomenon, power.

The momentary resurrection of the Panslavic idea is another aspect of Soviet evolution during the war years that though little known should not be underestimated. Panslavism, an idea that had mobilized prestigious Russian intellectuals in the nineteenth century, had disappeared in the First World War. The isolation of the USSR in the years following the revolution and the Europe of nations shaped by the Treaty of Versailles were hardly propitious for the development of tendencies toward the cultural and political unification of the Slavs. Broken by one war, it is not surprising that the idea resurfaced in the course of another.[7] Stalin, who had encouraged studies of the Slavic world as early as 1939, understood in 1941 the usefulness of the Slavophile theses. The conception of the Slavic world that he had encouraged in 1939 was that of a universe of states, connected through their cultures and attracted by a powerful magnet, Russia. In his perception of the history of Slavic Europe, Slavism and Russian influence were indistinguishable.[8] It is consequently not surprising that during the war he used the Panslavic idea to group around a revived Russia the Slavic peoples engaged in the same struggle for their national survival. The establishment and development of the Slavophile movement corresponded to the necessities of the war; the movement was one of Stalin's political weapons at the time.

The movement took the form of a Panslavic Committee organized by the Central Committee of the Communist Party of the USSR, which maintained constant control over the institution.[9] The committee was created in August 1941 at the First Panslavic Conference, which met in Moscow and brought together many representatives of the Slavic peoples who were then present in the Soviet capital. This conference, which met while the USSR was experiencing a military disaster without precedent since the Napoleonic Wars, while the German armies were in the process of taking Kiev and preparing to launch an offensive against Moscow, was unquestionably a reflection of the panic of the moment. But it is remarkable that in this nearly desperate situation when German victory seemed unavoidable, an entire structure organizing the solidarity of the Slavs and propagating that idea was put in place. The Panslavic Committee established a journal, *Slaviani* (The Slavs), and prepared future conferences. In April 1942 the movement held a second conference and then a third, the last of this kind, in May 1943. Panslavic meetings were organized for the army during the same period. In addition to the conferences, which were widely publicized, the committee organized its own plenary sessions in which it developed a Slavophile strategy that would be widely propagated by the two large conferences of the movement. This strategy was limited to developing the solidarity of the Slavs around themes that varied in the course of the two years in which the movement was active. Through these activities of the Panslavic movement, we can see a clarification of the ideas of the USSR about its future role in Eastern Europe. Panslavism throws a useful light on inter-Allied conferences during the war years because it helps to explain the turnings of Stalin's thought and strategy. In 1941, at the moment of greatest danger, it was simply a matter of calling on the patriotism of all Slavs, of emphasizing what united the Slavic peoples, and of bringing them closer to the USSR. Because the governments in exile were not communist and the USSR did not want to alarm either its allies or the national authorities that had taken refuge in London, and because it sought to build bridges between those exiles and the communists of Eastern Europe who had taken refuge in the USSR, Panslavism was infinitely preferable to communist theses. It replaced them with an appeal to a feeling of belonging to a common universe acceptable to all—Western democracies, Slavic democracies, but also communists. The silence imposed on the Comintern also suggests that the USSR felt the necessity of finding another framework for defining regional solidarities and centralizing resistance movements. The themes developed in 1941 at the Moscow conference were thus all oriented around patriotism and common Slavic feeling. The word most frequently used by the movement to define what was common to all was *Slavianstvo*, the Slavic world, which became the framework within which all particular patriotisms were to develop. Old Russia, the greatest of the states of this *Slavianstvo*, was by definition the rallying point, the one that was capable of helping the others in their struggle, the one that could negotiate the future status of the Slavic universe. Two ideas stood out from this very simple program. One was the central, protective position of the USSR in this cultural community; the USSR (identified with Russia) thus became the older brother of the Slavic peoples, as Russia was tending again to become the older brother of the peoples of the USSR. The second idea, linked to the historical Slavophile movement, was a certain anti-Western orientation that had always been a part of Panslavism. Implicit in 1941, these orientations later took on great importance.

The Second Panslavic Conference gradually gave more precision to the contours of the future Slavic world and not only to the framework of the common struggle. In 1941 the movement had refrained from discussing international politics or the organization of society; the call for national struggle dominated all debates. In 1942, things were quite different. The conference first of all set out the permanent international framework of the life of the Slavic peoples. As a cultural community, the Panslavic world was integrated into the great wartime alliance and was mobilized around the older brother. Thus, the USSR acquired a kind of legitimacy to bring the fraternal Slavic peoples together in the struggle and to represent them in international life and in negotiations for the future. The postwar world—with Eastern Europe dominated by the USSR—was outlined in this Slavophile vision at a time when the USSR was still extremely weak and the Allies had not yet begun to negotiate about the Europe of the future. In the Panslavic meetings of 1943, the conceptions of internal political order also became clearer, since the movement emphasized the virtues of the national front and the virtues of a nationalism that was pro-Soviet because it was Panslavic (and only that kind of nationalism); finally, the conference offered the proposals of the Czech leaders (who were very Russophile) as a model for the whole Slavic world.

Even before all these problems were discussed with the Western Allies, Stalin had used the Slavic movement to gather around the USSR the Eastern European states or their provisional authorities to elaborate a few common principles that already sketched out the broad outlines of future choices. Russia was placed at the center of the constellation of Slavic nations, a constellation of equals, a fraternal constellation, one that it protected and dominated by means of its status of *primus inter pares*. The Slavic family was organized both within this common framework and on the basis of bilateral relations between Slavs, excluding partial groupings that would dislocate the community, that is, the small federations favored by the West, like the Balkan federation. From 1944 on, when victory was clear and when he negotiated about the political organization of certain neighboring states, Stalin let the Panslavic idea fall by the wayside. It had served well enough, but the time for more precise plans had come. Nevertheless, Panslavism went through some further developments in the Eastern European states, where it sometimes served to legitimate the establishment of privileged ties with the USSR. But it was no longer anything but an attenuated and local movement. Elsewhere, it had performed a useful function by welding together, if only momentarily, a community of peoples linked by culture and a danger experienced in common and by suggesting that Eastern Europe is a coherent territory whose history and particularity have followed a specific path, foreign to the rest of the continent.

Stalin's Ambitions: Security and Influence

In Bolshevik political thought, war holds a central place; it generates change. This does not imply that Bolsheviks tend to unleash wars but rather that they consider wars as privileged moments for the progress of their cause. This was Lenin's conviction and he relied on the defeat of his country to bring about the collapse of the czarist regime.[10] And this was Stalin's practice from 1938 on. The German-Soviet pact of August 1939 and the war in the west allowed Stalin for the first time to express his international ambitions. Rejecting the German suggestion to concentrate on the Middle East, Stalin used this period to enlarge the territory of the USSR at the expense of Poland, the Baltic countries, Finland, Bessarabia, and Bukovina. To justify these territorial acquisitions, Stalin invoked various arguments, but they were all based on national interest, which was rediscovered by the USSR in the thirties. Historical arguments were made to support the invasion of the Baltic states and the annexation of a Finnish province. What had been part of the empire ought to return to the USSR, although Stalin stage-managed a stimulacrum of a revolutionary movement in the Baltic states. Ethnic arguments were made when it was a matter of attaching territories populated by Ukrainians to the Ukraine. And there were finally, ubiquitously, arguments based on security.

When the second phase of the war began after June 22, 1941, Stalin, stricken by the disasters of the moment, articulated few demands in negotiations with his new allies. Nevertheless, on certain points he was already clear about his objectives. During his first meeting with Anthony Eden on December 15, 1941, he attempted to obtain from his interlocutor recognition of the Soviet borders of 1941, that is, of the annexations that had recently been carried out.[11]

With respect to Germany, Stalin then suggested that East Prussia should be attached to Poland. Even though his ideas at the time had very little effect because of the desperate position of the USSR and because of British firmness, it is clear that Stalin's views on the territorial future of Poland and

Germany were already established and would remain unchanged. After Stalingrad, Stalin had much more room to expound his views and to counter those of his interlocutors. From that moment in 1943 on, inter-Allied negotiations, which had until then been concentrated on the organization of military cooperation, became more clearly political, directed as well toward the discussion of postwar problems. And in these meetings—the conferences of Teheran (1943), Yalta (1945), Potsdam (1945), and the conferences of foreign ministers in 1943—the respective positions of the Allies considerably changed. The USSR, strengthened by its victory at Stalingrad and the consequent certainty of German retreat, and strengthened as well by the delays of the Anglo-American forces in opening a second front in Western Europe to relieve it, became distinctly more demanding, while its allies, on the defensive, had to justify both their strategic hesitations and their choice of North Africa for the first landing, which the USSR considered hardly helpful.[12]

The conference of foreign ministers held in Moscow from October 18 to 30, 1943, gave the Soviet representative, Molotov, the opportunity to indicate more clearly certain preferences of the USSR for the future organization of Eastern Europe.[13] The Allies were then concerned with the region [i.e., Eastern Europe] in which Soviet troops were about to become engaged. Still absent from the continent—the question of the second front was still on the table—the English and Americans feared that the advance of Soviet troops in the region would in the long run bring about the division of Europe into zones of influence, with a large zone dominated by the USSR. To ward off this danger, they attempted to get Soviet agreement to a four-power declaration on war aims and on an international organization. In this connection, the essential point in the declaration was the clause on the renunciation of the use of armed force on the territory of another state. Molotov firmly rejected it and his attitude has to be understood in the perspective of future Soviet actions in Eastern Europe. In effect, he declared that the USSR could not subject its decisions in this region that was central to its security to the agreement of its allies. What Molotov was clearly asserting was that the USSR had too many responsibilities and interests in Eastern Europe to accept international limitations on their exercise. In the same way, he opposed the British proposal to urge the states of Central and Eastern Europe to establish a federation to assure their survival. This plan tended to protect a Balkanized Europe from the weight of the USSR, which had been strengthened by its military successes, and to prevent Soviet troops from changing their liberating activity into authoritarian protection. Here, too, Molotov was extremely firm in his hostility to a proposal that, in his view, uselessly prejudged the future. Hostile to any plan for a federation, to any change in the regional balance, Molotov offered in exchange his personal guarantee that the USSR had no intention of consolidating a divided Europe or of imposing zones of influence.

And he suggested in conclusion that the future of these countries should be discussed at the summit, during the conference of heads of state scheduled to meet shortly in Teheran.

On the eve of the Teheran conference, the dialogue between the Soviets and the West was already thoroughly ambiguous and weighted with the misunderstandings that would characterize the future. Suspicious of his partners, convinced that after the war they intended to reestablish the *cordon sanitaire* that had isolated his country between the wars, Stalin negotiated by constantly adopting two contradictory attitudes. He moved without interruption from vehement reproaches to a conciliatory attitude that bewildered the representatives of the West.[14] The latter were attempting above all to protect the existing alliance; for the future, they believed in the virtue of great principles like the right of peoples to self-determination, and they believed in international institutions. This explains their insistence on getting Soviet agreement for the establishment of the United Nations, which would become, they hoped, a privileged setting for the pursuit of cooperation between East and West. This forced agreement sowed the seeds of future disillusionment. The Western allies hung on the good words lavished on them by the Soviets and on their agreements in principle, while Stalin was gradually setting out the boundaries of a Europe that corresponded to his wishes. As long as he was weak, he was more inclined to emphasize the links to his partners than his ambitions. And his partners concluded that their arguments had succeeded or that Soviet ambitions were limited.

The Teheran conference, held from November 28 to December 1, 1943, was the first meeting of the three leaders of the alliance, Churchill, Roosevelt, and Stalin. At that moment, the outcome of the war was becoming clear and the political and military position of the USSR was constantly growing stronger. The Red Army, engaged in a counteroffensive that had stalled for a while outside Kiev, was already on the point of advancing into Eastern Europe, while the Allies, despite a series of successes in North Africa and Italy, were still debating about a landing that would not take place until June 1944. It is therefore easy to see how Stalin could be more precise about some of his intentions, asserting without constraint his wish to see Germany permanently divided and to maintain the territories conquered before June 22, 1941, under Soviet control. Similarly, he did not conceal his interest in East Prussia[15] and the Finnish territories near Leningrad.[16] But when it came to Poland, although he raised the question of borders, he still remained very prudent about details and answered Churchill's request for more precise views with the statement that it was better to wait for the end of the war before debating the question.[17]

The militarily unequal conditions under which the three leaders arrived in Teheran were further aggravated by their differences in temperament and the misunderstandings that developed. After a period of disarray caused by the early military failures of the USSR, Stalin had been reassured by his successes. His authority within the country had been restored. The revolutionary leader had strengthened his legitimacy with historical support since he relied on the spirit of 1917, of course, but especially on the long line of defenders of Russian soil whose portraits in his office surrounded the gallery of communist ancestors. This ideological modification, this broadening of the basis for the legitimation of Soviet power, were accompanied by visible symbols that were far from negligible in the evolution of relations between Stalin and his allies. In the course of the war, Stalin's costume changed. He replaced the simple pea coat he had long been attached to with a military costume befitting his title of supreme commander. This vestimentary transformation, combined with an environment in which historical Russia had taken on new prominence, helps to explain why Stalin's interlocutors judged him more on his national appearance than on his communist background and took more account of or implicitly accepted his demands. Stalin, in fact, as his Western counterparts, Churchill, and later de Gaulle, testified, was able to present to them a relatively charming exterior. He was armed with deliberate simplicity and peasant cunning and he knew how to alternate between insistence on his demands and appearing to give in gracefully to others' arguments. His outbursts of anger, which sometimes came close to being insulting, only served to set off his conciliatory moments.[18] Churchill, who had experienced Stalin's mood swings during his Moscow visit in 1941, concluded from his relative familiarity with the Soviet leader that he had to deal with a head of state who was deeply attached to his national interests, a hard man no doubt, but one whose ambitions were located within a known framework, the classic concern to extend his influence.[19] In other words, he saw in Stalin's demands a variant of traditional Russian ambitions, inspired by the combined impulses toward power and security; and he thought for that very reason that it was possible to negotiate with Stalin by remaining aware of these known elements and by discussing spheres of influence. Stalin's ability to charm, more or less, his interlocutors, to conceal his brutality behind symbolic gestures and reasonable ambitions, deceived Roosevelt even more.[20] It is important to understand clearly Roosevelt's conception of the USSR at the moment when he was about to meet Stalin for the first time in Teheran.

In fact for the United States and not only for Roosevelt, the USSR had long been a distant world, indeed a *terra incognita*.[21] The German invasion of the USSR on June 22, 1941, was to reverse this ignorance and the distance that derived from it and to give birth to considerable interest in the United States about the Soviet Union, while American leaders remained uncertain whether it really should be considered different from other countries. No doubt, George Kennan, who was then a young diplomat but already a respected specialist on the USSR, warned Roosevelt in June 1941 against the temptation of considering the USSR as a possible ally for democratic countries; he pointed out that, to an even greater degree than was true for Germany, it was hated and feared by its neighbors.[22] Roosevelt was nevertheless more receptive to the views of those who advised him to deal with Moscow, to "find a way to work *with* rather than *against* the Russians."[23] This relative confidence in the possibility of having a common policy with the USSR had been strengthened by the indirect contacts he had had with Stalin at the time when the latter's difficulties had made him more receptive to his partners' arguments. During the initial phase of the German-Soviet conflict, Roosevelt had sent Harry Hopkins to Stalin to negotiate the lend-lease agreements. Hopkins's impression could only comfort Roosevelt, when he wrote: "The caviar and smoked salmon were almost excessive. I wouldn't call Uncle Joe a friendly man, although he is rather interesting; I think I've got what I wanted."[24] "Uncle Joe" was in the end the image that Roosevelt took back from Teheran. This familiar and reassuring expression was further developed after the meeting. Roosevelt, in fact, gradually became convinced that Stalin was after all a political man, who like all other political men had to fight against colleagues determined to limit his power and had to listen to his constituents. From this came his conviction that dialogue between them was possible and that they shared a common language because common concerns united them.

Against Roosevelt's rather naive perception of the USSR and its leader, we should set Soviet lucidity about divisions in the Western camp which they could use. In 1942, Molotov had negotiated with Churchill, and then with Roosevelt, about the problems of the 1941 borders and the second front. From these contacts, he had learned of the profound differences of views about the postwar world dividing the two allies. At this early stage, he had understood that American hostility to colonialism and Roosevelt's desire for rapid decolonization after the war included the British colonies, while Britain's primary concern was precisely to preserve its empire.[25] On the theme of anticolonialism, the USSR could thus share a common language with Roosevelt, and this helped to conceal Stalin's territorial ambitions from the American leader. Roosevelt's conviction that the postwar order would depend on the Atlantic Charter, that is, on the right of peoples to choose their own political systems and to decide on territorial changes that affected them, was strengthened by Soviet adhesion, reticent but nonetheless given, to the charter.[26] Roosevelt's illusions, his confidence in the possibility of establishing relations with the USSR on the basis of certain common views, however ambiguous, explain his attitude in Teheran. He devoted most of his attention to negotiating with Stalin about the organization of the postwar world. In this connection Stalin demonstrated great cleverness, at first challenging Roosevelt's ideas,[27] then announcing that he accepted the American point of view.[28]

Confronted with what he considered a resounding demonstration of Stalin's good will, Roosevelt was all the more inclined to avoid involvement in discussions about an area that was essential for Stalin, Poland. Roosevelt was in a bad position to discuss this issue. His trouble had a domestic cause. American elections were approaching, and Roosevelt was anxious to avoid antagonizing the significant Polish sector of the electorate in the United States.[29] This explains his wish to give Churchill the responsibility for discussing the question, which had become urgent by the end of 1943.

In fact, for the first time since 1941, Stalin in Teheran clearly revealed his country's ambitions, even though he still refrained from expressing all the details. But his wishes concerning the Polish borders were perfectly clear. He was asking for recognition of the Curzon Line,[30] for which Poland would receive compensation in the West by other concessions from German territory. Although agreement was nearly reached on the Soviet-Polish border, ambiguity remained about the rest. Even at that point, Stalin was still discreet about Soviet intentions toward the territories liberated by the Red Army, notably toward their political future. On various occasions, he emphasized that the natural borders of the USSR were those that established its security, as history, he added, had often demonstrated. Thus in late 1943 Stalin's position seemed to be much more modest than his later demands. He spoke only of a limited reorganization of neighboring territories, he was determined to preserve what had been gained in 1941, and he justified everything in terms of national security. Because the USSR had experienced considerable losses and its allies had delayed drawing German forces away from the Russian front, and because English and Soviet notions about the importance of military operations in the Mediterranean were totally opposed to one another, Stalin was in a good position to defend his concern to assure secure borders for his country. He found in Roosevelt a distracted, and therefore conciliatory listener; in Churchill an embarrassed, and therefore also conciliatory listener.

The debate in Teheran over the future of Poland was shrouded in ambiguity. The question appeared to be less one of Poland than one of a border problem affecting Soviet security. At the conclusion of the Teheran conference, it might have been thought that because Stalin had demanded little, his ambitions were limited and that nothing in the future was fixed. However, the fate of Poland had already been almost sealed.

Discreet in his "summit" talks with the Allies, Stalin nevertheless showed immediately after the Teheran meeting that his views about the future of Eastern Europe went far beyond the limited framework of border problems. On December 12, 1943, a Soviet-Czech treaty of friendship and alliance was signed in Moscow. President Beneš, head of the Czech government-in-exile in London, who had been warned by the British government about such an agreement, went to Moscow in person for the negotiations. The Teheran conference showed the Czechs and other Eastern European leaders that the USSR was in a position of power in that part of the continent. And President Beneš considered it wise to turn toward the USSR before Soviet troops entered Czech territory in order to be able to negotiate later with the USSR about the fate of his country. Here too, as in the case of Poland, but this time without consulting his allies, Stalin was concerned with borders.[31] He informed Beneš of the Soviet wish to "rectify" the northeastern border of Czechoslovakia, which later resulted in Soviet annexation of the sub-Carpathian Ukraine. In exchange, the USSR recognized Czech borders before Munich, that is, on its own it "restored" Teschen and the Sudetenland to Czechoslovakia, showing little concern for future allied negotiations. But, beyond territorial problems, the discussion also focused on the future political organization of Czechoslovakia. President Beneš had to accept the idea of admitting Communist ministers into the government that would be established after the liberation. This treaty, which already integrated Czechoslovakia into a Soviet zone of influence—though it was still nonexistent and something Stalin had not negotiated with his allies—placed before the Allies a dual *fait accompli*. It put an end to the plan that Anthony Eden had attempted to promote at the 1942 Moscow conference of a federation of Eastern European states, in which the two countries of Poland and Czechoslovakia would have been an essential pillar.[32] This plan, which would have strengthened the independence of the two states, was devoid of meaning from the moment that the USSR had turned Czechoslovakia in its direction. Moreover, the Soviet-Czech treaty informed the West that the USSR had taken on itself particular responsibility—territorial but also political—for the organization of this part of Europe. While in negotiations with the Allies, Stalin had constantly reiterated his concern not to become prematurely involved in postwar matters, in Eastern Europe he was outlining, during the war and unilaterally, the essential features of the Europe of the future. And although in his dialogue with the Allies, Stalin referred to his ambitions only in terms of security, as soon as he took the initiative, as in Czechoslovakia, he thought and acted in terms of spheres of influence.

Thus, by the end of 1943, while Soviet troops had not yet undertaken their triumphal march through Eastern Europe, the dual character of Stalin's policies was becoming clear: the policy of a great power negotiating with its allies; the policy of influence and expansion of a major communist state imposing its will on them. The future of Eastern Europe was already taking shape at that moment, even if the alliance was not shaken by that fact. Similarly, the future of Poland had already been sketched out; the foundations were established by the Teheran conference, insufficiently recognized at the time, but difficult to change thereafter.

The Polish "Ghost"

"Poland, like Banquo's ghost, hovered over all succeeding summit meetings, and it increasingly poisoned the political and diplomatic atmosphere of the grand alliance," according to Adam Ulam in his history of Soviet foreign policy.[33] This remark provides a good summary of the substance of allied relations after the Teheran conference. Poland was in fact at the heart of Stalin's concern; moreover, Poland was a constant element of regret and greed in Soviet foreign policy.[34] Relations between these historically linked neighbors were dominated by two problems during the war years: the border, which referred to two opposed conceptions of Polish territory; and the future government of Poland, which the Allies for a while reduced to the more immediate and visible problem of bad relations between the Soviet and Polish governments, thereby underestimating the seriousness and breadth of Stalin's plans.

Having escaped from the Russian empire thanks to Russian defeats in the First World War and thanks to the revolution, Poland had always seen its independence challenged by the USSR. Lenin along with Bukharin thought that the right of the Polish bourgeoisie to have an independent state was highly dependent on circumstances. The Soviet attitude toward Poland between the wars was always made up of a mixture of nostalgia for the failed revolutions of 1920, of rancor against Polish anti-Sovietism, and of a growing certainty that historical rights and revolutionary necessities combined to "correct" the independence that Poland had obtained in 1917. This is why the secret protocol of the 1939 Nazi-Soviet treaty provided that the Soviet sphere of influence would encompass Polish territory.[35]

The entry of Soviet troops into Poland on September 17, 1939, in conformity with the secret protocol, led to a delimitation of the Soviet and German occupation zones, which was confirmed in a convention signed by the two states on September 28, 1939. From 1941 on, this border was constantly claimed by Stalin as the prewar border.

However, the debate on the border remained obscure until the Yalta conference because of the complexity of the subject and the confusion in the minds of the negotiators, with the exception of Stalin. In fact, while Stalin held firmly to the demand of Allied recognition of what he had gotten from Hitler, Churchill was willing to accept at most a return to the border negotiated in 1920 after the war at the Soviet-Polish conference, known as the Curzon Line. But because of a transmission error, the Curzon Line that had been definitively established followed a different path from the one that had been negotiated by Lloyd George and Polish Prime Minister Grabski. This mistake left Lvov on the Soviet side, while it was supposed to be located on the Polish side.[36] This negligence had had few concrete effects in 1920, because the Soviet-Polish border finally adopted by the Treaty of Riga was located east of the Curzon Line and was thus much more favorable to Poland. But at the time of the Teheran and Yalta negotiations, Stalin played with these ambiguities, and each of his interlocutors referred to different borders. Roosevelt, barely familiar with the map of Europe and the subtleties of past negotiations, had accepted, at least according to Stalin and Molotov, the idea of setting the border at the Curzon Line, without specifying which of the two lines he had finally settled on.[37] The complexity of the problem led to a decision at Teheran to leave uncertain a precise definition of Poland's eastern border; but at the same time, to calm Stalin's impatience, Churchill suggested the broad outlines of compensation that would be granted to Poland at Germany's expense.

On January 11, 1944, the USSR published an official communiqué specifying that the Curzon Line would indeed be its western border; but the definition given to this Curzon Line simply corresponded to the border established by the Nazi-Soviet pact of 1939.[38] There was thus agreement on terminology and disagreement on fundamentals. What could the Allies do? The landing was not yet on the agenda, Soviet sacrifices were obvious, and Churchill had no choice but to accept Stalin's ultimatum and to make the Polish government-in-exile swallow it. It was in fact important that Churchill secure a declaration of good will from the head of the Polish government, Mikolajczyk, the successor to General Sikorski who had died in an airplane accident in July 1943. In fact, the border question was already connected with a sharp conflict over the Polish government. Churchill wanted, at any price, to avoid having Stalin use the pretext of Mikolajczyk's hostility toward him to assert that he could not deal with Mikolajczyk and the Polish government in London on any question.

Soviet hostility to the Polish government-in-exile, created in November 1939 in France and transferred to London in 1940, went back to its beginnings, when it was recognized by all the Western powers. As an ally of Germany, the USSR obviously had no diplomatic relations with the Polish government. In 1941, with the reversal of alliances, this situation became intolerable and Britain attempted to normalize relations between the Sikorski government and the USSR. From this moment on—negotiations began on July 5, 1941—it was clear that Polish-Soviet hostility would remain a constant stumbling block for allied relations. The Poles of London, aware of the weakness of the USSR after the invasion, attempted to secure British support for their demands. For them, it was necessary that the USSR commit itself to restoring in the future Polish territory as it was in 1939. For Stalin, on the contrary, the real Poland was what he called "ethnic" Poland, with the territories annexed by the USSR cut off from it. Despite, or because of, the nearly desperate situation of the USSR at the time, Churchill declined to support Polish demands, inviting Sikorski to accept as the price of a reconciliation with Moscow a hardly satisfactory solution and the hope of a moderate Soviet attitude after the war. Forced to give in, Sikorski signed an agreement with the USSR on July 30, 1941. Diplomatic relations were thereby reestablished between the two governments, and the treaty seemed to open the way to genuine Soviet-Polish cooperation. A Polish army was set up in the USSR, confirmed by the signature of a military convention on August 12, and the clauses of the Nazi-Soviet pact concerning Poland were abrogated. On August 4 a *Pravda* editorial dealing with Soviet-Polish relations even suggested that the territorial questions remained open. For two years the USSR and the Sikorski government maintained strained relations marked by incidents in which the USSR continually attempted to gain British support against Sikorski, who was presented in Moscow as a demanding and irresponsible head of government. Moreover, despite the official reconciliation of 1941, by 1943 the USSR had set up against the "reactionaries" of London the embryo of a Polish government formed on Soviet territory. At its head was the writer Wanda Wasilewska, who had been a Soviet citizen since 1939 and was a deputy to the Supreme Soviet. Her Union of Polish Patriots organized Polish military units that fought alongside the Red Army on the eastern front and would probably make up the core of the future Polish army. Although the Soviet-Polish conflict was partially concealed from 1941 to 1943 by the official reconciliation (Sikorski's trip to Moscow in December 1941 supports this), it nevertheless helped to weaken the government-in-exile even at this early date. Sikorski was obsessed by his Soviet neighbor and convinced of the urgency of negotiating the postwar status of Poland. The members of his government were divided over a strategy that would permit a strengthening of the Polish position, and these divisions fostered factional and personal conflicts that in turn helped to undermine the general position of the government-in-exile. Churchill was exasperated by these conflicts, as he was exasperated by the illusions and the demands of the Poles, who sometimes overestimated their own importance. All of this, in the long run, supported the position of Stalin, who was convinced that his allies were not ready to sacrifice their interests and the cohesion of the alliance to the cause of the Polish government.

This very precarious "armed peace" could not last. It was brought to an end by the Katyn affair, which led to a definitive break between the USSR and the government-in-exile and allowed Stalin to reveal his hand.

On April 12, 1943, the Germans dug up 4,321 corpses in the forest of Katyn, not far from Smolensk. These men, in military uniforms, had all been shot in the back of the head. Everything indicated that they were Polish officers who had been missing for months in Soviet territory. The deaths were attributed by the German authorities to the Red Army. Berlin asserted that these men had been killed during the summer of 1940. The deaths were immediately blamed by the USSR on Germany, which according to the

Soviets had committed the massacre during the winter of 1941. For the Polish government-in-exile, the truth was indisputable and demonstrated by the fact that the victims were wearing summer clothes. The massacre was indeed the act of the Red Army, and the Sikorski government loudly demanded that the Red Cross investigate the affair. For the USSR, this demand was intolerable and relations with the government-in-exile were immediately broken off. Later, Soviets and Germans each set up an investigating commission, each of which, as one might expect, concluded that the other army was guilty. However, after long historical investigations, everything points to the USSR as the guilty party.[39]

The most serious consequence of this break was a decisive weakening of the government-in-exile. Linked to Great Britain, it was from this moment on ignored by the USSR. When Polish territory was liberated by the Red Army, the government in London, cut off from the USSR, could not participate in decisions that were made on the spot, and it was absent from all the negotiations taking place in Poland.

There is no doubt that the USSR found cause for satisfaction in this break. Reconciliation with the Sikorski government had been extorted from it in its worst period of military weakness, and it presented the inconvenience of tying Moscow to a particular solution. A government recognized by the Allies was a valid interlocutor for postwar negotiations, and Stalin wanted to avoid that at all costs. The Anglo-Soviet treaty of May 1942 threw into relief Britain's difficulty in reconciling their alliance with the Soviet Union and Polish interests. When Sikorski demanded an international investigation of Katyn, Stalin more or less ordered Churchill to denounce what he called a provocation designed to ruin the Alliance.[40]

From this point on, bad Soviet-Polish relations took on the form of a more precise problem, that of a Polish government that the USSR was willing to accept. In conveying to Churchill Stalin's indignant message about the Katyn affair, Soviet Ambassador Maisky had indicated that, for Moscow, the government in London was made up of enemies of his country, hence of men who had to be forced out. When Sikorski was replaced in July 1943 by the leader of the Peasant Party, Stanisław Mikolajczyk, he was subjected to very strong pressure from the British to abandon the pretentions and the rigidity of his predecessor and to compromise with the USSR.[41] This implied both that he keep silent about the Katyn affair and that he accept Stalin's territorial notions. Urged on by his ministers, Mikolajczyk maintained his intransigence and sought support from Roosevelt, hoping to benefit from the help of the Polish community in the United States and the influence of the Polish vote. But Roosevelt was hardly inclined to confront Stalin on this point. Thinking of his Polish constituents, he received Mikolajczyk in 1944 and showered him with encouraging words. At the same time he sent Ambassador Harriman to Stalin to explain to him that he could not reject Mikolajczyk because of his Polish constituents; but, Roosevelt asserted, that in no way implied that he had the slighest intention of intervening in what was a conflict between the USSR and the Polish government-in-exile.[42] Again to satisfy his constituents, Roosevelt expressly asked that Stalin receive Mikolajczyk. Lulled by encouragement from Roosevelt that had no content and subjected to strong British pressure, Mikolajczyk went to Moscow in July 1944. At that point, the situation had already been clarified. In Poland, the USSR had taken two initiatives. Its troops, which had crossed the border on January 4, 1944, were advancing rapidly toward Warsaw. On July 21, the USSR sponsored the creation of the Committee of National Liberation (PKWN), which brought together Wanda Wasilewska's Union of Polish Patriots (ZPP) and the National Council (KRN) formed on January 1, 1944, by the Polish communist organization. This Committee of National Liberation, established in Lublin under the presidency of the communist Bolesław Bierut, was given by Moscow all civil and administrative powers over the liberated regions west of the river Bug, that is, in what Stalin considered the "real" Poland.[43]

Thus, the arrival of Mikolajczyk, head of the government-in-exile, practically coincided with the Soviet creation of the embryo of a provisional government under Soviet authority. The question of the relations between these two power structures and the question of their legitimacy were thus posed from the outset.

Stalin invited Mikolajczyk to join the Lublin Liberation Committee. This reveals how Stalin's views had evolved in this brief period marked by the Red Army's military successes. From 1943 to 1944, discussing the Polish government with his allies, Stalin emphasized that the hostility he encountered in the government-in-exile required that it get rid of its most anti-Soviet elements. At first, he was ready to agree—at the price of Mikolajczyk's falling into step—to recognize a transformed government-in-exile. In June 1944, in his exchange of correspondence with Roosevelt, Stalin changed his mind and suggested that the government-in-exile should not only reject certain "anti-Soviet" elements, but also should open itself to "Polish democrats struggling in their country," that is, clearly, to the Polish leaders of the KRN, under Soviet domination.[44] Speaking to Mikolajczyk in July, Stalin was even more precise. He wanted to draw Mikolajczyk into the structures he had established in Poland to give them the dual support of the government-in-exile and of Britain. He thus hoped to have his allies agree to the substitution of a communist government for the Polish government in London. To accomplish this, he was counting on Mikolajczyk's moral authority and the influence of the Peasant Party he represented; everything suggested that he use Sikorski's successor. Similarly, thinking he would charm Roosevelt, he informed him on August 9 that the Lublin Committee would like to call on the expertise of emigrés, like the Polish economist Oskar Lange of Chicago.[45] The government-in-exile thus found itself in a very delicate posture because it could not once again break with the USSR, since that would risk the loss of all legitimacy, and because the "broadening" solutions proposed by Stalin were only very tentatively rejected by Roosevelt. The Warsaw insurrection represented a decisive moment in this conflict over the Polish government. In July 1944, the retreat of the German army was accompanied by an accelerated pace in the establishment of Soviet authority over Polish territory. On July 26, the Lublin Committtee signed an agreement with the USSR that stipulated in Article 9 that security problems would be referred to Soviet authorities in the zones they controlled. The Polish resistance in those zones was immediately enrolled in units dominated by the USSR. Aware that they were witnessing a rapid Sovietization of the liberated territories in which the Allies, preoccupied by the Normandy front, showed little interest, the government-in-exile and the Polish Army under its command decided to revolt and to liberate Warsaw without Soviet help. They thought that they could thus recapture the initiative and impose themselves as unchallengeable participants or representatives. The Warsaw uprising—which took place from August 1 to October 2, 1944—was a bloody tragedy that cost Poland 250,000 dead (225,000 civilians, 20,000 members of the Polish Army), hundreds of thousands of people wounded and prisoners taken, and the destruction of the capital. Warsaw, which had had a population of 1,300,000 at the beginning of the war, was nothing but a field of ruins deserted by all its inhabitants. The history of the last war contains very few such bloody examples.[46] But to the human losses, to the disaster of the total annihilation of a city, was added the political disaster. By deciding to launch this insurrection when the Red Army was approaching the left bank of the Vistula, the government-in-exile and the internal resistance forces were betting on the rapid advance of the Soviet Army, on the defeat of the German Army, and on their capacity to demonstrate their legitimacy with the support of the Polish population all joining in the insurrection. But Soviet troops did not cross the Vistula, leaving the resistance alone against the German Army. To Churchill's anguished appeals, Stalin answered that it was an ill-considered adventure and that, as for an insurrection, there was in Warsaw only "a group of criminals determined to seize power." Aid to the insurgents was limited to a few parachute drops.[47] Stalin always denied that he had urged the Polish resistance to insurrection, as the resistance asserted. While Churchill attempted to bring Stalin to a more humane attitude and to get support from Roosevelt in this effort of persuasion, Roosevelt was from the start convinced that he could do nothing. Moreover, the Allies' principal concern was to avoid conflicts with Stalin, even on the Polish question.[48]

Armed with the freedom of action that he was thus granted, Stalin quickly created a *fait accompli* in Poland. On December 31, 1944, the Lublin Committee proclaimed itself as a provisional government (RTRP) and was recognized a few days later by the USSR. January 1945 was marked by the liberation of all Polish territory and the installation of the Lublin government in Warsaw. The mayoralty of the city was at the same time and in anything but a democratic manner conferred on an unknown communist, Marian Spychalski. Thus Stalin unilaterally imposed his control and his representatives on Poland, whose fate was supposed to have been determined during the coming summit meetings of the Allied leaders. Confronted with this Soviet coup, the government could only recognize that it had been the victim of abandonment. In October 1944, when Churchill and Stalin were debating the future of Europe in Moscow, Mikolajczyk was summoned and subjected to the combined pressure of the two leaders. Stalin and Churchill too insisted that he adopt a compromise position on the location of the border and on his relations with the Lublin government. The coalition taking shape in Moscow opposed Stalin and Churchill to the intransigent president of the government-in-exile.[49] His intransigence was however less than that of his government, which accused him on his return to London of having betrayed Polish interests and drove him to resign in November 1944. The Lublin government, supported and recognized by Moscow, was thus confronted by a very weak counterpart, a government-in-exile without a respected leader, controlled by a group of agitated politicians who were dangerous because of their exaggerated demands. Even if the Western allies did not accept the Soviet *fait accompli*, they were hardly inclined to fight for the defense of the cause of their Polish protégés.

The difficult situation that Mikolajczyk confronted in Moscow in October 1944 is easy to understand, even if history recalls from the later Stalin-Churchill encounter only its most extreme aspects. When he came to Moscow on October 9, 1944, Churchill was concerned in the light of military developments to reduce Stalin's ambitions, or at least to turn them toward regions distant from the British Empire and from Europe. By insisting on Stalin's commitment to participate in the war against Japan and listening to him develop his ambitious views about Manchuria and the northern Chinese territories, Churchill clearly hoped to restrain him elsewhere. This is the troubled perspective in which we must place the badly understood episode of the division of spheres of influence. By noting on a piece of paper what territories could come under the respective influences of the various powers, by discussing spheres of influence, Churchill hoped above all to define those places that would escape the voracity of his opponent.[50] This acute awareness of a situation in which the USSR was in the process of making irreversible progress also explains Churchill's pressures on Mikolajczyk. By pressuring him to give in on points that had already been won by Stalin, he wanted the exiled leader to maintain his presence in the debate on the future of Poland and to force Stalin to take the government-in-exile into consideration, despite its weakness.[51] That the maneuver was useless or clumsy is subject to another debate. But the fact remains that Churchill was dominated at the time by the desire to win Stalin over to his views, and this explains the fleeting optimism he felt from Stalin's cordial remarks.[52]

Yalta: The Myth and the Reality

When the Yalta conference opened on February 4, 1945, the military and political situation in Europe ensured that the USSR would be in a remarkably strong position. From the time it had entered Polish territory, the Red Army had progressed in all directions. Rumania had capitulated in August and declared war on Germany, which had until then been its ally, while these events did not prevent the Red Army from occupying the totality of Rumanian territory. Bulgaria, which was not at war with the USSR and tried in September to make peace with the West, was caught short by the USSR, which declared war on it and also invaded the entire country. At the same time, Hungary served as a theater of operations for Germany, which by maintaining substantial forces on its territory prevented that country from following the Rumanian path and from escaping from the USSR, which also had committed numerous troops there.

Of all the allies of Germany, the only country that succeeded in coming out of the conflict without keeping the Red Army on its soil was Finland. By signing an armistice on September 19, by accepting territorial amputations that more or less corresponded to Soviet conquests in 1940, and by slipping into the Soviet sphere of influence without hesitating, Finland escaped from both armed occupation and later political changes. But everywhere else military occupation followed capitulation, and the USSR clearly showed that beyond strategic objectives a whole political program was taking shape. The Balkans were physically swallowed up in its sphere of influence. When Churchill noted on his little piece of paper in Moscow in October 1944 that Bulgaria would be 25 percent under British influence and Rumania 10 percent, he was expressing a pious wish for those countries that were in fact occupied 100 percent by the USSR. In Western Europe, the military situation was also relatively favorable for the USSR. Von Rundstedt's offensive had no doubt been turned back; but the Allies had insisted so much that Stalin increase his efforts in the East that they gave him the feeling that he had enabled them to avoid a defeat. Stalin thus arrived at Yalta as a victor; but he had not won everything yet. He had to obtain his allies' agreement to his conceptions of the organization of Eastern Europe.

It is the real facts—the omnipresence of the Red Army and behind it new governments being established on the ruins of the old systems of authority— that explain what happened at Yalta, or what did not happen there. The behavior of the three leaders reveals their respective strengths. Just as revealing is the fact that the conference was held in Yalta on the Black Sea in Soviet territory. Stalin had imposed his choice on his allies, arguing that military operations prevented him from leaving his country. And Roosevelt, exhausted as he was, agreed to go. The Anglo-Americans wanted to obtain a good deal from Stalin: a more or less rapid entry into the war against Japan; agreement that he not consider Eastern and Central Europe, where his armies were camped, as a private preserve where he could do as he wished; and that he not move toward the Mediterranean and Western Europe. Their anxious position can be very simply summed up: How to convince Stalin, who had military control of half of Europe, to go no further? How to contain him geographically where he already was? And how to prevent him from turning military occupation into political revolution or annexation? The history of Yalta is not the history of a cynical bargain made with the USSR, but one of arduous negotiations to convince a victorious and dynamic country to stop its forward movement and not to abuse its victory. This was indeed Roosevelt's vision; he remarked in a conversation with a group of American senators in January 1945: "The Russians have power in Eastern Europe," thus "the only possibility is to use our influence to ameliorate the situation."[53]

Roosevelt's clearly defensive attitude and Churchill's fears for the Mediterranean contrasted with the solidity of the Soviet position. The Red Army was close to launching its assault on Berlin and Stalin no longer concealed his European amibitions, notably in Poland, where his representatives, the Lublin authorities, were showing themselves to be intransigent in negotiations with the government-in-exile. In Moscow, Ambassador Harriman had been perfectly aware of this evolution of the USSR, of the more and more brutal tone adopted by Stalin toward his allies, and of his hardening on the problems he considered decisive. Informing his government of these developments, Harriman insisted on the importance of the Polish question, which was and would increasingly be, he said, the touchstone of Allied relations.[54] Harriman added to this warning a lucid observation on the behavior of the Soviet ally, writing: "These men know their power and are counting on it to force us to accept their will."[55] At Yalta, although the Western representatives were fully aware that they were confronted with an unfavorable situation, they perhaps had not evaluated at the outset the importance of their own dissensions, which further complicated the debate. In fact, each leader came to Yalta with his own dominant preoccupations, which prevented the formation of a common Western front against Stalin. But even if this common front had really existed, it would nonetheless not have changed the initial situation: the presence of the Red Army in the heart of Europe.

For Stalin, the first goal to attain at Yalta was the definition of a Polish status in conformity with his wishes. What he intended was to give to the *de facto* domination exercised by the USSR in Poland international legitimacy, allowing him to transform momentary military advantage into permanent influence. For Churchill, the fate of the European continent was a primary concern, which he attempted to articulate while taking account of the present reality. To the preeminence acquired by the USSR in Eastern Europe, Churchill wished to counterpose a balance of the entire continent based on the strengthening of France and the maintenance of German unity. He considered that only the reintegration of those two countries into the European concert would counterbalance Soviet power and perhaps in the long run erode it. But at the same time, Churchill was concerned with the British Empire, which he intended to preserve. Roosevelt's thought was less European, or in any event less immediately tied to the situation on the continent. For the moment, Roosevelt was above all concerned to assure Soviet participation in the Pacific war. For the future, he thought that continental difficulties would find a solution only by perpetuating the wartime alliance in peacetime, that is, in the framework of an international organization that would bind the USSR to principles and rules of conduct it had accepted. This explains the importance Roosevelt attributed to securing Soviet agreement to the creation of the United Nations, the most favorable framework in his view for future international relations.

This is not the place to analyze the entirety of the Yalta discussion, even though it is difficult to understand the decisions that were made there without taking account of the multiplicity of subjects considered. But for the future of Eastern Europe and for Stalin as well, the two important questions were Poland and Germany. In these two countries events had preceded the Yalta debate. Stalin was master of the field, and his partners could do no better than to attempt to moderate his triumph. Their task was complicated not only by the facts, but by the way in which Stalin approached the problem. What he invoked to support his demands was the security of his country, which had been perpetually challenged by its two neighbors. He multiplied long references to history to demonstrate that the USSR, following imperial Russia, had constantly been subjected to the German threat and that Poland had been the pathway and the intermediary, often quite willing, for these invasions. For the USSR, said Stalin, the status of Poland is a matter "of life and death." And Bohlen, who was Roosevelt's interpreter and one of his closest advisers at Yalta, noted that one could measure Stalin's passionate interest in Poland by the quality of his speeches and by his perfect knowledge of the subject in all its aspects, historical, geographical, and so on.[56]

What could one negotiate at Yalta about the future of a Poland that had already been conquered by the USSR and whose many aspects had already been debated at Teheran and elsewhere? Once again the problem of the Polish-Soviet border and that of the government were put on the table. With respect to the border, the Teheran conference had without any doubt settled the future by the agreement reached on the "Curzon Line." However, the lack of precision of this demarcation and the question of Lvov allowed the Anglo-Americans to reopen the debate.[57] Roosevelt asked Stalin to leave Lvov and the oil fields of the region to Poland. The British and the Americans emphasized their acceptance, established at Teheran, of the Curzon Line as the eastern border of Poland, but at the same time asked for this concession. It is remarkable that their request did not rely on the misunderstandings that the two border lines of 1920 might have engendered at Teheran, but that they simply appealed to Stalin's magnanimity and suggested that he make a gesture of good will. This argument—the only one possible in the general context of Yalta—clearly expressed the power relations that existed in February 1945. These power relations also explain why Stalin could be much clearer in his intransigence than he was at Teheran. But having explained that the security of the USSR as well as legality (for Stalin, Lvov was east of the Curzon Line as he understood it) demanded that he keep Lvov, he asserted that he understood the necessity for Poland to preserve a viable territory. And for that purpose he maintained that the Polish border could be extended in the west up to the Neisse. Although on the question of the western border of Poland defined at the expense of Germany agreement could not be reached at Yalta (the English and the Americans did not accept the extensions of Polish territory in the west proposed by Stalin), the Curzon Line in its Soviet version was definitively accepted as the border with the USSR.[58] Stalin had won on a point that he refused to discuss, and the monopoly situation of the Red Army in Poland made any attempt to make him change his mind futile.

The problem of the Polish government, like the border problem, was in part resolved by the factual situation, the existence of a provisional government recognized by the USSR. But it was also partly open, precisely because the Western allies continued to locate legitimacy with the government-in-exile. The Yalta debate was therefore not useless. Moreover, the Warsaw government was identified as provisional, and it seemed possible to negotiate an accommodation that would have recognized the two opposed legitimacies. The stakes were large in terms of both present and future. For the present, it was necessary to set up a provisional government that had the assent of all the allies and could reconcile all the Polish interests. For the future it was necessary to specify the conditions under which Poland would choose its system of government. On the first point, two arguments divided the Soviets from the West. For Stalin, the provisional government derived from the Lublin Committee was already the true representative of the popular will. Any political construction had to begin with that reality and consequently the provisional government would be the kernel around which a provisional government of national unity could be set up. Stalin thus rejected from the outset the idea that one could start from scratch by establishing competition or cooperation between the political forces of Lublin and London. He accepted only one possibility, the entry of a few "Londoners" into the existing provisional government, that is a carefully controlled broadening of that instrumentality. Legitimacy in Polish territory was to be found, in his view, in the government whose establishment he had fostered, and he depended on this government to open itself to the London exiles.

The Western argument was entirely different, even though it was already marked by substantial concessions. The Western leaders, who had long considered only the government-in-exile legitimate, had later come around to the idea of mingling the two authorities, the government in London and the one in Lublin. But at Yalta the progress of events suggested that this compromise solution was already out of date and that if the object was to avoid granting superiority to the pro-Soviet Warsaw government, the only solution that would not unduly compromise the future was the establishment of a new provisional government, more representative of the diversity of political forces, which would have the task of preparing for elections. That was the essential element for the future choices of the political organization of Poland. For the West it was important to get from Stalin a commitment that free elections would be organized as soon as the situation permitted in order to decide on the Polish political system and its leaders. Stalin agreed to accept this decision as set out in the final communiqué. But he also inserted into the communiqué that all the "anti-Nazi and democratic" parties would participate in the elections.

Having gotten satisfaction on the question of the provisional government, Stalin knew from that moment on that he could also control the elections and even the definition of the "democratic" parties that could take part in them. The solution that was finally adopted for the provisional government corresponded to his views. The provisional government after some adjustments was to form the core of the future government and administration. As an apparent concession the readjustment was to be carried out under the auspices of a tripartite commission made up of Molotov and the British and American ambassadors to Moscow, who would associate with their work the "Polish democratic leaders of Poland and the exterior."[59] In the texts, the superiority granted to the provisional government seemed tempered by this international control as well as by the association with it of political leaders of the noncommunist internal resistance and the government in London. The USSR thus implicitly accepted the broadening of the government, even though in contrast to the position defended by the West two years earlier, it was the government in place and not the one in London that was being broadened. But in practice, the imprecision of the compromise also served Stalin's ends, as Bohlen noted in his memoirs.[60] To begin with, the text accepted by all negotiators did not specify how many "democrats" were to be associated with the provisional government, nor did it indicate who would be the members of the commission who would have the burden of choosing the participants in the broadening of the government. Stalin was thus free to consider that the reorganization of the government could be reduced to the distribution of a few secondary positions to politicians who could be manipulated. Above all, he concluded that the best way of carrying out this operation was to negotiate in Moscow only with the government in place; his protégés thus became the arbiters of future choices and thereby had extensive authority over the Poles of London.

On one point—which might have been very important for the future—he remained intransigent. This was the question of control over future elections. The West, aware that they had been obliged to recognize the superiority of the government installed in Warsaw, tried to moderate its influence on the elections in order to preserve the future choices of the Poles. They knew that control over the frequency and freedom of elections would be decisive. This is why they attempted to obtain agreement that the ambassadors of the three allied states, present in Warsaw, would be charged with controlling electoral operations; this presupposed that they would be given all the means needed to carry out the task. On this point, Stalin was inflexible. The Yalta conference, while accepting a few comforting principles—free elections, joint Allied responsibility—did nothing but confirm the existing situation in Poland. The eastern borders gave the USSR the territories it had demanded; the western borders of Poland, imprecisely set, would be a source of conflict between the West and the Soviets and would above all be a source of frustration and hostility for the dispossessed Germans, thereby establishing a certain dependence of Poland on the Soviet Union.[61] The Polish government that would have the task of organizing free elections—despite the negotiated broadening—was made up essentially of pro-Soviet elements who agreed with the positions of and were controlled by the USSR. No doubt Molotov had accepted a few minor border adjustments on the Curzon Line to compensate for the major Soviet acquisitions, and the terms "free elections" and "control over elections" were inscribed in the communiqués. But none of all that was enough to conceal the real situation: The fate of Poland depended on Stalin's designs.

Western acquiescence to Stalin's demands on Poland resulted from the fact that the situation there was already fixed and the war was over. Because, on the other hand, the German front had not yet been definitively broken, the future organization of Germany remained ambiguous, and Stalin attempted on this point to obtain the definition of a consensus on the dismemberment of the country.[62] But although the word "dismemberment" had been accepted, the status of conquered Germany remained to be discussed. Stalin was inflexible on questions on which he had very precise ideas—Poland, German reparations—and more hesitant when his objectives had not been definitively established or when the situation in the field had not created an irreversible position.[63]

This pragmatic vision of the future explains Stalin's acceptance of the Declaration on Liberated Europe that had been prepared by the American delegation and that tried to define for all the countries of Europe that had been occupied the conditions for a return to democratic political life. The declaration, which was clearly inspired by the principles of the Atlantic Charter, asserted that in all the occupied countries the future required the destruction of Nazism, the creation of democratic institutions, and economic reconstruction. To succeed in attaining these goals, "provisional governments containing representatives of all democratic elements of the population would be set up, and they should prepare free elections that would allow as quickly as possible for the establishment of governments responsive to the popular will." The three great powers were jointly to ensure the realization of this plan by helping the liberated states to restore their institutions to working order and even to defend their domestic peace. This declaration, which extended to all European countries that had fallen under German domination the principles that had been accepted for Poland, was sufficiently vague so as to obtain the support of the three great powers. It is easy to understand why Stalin ratified it without hesitation, because it imposed no precise obligations on him. In an initial draft prepared by the State Department, the idea had been proposed of an authority charged with the duty of really controlling the application of the declaration's provisions. This High Commission for the Liberated Regions was considered too constraining and was abandoned in favor of the responsibility of the three great powers that was to be carried out under conditions that remained to be defined.[64] Roosevelt was nevertheless satisfied that he had obtained a general agreement on this text. He was anxious above all to show his public that the populations of Europe had not been turned over to the USSR. He also considered that the provisions whereby "the three great powers will jointly give their aid to the peoples of the liberated states . . . to assure domestic peace," preserved the possibility of intervening in Europe if necessary to preserve the independence of the various states.[65] Of all the states present at Yalta, only one, the USSR, later took advantage of that latitude. But it did so unilaterally and by relying on entirely different principles from those in the Declaration on Liberated Europe, which quickly fell into oblivion.

In considering the unfolding of military events and the political debate at Yalta, can it be maintained seriously that the West turned Eastern Europe over to the USSR? There is no doubt that the conference suffered from a sharp disparity between Stalin's negotiating abilities and the weakness of his interlocutors. The military situation was aggravated by the inequality among the negotiators and also by the very organization of the discussions. Stalin at Yalta, in conditions that were favorable to him, was a brilliant defender of his positions. Constantly invoking the security of his country—an argument confirmed by the civilian and military losses of the USSR—and keeping silent his future political objectives, he strengthened his position through a remarkable knowledge of the questions close to his heart, particularly the

Polish question. Confronting him, his interlocutors were sometimes weakened by their differences over objectives, by a lesser knowledge concerning certain questions—Roosevelt's hesitations and confusions about Poland, for example—and probably by the state of Roosevelt's health.[66] But the organization of the conference was perhaps the major cause of the Western delegates' difficulties. Jean Laloy has very properly emphasized the regrettable effects of a procedure according to which each subject was discussed separately.[67] This prevented any more general negotiations and the elaboration of an overall Allied strategy, and it limited the capacity of Stalin's interlocutors to correct or to apply counterweights to an initial situation that was very unfavorable for them. But even if these Western weaknesses had not existed, one may doubt that the final result of Yalta would have been different. Stalin's determination in relation to what he considered essential, Poland, was obvious. He had the means to support his determination because Eastern Europe was under his control; in Poland particularly the forces capable of resisting him had been annihilated by the Germans in the Warsaw uprising or else were exiled and therefore in no position to affect events. The Yalta conference merely confirmed previous decisions and a situation that favored Soviet demands. As a price for the recognition of his Polish ambitions, Stalin accepted Churchill's conception of a Western Europe from which he would be excluded. Although the Yalta conference was not characterized, as E. Stettinius would have it, by the fact that "the USSR made greater concessions to the United States and Great Britain than they made to the USSR,"[68] it did ratify a concrete situation, the presence of Soviet troops in the eastern half of Europe, and it attempted to define the means of temporarily limiting that situation. Stalin's real victory at Yalta was his obtaining agreement on his most demanding views without his intransigence shaking the Alliance. No doubt at the conclusion of the negotiations his interlocutors sensed that behind apparent or real concessions by Stalin, behind the calming words—free elections, self-determination—his position of strength remained and attenuated the content of his concessions. But for the time being the agreement prevailed; and Roosevelt hoped that the international structures negotiated at Yalta—the United Nations—would force the USSR into behavior in conformity with the principles that had been defined in common.

*   *   *

From the military disasters of 1941 to the Yalta conference, the change in the Soviet position allowed Stalin to show himself constantly more demanding in his territorial and political ambitions and to impose on Eastern Europe an authority that from February 1945 on allowed for little to counter it, at least in practice. This continuous progress of the USSR immediately raises a question. Was it the result of circumstances and Stalin's capacity to exploit them? Or else must we admit that as early as 1939 Stalin had a vast program of conquest and revolution in Europe in mind that the war allowed him to bring to fruition? If we consider attentively Stalin's conduct in the Nazi-Soviet negotiations and in those with the Allies, we are led to question the existence of such a program. What stands out from the complex course of this history is a constant pragmatism and a definite capacity to adapt to events that Stalin had sometimes failed to foresee. No doubt as early as 1939 Stalin took advantage of the war to reestablish a footing in Poland, to try to do the same in Finland, and to incorporate the Baltic states within Soviet territory. In these various steps, from which he did not allow himself to be diverted by German attempts to interest him in the oil regions of the Middle East dominated by Great Britain, Stalin aimed at the recovery of territories lost in 1917. Historic Russia, whose renaissance had been marked by the 1936 Constitution, showed through the mask of the Soviet state and its ambitions in the war years. But there was nothing new in this desire to reconstitute the territory that the war and the revolution had dislocated. The Bolsheviks had only provisionally accepted self-determination for the peoples subject to the empire, as a concession to exceptionally unfavorable conditions. The independence of former imperial possessions had always been considered a regrettable parenthesis. In the same way the Bolsheviks had always thought that the halt to revolutions they recognized in 1921 was only momentary, and they hoped that the forward march of the revolution would resume at a more propitious moment.

As an heir of Lenin and one of the original Bolsheviks, Stalin had shared this regret for the lost territories and the hope for future revolutions. But beyond these muddled regrets and hopes, hardly clear in temporal terms, he does not seem to have developed a precise revolutionary program in the early forties. The war favored territorial enterprises and he took advantage of it, as soon as and wherever possible. However, a transformation in Stalin's strategy took place after the battle of Stalingrad because postwar political perspectives began to take shape. The role played by communists in resistance movements everywhere suggested that the postwar European political order could be changed. In certain cases, events went beyond Stalin's intentions; the Yugoslav example is an enlightening illustration. While Tito emphasized the role of the communists in the resistance and wanted to dissociate from the resistance Mihajlović's troops, who were loyal to the monarchy, and also wanted to reshape the political future, Stalin forced him to accept a nationalist line and allegiance to the sovereign in exile in London. Was there a logical connection between this Yugoslav resistance, with its political center in London gathered around the monarchy, and the hostility to the Polish government in London? In the same way, we must observe the different treatments imposed on independent countries in which the Red Army exercised its authority between 1941 and 1945. Why reincorporate the Baltic states into the USSR and totally annihilate their independence? Why impose only Soviet control on the Polish government? Why be satisfied with rectifying Soviet-Finnish borders and impose on that country only benign neutrality toward the USSR? In these three situations, which were all clear by the time of Yalta, can we find the expression of a master plan?

These differences reveal in reality the changes that had taken place in Stalin's perceptions of his strength and of the future possibilities created by the war. If we take once again the example of Poland—an obsession of Stalin's—we can measure these changes. In 1939 Stalin participated in the annihilation of Polish sovereignty, and for two years in those areas where he controlled the situation he attempted to eradicate all elements of Polish national life. After 1941, on the contrary, he asserted his will to restore the Polish state and to assure the survival of a "strong" Polish nation. And the territorial extensions at the expense of Germany that he proposed indicate in fact that he wanted to have a "viable" Poland on his borders, even if its limits were to be defined by the USSR. These variations in his attitude toward Poland, like the differing treatments he imposed on the various resistance movements and states in the east, reveal that Stalin's views were forged by the course of time and events. Before 1943 he had to survive, and he negotiated with his allies only about what seemed essential to him, his conception of security. After 1943, when he glimpsed that behind victory a new political order could be encouraged, he prepared the ground for it by constantly insisting on what was the most urgent thing for him, the security of Soviet borders. The war had showed him that this security was tied first of all to military power, to Soviet capacity, thanks to this power, to impose its will on its neighbors and its desire on its allies. This explains why Stalin's ideas concerning the organization of Eastern Europe were expressed first of all in terms of control and not in terms of fundamental political change. The transformations that he imposed or supported later in the territories that had become by force of circumstances the Soviet sphere of influence were the product of the privileged place that had been given to Soviet power, to his decisions, and to his experience of revolution. Stalin's mental universe and his programs were constantly being shaped by facts, by experience, and always dominated by one certainty: the primacy of force and of the balance of forces; the necessity of making the future of neighboring states depend on Soviet decisions and on the interests of the Soviet state. If, during the war, Stalin did not yet have a grand design for the organization of the world, he was on the other hand guided by a clear determination: to maintain definitively the influence of the USSR in those areas to which the war had led Soviet armies. When the besieged citadel had disappeared, it was time to organize the conquered territories to assure the permanence of those conquests. All empires begin in this way.

NOTES

1. On the disastrous effects of the purges and on the lack of preparation for war, see Khrushchev's Secret Speech to the Twentieth Congress.

On the beginning of the war, it is interesting to read Zhukov's memoirs, *Vospomineniia i razmyshlenia* (Memories and Reflections) (Moscow, 1971), 189–235 (on the eve of war) and 235–40.

2. A. Nekrich, *Nakazannye narody* (The Punished Peoples) (New York, 1978), particularly 7–24.

3. E. B. Pashukanis, "Gosudarstvo i pravo pri sotsializme," *Sovetskoe Gosudarstvo* 3 (1936):3–11. This article established the change in direction of 1936.

4. Speech of July 3, 1941. On this period, see H. Carrère d'Encausse, *Staline* (Paris, 1979), 132.

5. J. Degras, ed., *The Communist International 1919–1943—Documents* (London and New York, 1965), 3:476.

6. The theses of the Seventh Congress of the Comintern shed light on this shift; see *Contre la guerre et le fascisme: l'unite—Résolutions et décisions* (Paris: Bureau d'éditions, 1935), 11.

7. On the theses and the organization of the movement, see G. D. Komkov, "Politicheskaia propaganda i agitatsia v gody velikoi otechestvennoi voiny," *Istoria SSSR* 4 (July–August 1972):102–4. On Stalin's Panslavism, see the very important work by V. C. Fisera, *Le Mouvement socialiste et les slavismes des origines à 1945* (thesis, University of Paris I, 1973); and by the same author, *De l'idéologie diplomatique à la diplomatie idéologique, la pensée politique de Staline de 1939 à 1947* (Paris: I.E.P., 1971).

8. This was the direction given to the work of the chair of the History of the Slavs created at the University of Moscow on May 10, 1939. Fisera, *Le Mouvement socialiste et les slavismes*, 467.

9. Komkov, loc. cit.

10. G. Haupt, "Guerre et révolution chez Lénine," *Revue française de science politique* 2 (April 1971):256–281.

11. This is confirmed by Ambassador Maisky in his *Memoirs of a Soviet Ambassador: The War 1939–1943* (London, 1967), 231ff.

12. Winston Churchill, *The Second World War: The Hinge of Fate* (Boston, 1950), 477–78. See also V. M. Kulish, *Istoriia vtorogo fronta* (Moscow, 1971), 150ff.

13. Averell Harriman and Elie Abel, *Special Envoy to Churchill and Stalin, 1941–1946* (New York, 1975), 244.

14. Phillip Moseley, in R. Dennett and J. Johnson, *Negotiating With the Russians* (Boston, 1951), 282ff., quoted in *Soviet Diplomacy and Negotiating Behavior* (Washington, n.d.), 162.

15. R. E. Sherwood, *Roosevelt and Hopkins: An Intimate History* (New York, 1948), 561.

16. Herbert Feis, *Churchill, Roosevelt, Stalin: The War They Waged and the Peace They Sought* (Princeton, 1957), 272–73.

17. Ibid., 285.

18. Maisky, op. cit., 176.

19. Churchill, op. cit., 486.

20.   On the "personal" relations with Stalin reported by Churchill, see the memoirs of Lord Moran, *Churchill Taken from the Diaries of Lord Moran*, quoted by Adam Ulam, *Expansion and Coexistence* (Cambridge, Mass., 1968), 351.

21.   See the excellent thesis by A. Tinguy, *Commerce et coexistence. Aspects politiques et historiques des relations économiques et culturelles soviéto-américaines* (Paris, 1981), 4–48, and Daniel Yergin, *Shattered Peace: The Origins of the Cold War and the Division of Europe* (Boston, 1977).

22.   Yergin, op. cit., 40.

23.   Ibid., 42–43.

24.   Ibid., 53–54.

25.   Sherwood, op. cit., 572.

26.   Feis, op. cit., 23.

27.   Ulam, op. cit., 352.

28.   Feis, op. cit., 270.

29.   Harriman and Abel, op. cit., 279.

30.   W. Sworakowski, "An Error Regarding East Galicia in Curzon's Note to the Soviet Government," *Journal of Central European Affairs* 4 (1944):3–26.

31.   In question was the Sub-Carpathian Ukraine in the 1943 treaty, *Shornik deistvuiushchih dogovorov, soglashenii i konventsii zakliuchennyh SSSR s inostrannymi gosudarstvami* (Collection of treaties, agreements, and conventions between the U.S.S.R. and other countries), vol. 11, no. 406, 31–32.

32.   E. Taborsky, "Polish-Czechoslovak Federation: The Story of the First Soviet Veto," *Journal of Central European Affairs* 9 (1949–50):379–85, and Harriman and Abel, op. cit., 244.

33.   Ulam, op. cit., 276.

34.   *Documents on Polish-Soviet Relations, 1939–1945* (London: Sikorski Institute, 1961).

35.   The text of the treaty is in R. J. Sonntag and J. S. Beddie, eds., *Nazi-Soviet Relations, 1938–1941, Documents from the Archives of the German Foreign Office* (Washington, 1948), 78.

36.   For an excellent synthesis on the questions of the various borders, see N. Davies, *God's Playground: A History of Poland*, 2 vols. (Oxford, 1981), 2:504.

37.   Feis, op. cit., 285.

38.   *Pravda*, January 12, 1944; note the tone of the editorial in *Pravda* on August 4, 1943 on this problem.

39.   See the very good synthesis by A. Kwiatkowska-Viattean, *1940–1943, Katyn, l'armée polonaise assassinée* (Brussels, 1982) and Sir Owen O'Malley, *Katyn Dispatches of Sir Owen O'Malley to the British Government* (Chicago, 1973).

40.   Churchill, op. cit., 761.

41.   Ulam, op. cit., 356, notes that the leader of the Peasant Party had neither the prestige nor the authority of Sikorski.

42.   *Perepiska predsedatelia soveta ministrov SSR s presidentami SShA i premier ministrami velikobritanni vo vremia velikoi otechestvennoi voiny, 1941–1945* (Correspondence of the president of the Soviet Council of Ministers with the presidents of the U.S.A. and the prime ministers of Great Britain during the Great Patriotic War, 1941–1945) (Moscow, 1957), 2:145.

43.   The Soviet concept of ethnic Poland was opposed to the Polish concept of historic Poland, whose borders were defended by the Polish delegation to the Paris conference.

44.   *Perepiska predsedatelia soveta*, 145.

45.   Ibid., 153.

46.   J. Ciechanowski, *The Warsaw Rising of 1944* (Cambridge, 1971), 217ff.

47.   *Perepiski predsedatelia soveta*, 1:252ff, 255, and 257.

48.   Feis, op. cit., 386.

49.   E. Rozek, *Allied Wartime Diplomacy: A Pattern in Poland* (New York, 1958), 282–83.

50.   Winston Churchill, *Triumph and Tragedy* (London, 1953), 226–27.

51.   The very negative position that Roosevelt communicated to Stalin contributed to this weakness. See Roosevelt's message to Stalin on the Polish border: *Foreign Relations of the United States—Diplomatic Papers* (Washington, 1968), 3:332–36.

52.   Churchill, *Triumph and Tragedy*, 242.

53.   Quoted by Yergin, op. cit., 58.

54.   Harriman and Abel, op. cit., 317.

55.   Ibid, 343–44.

56.   Charles Bohlen, *Witness to History 1929–1969* (New York, 1973), 187.

57.   Feis, op. cit., 285.

58.   Churchill, *Triumph and Tragedy*, 377.

59.   Bohlen, op. cit., 191.

60.   Ibid., 191–92.

61.   *Tegeran-Yalta-Potsdam—Sbornik dokumentov* (Moscow, 1967), 97ff.

62.   *Foreign Relations of the United States: The Conferences of Malta and Yalta 1945* (Washington, 1955), 176.

63.   Ulam, op. cit., 370.

64.   *Tegeran-Yalta-Potsdam*, 122–23; for the background and the communiqué by the three great powers of February 11, 1945, *Department of State Bulletin*, 12/1945, pp. 213–16.

65.   Communiqué of February 11, 1945, Title V; the French text is accessible in A. Frink, *De Yalta à Potsdam* (Brussels, 1982), 207–11.

66.   Bohlen, op. cit., 172.

67.   J. Laloy, *Entre guerres et paix* (Paris, 1966), 112–14.

68.   E. Stettinius, *Roosevelt and the Russians*, 2nd ed. (London, 1950), 261.

2

THE MANIPULATED REVOLUTIONS

By negotiating with Stalin from 1943 to 1945, the Americans and the British hoped to contain not only the territorial but also the political ambitions of the ally that they were gradually getting to know. In this respect, the notion of spheres of influence, even though it was constantly disavowed, was implicitly considered a necessary evil by the West.[1] The West hoped that the USSR, reassured by the recognition of its regional interests, would gradually adapt its political behavior to a pacified environment. The free elections that were to be held throughout Eastern Europe, according to the agreements that had been reached, seemed to be the surest way of reconciling Soviet interests, the independence of the states concerned, and international morale. Beyond the perpetuation of spheres of influence, the Allies hoped that the USSR would be satisfied by the installation of governments aware of its power and of its desire to consolidate its security. The notion of friendly governments, steadfastly defended by Stalin, suggested that the USSR would be satisfied with a layer of states well disposed toward him in which international alignment with the USSR would be compensated for by relatively autonomous domestic policies.[2] In fact, Finland later demonstrated that it was possible to have such illusions in 1945 without being ridiculous. Stalin's determination to defend his conception of the Polish government did not completely destroy this illusion, because Polish-Soviet relations had traditionally been marked by passion, the Polish attitude between the wars lent support to Stalin's position, and finally, the anti-Sovietism of the government-in-exile was glaringly obvious.

The Anglo-American allies were not really wrong in 1945 when they guessed that Stalin had no clear idea about the way in which he intended to exercise his authority over Eastern Europe. In this area too his intentions became clearer as circumstances changed, and the international climate sometimes had the effect of radicalizing his activity. The euphoric atmosphere that marked the conclusion of the Yalta conference, the illusion that understand-

37

ing had been created among the major victors in the conflict, very soon gave way to a clarity that darkened Roosevelt's final days. Hardly had everyone left Yalta when Stalin multiplied actions that changed, before the promised elections, the provisional political balance of Eastern Europe. The actions taken by Vyshinsky, vice-minister of foreign affairs of the USSR, to force King Michael of Rumania to include communists in a liberal government had a brutal effect, revealing Stalin's lack of respect for the right of the liberated peoples to determine their future fates. The cynicism that Stalin demonstrated in the spring of 1945 within his sphere of influence also extended to his relations with those who were still his allies. He violently accused Roosevelt of looking for a separate peace with Germany. This incident, which overwhelmed him, led Roosevelt to this startling confession: "Harriman was right, you can't deal with Stalin. He has betrayed all the commitments he made at Yalta."[3]

In this deteriorating international climate the explosion of the first atomic bomb over Hiroshima on August 6, 1945, helped to exacerbate relations with the USSR and to push Stalin toward a more militant attitude in Europe. For the West, the bomb had created a new international balance that Churchill explained in the most explicit manner: "Now we have in hand a way to restore the balance with the Russians."[4] This new confidence of the Western powers in their strength had as its counterpart on the Soviet side a feeling of frustration and anxiety that expressed itself in aggressive behavior. George Kennan, who participated in most Soviet-American meetings at the time, has provided a perfect description of this evolution of the USSR from a still prudent attitude to growing hostility, implying an eventual break in the alliance established during the war.[5] At the conference of foreign ministers in London in September 1945, Molotov asked point-blank of Byrnes, secretary of state since July 3, 1945, who had come to London determined to make use of the bomb as a negotiating point, whether he "was carrying one in his pants pocket."[6] This episode provides clear evidence of the tense nature of Allied relations after August 6. The Soviet response to this new balance as Molotov provided a glimpse of it in London and as Stalin suggested to Harriman during their meeting in Gagra in October 1945, was that the USSR felt released from its commitments to its allies because of their intention to dominate it strategically. If the USSR was thus subjected to an implicit threat, the alliance no longer had a raison d'être, and isolation would return to the fore. Isolation, for Stalin, meant that the USSR had to emphasize its security and to be solely responsible for that security. The plans developed in common during the war, the common guarantees developed in the recent past were obsolete once the balance of power had changed; as soon as the Allies, said Stalin, had used this new balance to put pressure on the USSR. And Soviet security was now at stake on the western borders where the USSR and its recent allies were confronting one another. From this moment on, the

USSR could only strengthen its control over Eastern Europe. Three consequences derived from this new international context, which imposed itself on all the Allies in a few weeks, as soon as the war was over. There was first the cold war, which began to be sensed when the guns had hardly been silenced. Beginning with suspicious or brutal statements, it developed in the interstices of the alliance that the conferences of 1945 and 1946 had attempted momentarily to preserve, before the alliance and its final illusions collapsed in 1947.[7] Second, Soviet activism was transforming Eastern Europe definitively into its sphere of influence. Finally, the American political elite adopted a new conception of relations with the USSR. The desire to cooperate was followed by the determination to contain the Soviets, according to the expression and the doctrine formulated by George Kennan in 1946.[8]

Once again in this period Stalin's way of expressing his concerns was prudent, always suggesting that, aside from his security concerns in Poland, everything was provisional, and connected to the war that was coming to an end and that everything therefore could be changed. This presentation of Soviet activities, which was in reality directed toward the creation of positions of strength that it would be difficult to reverse, is clearly demonstrated by the conversations that took place between Stalin and Harry Hopkins in Moscow in May 1945. When Hopkins expressed concern about the changes that were taking place in Eastern Europe, Stalin responded by making conciliatory statements about his own concern for democratic freedoms. But, he added, these freedoms would obviously be subject to certain limitations in wartime and they could not, moreover, be extended to "fascist" elements. And speaking to an interlocutor who had little familiarity with the real situation in the countries in which the Red Army exercised exclusive control, he concluded by saying that after all, he, Stalin, was well acquainted with the facts and was in a better position than his Western allies, who were unfamiliar with the region, to judge what was necessary and to recognize the divisions between democrats and fascists. Stalin thus presented to Hopkins and to all his Western interlocutors a flawless argument based on his total acceptance of democratic principles and his unique knowledge of local political conditions. He explicitly denied that there was the slightest program governing his actions in Eastern Europe or that any such presumed plan would tend toward a radical transformation of the political framework of the countries concerned.[9]

The Russian Revolutionary Model

What exactly did Stalin want during the years in which the fate of Eastern Europe was determined? Revolution? The creation of puppet powers masking Soviet control? In order to rediscover the thread connecting his various actions it is important first of all to consider his notion of revolution in general, to locate the model that provided his terms of reference. Revolution as Stalin understood it was indeed linked to the experience of his country and to his interpretations of the Marxist model, of Lenin's actions, and of his own choices. From the Marxist program, of which Stalin claimed himself the faithful heir to his dying breath, the Russian Revolution had retained nothing, or rather, it had demonstrated that the program was inapplicable. The revolution, according to Marx, was to be the outcome of capitalist development and advanced industrialization, which should have produced a large working class that was conscious of its alienation. The Russian Revolution, far from having been the product of this kind of collapse of over-developed capitalism and industrialism, took place in a country in which capitalism had barely begun to flourish; and it had as an effect—not a cause—a tumultous industrialization that generated a working class long after the revolution. The Russian Revolution had demonstrated the importance or the revolutionary virtue of elements that Marx had hardly suspected: the rural milieu, authoritarian political structures within which the society found few opportunities to develop its political experience, national solidarity, the activism of intellectual circles isolated from the workers but prepared to lead them, and social instability and anxiety. In this volatile social context, war had played a determining role. It had disorganized existing structures and created conditions favoring every kind of change. From this initial situation Stalin had drawn a conclusion that unquestionably dominated his perception of the revolutionary process. He always saw revolution as a consequence of war, and the internal structures of societies remained for him a negligible if not nonexistent component of the revolutionary movement. He thought of the revolution in terms of an international, not a domestic and social context. This is why for him the revolution was also linked to the international status of the USSR and to the advantages and disadvantages for his country of international relations that could flow from that status. Stalin's entire set of attitudes toward national communist parties and toward the Comintern derived from that perception. In the interwar years, Stalin had forced the Comintern to agree that the notion of revolution was identified with the notions of defense of the USSR and loyalty to the motherland of revolutions.

But the Russian Revolution and the Russian conception of revolution cannot be reduced to the Bolsheviks' success in October 1917. The Russian model had the peculiarity that the seizure of power was not the outcome of class struggle but its beginning; it was the point of departure for the more profound revolution, the revolution in the values and the organization of society. This is where the Russian experience becomes particularly interesting and where the question of its validity for other societies arises. From the outset the revolutionary explosion had been characterized by the unequal relation—not foreseen by Marx—between the masses and a group of organized revolutionaries. Popular spontaneity, the motive force of the revolutionary movement, was led, contained, channeled by a perfectly structured organization of professional revolutionaries, Lenin's Bolshevik Party. Although the blows struck against the old order, fostered by the chaos created by a disastrous war, came from the depths of society in February 1917, the choices concerning the new order that were imposed after October 1917 were made in the narrow, marginal circle represented by Lenin's political organization. In *What Is to Be Done?*, written at the beginning of the century, Lenin had already developed the essential elements of his conception of the relations between the masses and a party whose acute consciousness of the laws of history made it capable of embodying and guiding the future of the masses, even if those masses were made up of workers. There are many signs in Lenin's work and his actions that reveal this consistent conception of revolution in which the dictatorship of the proletariat, carried out through new state structures, was the legitimate form of a permanent class struggle. And it was the party that exercised this dictatorship of the proletariat. The revolution from beginning to end was thus carried out from above, from the seat of awareness of history and class consciousness. This legitimation of the party, of a power that was not of the people but was exercised in its name and over it, of a lasting revolution that was first of all to break the old order (with the help of the war), and then to create a political power, and finally to shape society and its surroundings, all of this was the lesson that Lenin's successors derived from his experience.[10] The essential elements of the model lay of course in the paths leading to the seizure of power and even more in the tasks that would be accomplished thereafter.

It was at this point that Stalin made his own contribution to the Russian model. Until 1929, in the great debate over the road to follow that divided Lenin's successors into supporters of gradualism and supporters of radical revolution, Stalin adopted a middle position and presented himself as a loyal follower of the Lenin who had proposed the NEP.[11] But in 1929 he linked his name to radicalism, to the new revolution. Historians have for a long time discussed the basis for Stalin's shift in attitude to this decisive problem. Was the shift a circumstantial decision or the product of a personal conception of the revolution? Had Stalin as a pragmatist chosen to commit his country to the radical break of 1929 because the difficult economic situation led him to conclude that this break was the only way of dealing with it? Or, on the contrary, did he finally have the opportunity to resume the revolutionary thread that had been broken or loosened during the NEP? Was he then able, thanks to the economic circumstances he could cite, to apply his radical conception of change, his own plan for a new society?[12]

This is not the place to argue the matter, but the hypothesis I have adopted is that Stalin's choice was not the product of circumstances or of pragmatism. For Stalin, communist society was a society of a new kind, based on a totally unprecedented political culture that could not be imposed gradually nor by respecting the popular will. He interpreted social revolution merely as a continuation of the political revolution whose paths had been traced by experience. Because it had to create a new world, the revolution had first to sweep away the old order. But the old order was not simply a concept, it was the very warp and woof of history and human will. It was a political culture made up of adhesion to values, forms of solidarity, and patterns of behavior. Never in history had human societies accepted such radical breaks, freely agreed to be the raw material consumed in order to produce the new substance of the world of the future. Just as industrialization and the transformation of the economy had been nothing but the consequences of the revolutionary and political change of 1917, so, when the stage of social revolution had been reached, it was the moral change of man and society that would determine the rest, that is, the economy. This primacy of political revolution, and then of the essential components of social revolution, values and behavior, over the economic sphere, which was the central choice of Leninism and Stalinism, explains the concept of revolution from above or forced revolution. Social and moral revolution was to change mankind as a whole, and it was therefore total (indeed totalitarian) and totally unacceptable to mankind. It was therefore necessary for this kind of revolution to be imposed on mankind. The concrete elements of the Russian model derive from this conception of revolution. Its political elements were systems predicated on a single ideology and a single organization, which automatically condemned the intrusion of ideas unrelated to the plan in a society subject to such ordeals. There was also a radical economic revolution—involving industrialization and collectivization—whose first effect was to disrupt all previous patterns of life and work, to create unprecedented social mobility that atomized society, disabled it, and finally left the individual face to face with absolute power, whose usual means of government was terror. In this context economic choices—like the absolute priority given to heavy industry—had a dual rationality, economic of course, but above all political. Economically, these choices reflected the will to mobilize all resources for the program of industrialization, for modernization of a new kind, concentrated on the progress of the economic power of the state. But the political reasons for these choices were perhaps more decisive. The growth of heavy industry was at the heart of the development of Soviet state power. In the last analysis, what Stalin was constructing was an omnipotent state based on a modern or modernized economy mobilizing all the human and material resources of the country for its benefit.[13]

Was this model, which the Second World War had shown in 1941 to be precarious but had later revealed to be capable of adaptation and survival, necessarily the template for all subsequent revolutions? In an interview with Roy Howard in 1936 Stalin vigorously rejected that hypothesis, asserting that "the idea of exporting revolutions is an absurdity."[14] However, the leaders of the USSR had already exported revolution on several occasions and in the process had imposed a strict imitation of their experience. In 1920, Outer Mongolia, occupied by the Red Army, experienced the imposition of a Leninist style revolution and a regime that slavishly imitated the political structures of the USSR. Between 1939 and 1941 when the USSR was able to annex the Baltic states and the eastern part of Poland, it immediately imposed on them a replica of its political and economic structures. Before being invaded by the German armies, the Baltic states had been subjected to collectivization and the beginning of a veritable "cultural" and political revolution that went as far as Soviet activities had in the thirties.[15]

Although it was occupied by the Red Army, Eastern Europe was not automatically attached to the USSR. For that very reason, the brutal imposition of the Soviet system in the way it had been carried out in the Baltic states was unthinkable, and a pure and simple export of the revolution was equally difficult to accomplish. In these circumstances and in this region, how could Stalin use the favorable conditions that the war had created to ensure with some stability an extension of Soviet influence or domination? How could be perpetuate a situation—Soviet authority over neighboring countries—which was, as the Allies had endlessly discussed, supposed to evolve toward normalcy, that is, toward a return to national independence and the expression of the popular will? The period during which Stalin could organize Eastern Europe according to his views was by definition very short. This explains why the countries of the region experienced in a compressed time period—the eight years from 1945 to 1953—the entire cycle of changes that had taken twenty years in the USSR. In this brief period, the populations involved went through the ordeals of political revolution, economic revolution, and the creation of a new social and moral order. Because of the extraordinary rapidity with which events unfolded, it is difficult to discern their logic, their essential characteristics, and it is clear that such short historical periods were often telescoped and overlapped from one country to another.

The historians who have attempted to recount this brief and tragic history[16] have generally agreed that it could be divided into two periods, the first, when diversity and a certain freedom of action by the governments prevailed that lasted from 1945 to 1947, and the second, after 1947 when the USSR imposed conformity everywhere.[17] The initial period of the history of Sovietized Europe was, of course, the years that immediately followed the war. This period determined the fate of those countries because it determined the matter that Lenin had always asserted controlled everything else, state power. The Russian revolutionary model had as its mainspring the problem of the conquest of power and of the definition of the center of power. The extension of the model to Eastern Europe was carried out in the same terms—the conquest of state power was identified with the revolution. If we look at the history of Eastern Europe in this perspective, we can discern in the variety of existing situations three cases, three revolutionary strategies: revolution as the seizure of power made from within the society, as in Yugoslavia and Albania; revolution that took place under pressure from the USSR (almost all other countries except Czechoslavakia); and finally the case of Czechoslovakia, which began by resembling Yugoslavia and Albania and ended by imitating the others.

From National Resistance to Social Revolution

The Leninist strategy for the seizure of power was enriched during the Second World War by a variant in which war and revolution were mingled as in the Leninist model, but according to different patterns. This strategy, of which China is the best example, triumphed in two European countries, Yugoslavia and Albania, and it should be briefly recounted here because it permanently influenced Soviet perceptions of the export of revolution.

At the origin of this strategy for revolution there were common elements all linked to the war. Foreign occupation simultaneously destroyed national independence, existing structures of authority, and social solidarity. From the political void that was thus created, the communist parties drew new strength and a hitherto untapped social audience; their prestige depended on their capacity to transform themselves into national resistance movements or else to organize and lead the resistance. By uniting society around the theme of the liberation of the national territory, the communist parties achieved a broad consensus and the capacity to influence social structures. And the liberation of the land everywhere allowed them to move without transition from the nationalist to the revolutionary attitude, because they were gradually able to establish a new social and economic order in the liberated territories in the void created by the war, or else by opposition to the structures maintained by the occupying power. The evolution of Yugoslavia provides a good illustration of this process. A multiethnic state, created by war and the Versailles Treaty, and as precarious as many of the other creations of that treaty, Yugoslavia collapsed in a war that destroyed what the Versailles Treaty had constructed. It was occupied and dismembered by all the neighboring populations—Italians, Germans, Bulgarians, Hungarians— who thought they had rights over some fraction of Yugoslav territory or over the peoples of Yugoslavia. The state created in 1919 was weak from a lack of national unity and even more because it had no symbols of unity or institutions to encourage the integration of its diverse peoples. The Serbian monarchy could not possibly suffice to compensate for the variety of ethnic groups, languages, religions, and alphabets grouped together in a single state. The elements of diversity and historically based ethnic and cultural quarrels were too powerful to enable political determination in the course of the twenty years from 1919 to 1940 to overcome them in favor of a will toward a common life. Yugoslavia disappeared, victimized because it had lacked the time to establish a correspondence between state and nation. Within this diversity, two institutions survived the time of the division as they had existed while the state was alive, the monarchy and the communist party. These two institutions both claimed to represent the interests of all the different national and ethnic groups; they claimed to have the capacity to unify. On the eve of the war, the Yugoslav Communist Party, sprung from a brilliant Serbian Marxist tradition, was a solid, relatively popular organization, thoroughly controlled by Tito.[18] The evolution of the USSR during the war and the emphasis placed on defense of the nation at the expense of communist themes allowed Tito to present himself as the leader of the internal resistance and of the reconquest of independence and to unify all the national components of the Yugoslav state. At the outset, his partisans had mixed results, but a precise strategy very quickly emerged that consisted of the establishment of a territorial base in which, in the framework of a controlled region, the movement developed real power. Thus in autumn 1941, Tito's partisans created the Republic of Uzhice in the northern part of Serbia, then they retreated to the mountainous regions of Bosnia. But everywhere they established new political structures, popular committees charged with administering the territories in which the invasion had destroyed all national authority. It was the political void created by the occupying forces that granted spontaneous legitimacy to the popular authorities set up by Tito, authorities that recruited their leaders from a broad spectrum of the population, paying no attention to political affiliations. Supported by this popular rearguard, Tito developed his forces, and by February 1945 he could pride himself on having under his command fifty-four divisions numbering more than eight hundred thousand men. Tito found his partisans in the countryside, where a harsh occupation made them inclined to join the ranks of those who appealed to their patriotic feeling. Of course, Tito was not the only organizer of resistance. But he was able gradually to force out his principal domestic rival, Mihajlović, because he relied more heavily on disciplined military organization, and in that period of disarray, violence and organization were most fruitful. He also succeeded perhaps above all because as a communist from the harsh school of the Comintern, he adroitly practiced the art of eliminating his rivals by all available means.[19]

The Soviet attitude toward Tito sheds light on their conceptions of the war and the postwar world. Although Tito had been formed by the Comintern and was then very close to the USSR, Stalin long delayed recognizing him as the future leader of Yugoslavia. While he showed himself constantly hostile to the Polish government in London and looked instead for allies within Poland itself, when it came to Yugoslavia, Stalin adopted the opposite position. To Tito's requests for aid he responded with delaying statements and a precise piece of advice: Tito should cooperate with the legitimate leaders of the Yugoslav state, King Peter and the government-in-exile in London, who supported Mihajlović. The USSR, which was at the time downplaying the Comintern and preparing to suppress it, was not eager to frighten its allies by supporting a communist who was setting up popular authorities behind the lines. More than this prudence, what explains Stalin's reservations about Tito was probably his suspicion of Tito's strategy and Tito's political stature. The USSR finally acceded to his claim to embody the Yugoslav resistance, because Stalin had in 1942 been unable to obtain the signature of the government-in-exile on a treaty of mutual assistance.[20] It was also because at the Teheran conference the Allies turned away from the exiles and supported Tito, even though the British government tried for a time to reconcile Tito and the king.

But the reticence of the USSR toward the Yugoslavian communist leader remained a permanent characteristic of the relations between Stalin and Tito. In 1945 the liberation of Belgrade was the object of a veritable race between Soviet tanks, which by entering the capital first would symbolize the decisive role played by the USSR in the victory, and Tito's troops, since Tito wanted to show Stalin that the fate of Yugoslavia had been determined principally within the country.[21] Having stood up to Stalin during the war in his rejection of any compromise with the government-in-exile and having already established communist political leadership in the liberated territories, Tito remained master of the field. As a sincere communist and despite past friction, Tito did not envisage in 1945 an isolated revolutionary solution. The USSR was the motherland of revolutions. The Titoist conception of the development of postrevolutionary societies was open and he attempted to balance internationalism and the national interest. In 1945, in an exchange of letters between the Yugoslav and Soviet Communist Parties, Kardelj spelled out these views. Yugoslavia was one of the "future Soviet republics, and . . . relations should be constructed with a view toward Yugoslavia becoming in the future an integral part of the USSR."[22] While awaiting this development, Yugoslavia was led by Tito in a way that took into account the profound changes that the war had brought about. In November 1945 he organized elections that gave 90 percent of the vote to the popular front that he had established. The victory was an expression of the domestic domination already exercised and also of a political context that, without being openly terroristic, was characterized by intimidating measures being taken against all possible opponents and according to numerous indications by electoral irregularities. Although democracy was rather roughly handled in this period, Tito's accomplishment was unquestionably to have brought out of the war a multiethnic state in which national communities that the common struggle for liberation had brought together could live side by side. The constitution adopted on January 31, 1946 was inspired by the Soviet Constitution of 1936, particularly with respect to federal organization.[23]

Thus, without the USSR having to intervene, Yugoslavia changed a war of liberation into a revolution at a moment when the fate of Europe, debated by the Allies, was far from being fixed. From this change the USSR gained definite revolutionary progress that did not place it in a difficult situation. Tito had been supported by the Allies, particularly by Britain; considered the true leader of the Yugoslav resistance since 1943, he met no opposition to the authority he had assumed over his country. In neighboring Albania, the revolution followed the same path. The USSR thus found itself in a strong position to assert that revolutionary development owed nothing to its intervention and everything to the popular will. This is the thesis it upheld in countries where the weakness of communism and the survival of democratic parties led it into various kinds of intervention and a complex strategy that came to be known as the "salami strategy."

The "Salami Strategy"

The revolutions of 1945 and 1946 in Yugoslavia and Albania owed their successes to the war and were the product of domestic developments. No doubt if the Red Army had been totally absent from the region, Tito's task would have been more complicated; existing conflicts in Yugoslavia among distinct national groups and political forces would probably have assumed different dimensions. But in the other countries of the region, the situation in 1945 was characterized by contradictory phenomena. On the one hand the Red Army was present everywhere. But on the other none of the states except for Yugoslavia and Albania had been liberated by their own forces. Their communist parties were not partisans of political change. And the Allies thought that in the course of negotiations they had set up some protective devices over these states. To maintain lasting control over these countries, whether allies or enemies, Stalin had to choose between two strategies. The radical solution was pure and simple annexation and the Sovietization of these countries along the lines of what he had done in the Baltic states. The other, more subtle strategy, involved imposing control over the governments while taking into account the real condition of political forces in each country. The whole evolution of the war—the alliance with the great powers, the egalitarian theses of the Slavophile movement, the appeal that had been made to nationalist feelings—precluded recourse to annexation, which would have been from the international point of view more than dangerous. What remained was to find the means to control local governments, to make them, in conformity with the agreement defended in all the inter-Allied conferences, friendly governments. Confronted with this problem, Stalin gradually elaborated a "front" strategy, which he applied at first in a very pragmatic way. It involved the restoration or maintenance of independent states under the leadership of coalition governments that would include communists. This strategy, reconstituting the constellation of forces brought together by the internal resistance, was in principle supposed to take into account the respective weight of each political tendency. The front policy in principle offered the Allies the guarantee that local political situations would determine the composition of each provisional government that would remain in place until "free" elections could be held and would ensure an acceptable transition to democracy. This was a reasonable hope considering the general weakness of communist forces in Eastern Europe and the anti-Soviet sentiments of several peoples, particularly the Poles and the Hungarians.

Did Stalin foresee at the outset the means for developing during this transitional stage an offensive revolutionary strategy? Nothing is less certain. His efforts to restrain Tito are evidence of his hesitations concerning the best organization for the countries not incorporated into the USSR. But the facts rapidly suggested to him a strategy for wearing down the national fronts that would allow him to push communists to power at the expense of all other forces. This "salami strategy" had a precise meaning, it implied the gradual absorption in carefully calculated stages of all the forces participating in power that kept the communists from a monopoly position. Two elements operated in favor of this strategic shift, one internal, the other external. The favorable internal element was the collapse, because of the war, of all the political structures of the Eastern European countries. The external element was the presence of the Red Army. Having penetrated, alone, all the Eastern European countries, the Red Army was the arbiter of their first postwar political orientations. When it remained as an occupying force in the territories it had "liberated," it was in a position to impose its choices, to authorize or forbid, to exercise constant pressure on local political life. This was particularly easy in the case of conquered countries like Hungary that were permanently treated as enemies and thereby incapable of any reaction. But in the countries to which the Red Army came not as a conqueror but as a liberator and from which it was supposed to withdraw, the consequences of its passage were no less important. In the course of the liberation, the Red Army was able to choose those to whom it would turn over the power seized from the enemy. Just as Tito put his own representatives in place as he progressed, so the Red Army established, no doubt provisionally, leaders who by definition would be favorable to it and whose authority would weigh decisively on future developments. We can agree that the political choices of the Eastern European countries—put off by the Allies until a more peaceful period when the conduct of free elections could be contemplated—were distorted from the outset by the authorities put in place by the Red Army where it alone was present. When Allied commissions arrived on the spot to supervise resumed political life, that life had already been so sufficiently consolidated as to make their intervention futile. This state of affairs was aggravated by a political factor common to all these countries, a consensus around the idea of change.[24] Because the war had destroyed political and social structures, organized systems, and accepted ideas, the slogan of necessary or inevitable change was established everywhere. Nowhere in Eastern Europe, but also among the Allies did anyone imagine that any kind of restoration of the old order could take place. The postwar world had to be a new world in which democracy would wear the colors of socialism. This was one of the givens of those years, surprising from the perspective of today. The antifascist crusade had been conducted by the liberal democracies as well as by the USSR. But in the world of ideology, liberal democracy was almost disqualified in favor of socialism. All the countries emerging from the war were more or less condemned to organize social change. Since the communists were the spokesmen of political and social change, they found legitimacy for their will to exercise a leading role that took no account of the social and political realities of the countries in which they established themselves. In advocating change as an absolute and general necessity, it was forgotten that Czechoslovakia between the wars had been a democratic country. This creeping ideology that was not yet communism but would lead to it—the indispensable transformation of all prewar structures and social relations— had the immediate effect of weakening the democratic forces in the Eastern European states during these decisive years.

The USSR was able to develop the salami strategy easily and very quickly in the conquered countries. Because they had been on the losing side, they were both occupied and subjected more than others to the ideology of change.[25] Having been allied to Germany, they saw their entire past condemned and all their political leadership discredited, and they were thus impoverished in confronting the political forces that the Red Army supported. The communists in Rumania, Hungary, and Bulgaria, even though they were not very representative, had the triple advantage of having been persecuted before and during the war and thus they escaped from the rejection of the past; also they embodied change; and finally they were the most trustworthy friends of the USSR. It is hardly surprising that the communists in these countries quickly moved away from the broad coalitions established immediately after the war. Having come out of the war in difficult conditions, these countries occupied very different positions with respect to the USSR and these differences affected their futures. Bulgaria, although it had been defeated, had always had close ties with Russia and then with the USSR, ties consolidated by history, culture, and religious and linguistic kinship. The appeal to Slavic solidarity launched by Stalin had had profound repercussions in Bulgaria, as evidenced by the organization there of a conference of Slavs in March 1945, the first of its kind.[26]

In fact, while the movement seems to have been relegated to the background in the USSR—it no longer had much usefulness—the Slavic countries under Soviet occupation took up the torch. They thereby suggested that what was seen from the outside as a symptom of Soviet domination over its smaller neighbors was in fact a manifestation of a historical solidarity unknown to the Western world. As early as 1945, Bulgaria, despite contrary choices during the war, presented itself as a privileged ally of the USSR. The existence of a long communist tradition in the country and the personality of Georgi Dimitrov, who had long been involved with the Comintern, all prepared Bulgaria to evolve quickly toward the USSR. It is remarkable in this case that other political forces, like Petkov's Agrarian Party, were not generally hostile to the USSR. Things were entirely different in the two other conquered countries. In Rumania, the "Westernizing" tradition prevailed. The absence of a history of solidarity with Russia was made worse by the weakness of the communist movement, obviously incapable of being the mainspring of a national front, which would have brought out its minority position. The situation of the communists was even less favorable, if possible, in Hungary, where the unpopular memories of the Soviet Republic of Béla Kun were grafted onto the terror created by the attitude of the Soviet occupation troops in the country that had had the most difficulty in extricating itself from the German alliance. The difficulty of assuming that the communist party held a position of strength in the country can be judged from the results of the November 1945 elections, controlled by the Red Army though they were. The Smallholders' Party achieved the prodigious result, considering the political context of the time, of winning 59 percent of the vote, and democratic parties taken together retained 83 percent of the seats in the assembly.

In these circumstances, it was clear that the political evolution of these three countries could not follow a uniform pattern. However, certain common traits also characterized their situations at the time the decisive choices were made. The Red Army was present in all three countries. The defeat they had experienced subjected them to control by occupying forces that were supposed to be tripartite according to Allied agreements, but were in fact a Soviet monopoly. In all three of these countries, the decisive months—from the installation of provisional governments to the organization of elections—were marked by identical processes of penetration of the mechanisms of the state by the communist parties, whatever their strength may have been initially. While the democractic parties, loyal to a classical conception of political life, took possession of the state or played a role in its management in government, or in economic life, the communist parties laid claim to sectors whose importance no one else recognized. Everywhere they gained control either directly or through stand-ins of the Ministry of the Interior, which was in most European countries the government department responsible for internal security. They thereby controlled public order and the elections. Thus in Bulgaria the Ministry of the Interior fell immediately into the hands of the communist Yugov, who placed members of his party at all levels of the department. In Hungary, the party's seizure of the entire apparatus of repression was carried out more subtly through the intermediary actions of a minister from the National Agrarian Party, Erdei, who had been totally won over by the communist party. In Rumania, a "Hungarian" situation prevailed for a time, when the first minister of the interior, Penescu, who was a member of the National Agrarian Party, was violently attacked by the communists, who accused him of protecting fascists. His replacement, General Radescu, who was also prime minister, was placed at the head of the government under pressure from the Soviet occupation authorities, attracted by his notorious philo-Sovietism. Unable simultaneously to carry out his functions as prime minister and as interior minister, Radescu left this key department in the hands of his deputy, the communist Georgescu. One can see how subtly the seizure of control of a position that was decisive for shaping political life was carried out. The communists were installed in visible positions only where their places in the political constellation justified it and where opposition to their presence did not exist. But where communist parties were weak and mistrust of them obvious, they benefited both from intermediaries favorable to their position and from opportunities to put members of the party in place in the state apparatus. This penetration—more or less rapid according to the circumstances—of the apparatus of the state was all the more effective because it was barely visible and was often carried out with the cooperation of noncommunists. It allowed communist parties that were often very much in the minority to impose themselves through "democratic" elections. There were thus two situations that differed at the outset but quickly converged. Where the communist party was in a position of strength, the national coalition, the first stage in the seizure of power, was organized around the party. Elsewhere, the communist party was only one element of the coalition, and at first it concentrated on breaking up the unity of the democratic forces by discrediting them and sowing discord among them.

The first case was that of Bulgaria. The Patriotic Front formed on September 9, 1944, was a coalition in which two communists occupied the vice presidency and the interior and justice ministries, which allowed them to unleash an immediate purge campaign against the "fascists," a campaign facilitated by the existence of a militia established by the communist party at the time. This conditioning of public opinion was accompanied by the systematic persecution of the opposition parties, which were attacked by the police and slandered and had their paper supplies restricted, interfering with the distribution of their newspapers. Finally, the communist party adroitly managed to divide the political parties belonging to the coalition whose prestige was still great in early 1945. In these parties—Petkov's Agrarian Party and the Social Democratic Party—the communists, by means of alternating or simultaneous threats and promises, supported generally pro-

Soviet left-wing factions and gradually made these factions the official governmental representatives of the parties, whose majorities were then shunted into the opposition. Thanks to this "entryism" we can see the development of a split between the "leftist" fractions of the other parties, integrated into the Patriotic Front and with access to newspapers, and the "reactionary" fractions subjected to all sorts of humiliations.[27] The Patriotic Front seemed to attest to the existence of a multiparty state, but the reality was being rapidly transformed through these manipulations and the continuous intimidation tactics against noncommunist elements. It was in this deeply deteriorating context that elections, provided for in the Allied conferences to assure the return to normal conditions, were to take place. In fact, the situation was so abnormal that the Western governments submitted their complaints to Moscow during the summer of 1945 and demanded that elections be postponed until an atmosphere of freedom had been restored.[28] The elections finally took place in November 1945 with a single list of candidates offered by the communists, while the opposition advocated abstention because of the obstacles and the frequent violence to which they had been subjected. It is not surprising that the Patriotic Front, that is the communists, won the elections with 88 percent of the vote. The Allies, who completely contested the validity of the elections, had to ask themselves whether they should accept the government reflected by these results. They expressed their concern at the foreign ministers conference in Moscow in December 1945, but, and here we can see how the actual situation prevailed over all past agreements, the USSR took upon itself alone the task of imposing on Sofia the task of "broadening" of the Bulgarian government that had been decided on in Moscow under Western pressure to reestablish a certain pluralism. Vyshinsky, who was supposed to represent the joint determination of the Allies in Bulgaria, far from helping to broaden the government, restricted it, and in the end caused all possible compromises to fail. In July 1946—the monarchy having been abolished by referendum in September 1945—new elections were held to establish the republic. In the same climate of terror that had prevailed the year before, the Patriotic Front received 78 percent of the votes (277 seats for the Communist Party and 87 for its allies, as opposed to 101 for the opposition), and the former member of the Comintern, Georgi Dimitrov, became prime minister. Challenged by the West, these elections nevertheless turned Bulgaria in a henceforth irreversible direction.

In this evolution, several facts deserve emphasis, all converging toward one reality, the importance of the role played by the USSR. Bulgaria was as we have seen the country in which conditions for such a change were most favorable. However, despite the obvious Russophilia of all political groups there, opposition to a well-established communist party continued to grow. The fact that the opposition in 1946, terrified, hunted, subjected to violence from the communist militia and police, still won 101 seats is definite evidence of the response evoked by their hostility to the Sovietization of their country. The USSR directly and not only through the presence of the Red Army affected this evolution. By taking charge of the broadening of the government demanded by the Allies in 1945, Stalin provided a clear sign that Bulgaria came under his exclusive responsibility. At the moment of a decisive choice, when the Bulgarian communists were hesitating over whether they should open the ranks of government to an opposition whose popularity they could measure, it was Vyshinsky who opposed a compromise solution. This solution would have preserved the coalition for a time instead of shifting Bulgaria to the stage of a system totally dominated by the communists, associating a few fellow-travelers with their power. The very choice of Dimitrov as prime minister demonstrated the degree of Bulgaria's subordination to the USSR from that moment on. Dimitrov, who had been general secretary of the Comintern, had remained in Moscow until November 1945. At the moment when the coalition gave way to a seizure of the state by the Bulgarian Communist Party, it is significant that it was a man coming from the USSR and not a communist of the interior who was placed at the head of the government. More certain than his colleagues, who had momentarily hesitated over whether to prolong the coalition, Dimitrov was Stalin's man, and Stalin's authority over Bulgaria was thus openly confirmed. If the USSR had to support in this way the communist seizure of power in a country in which it was the easiest to carry out, it is easy to see that elsewhere, where the communists' position was weaker, Soviet intervention was even more urgent.[29]

In Rumania, Soviet pressure appeared the moment the Red Army arrived. General Vinogradov intervened with the king in September to demand a reorganization of the government established on September 23, even though it contained a communist. But the Communist Party's situation remained precarious, and its leaders, Ana Pauker, who had just arrived from Moscow, and Gheorghiu-Dej, who had recently come out of prison, had no popular support. Once again, it was by intimidation conducted from outside the coalition government that the communists eroded the position of their rivals. A small minority in the government—one minister without portfolio, but also the vice minister of the interior—their activity was concentrated on the organization of street demonstrations and challenges to the government in place. The theme of their campaign was "fascism," which, they said, had not been uprooted and was "protected" by the authorities in place. In this connection, the Soviet occupation authorities argued that democracy demanded both respect for the popular will and the suppression of the remnants of fascism and its supporters. The Communist Party found itself, thanks to Soviet support, the representative of the people and the antifascist struggle. Paralyzed by Soviet pressure and the maneuvers of Soviet officials and by the gradually increasing control of the press by the Communist Party, in February 1945 Radescu attempted a test of strength and called on all the "vital forces of Rumania" in a radio address. The Soviet reaction was immediate and direct. Soviet troops occupied all the strategic points of Bucharest and disarmed the Rumanian troops. Vyshinsky, urgently sent to the capital, demanded from the king the dismissal of the Radescu government and the appointment of a "front" government representing "the popular forces." The government formed on March 6 clearly reflected the dual Soviet concerns, to have communists preeminent in Rumania, but without the appearance of a coup that would be unacceptable to the Allies, who were already troubled by the Bulgarian situation. The government was headed—because of the necessity of concealing its orientation—by a fellow traveler, Groza, and contained only three communists among a significant number of liberals. But the communists obtained two ministries that allowed them to control all of Rumanian political life, the Ministry of the Interior, which was given to Georgiescu, and the Ministry of Justice, given to Patrašcanu.

Although the Allies had practically given Stalin a free hand in Bulgaria, in Rumania they refused to accept the *fait accompli* and swung their support to King Michael. They thus gave him a final opportunity to rectify the situation. Arguing that the USSR had determined the fate of the Rumanian government without consultation with its allies in flagrant contradiction to the Yalta agreement on obligatory cooperation, the British and the Americans refused to recognize the Groza government. The king, for his part, tried to get Groza to resign and asked for Western mediation. At this point in the conflict, Stalin committed his authority to save the man put in place by Vyshinsky. The USSR had immediately given official recognition to the new government, had granted it authority over Transylvania as a clear indication of its representative nature, and finally had invited it to Moscow to provide Stalin's solemn support for its authority. For the first time, it was obvious that there was dissension among the Allies about their visions of the future of Eastern Europe. And the resistance of King Michael of Rumania against the USSR showed that there was a legitimate solution to the conflict. At the foreign ministers conference of December 1945, the USSR, careful to avoid any breaks and responding to Allied protests against events in Bulgaria and Rumania, agreed to help produce a compromise solution. A tripartite commission[30] in which Soviet influence was dominant negotiated a broadening of the government with the king. The compromise was in fact favorable to the USSR. In return for the broadening of the government (two ministers from the opposition were added), the USSR obtained its allies' recognition of the Groza government. Moreover, even though it had been broadened, the government retained its procommunist orientation. The two opposition figures remained confined to a purely representative role. Finally, the negotiations conducted by Vyshinsky clearly demonstrated that the influence of the USSR in a country occupied by the Red Army was determinative. The real negotiator was Vyshinsky; he was the one from whom the West tried to get concessions and he was also the one who influenced the local situation. Although the process of the communization of Rumania appeared momentarily to be interrupted, Sovietization continued. And the Allies, although they challenged communist influence, were more discreet in their criticism of Soviet actions.

As in Bulgaria, the *de facto* situation went far beyond the legal situation. The coalition government was overwhelmed by the incessant activity of the Communist Party, which multiplied its attacks against the opposition, its newspapers, its political parties, and its personnel. Groups of communist militants disrupted meetings of adversaries of the party, attacked them violently, and demanded that "fascism" be punished. As in Bulgaria, the theme of the collusion of the opposition with the fascists served as the slogan for groups acting on behalf of the Communist Party. This strategy paralysed the opposition and cut it off from a society that was overcome by fear; and the government refused to act, using as a pretext its duty to listen to the "will of the people."

The elections that took place on November 19, 1946, against this background of growing terror and illegitimacy, covered by the government, obviously produced predictable results. Three hundred forty-eight seats went to the government coalition, to which could be added the twenty-nine seats of a satellite party representing the Hungarian minority of Transylvania. The weakened opposition gained only thirty-five deputies, including twenty-nine Agrarians and three Liberals. The Allies had long given up a battle whose futility they recognized. The Rumanian government had in advance answered all their warnings with an argument that was new but was to have a long history. It asserted that only two of the Allies suspected the impartiality of the political authorities and the serenity of the electoral atmosphere, while the USSR was on the contrary quite pleased. In these circumstances Groza in turn denounced what he called an intolerable interference in the domestic affairs of Rumania and emphasized how necessary Soviet support was to him in order to counteract that interference.[31] The government was moreover to perpetuate this support, since the peace treaty of February 10, 1947, established the permanent presence of the Red Army. There remained the obstacle of the form of government. The monarchy had survived the ordeal of 1944; the political parties that still existed, particularly the Peasant Party, had certain legal rights. The Social Democratic Party, subjected to pressure from the communists who wanted to impose a merger, was more and more divided, and its leadership was attacked by both militants and local leaders who were mobilized by hostility both to the USSR and to communism. The year 1947 was devoted to completing the process of the suppression of these obstacles through increased terror. But in essential respects the alignment of the Rumanian regime with the Bulgarian regime was complete with the elections. All the struggles conducted thereafter, until the adoption of the republic, were only rearguard battles. Against the oppressive Soviet presence and the incessant intervention of Stalin's representatives, the will of Rumanian politicians and the local population that was so unfavorable to communism carried no weight.

In the initial phase, Hungary offered a less distressing spectacle to the superficial observer. In this country that had been devastated by the Red Army, the communists, who were in the minority, attempted to move into power, not openly but through the intermediary of Committees of National Liberation including all the parties in order gradually to limit the authority of the very popular Smallholders' Party. In this case, the model was clearly that of the soviets to which Lenin had promised all power in April 1917, while secretly intending to penetrate and ultimately Bolshevize them.[32] However, despite Soviet pressure (Marshal Voroshilov, president of the Election Control Commission, personally intervened to support the communists),[33] and despite the Communist Party's cleverness in penetrating the security services and the unions that it made into a tool for its demonstrations, the political climate in Hungary remained relatively peaceful. At this stage, the place of the Smallholders' Party in society constituted an obstacle that it was difficult to get around. This explains why the elections in November 1945 were conducted under nearly normal conditions and why the communists with 17 percent of the votes momentarily had to bow before the Smallholders' Party, which itself obtained 57 percent of the votes and the leadership of the government.

In the minority, as might be expected, they fought to obtain the only position in the coalition that could compensate for their weakness. They demanded the Ministry of the Interior as a condition of their participation and confronted with this intransigence, the government capitulated. The reason for this capitulation is obvious. Soviet troops were present and any government that was not accepted by the USSR would have been unable to function. For more than a year the Communist Party's activities were directed toward disorganizing the majority. It created a Bloc of the Left within the front, which demonstrated its power by organizing a mass demonstration in Budapest on March 12, 1946, intimidating the Smallholders' Party by accusing it of sheltering fascist elements in its ranks. Once again, the use of the formidable weapon of the accusation of fascism produced its effects. The Smallholders' Party carried out its own purge of its ranks. The police became involved and denounced plots supposedly fomented by important personalities in the party. This harrassment divided it, weakened the popular confidence that had until then been its principal strength, and more or less turned it over to prosecution by the Minister of the Interior, Rajk. This "psychological preparation" of public opinion, domestic and international, explains the shift that took place between 1945 and 1947. The 1945 elections had showed that Hungary was not at all inclined to turn toward communism. The August 1947 elections were prepared with extreme care by the Communist Party and the Soviet authorities. On several occasions in 1946 General Sviridov, commander of Soviet troops in Hungary, intervened to impose the choice of pro-Soviet candidates for government positions and even to arrest men suspected of "fascist sympathies." The Hungarian government was thus step by step presented as incapable of exercising its authority. Communist control over the police apparatus during this period was on the other hand completely effective. In fact, the new electoral law prevented from voting anyone who had been convicted or had had any trouble, very broadly defined, with the police.[34] This provision was particularly serious because the police engaged in a veritable harrassment of the opposition in the months preceding the elections. The communists were already presenting themselves as victims of a future purge and constantly repeated that the "democratic coalition" was held in place only by the presence of the Red Army, guarantor of its survival. Thus the relatively peaceful electoral climate of 1945 was replaced in 1947 when the communists were still in the minority by an oppressive and threatening climate and by fraudulent practices that had been absent from the previous election. Despite this obvious degradation of political debate, the communist position was far from satisfying. From 17 percent, their votes increased to 22 percent. Parties within the communist sphere of influence also won votes, enough to give the procommunist coalition a doubtful majority. But on the other side, the persistence of an opposition vote representing 35 percent of the electorate showed how much in the way of manipulation and Soviet intervention was required for the conquest of power in this country that had been so battered in 1945.

More or less quickly, through various techniques, the three former allies of Germany found themselves in the space of two event-filled years in comparable situations. The communists dominated everywhere, even if they had not yet finished off their adversaries. Everywhere as well the USSR had demonstrated with some minor variations that it alone was in control of political evolution; and it showed an increasing lack of concern for the timid protests of its allies. It is true that for the latter the real test of strength was located elsewhere, in Poland, where the existence of political leaders supported by the West and the status of an ally rather than of a conquered enemy ought in principle to have allowed them to react to Soviet violations of past agreements.

In contrast to what happened in Yugoslavia and the conquered countries, the evolution of Poland was in part irreversible from the very moment when the Polish government was put in place. The communists of the Lublin government had several powerful elements on their side.[35] First of all, they were in place while their adversaries were still in London. This circumstance mandated the solution of a broadening of the government advocated by

Stalin, at the expense of the Anglo-American argument. They had been able, like Yugoslavia in some respects, to set up their own institutions in former German territory over which the USSR had given control to Gomułka, thereby creating a *fait accompli*. Finally, they had ensured Moscow's primacy in Poland's foreign relations by signing the bilateral treaty of April 21, 1945. The Western allies, who had not been consulted beforehand, thus found themselves deprived of any real influence. However, the integration of Poland into the Soviet sphere of influence was not absolute, because despite the conditions under which the provisional government was installed, the USSR did not really control the country. Stalin, having taken the trouble to become personally involved in the making of the government, choosing the "key" men (Radkiewicz at Security and Rola Zymierski at Defense), knew that the Polish population saw his protégés as puppets, and that for that very reason, Soviet ascendancy over Poland was insufficient, at the mercy of uncontrollable events and even of a civil war.[36]

Confronting this group, strong because it was in place but without popular support, Mikolajczyk, leader of the Peasant Party, could pride himself on his popularity, his international recognition, and the place of his party in Polish society. His principal weaknesses stemmed from his hesitation in joining the coalition and especially from the *de facto* situation with which he was confronted. It was precisely the implantation of the communists in Poland that explained his delay in returning to the country and agreeing to sign the Yalta accord on the broadening of the Lublin government. In 1945 Mikolajczyk had hoped for a time to persuade the West that they had made a fool's bargain, that Soviet control over Eastern Europe was already in progress, and that the only solution was to harden their positions toward the USSR and not to compromise. When he finally returned to Poland at the urging of his allies it was too late. No doubt Mikolajczyk was treated in a way that appeared to satisfy the requirements of a coalition government in which his party was an important element. He was named vice premier and minister of agriculture. And in the government reorganization one of his associates was placed at the head of the administration in order to satisfy him. But in fact communist infiltration of the state apparatus was already very advanced. To counteract the activity of the head of public administration, it had been decided before his return to Poland that within the Interior Ministry, the security services would be separated from public administration. The communists had reserved security for themselves and they thereby dominated as they did everywhere else the secret police, military security, and the popular militias. Control of the army and law and order were thus all concentrated in the hands of the communist Radkiewicz, the man whom Stalin had personally chosen as interior minister of the provisional government a year earlier. The head of public administration was left with a position that carried few responsibilities and he was excluded from all questions involving security. His impotence was accentuated by the fact that his authority was exercised only over a part of Polish territory. The rich lands seized from Germany were placed under the exclusive authority of the communist Gomułka and his Ministry of Reconquered Territories. Behind the appearances of coalition, there were in reality two unequal groups, and indeed two Polands. In the "reconquered territories" a veritable communist state was created from the beginning, and the Poland of the 1945–47 coalition found itself under pressure from this "communist state within the state," which presented itself as a model and accelerated the whole process.[37] It was also under pressure from a party that was elsewhere in a dominant position. Finally, we have to take account of the Red Army present in the reconquered territories and also present from 1945 on in the Polish Army through the intermediary of Soviet officers of Polish origin. Mikolajczyk had hoped that the return to the country of the army of General Anders would allow him to counteract the rapid Sovietization of the Polish Army. But on this point, too, the initial situation shattered his hopes. The Polish troops that had fought on foreign soil were subjected to such control and pressure that they were unable to restore a minimum balance in favor of noncommunist forces.

Isolated within the government and without control over decisions, Mikolajczyk placed all his hopes in "free elections," believing that they offered him an opportunity to eliminate the communists completely. Convinced that he represented popular opinion, he underestimated the work that had been accomplished by his adversaries to control the electoral procedures, and he prepared for the free elections provided for by the Allied agreements. In 1946, instead of elections, he had to confront a complicated referendum, mixing three problems together and notably asking the voters to express their approval of the annexation of German territories, which could only bring a positive response. Mikolajczyk was unable to detect the trap, called for a negative vote on another question in order to measure his support, and found himself in the minority, although he always maintained that only the most shameless fraud had produced that result.[38] From that point on, Poland slid rapidly toward satellization. The West, taken in by the small number of communists in the coalition government (seven positions out of twenty-four; but the high number of fellow travelers and the distribution of positions compensated for this apparent weakness), reacted too late. Violence had been installed; the elections that the communists had dreaded until then were organized against a background of open crisis and flagrant voting irregularities. On January 19, 1947, the effects of this evolution could be easily measured. The government's Bloc of the Left obtained nine million votes and 392 seats, the opposition 2.2 million votes and fifty-two seats. Mikolajczyk had to leave the government and he became the target of communist attacks. Soon there was nothing he could do but take the road of exile.

If we confine ourselves to appearances, the history of Poland from 1945 to

1947 suggests that there was less direct intervention by the USSR there than in the conquered countries. There was no Soviet minister or general to dictate conduct to the local authorities. Nor were there any Soviet troops to put the national army under arrest or to take part in maintaining public order. But although the Polish political arena seemed open only to the national parties, it should not be forgotten that this was because Stalin had had ample time to organize the structures of power and to guide the operations of the government before the coalition was formed. In the conquered countries, the "patriotic" or "national" coalition was the first form of autonomous political power established at the end of the war. It was the framework for competition between the communists and the other parties; and within this coalition, Soviet activity had had the effect of leading the communists from a minority to a dominant position. In Poland, on the contrary, the coalition was the product of a broadening of the power held by the communists. And competition was much more restricted because all the positions that gave access to decision making and control had already been distributed. Soviet support was necessary in this case to allow the communists to hold on to positions they had already won. It can be asserted that in Poland the breakup of the coalition in 1947 was already guaranteed in 1945 and the coalition itself was never anything but a trick.

Revolution by the "Parliamentary Path"

Beginning in 1956, Stalin's heirs insisted on the possibility of not following the revolutionary example of the USSR in every circumstance. And as an example of the "democratic passage to socialism by the parliamentary path," they offered Czechoslovakia.[39]

It is indisputable that the case of Czechoslovakia during this period was very different from that of the other countries discussed here. Out of all of Eastern Europe, Czechoslovakia was the only country in which the establishment of communism was possible as early as 1945. It was the only country in which the USSR exerted pressure to delay the process. Hubert Ripka, one of the best placed witnesses of the period, noted this anomaly and concluded that what Stalin had "prefabricated" was not revolution, which was possible and plausible in 1945, but on the contrary, restraint at that moment, in order to impose a simple coup later in 1948.[40] In fact, everything about the situation of Czechoslovakia in 1945 favored a peaceful evolution toward socialism: a powerful communist party; a certain degree of solidarity between the government-in-exile in London and the communists, whom Beneš invited to participate in the Czech national government; a head of state who, unlike Mikolajczyk, was ready to participate in a coalition government; and a people whom the West had discouraged by abandoning it at Munich and who had emerged from the ordeal of 1938 to 1945 dominated by unconcealed pro-Soviet feelings. All the parties making up the coalition in London were, moreover, convinced of the need for profound structural reforms—widespread nationalizations and agrarian reform—that would have the effect of changing the conditions under which authority would be exercised in liberated Czechoslovakia, giving the state economy and those who were to control it considerable importance.

It was in this context that the USSR conducted a veritable experiment with the popular front as a transitional path toward a controlled revolution. This strategy, baptized by Gottwald "democratic national revolution," seemed to provide equal places for the supporters of democracy and the communists. The former won recognition for pluralism and for democracy in political life and within the parties. The latter were the bearers of a program of nationalizations and planning. Cooperation between communists and noncommunists in the National Front involved, however, an important political concession to communist conceptions. Pluralism operated "within" the National Front, which was recognized as the only framework for political activity; and certain parties were from the beginning excluded from it (the Agrarians and the Slovak People's Party).[41] The Communist Party derived from this coalition a legitimation of its position in power and of its program, and the values defended by the party and those of the whole nation quickly became identified with one another. Imperceptibly, the coalition began always to favor the communists. In the first government, led by the Social Democrat Fierlinger, the communists held the traditional key positions—Interior, Information—but also ministries that granted them more subtle control over public opinion—National Education, Social Security—to which was added control of the army through the intermediary of a sympathizer, all the more useful because he was not a communist, General Svoboda; they also had control of Foreign Affairs, thanks to Vice-Minister Clementis. Finally, the Ministry of Industry, also a decisive sector in a developed country with a large and educated working class, was under the communists' thumb through the intermediary of a Social Democratic minister sympathetic to the party, Lansman.[42]

It is clear what made the coalition strong at the time. The communists had penetrated the state apparatus thanks to a few men installed in strategic positions. But they had penetrated it even more because they had "satellites" in the Social Democratic Party who were completely devoted to them and who at the same time seemed to guarantee the balance of the coalition. Although the Communist Party completely controlled the unions, various organizations escaped from it and the noncommunist parties enjoyed indisputable popular support. The 1946 elections showed how balanced the situation remained, since the Communist Party won 38 percent of the vote and 114 out of 300 seats. However, in Slovakia, the elections resulted in a communist defeat and that accentuated the struggle for power that was already developing under cover of the coalition.

While the rise of communists to total power was taking place elsewhere in a climate of violence, Czechoslovakia continued to offer the image of a successful wager on "parliamentary socialism." The political struggles, the intimidation of a few ministers, and the Tiso trial in Slovakia could not obscure two phenomena that were exceptional between 1945 and 1948 in that part of Europe: Czechoslavakia was not under the control of the Red Army, which had left the country in 1945; and debates in Parliament and in public life remained despite undoubted violations and excesses open to several parties struggling every inch of the way to maintain their places in the coalition. In the general shift of Eastern European countries toward communism and Soviet control, Czechoslovakia remained a reassuring exception. It seemed to show that the USSR was not determined in all circumstances to transform its military victories into revolution and domination over other peoples. It especially seemed to suggest that nothing was yet final, that a return to normalcy was not impossible. If democracy survived in Czechoslovakia, if a mixture of democracy and socialism were to be preserved there, wouldn't it be a model for the future for those countries in which the withdrawal of the Red Army would permit similar developments? There is no doubt that the USSR decided that Czechoslovakia was the perfect place to maintain this kind of illusion and to give some assurances to its allies. As long as international conditions forced it to be prudent, Czechoslovakia was left free to pursue a relatively democratic life and to demonstrate that communists could live together with other parties while respecting political rules that they had not completely defined. The choice of Czechoslovakia for such a demonstration is easy to understand. Of all the countries in Eastern Europe, it was the only one that had really greeted the Red Army as a liberating army. It was also the only one ready to accept the idea that the USSR was the best guarantor of its survival and thus that policies giving the USSR a privileged place were natural and desirable.

Maintained for international reasons, the "Czech path" that reconciled democracy and socialism was brutally suppressed as soon as the reasons encouraging the USSR to preserve it had disappeared. When the USSR feared that the West would reestablish a foothold in Czechoslovakia through the Franco-Czech treaty and the Marshall Plan, it stopped the experiment short and with the Prague coup of February 1948 aligned Czechoslovakia with the other countries it controlled. In a few weeks, the political system that had seemed to have proved its capacity to survive was destroyed. In a few weeks, the coalition succumbed to the maneuvers of the communists, who used against it forms of pressure they had held in reserve since 1945. The Prague coup demonstrated that in 1945 Czechoslovakia had not been saved from communization, carried out at full speed elsewhere, by an exceptional aptitude for democracy, but on the contrary that despite a democratic tradition and a pluralist political culture, it could at any moment under certain conditions be forced to follow the path taken before it by countries without democratic traditions, like Bulgaria. The first lesson of the Prague coup was that the techniques and instruments for the communist seizure of power were infinitely more decisive than the local conditions and democratic aptitudes of any particular country.

Stalin's Program and His Means

The three years from 1945 to 1948 were enough for the USSR to transform into lasting domination what was to have been only a momentary influence. Three years were enough for it to remove from Europe countries that, located in its center, had almost always succeeded in maintaining a balance between the two European poles. Three years were enough to commit unprepared and unwilling countries to a revolutionary path with no turning back.

This transformation of Eastern European political systems and outcomes that had started from different situations—as winners or losers, as industrialized or predominantly rural countries, as Slavic or non-Slavic countries, as democratic countries or countries with an authoritarian tradition, as nationally homogeneous or multiethnic and thereby divided countries—was marked by certain common characteristics, which outline a new kind of revolutionary strategy, unknown to Lenin though carried out in his name. In the first place, everywhere, despite initial differences, it was the USSR that decided the fate of each of these Eastern European countries with the exception of the two "loners," Yugoslavia and Albania. Elsewhere from beginning to end the USSR had imposed the strategy, defined the rules of the game, and decided at what moment the revolution should take place. From one end of Eastern Europe to the other, revolutions were made from above and from the outside, that is, decided and organized by the Soviet Union. When he rejected the idea of exporting revolution, Stalin was not really contradicting his future actions. He did not export revolution; he extended the Russian Revolution to the countries over which he had control.

These extensions of the revolution and the authoritarian and generally violent imposition of this process of change were not carried out by improvisation. Domestic situations were never the determining factor in Stalin's decisions. What determined his choices was the international situation. War had installed Stalin's armies in the heart of Europe and forced the Allies to pay attention to his demands. Stalin had a warlike view of the extension of the revolution. The function of these revolutions was to assure his control over the occupied territories. And because postwar international life prohibited or limited annexations and permanent occupations, he was led to substitute, as soon as he could, political for military control. This did not at all mean that for Stalin the revolutions were only disguises for pure and simple occupations. It meant that his conception of world revolution—and he was the first to have the opportunity really to extend the revolution—made revolution depend on the USSR and represented an extension of Soviet power, which he identified with the power of the revolution.

But although the war provided him with the opportunity, finally, to bring about this revolutionary progress, the military means that the war put at his disposal, the armies of occupation, were always subordinate to the ultimate program, which was political, and thus to political tools. No doubt, the Red Army facilitated the communist seizures of power in several East European countries, but it was absent from Czechoslovakia where the coalition had had time to consolidate itself and where the democratic tradition was most vital. It is thus inaccurate to reduce the success of the revolutions solely to the presence of Soviet troops. Moreover, in the countries where it played the greatest role, Rumania and Hungary, the war had already shattered previous political structures and the systems in place were very vulnerable. The common characteristic of all these revolutions, aside from the Soviet desire to bring them about, was the use of the salami strategy. Everywhere coalition governments evolved, at various rhythms but in an identical manner. The communist parties had seized strategic positions, almost always the Ministries of the Interior, although beyond that, the definition of strategic positions varied from country to country. In some instances, the communists were even able to give up the Ministry of the Interior and to control the apparatus of repression and security by other means or through the intermediary services of cleverly manipulated noncommunist ministers. And they used these positions of strength in two directions: to divide the adversary parties, weaken them, discredit them, and then destroy them; and to terrify, or in any event control, the population. Within the fronts, whether they were called "patriotic" or "national," the communists practiced a dual strategy: the salami strategy, and the Trojan horse strategy. "Day by day, slice by slice," they "cut up the reactionary positions concealed in other policies," as Rakosi later defined the salami strategy.[43] The slices went from the right to the center and finally to the left in a process of elimination that the communist parties orchestrated at every stage. Although the parties of the "right" and the center were often aware that they were the preferred targets of this strategy, and although they attempted to defend their positions in the coalition, the communist parties generally had a naive ally, the last slice of the salami, which ended up suffering the fate of those it had helped to eliminate, and that was the Social Democratic parties. The most spectacular illustration of the Social Democrats' errors in judgment is the case of Fierlinger in Prague, who was the communists' most loyal ally and the zealous artisan of their final victory.

The use of the Social Democrats was also an element of revolutionary manipulation through a second strategy, "entryism" or the Trojan horse. The communists constantly penetrated the noncommunist parties by using for this purpose either their own agents or more frequently sympathizers from other parties.[44] This infiltration of the opposition parties effectively contributed to their destruction.

It was in the realm of infiltration, of police control and violence that the communist parties joined battle and won. The existence of fronts intended to manage the transition until free elections could take place should not conceal the fact that communist strategy granted elections an ambiguous function. The fronts were broken by the elections. In each country, the movement from the coalition to party hegemony took place on the basis of elections won by the party allowing it to eliminate its adversaries in an apparently democratic confrontation. This consistency of electoral success should not conceal the essential fact that at the moment when the break-up of the coalition had been decided upon, elections had to be won. They were not the expressions of popular choice but an obligatory stage in the process of the seizure of power. Nor were they expressions of the real strength of the party. The communist parties were in the minority almost everywhere, and the coalitions allowed them to manipulate, under the cover of a fiction of democracy, the conditions under which the elections would finally take place. Where the communist parties were extremely weak, violence and fraud were barely concealed. Where they were stronger, intimidation and manipulation of the crowd could be subtler; this was the case in Czechoslovakia. But everywhere, at the moment the coalition came to an end, in a final effort the party set in motion the police resources it had acquired from the very beginning of the front in order to ensure electoral success. The elections thus had the function of concealing the violence of the move toward the seizure of power. They were a screen for the seizure of power, which was in reality carried out by communist party organizations, not by votes in voting booths. In the last analysis, the electoral weight of the communist parties of Eastern Europe was of little importance; the only things that counted were the communist party organizations and the degree of control they had achieved over the state apparatus.

The relations between the communist party and the masses varied from one country to another according to how well established it was and how it related to the country's political traditions. Terrorized or mobilized masses were the two polar extremes of the strategy of the Eastern European communist parties. In any event, the parties were everywhere able to manipulate at a minimum a part of society. Peasants in Poland were momentarily won over to the party by the distribution of German lands. Slovaks were united around the popular themes of the Slovak nation. Workers in Prague staged street demonstrations under the leadership of their unions. Czechoslovakia, which was industrialized and enjoyed a democratic tradition, offered an extreme example of the strategy of well-controlled mass mobilizations. The masses that took to the streets of Prague after February 20, 1948, where they proclaimed that the Communist Party embodied the popular will against the still existing legal government, were tightly controlled. Like Lenin before them, the Czech unions knew that spontaneity was dangerous and that the only useful kind of demonstration was one that was well prepared and remained under their control.

In this context, there came into play another aspect of the strategy that the Eastern European communist parties had inherited from the Leninist model, the extension of the political battle to all social forces to suppress possible counterweights to their ascendancy. The penetration of the state apparatus was in fact the surest method of neutralizing the other political parties before annihilating them. It remained to neutralize society, to deprive it of its means of expression and self-defense. The unions, where they existed, carried out this function. Czechoslovakia again provides the best example. The unions, dominated by Zápotocký, were an emanation of the Czech Communist Party. They were able to organize and channel a "popular will" that had no other places in which to express itself, because following the unions all social organizations had been infiltrated and coopted by the Communist Party. This was a faithful application of the Leninist model that made the communist party the bearer of social consciousness and gave it the task of organizing and controlling society at all levels, depriving it of any other mode of expression. From the party to society, all countervailing powers were suppressed, and the organisms of social representation and association—unions, youth associations, and so on—were reduced to the state of transmission belts for the political authorities. In the last analysis, this revolutionary strategy was characterized by the gradual destruction of civil society before the official transition to another system through elections. The elections were simply an acknowledgment that the coalition had disappeared. They consolidated what the whole intermediate phase had prepared for and theorized about, a revolutionary legitimacy that had gradually, insidiously, replaced the legitimacy defined by the constitution and traditional political institutions. This *de facto* legitimacy prevailed over the law, even though it was concealed behind the false appearance of the popular will; everywhere it was a deliberate creation of, and was imposed by, the communist parties, who had defined their programs and their plans of action in agreement with Stalin and under his aegis. The Leninist conception of a communist party responsible for forging consciousness and the social interest was at the heart of the revolutionary history of Eastern Europe in the years from 1945 to 1947.

We should also emphasize another important aspect of these manipulated revolutions: the simultaneous use of an ideology of national consensus and one of internal struggle, which together made up a contradictory whole.

The phase of the coalition was presented in all these Eastern Europe countries as the expression of a national consensus around a program of reconstruction and profound change accepted by all. But this consensus, which by definition integrated all political forces into a common program, also made the progression of communist parties at the expense of other political forces that much more difficult. In this context, the notion of an internal enemy took on all its significance and became a powerful means for destroying all the noncommunist forces. The internal enemy was first of all fascism, which had already been destroyed. In the name of the struggle against fascism or against "protection granted to fascists," the communist parties, which identified themselves improperly and exclusively with anti-fascism, were able systematically to ban political parties and newspapers, to persecute individuals and groups, and to impose their will. Where fascism could not be invoked, the internal enemy had no identity; but through the processes of identification, because communism was by definition identical to antifascism, this adversary, because he was an enemy of the communists, was by definition a fascist. Hubert Ripka in his penetrating analysis of the Czech tragedy shows clearly how the party was able to monopolize the antifascist struggle in order to justify both its control over the police and its image of exemplary antifascism; how it then imperceptibly transferred this argument to the people's democracy with which it was identified and which it claimed was threatened by an "internal enemy," a term which gradually came to encompass everything that was not communist.[45] The great error of the democratic parties was to accept without resisting the vocabulary and the postulates of the communist parties. By their silence they legitimized the communists' claim that they embodied the values of freedom, democracy, and struggle against fascism; they legitimized their claim of identification with the threatened people's democracy. By their silence they allowed themselves to be trapped by rules of the game decided upon by the communist parties. Although some noncommunist leaders, like Mikolajczyk, were lucid about this trap and hesitated to participate in coalitions whose logic they knew to be fixed in advance, others, like the Czechs, demonstrated unmistakable complacency in the face of a process that was going to destroy them. In this respect, the history of Eastern Europe is far from uniform and different degrees of lucidity and resistance on the part of noncommunists can be discerned from one country to another. Although in the conquered countries, the noncommunist parties had few opportunities to address communist claims to embody the defense of democracy—the defeat and the very weighty presence of the Red Army favored the communists from the outset—the situation was different in Poland and Czechoslovakia. In those two countries, the contrasting attitudes of the noncommunists toward the communist parties— Mikolajczyk's desperate defiance, and Beneš's weakness—were the result both of their respective positions with respect to Russia and of the political traditions of each country. For Mikolajczyk, after the defeat of Germany, the

USSR was the only threat hanging over Poland. This is why he did not hesitate to identify the communists with the USSR and to reject them altogether. For Beneš, the USSR was not Czechoslovakia's enemy, and Slavic solidarity was not an expression devoid of meaning. Although they were opposed on this point, and therefore adopted different attitudes toward the coalition, Mikolajczyk and Beneš both shared the hope of saving democracy through the popular will; that is, they shared in an underestimation of the communists' ability to reduce elections to a stage of and a means for their march to power. Mikolajczyk believed in his influence over the society and Beneš believed in the strength of the democratic tradition in Czechoslovakia. Although both were right in their evaluations of these factors, both left out of account the fact that harmony with society and with democratic traditions carried little weight in a confrontation with the perfected apparatuses of the communist parties and their strategies. Forgetting the example offered by the Bolsheviks between October 1917 and February 1918, when Lenin dissolved the Constituent Assembly, they seemed unaware that, confronted with the communist program, formal democracy had proved defenseless.

This leads to two final questions. Could other men who were more combative and opposed to the communists have avoided or retarded the course of events from 1945 to 1948? Was Stalin's program in those years coherent and in conformity with history as it developed?

To make a judgment about the quality of the men who participated in this troubled period is risky, for the problem is not only the relative abilities of the protagonists of this history. No doubt we can agree with the remarks of François Fejtö at the conclusion of his excellent analysis, *Le Coup de Prague:*

If the USSR, through the intermediary of the Czech Communist Party, was able to win, this was primarily because of the division, the mediocrity, the indecision, the lack of imagination, and the lack of courage of the defenders of the democratic order in Czechoslovakia; and secondly, thanks to the power of the Czech Communist Party, the tactical cleverness of its leaders, and the discipline and combativeness of its militants.[46]

On the one side were indecisive and bewildered men, on the other decisive men. This severe judgment has been made by other writers about other countries. It has been used to explain Tito's victory over Mihajlović, Gomułka's victory over Mikolajczyk, and so on. It was often true that noncommunist leaders lacked lucidity, that they agreed too easily to be locked into a system whose principles were defined by the communist parties, that they believed in democratic virtues and did not always fight with enough decisiveness to impose them, but this was not always the case. Moreover, we cannot forget how unequal the struggle was. Whether the Red Army was present or not in the countries where these confrontations developed, the shadow of Soviet power extended over all of Eastern Europe. On the other hand, the retreat of the West in the face of Soviet demands was obvious. The communists could at any moment turn to a nearby protector; the noncommunists called unavailingly on distant powers who generally relied on Soviet mediation to resolve conflicts. The isolation in which noncommunist leaders and parties found themselves in the face of the powerful assistance the USSR provided for their adversaries helps us to understand their feelings of helplessness. Although they gave legitimacy to the communists' claim to embody the national interest and the struggle against internal enemies, were they not simply echoing the West's acceptance of similar claims by the USSR on an international scale? The idea that the alternative to fascist totalitarianism was communism was not born in Eastern Europe in 1945. It was the product of a general weakening of confidence in the virtues of parliamentary democracy. All of postwar Europe was haunted by the idea of a new political and social order, to which only communist ideology gave some consistency. The ideological weakness of Eastern European noncommunists, their tendency to locate themselves within the sphere of influence of the "revolutionary" call launched by the communists, was connected with this evolution of political ideas in 1945 in all of Europe. Communism was a symbol of progress, almost everyone agreed. This certainty was mortal for the democracies. In the light of this political and ideological solitude on the part of the adversaries of communism, it is of relatively little importance whether they were men of character or indecisive men. For their adversaries were no more exemplary personalities than they. We always tend to attribute to conquerors the virtues that would explain victory. But was Stalin really more remarkable in character and intelligence than Bukharin or Trotsky? Or did he perhaps simply understand immediate situations better than they did? Were Gottwald, Gomułka, and Dimitrov incomparably superior to Beneš, Mikolajczyk, and Petkov? Or were they perhaps only the clever tools of a global plan for the expansion of Soviet power? If the noncommunist protagonists of this history had been more decisive, more attentive to the lessons of the past, which would have enlightened them about the nature of the communist party and its programs, perhaps they would have complicated Stalin's task. But could they, alone, have radically changed a situation in which they were so disfavored?

Although the course of events in Eastern Europe between 1945 and 1948 was more or less ineluctable, this was not by virtue of so-called historical laws or some meaning of history, but because Stalin the conqueror had developed a plan that allowed him to consolidate his victory in a lasting way. Hence, we must be more specific about his program.

During the war Stalin had been careful not to frighten his allies with exorbitant claims; what is more, the course of the war, which was long uncertain, forced him at first to limit himself to the realm of defense.

However, even in the most difficult years, Stalin continued to think that the countries located on the western borders of the USSR had been the perennial stakes in the rivalry among the great powers. With the exception of Poland, which had taken on at the time a genuinely international status and laid claim to its own role, the other states were staging posts for the great powers and for that very reason susceptible to penetration and influence. The USSR had felt threatened before 1941 by the neighboring states of Eastern Europe, confirmed by the French policy of the *cordon sanitaire* and the ambitions of Nazi Germany. The war, which allowed the Soviets to penetrate the region, changed the map of the powers exercising influence there, but it did not change the permanent realities of a zone open to the competition of the great powers. France and Germany were replaced by the USSR and the United States. But, in this new confrontation on Eastern European territory, the balance had shifted. Although the United States in 1945 thought of itself as a protector of the democracies, it had no direct interests in the region, as France and Germany had had in 1939. The USSR, on the contrary, had always thought that its security was located primarily to the west of its borders. This unequal interest in Eastern Europe by the two powers confronting one another there explains the boldness Stalin demonstrated from 1945 on and it defined the outlines of his program. For the USSR, Eastern Europe, suddenly available to its ambitions because it was present there and because the United States was not inclined to take risks for a region it considered secondary, presented a threefold interest. It could be transformed into a defensive barrier, closed off to the other powers and subjected to the influence of the USSR, thereby securing its western borders. This was the thesis Stalin defended during the war, and his allies accepted it. But in the end the region could also become a link in a revolutionary chain that would connect the USSR to Western Europe. In Stalin's conception of revolutions—which were to take place in the framework of territorial continuity, extending the Russian Revolution and Soviet space—the revolutionary transformation of Eastern Europe constituted an indispensable prerequisite to the forward march toward the West. It is doubtful that Stalin had incorporated into his plans by 1945 the systematic transformation of Eastern Europe. But it is certain that, as a pragmatist taking advantage of the defensive barrier that had been conceded to him, he determined to prepare for the revolutionary alternative where that could be accomplished without provoking international incidents. In the years from 1945 to 1947, careful not to disturb excessively the weakening alliance of the great powers, he precipitated the movement whereby local resistance was attenuated enough to allow him to confront the West with a *fait accompli* (in Rumania and Bulgaria). He acted in the same way in Poland where resistance was relatively strong, because he wanted to avoid the consolidation of an opposition force which the West might later be tempted to support. And he preserved the Czech status quo, aware that at any moment he would be in a position to bring about the defeat of any political compromise.

Stalin's strategy was thus organized in temporal stages. In the short term, it was aimed at consolidating a defensive barrier without excessive risks by imposing political systems infiltrated by communist parties loyal to the USSR. It was thus a procedure for indirect control over nominally sovereign countries. In the long term, he prepared for the revolutionary alternative by giving local communist parties the means to dominate society. But during this period, his long-term program remained hazy. Did it go beyond the will to control the governments, beyond the vision of a comfortable and diverse defensive barrier? As long as Stalin felt the necessity of having the international community recognize the legitimacy of his defensive aspirations in Eastern Europe, the offensive alternative was implicit in his reasoning. And probably the means for putting this alternative fully into operation were not defined. On the other hand, when the international context was changed at the end of 1947 and the alliance was seen by Stalin as a threat to his established positions in Eastern Europe, he developed his strategy in an offensive direction and transformed the defensive barrier into satellites of Soviet power.

NOTES

1.   Charles Bohlen, *Witness to History—1929–1969* (New York, 1973), 175ff.

2.   See the conversations between Stalin and de Gaulle of December 1944. Charles de Gaulle, *Mémoires de guerre. Le Salut, 1944–1946* (Paris, 1969), 83–92.

3.   Averell Harriman and Elie Abel, *Special Envoy to Churchill and Stalin, 1941–1946* (New York, 1975), 444.

4.   Quoted by Daniel Yergin, *Shattered Peace* (Boston, 1977), 104.

5.   George Kennan, *Memoirs, 1925–1950* (Boston, 1967), 1:283ff.

6.   Quoted by Yergin, op. cit., 105–6.

7.   Harriman and Abel, op. cit., 518.

8.   George Kennan ("X"), "The Sources of Soviet Conduct," *Foreign Affairs* III, 25 (1947):566–82.

9.   Harriman and Abel, op. cit., 542.

10.   See Robert C. Tucker, ed., *Stalinism* (New York, 1977), 81–91.

11.   Moshe Lewin, *Political Undercurrents in Soviet Economic Debates* (Princeton, 1974), particularly 73–96.

12.   Ibid., 97–124.

13.   Lewin discusses this problem at length in Tucker, *Stalinism*, 115ff. See also the collection edited by Charles Bettelheim, *L'Industrialisation de l'U.R.S.S. dans les années trente* (Paris, 1982).

14.   *Pravda*, 5 March 1936.

15.   J. Cathola, *Sans fleur ni fusil* (Paris, 1981), 73–85.

16. In this part of this chapter, I have relied particularly on the pioneering and still unsurpassed work of Hugh Seton-Watson, *The East European Revolution* (Oxford, 1950; 3rd ed. 1956), especially 167–230; Zbigniew Brzezinski, *The Soviet Bloc, Unity and Conflict*, rev. ed. (Cambridge, Mass., 1967); François Fejtö, *Histoire des démocraties populaires* (Paris, 1956), vol. 1.

17. See Brzezinski, *The Soviet Bloc*, 4.

18. Tito, *L'édification du socialisme et le rôle et les tâches de l'alliance socialiste du peuple travailleur de Yougoslavie*, (Belgrade 1960).

19. On the relations among Tito, Mihajlović, and the British, see S. Clissold, *Whirlwind: Tito's Rise to Power* (New York, 1949), 213ff.

20. Tito, "L'armée populaire dans la guerre et la révoluion," *Questions actuelles de socialisme* 1 (Jan.–Feb. 1952):58ff.

21. Seton-Watson, op. cit., 222.

22. Echange de lettres entre le C.C. du P.C.Y. et le C.C. du P.C.(b) de l'U.R.S.S., *Le Livre Yougoslave* (Paris, 1950), 84.

23. The republic was proclaimed on November 29, 1945. On this period, see *Foreign Relations of the United States. Diplomatic Papers* (1945), 5:1203–6; 6:1104–92.

24. C. E. Black and T. G. Thornton, *Communism and Revolution: The Strategic Uses of Political Violence* (Princeton, 1964), particularly chapter 4.

25. Bulgaria had declared war on Germany in September 1944; Rumania in August 1944; only Hungary did not manage it.

26. *Slavianskii Sbor v Sofiji* (1945). I am indebted to Antonín Snejdárek for this information.

27. Seton-Watson, op. cit., 222.

28. Kennan, *Memoirs*, 1:284.

29. See Seton-Watson, op. cit., 215.

30. It was made up of Vyshinsky and the American and British ambassadors, Averell Harriman and Sir Clark Kerr.

31. Seton-Watson, op. cit., 207.

32. For the communization of Hungary, see François Fejtö, *Histoire des démocraties populaires*, vol. 1; Seton-Watson, op. cit., especially 191.

33. Seton-Watson, op. cit., 193.

34. In early 1946, the commander of Soviet troops put pressure on the government to prevent the adoption of a law providing for amnesty or for the reduction of punishment in the case of minor political offenses, see Seton-Watson, op. cit., 196.

35. On this phase of Polish history, see S. Mikolajczyk, *Le Viol de la Pologne* (Paris, 1949); J. Czewanowski, *La Rançon de la victoire* (Paris, 1949). H. Stehle, *The Independent Satellite: Society and Politics in Poland Since 1945* (London, 1965); P. Hiscocks, *Poland: Bridge for the Abyss? An Interpretation for Development in Postwar Poland* (London, 1963); Davies, *God's Playground: A History of Poland*, vol. 2 (Oxford, 1981; repr. New York, 1982), ch. 23.

36. Davies, op. cit., 558. Davies quotes a remark Stalin made to his protégés: "When the Red Army has left, they will shoot you as traitors."

37. Czewanowski, op. cit., 111.

38. Mikolajczyk, op. cit., 183ff.

39. *Dvatsatyi s'ezd Kommunisticheskoi Partii Sovetskogo Soiuza* (Moscow, 1956), 1:32ff.

40.   Hubert Ripka, *Le Coup de Prague* (Paris, 1949), iv and 15ff.

41.   These parties were accused of collaboration, Ripka, op. cit., 19.

42.   Ibid., 21.

43.   Rákosi explained this strategy in a lecture given at the Upper School of the Hungarian Workers Party in February 1952; "The path of our people's democracy," translated by La Documentation francaise, *Articles et Documents*, no. 2536, November 19, 1952.

44.   The example of General Svoboda in Czechoslovakia illustrates this. In 1969, he admitted that he had asked to join the party and that Gottwald had answered him: "Stay independent; in that capacity you will perform much greater services for the party." Speech given to the Central Committee of the Czech Communist Party in 1969 and reproduced in Pavel Tigrid's periodical *Svedectví*, no. 38 (1970), quoted by F. Fejtö, *Le Coup de Prague*, 66.

45.   Fejtö, op. cit., 157–58.

46.   Fejtö, op. cit., 227.

3

STALIN SADDLES THE COWS

Evoking the future of Poland in 1944, Stalin declared: "Establishing communism there would be as difficult as saddling a cow."[1] This inelegant metaphor was not applicable only to Poland. It was one thing to have imposed revolutions on the Eastern European countries, thanks to propitious circumstances and Soviet power. It was another thing to transform unprepared countries into communist states, when social and psychological conditions were very distant from the model of communism, the Soviet model, that Stalin intended to impose. It was not only in Poland that he had to "saddle a cow," but in all of Eastern Europe, with the exception of the countries that had taken the path by themselves, Yugoslavia and Albania. The metaphor also expresses the abnormal and violent character of the enterprise. A cow is not made to be saddled. And even when it is saddled, it never stops being, in its heart, a cow. The notion of domestication implied in Stalin's remark sheds a good deal of light on his views about the future of these communist states.

Two years after the end of the war, a page had been turned in the history of Eastern Europe. By January 1947, the question of power had been settled, even though the settlement was not identical in all countries. But communists everywhere had seized power or were already in a position to be able at any time to impose their will on what remained of the democratic parties. Poland was about to grant a majority to the Communist Party in "free elections"; in Hungary, the Social Democratic Party, the only survivor of the coalition, was on the road to pure and simple absorption by the Communist Party; finally, in Czechoslovakia, President Beneš was engaged in a final battle that many of his associates knew was already lost.[2]

From 1945 to 1947, the Eastern European countries thought they would be able to follow different paths, the paths of "national-democratic revolutions" whose aim was to construct people's democracies in harmony with the particular nature and history of each society. Almost all the communist leaders had articulated their perceptions of their revolutionary objectives.

They had all emphasized the link between revolution and national particularity. Thus in 1944, Gomułka declared that every society should turn toward people's democracy, a new political form completely different from liberal democracy.[3] And he explained the meaning of this "new democracy." "In the conditions created by the people's democracy, thanks to the strengthening of state power and the state apparatus by democratic elements, thanks to the development of nationalized production, the road to social transformation and movement toward the socialist system has become possible, and possible through a gradual process."[4]

In November 1946, Gomułka spoke of the Polish road, compared it to the Soviet road, and rejected the idea of imitating the latter. For him, the originality of the Polish people's democracy was that social and political transformations had been carried out peacefully; that the dictatorship of the proletariat did not and should not exist; that the separation of powers had been maintained; and that state power was based on a pluralist parliamentary democracy.

Gomułka's remarks, repeated by other leaders of the people's democracies at the time,[5] in fact were the expression of a certain degree of optimism about the freedom Stalin had left to the various communist parties to move toward power according to the means they thought easiest to use.

But beginning in 1947 that freedom was taken away from them. This was the second phase during which Soviet domination was consolidated in part through the internal evolutions of the various states. The communist parties that dominated the scene were loyal allies of the USSR. But Stalin did not have complete confidence in them. There were several reasons for this: his congenital suspicion of all his associates; his conception of security and stability, which rested on total control over men and events; his certainty that the power of the national communists was uncertainly established, because they dominated societies that were not yet fully detached from the democratic phase and that did not recognize those parties as their representatives but saw them simply as agents of the NKVD.[6]

To Stalin's suspicion of any system that departed from the Soviet model and to his obsessional desire to control everything and to think of power only in terms of domination and control should be added the new international context that took shape during the course of 1947. The cold war replaced the postwar period. In truth, for Stalin, convinced of the permanent nature of the confrontation between the communist and capitalist worlds, the cold war was probably a logical continuation of the war itself. And the battle for a defensive perimeter, conducted during the war and up to 1947, expressed this concern. As early as February 9, 1946, in a speech delivered in Moscow, Stalin declared that the capitalist camp was by definition the source of war and that cooperation with it was not possible.[7] The idea of the cold war certainly emerged from this speech. At the time, George Kennan expressed his concern in a telegram he immediately sent to the State Department; and the following year he discussed the conclusions that should be drawn from it: a barricade had to be erected against the USSR. This was the beginning of the containment program.[8] Once the era of negotiations with the Allies had come to an end, the factors that had encouraged Stalin's prudence in Eastern Europe faded. On the other hand, his desire to establish permanent control over the satellites was strengthened by the fear that the area would become, as it had been between the wars, the focus of confrontations with the external world. The plan developed by General Marshall to help the reconstruction of Europe was in Stalin's eyes the first step toward reconquest of Eastern Europe by the United States, which claimed to be responsible for the sovereignty of individual states and for the salvation of the democracies.

There thus began in 1947 the process of the transformation of the people's democracies, which were still very different from one another, and this transformation had the effect of unifying Eastern Europe. It had the particular effect of changing all the states of the region into carbon copies of the USSR. To attain this uniformity, Stalin, who by this time was intervening quite directly in the affairs of the states he wanted to control, imposed his ideas on them in three areas: foreign policy, which was aligned with that of the USSR; the political system, which was reconstructed along Soviet lines; and the procedures of political life, which followed the Soviet pattern. Finally, the reorganization of the economy completed the establishment in the people's democracies of the Soviet model of the thirties.

The Fortified Camp

Was Eastern Europe the outer edge of the USSR or an intermediate zone between the USSR and Western Europe? This was what was at stake in the conflict developing between Stalin and the satellite states, at least those that were still attempting to preserve a certain autonomy. Following the war, Stalin had undertaken to forge a system of alliances uniting the people's democracies to the USSR and with each other. The Soviet-Czech treaty of 1943 had served as a model for this network of agreements. It was followed in 1945 and 1946 by the Yugoslav treaty (April 10, 1945) and the Polish treaty (April 25, 1945) and by bilateral treaties signed by Yugoslavia with its Czech and Albanian neighbors. The conquered states were as yet outside this process of the formation of a coherent bloc in the east.

The Soviet-Polish treaty, signed like its Soviet-Czech counterpart while the alliance was still the framework for international relations, was revealing about Stalin's plans to exclude the West from the entirety of his sphere of influence. The treaty was signed in Moscow with the provisional government whose composition had been personally supervised by Stalin in 1944 and whose legitimacy he had unilaterally recognized on the eve of Yalta. The

Soviet-Polish treaty of 1945 tied Poland to the USSR for twenty years. The opinion of the great powers had not been requested; no one made any reference to the government-in-exile and this was a clear indication that for Stalin the fate of the country depended on Moscow. On the eve of the first United Nations conference in San Francisco where the fate of Poland was to be discussed, this *fait accompli* ruined the opportunity for United Nations action in Europe.[9] Against this policy of exclusive orientation toward the east, Czechoslovakia, which still had some room to maneuver, attempted to carry out a policy of balance between East and West, by negotiating a treaty with France following the pattern of the system of alliances established before the war. The prospect of this treaty had been aired as early as December 1943. In the mind of the Czech exiles it was intended to complete the Soviet-Czech treaty in order to avoid opposition between two groups of émigrés, as had been the case with Poland. It was also intended to allow liberated Czechoslovakia to be free from exclusive dependence on a too-powerful ally. Begun in 1944, the negotiations with France arrived at a precise proposal in 1946. During the last phases of the war, Stalin could not prevent it. However, at that very moment there occurred a curious incident that shed light on Stalin's views of the future and at the same time announced the use that he would make of noncommunists in the salami strategy.

In 1944, Czechoslovakia was represented in Moscow by the Social Democrat, Fierlinger. On August 22, 1944, in response to the Franco-Czech statement declaring that "the two countries agree that, at the appropriate time, any changes and additions to existing treaties should be made if they are considered necessary to make cooperation between France and Czechoslovakia closer," he suddenly raised an objection that was unexpected at the time. The USSR, he said, could not agree to have such a statement made unless it had been consulted. Moreover, the Soviet-Czech treaty was incompatible with this way of proceeding.[10]

Even though the Soviet government could not at the time oppose the plan—it was, moreover, a declaration of intention and not a treaty—it expressed obvious hostility toward it. Fierlinger was indeed its spokesman in arguing that the countries bordering on the USSR had to harmonize their foreign policies with that of Moscow.

In 1947 hostility toward the treaty was no longer disguised; it was openly expressed by the communist members of the Prague government. They systematically held back the planned treaty, which had seemed acceptable to them as long as the French communists were in the government in Paris. Slowed down in Paris,[11] the plan was violently attacked in Prague. When he came before the Council of Ministers, Clementis, the communist undersecretary of state for foreign affairs, supported by Gottwald, asserted that it was useless and unacceptable.[12] In 1947, the positions were clarified. If, for President Beneš, the treaty with France "will be a window opened to the

West. The more the Soviet circle closes around us, the more important it is that we strengthen ties with France,"[13] for Stalin, it was precisely this window that was unacceptable. This was all the more the case because he was at the time sponsoring bilateral treaties between the eastern countries. Czechoslovakia was in fact on the eve of undertaking negotiations under his auspices with Rumania and Bulgaria. And Stalin wished to accept no counterweight to the "eastern" alliance system that was in the process of closing off access to the satellites. He did not conceal from the Prague government his hostility toward the policy of building bridges with the West. In 1947, receiving a Czech delegation led by Gottwald and Masaryk in the Kremlin, Stalin vehemently criticized the alliance with France. He thereby demonstrated that for him Czechoslovakia already belonged to the Soviet camp, despite the survival of a pluralist government. His hostility to the Franco-Czech treaty was matched with similar effectiveness by his hostility to a Franco-Polish treaty that he caused to fail in the same way.[14] More realistic than the Czechs, more dominated from the outset by the communists, the Poles went no further in their exploration of the ways in which they might still be connected to the Western world. The last chance for Eastern Europe to avoid being trapped in the "Soviet circle," which Beneš saw so clearly tightening around the satellite countries, was the Marshall Plan. This program led Stalin to give up all precautions in order to define clearly the "duties" of the Eastern European states to the USSR and his exclusive conception of alliances.

The Marshall Plan was a key element in the American reaction to a Soviet expansion that could no longer be ignored. It was an extension of the Truman Doctrine presented in the president's speech to Congress on March 12, 1947, a speech that dramatically contrasted two worlds, the world of "terror and oppression," and that of "majority rule."[15] In order to attempt to prevent Europe from slipping into the first camp, the United States took the initiative of offering it an aid program for economic reconstruction, the Marshall Plan. The plan was largely inspired by the ideas and fears of George Kennan.[16] Designed primarily to block the communization of European countries, primarily Italy and France, the Marshall Plan was also offered to the satellite countries in the hope of building bridges with them and loosening the stranglehold that the USSR had on them. All European countries as victims of the war were covered by the plan, a last attempt to block the process of division of the continent. The USSR was supposed to respond to this offer for itself. Officially, it was not to take a position for the satellite states. The Soviet attitude was in the beginning very complex, probably reflecting hesitations about its long-range interest in accepting aid for which the Soviet economy, without question, had the greatest need. At first Moscow agreed to take part in the preparatory meeting held in Paris on June 27, 1947. Molotov, who represented his country there, was relatively cooperative, thus suggesting that the plan suited the USSR. On July 2 he completely reversed his position and announced to his negotiating partners that the USSR could not be associated with an operation whose "inevitable effect would be to limit the sovereignty of participating states."[17] This is not the place to comment on the causes of the Soviet reversal, but we must consider its consequences in the satellite nations.

The Marshall Plan had been greeted with enthusiasm in Czechoslovakia and Poland and had provoked a reaction of cautious interest in Hungary. In the countries in which the "democratic" stage had already been totally abolished, rejection was immediate. But in Prague, and to a lesser degree in Warsaw, there was a great temptation to rush toward this door opening on the Western world.[18] The Czechs, who had already tried to obtain economic aid from the United States in 1946, had the sense that they were returning to their earlier plan and following the same logic: to avoid making Czechoslovakia too dependent on the USSR.

But how could the USSR, which had just withdrawn from the meetings in Paris, allow its allies to take part? Within a few days, Stalin destroyed the illusions Polish and Czech leaders still held about their freedom of maneuver in the international arena. On July 4, two days after Molotov had left the Paris conference, Prague and Warsaw announced their wishes to receive Marshall Plan aid. Of course, during the cabinet meetings at which the decisions had been made, Gottwald had suggested the need for knowing the Soviet position on such a commitment before going further. And on July 9, a Czech delegation went to the Kremlin to clarify this point and to plead its case. But Stalin had not waited for July 9. He demanded that the Polish government purely and simply renounce Marshall Plan aid. In fact, the USSR took the initiative of announcing that neither Poland nor Rumania, also tempted by the prospect, would engage in discussions or participate in the Paris conference.[19]

From this point on, Stalin's position became more precise. It was no longer up to local communists to take the initiative in renouncing Western plans; it was the USSR that invoked the solidarity connected with the alliances among the Eastern European countries in order to cut off connections with the West. Stalin bluntly explained to the Czech delegation that the USSR had no intention of allowing its allies to follow policies different from its own. Moreover, he considered any policy involving association with the United States anti-Soviet. Summing up Stalin's position, Ripka writes: "Stalin confronted the Czech government with the choice either of immediately renouncing Marshall Plan aid or of entering into conflict with the Soviet Union. It was in fact nothing more nor less than an ultimatum."[20]

The brutality of the ultimatum was accompanied by demands that already revealed Stalin's determination to impose on the last country that was still independent in appearance the unanimist political style characteristic of Stalinism. Gottwald, who represented the authority of Stalin in this affair, demanded from his government an immediate decision and what is more a unanimous one. Stalin had always wished for the adversaries of his policies to become its defenders, thus legitimizing all his positions and weakening theirs. In July 1947 Stalin forced on the noncommunist members of the Czech government the same attitude that had led to the destruction of opposition leaders in the USSR in the twenties. He was thus already preparing for the "Prague coup," which would eliminate all those who at the beginning had given legitimacy to the Communist Party.

The rejection of the Marshall Plan had considerable importance in the history of Eastern Europe, going well beyond the immediate choice. For the first time, Stalin had expressed his conception of the alliances that had been concluded within his sphere of influence. These alliances—this is the precise meaning of his remarks on July 9, 1947—meant that friendship with the USSR was the point of reference for all international activities of the signatory states. The USSR was to be the sole judge and guarantor of that friendship and of the interests of the USSR and its allies. There could be no different positions within the alliance; the USSR alone defined the alliance's choices and preferences. Nor could there be different judgments within member states of the alliance. The link between domestic policies and external choices was clearly indicated. Until that point, Stalin had been satisfied with controlling his allies through the intermediary of procommunist governments or communist ministers who guaranteed the docility of the satellite states. From July 1947 on it became clear that this form of indirect control was too loose, that it did not guard the governments from the temptation of balancing their policies in the East with an opening to the West. The entire conception of the region was thus changed. The satellites, in order not to be subjected to any outside influence that might turn them away from their inevitable center of attraction, had to come to resemble the USSR in every respect. Only the total adoption of the Soviet model could guarantee total loyalty to the USSR. In 1945 Stalin had scoffed at the Yugoslav suggestion of integrating Yugoslavia into the USSR. In 1947, he took it up again in a disguised form. By imposing on the people's democracies, isolated from the external world by a foreign policy that connected them only to Moscow, a domestic transformation analogous to the one experienced by the USSR in the thirties, he completed his work. The people's democracies, like the national states incorporated into the USSR, became sister republics, differing from the federated republics of the USSR only because they were located in a second circle, theoretically sovereign. The demonstration of their international nonsovereignty was accomplished in the Marshall Plan affair. Until July 1947, doubt about the degree of Soviet control over those states could persist, and this explains the fact that there was still talk of the "Soviet sphere of influence." After July 1947, this fiction collapsed. This was also the point at which domestic alignments came out into the open.

The formative years of the Stalinist USSR from 1927 to 1938 were characterized by a closing off of the country from the outside world. The USSR, a besieged citadel, maintained diplomatic relations with the outside world, but those relations were a matter of state. The society was condemned to total isolation; neither people nor ideas from the outside penetrated into the USSR, and this isolation, justified by the notion of external threat, allowed Stalin to break down the society, its mentalities and its economic and social structures, in order gradually to bring into being the world and the "new man" of socialism. He repeated this operation by extending the besieged citadel to the satellite countries, by making Eastern Europe into a veritable fortified camp, closed off from the external world and receiving ideas and models only from the USSR. This unification of such a diversified part of Europe, which was carried out in the name of the satellite countries in a very short seven years, passed through all the stages of Stalinization that had taken nearly a quarter of a century in the USSR.

The Export of the Stalinist State

Stalin denied that revolutions could be exported. On the other hand, he never denied his intention of exporting a state model whose shape he had helped to establish from the early twenties on. This export of the state model contained several elements: the state, the party, and the men who would allow institutions to function in perfect harmony with the system of Soviet power. Democratic centralism was to become the pattern for relations between the satellite states and the Soviet center, with the understanding that as in all of Soviet history the emphasis would always be on the center. The period of Stalinization was marked by an intense institutional activity designed to bring the state forms of the satellites as close as possible to Soviet conceptions. The adoption of new constitutions, sometimes rewritten in a very short period of time, was only the most visible part of this rapid transformation of state norms. At the outset, two distinct situations prevailed. In the first, revolutionary will, that confirmed the elimination of old state forms or the necessity of finding a solution to their collapse explained why as early as 1946 Yugoslavia, Albania, and Hungary promulgated constitutions that owed nothing to the fundamental texts of the past. Elsewhere, prewar constitutions were slightly modified and then ensued a transitional stage. With the cold war and the break of 1947, this constitutional evolution accelerated and all the Eastern European countries defined their institutions in accordance with the demands of quickening Sovietization (Bulgaria: 1947; Czechoslovakia: 1948; Rumania: 1948, and a new constitution in 1952; Hungary and the GDR: 1949; Albania: 1950).[21]

All these texts imitated with remarkable fidelity the Soviet Constitution of 1936. Moreover, a surprising fact should be emphasized: their model was the Stalinist constitution of a Soviet state that had already gone through all the stages of internal transformation and not the constitutions of the postrevolutionary years (1918 and 1924), which took account of social differences and the fact that mental attitudes lagged behind the political system.

Stalin's determination to accelerate the process of change in Eastern Europe, to take short cuts, confirmed by the purges and the economic changes of this period, was thus present from the outset in this manner of writing constitutions. As always in the USSR, the superstructure, the world of ideas, far from reflecting social change, preceded it. Stalin's scorn for the realities in place and for everything that contradicted his own plans, and his voluntarism, were at the heart of the political evolution of Eastern Europe during those years.

The model he imposed under the name of people's democracy was the Soviet model of the one-party state; if it was absolutely necessary, he accepted a deceptive coalition in which the national front brought together all the parties accepted by the leading party, leaving no room for an external opposition and reducing the parties in the coalition to a purely decorative function. The state imitated Soviet institutions at every level. At the summit was an assembly elected by universal suffrage and endowed with legislative authority (the variations were only in name: the Sejm in Poland, Skupština in Yugoslavia; Great National Assembly in Rumania, and so on). An exception to this uniformity, the bicameral Yugoslav Assembly reflected the ethnic complexity of that country and perfectly copied the solution to this problem in the Soviet Constitution. In most East European states, the function of the head of state was as in the USSR held collectively by the Presidium of the Parliament, with the exception of Poland and Czechoslovakia which preferred to maintain a presidential function.

At lower levels, we find a pyramid of councils and committees patterned after the soviets of the Stalinist USSR; like their models, these were councils without power, hardly representative, totally foreign to the soviets that had emerged from the popular will in 1917. Centralization, which had been a permanent concern of all leaders in the USSR, was at the heart of this system in which the councils were an alibi for an extraordinary concentration of power. Like the USSR, the people's democracies displayed profound contempt for the bourgeois principle of the separation of powers, opposing to it the singleness of the people's power. And this adhesion to Soviet theses was demonstrated by the privileged role given to an office resembling that of an attorney general, an emanation of the state whose role was above all to protect the state.

Beginning in 1948, this imitation of the Soviet model was carried into the definition of the state. If until then the people's democracy had been described as an intermediate stage between the bourgeois republic and the Soviet republic, which justified the claim of national leaders to be following individual paths, this was because the USSR considered those differences necessary and reassuring. In the report he presented to the founding meeting of the Cominform in 1947,[22] Zhdanov defined this national version of people's democracy, as all Soviet theoreticians did at the time, by emphasizing its differences from the Soviet model.[23]

But a year later, Stalin decided that the time for variations and differences had passed.

It is not true that each country moves toward socialism on its own path, entirely individual; it is not true that there are as many roads to socialism as there are countries. To speak in that way is to deny the international value of the experience of Bolshevism. The general laws for the transition from capitalism to socialism, developed by Lenin and Stalin on the basis of the experience of the Bolshevik Party and the Soviet state, are obligatory for all countries.[24]

The Soviet model was the dictatorship of the proletariat, which had been rejected by the communist leaders of the satellites for nearly three years; all of them suddenly recognized its virtues. Then what was the meaning of the insistence on national paths but Stalin's wish to arrange for stages in a process of change that neither the Eastern European societies nor the West were ready to accept? Rákosi bluntly explained this concerted concealment of a radical objective: "The dictatorship of the proletariat envisaged as an aim would have frightened our allies in the coalition and made more difficult our attempts to rally the support of the majority, not only of the petty bourgeois, but also of the working masses."[25] And Gottwald, more precise in his confession, admitted that in 1945 Stalin in person had enjoined him to keep silent about the notion of dictatorship of the proletariat, invoking the example of Lenin who in April 1917 with the slogan "all power to the soviets," had thrown off the rivals of the Bolshevik Party. For Stalin, there would be plenty of time to uncover the real objectives of the communist party when it had no more rivals on the road to power.[26] This admission confirms that as early as 1945 Stalin had taken in hand the direction of the satellite states and that at no time did the local communist parties have the choice of an individual strategy. These communist parties, whose organization and functioning had never departed from the Comintern, that is, the Soviet model, obtained a leading position in all the Eastern European countries, either by virtue of the constitutional texts or through their own decisions. Thus Gottwald said in 1949: "Our Party embodies the unity of the working class of Czechoslovakia and its leading role in all spheres of social life."[27]

But as in the USSR of the Stalinist period, more than the communist parties as institutions, it was the leaders of the parties who held power in a Stalinist style, and each of whom represented the authority of Stalin in his own country.

The Instruments of Domination

Most of the leaders of the years 1948 to 1953 were linked to the USSR by their earlier activities: because they had been Comintern bureaucrats or because the reigning anticommunism of their countries had forced them to seek refuge in Moscow where they had for years swollen the ranks of communist officials, waiting for more favorable circumstances to allow them to return home. In the first category were men like Dimitrov who after leading the Balkan section of the Comintern became the general secretary of the world party of the revolution in 1935. From this position, which he held until the Comintern was dissolved in 1943, he derived immense authority. What was especially noteworthy about Tito in 1945 was that he had numerous links with the USSR. A prisoner of war in Russia since 1915, he had joined the Bolshevik Revolution in 1917 and had been incorporated into the Red Guard; in addition, he had worked in the Balkan secretariat of the Comintern in the mid-thirties. Rákosi had also been in Moscow in the early twenties before being imprisoned in Hungary. Bierut, Gottwald, and Ulbricht were all in various ways what could be called "old Muscovites." Among the national communists who were less visible in 1948, who waited in the background as eventual successors, Nagy, Gerö, Chervenkov, and many others shared this experience of the USSR. From this long familiarity with the motherland of the revolution, they all brought back to their countries a Stalinist style, imitating the man whom they recognized as a model for their manner of governing, but above all the "cult of personality" that they imposed. Gomułka referred to a dual hierarchy of the personality cult.[28] The first was located within each satellite state, where the leader of the party was a little Stalin, imposing the same undivided authority, demanding the same recognition of his omniscience and his infallibility as Stalin received in the Kremlin. But the real hierarchy of the personality cult was on a regional scale. At the summit was Stalin, whose cult radiated throughout the system, and this cult in turn was broken down within each country into a "national cult." The role of the personality cult as a unifying force in Eastern Europe was decisive. As in the USSR, it was the person of Stalin much more than communist ideology or the role played by the party that symbolized unity and the new world. The political revolution in Eastern Europe was above all the extension of the Stalin cult throughout Sovietized territory. Stalin was the "father of the peoples," just as he was the "father" of the Soviet people. Thus political frontiers, in principle maintained by the fiction of juridical sovereignty, collapsed. But it was not enough for Stalin to impose a rigid model, shaping the leaders and the methods by which power was exercised, even though his imitators repeated: "The Soviet Union is our model." Stalin conceived of the transformation and unification of Eastern Europe through direct control over the principal institutions—government, army, police—

which he filled with his representatives, whose hidden authority was often infinitely greater than that of the national leaders. Only the archives, if and when they are one day opened, will give a precise idea of the extent of this Soviet infiltration of national institutions. Without archives, we can only indicate in the light of a few revelations the methods of this direct control and identify its best known representatives.

The principal direct representative of Stalin in the field was everywhere the Soviet ambassador, whose function of control over the socialist states was never concealed. In this connection, Stalin wrote to Tito: "The Soviet ambassador, a responsible communist, representative of a friendly state that liberated Yugoslavia from the German occupation, has not only the right but the duty from time to time to speak with Yugoslav communists on all subjects of interest to them."[29] There is ample evidence of the nature of the conversations that took place between Soviet ambassadors and local leaders. The Soviet ambassador to Warsaw in 1947, Lebedev, who had earlier been the representative of the USSR to the Czech government in London, had taken advantage of his dual capacity at the time to paralyze the plan for a Franco-Czech treaty and to "warn" the Czechs against the anti-Sovietism of which he accused them. Now, what "anti-Sovietism" was in his eyes was the fall of the Social Democrat Fierlinger, a Trojan horse for the communists. For the Soviet representatives, Fierlinger's fate was nothing but an unbearable provocation.[30] This was indeed an instance of determining Czechoslovakia's internal choices, not of offering it vague advice. And this style of brutal repression was reinforced at every critical point by the dispatch of Soviet representatives who did not hesitate violently to demand respect for the Kremlin's will. In 1948, Zorin, who had been the Soviet ambassador to Czechoslovakia up to the preceding autumn, went to Prague where his presence and his advice assured Gottwald's success, while at the same time *Pravda* in Moscow confirmed that the only friends of the USSR in the country were the Czech communists.[31]

Less visible than the perpetual interventions in domestic affairs by Soviet ambassadors, the infiltration of institutions was particularly effective. The army and the police were the preferred targets of this technique of control. The Polish Army provides an excellent example of this. From 1949 to 1956 it was placed under the orders of a Soviet citizen of Polish origin, Marshall Rokossovski, whose entire previous career had been conducted in the USSR. Appointed defense minister in Poland, he was also vice-premier and a member of the Politburo. It was he who presided over the reconstruction of the decimated Polish Army, helped by Soviet military advisers and by officers, a large number of whom had served in the Red Army and lived for a long time in the USSR. And the high-ranking officers of this army were all Soviet representatives. In a few years he made the Polish Army into a most faithful replica of the Soviet Army. The army's Political Academy, created in 1951, permitted rigorous control over the entire officer corps by importing into the Polish Army the Soviet system of partisan selection, the *Nomenklatura*. The same system was applied in Bulgaria, where the Defense Minister appointed in 1950, General Panchevski, was also a pure product of the Red Army.[32] Sometimes the USSR avoided too blatant an intervention, either because the national army had too strong a tradition (as in Yugoslavia where it had been developed in the resistance), or else because the presence of Soviet occupation troops was enough to ensure direct control (as in Hungary). This is why the method most used was Soviet military advisers. At the time of the Soviet-Yugoslav conflict, the recall of these advisers to Moscow illuminated the nature of this "cooperation" that benefited the USSR above all. Occupied Hungary with a dismantled army depended completely on Soviet "military cooperation," that is, it received Soviet advisers and equipment and its officers were trained in Moscow. In a short time, according to General Béla Király, who presided over the Revolutionary Council of National Defense in Hungary in 1956, the Hungarian army, "under the vigilant eye of a growing number of Soviet advisers," had been transformed into a detachment of the Soviet Army. Nothing differentiated the two, neither weapons, nor training, nor military doctrine, nor spirit.[33]

The same fate was in store for the armies of the other conquered countries, which had been forced by the disarmament conditions of the peace treaties to eliminate a large part of their officer corps with a national background, paving the way for a restructuring organized by Moscow. Another decisive element in the Sovietization of these armies was the importation into all of Eastern Europe of the system of political control over the army—the *politruk*—which imposed on the army officers the absolute authority of political commissars. This political hierarchy was not only the means of bringing all the armies into line with that of the USSR, it was above all a means to infiltrate them. Almost everywhere, the political commissars were Soviets or men specially trained in the USSR. Thus the political commissars of the Rumanian Army were for the most part prisoners of war who, during their captivity in the USSR, had been subjected to special training before being sent back to their country.[34]

Although it had been in the camp of the victors and was liberated very early from the presence of the Red Army, the Army of the Czechoslovak Republic was nevertheless subjected to a Sovietization process analogous to that of the other armies. In this instance, Stalin's plan was facilitated by the war situation, since Czech units were present in both the Soviet and British Armies. From the very beginning of the republic, the communists launched incessant attacks against the officers who had been on the British side, strengthening the position of those who had come from the Red Army. The Prague coup permitted their complete elimination under the then-widespread accusation of espionage, leaving a free field for the officers who had been shaped by long experience in the ranks of the Soviet Army. There was another preferred method of Soviet intervention in the life of the Eastern European states, the police. Communist control over this institution seemed everywhere insufficient to Stalin, who merely applied in the satellite countries what he had established in the USSR. From the late twenties on, he had been determined to remove the police from the control of the party and the state and to make it an instrument of his personal power. After 1945 the police machinery of the people's democracies was placed under the authority of high-ranking Soviet advisers whose responsibilities in the purges and more generally in bringing these countries into line were revealed in the post-Stalin years. The role played by NKVD generals in the Rajk and Slánský trials is now well known thanks to the testimony of surviving victims like Arthur London and E. Loebel, who said of the Soviet advisers: "They were the masters of our country."[35] Furthermore, the debates that took place during the Prague Spring shed light on the extent of Soviet infiltration of the police and the control by the USSR of the whole life of the satellites. Loebel wrote that the sovereignty of Czechoslovakia had been turned over to Beria's agents.

The police forces of the satellites were supervised by advisers sent by the USSR; local police officials were recruited by the Soviet services to carry on direct surveillance of their fellow citizens for the benefit of the USSR without going through the channel of their superiors. Finally, as if this whole arrangement were not enough to reassure Stalin, every exceptional circumstance was an occasion for sending new Soviet officials to the scene to reinforce the advisers who were already there. A month did not pass in which Stalin did not give orders to arrest or release a high-ranking official; or else one of his close associates, like Mikoyan, would come bearing orders that had to be carried out immediately on pain "of interfering with the security of the communist world." In 1968 the Dubček government in Prague set up a commission—the Piller Commission—to bring these problems to light; and thanks to the documents published under the direction of Jiří Pelikan, we have a more complete view of the totality of methods put into operation by Stalin to break down any autonomous life in the people's democracies.[36] These documents shed particular light on two aspects of the Stalinization of the satellites: first, the close link and degree of cooperation that existed among the police, the party, and the state institutions. From 1945 on, the entire political systems of Eastern Europe were concentrated in the police function, where Soviet authority was preeminent. The second element concerns the scope of Soviet power. "The authority of the advisers was immense, their advice, suggestions, and decisions were in fact orders. The minister accepted their suggestions and recommendations, and had them carried out."[37]

The people's democracies were miniature Soviet Unions not only through the existing political systems, through the development of the personality cult, and through the constant surveillance carried out from Moscow; their environments and their political cultures were also transformed. It would be a serious error to reduce Stalinism to a simple system of oppression from above. It was, and this is one of the sources of its effectiveness, a prodigious enterprise devoted to the transformation of ways of thinking, through terror no doubt, but also through the imposition of a political culture cut off from the past. This expansion of the Stalinist model, designed in this respect as well to shape a new man, affected the environment, public mores, and political convictions. The environment throughout Eastern Europe was to resemble that of the Soviet citizen. Cities were sometimes renamed both to honor the "Great Leader" and to signify the unification of communist territory. Thus, Katowice became Stalinogród, public buildings became "palaces of culture" dedicated to Joseph Stalin, and gigantic statues of the master of the Kremlin dominated all the capitals, except for Warsaw. The style of buildings constructed during this period was a servile imitation of the style in favor in the USSR; socialist realism became the only style available to artists, Lysenko and his theories dominated the sciences, and "Diamat" (dialectical materialism) was the obligatory framework for all scientific research. A group of Russian or deformed Russian words concerned with political terminology or with the pattern of social relations in a communist world (the terms *pan* and *pani*, "Mr." and "Mrs." for example, were expelled from the Polish language), penetrated the national languages, which had been deprived of their own words. This unification of ideas and symbols was carried out by an organization of the press that also literally imitated the Soviet organization in which the essential elements were the daily paper and the monthly theoretical journal published by the local communist party, which reflected rather faithfully the organs of the Soviet Communist Party, *Pravda* and *Kommunist*.

It would be tedious to recite all the cultural institutions created at the time in order to propagate a common cultural model. Out of what would be a monotonous enumeration, perhaps we should focus on the changes brought about in the educational system and in the status of religion. The educational system that was then imported into Eastern Europe was guided by three principles designed to educate generations of true socialists. First of all, education was conceived as a means of destroying class society and of eliminating "bourgeois" elements from the society of the future. As had been the case in the USSR in the twenties, the schools gave priority in admissions and in grading to children of proletarian origins. Those who came from the privileged classes or the children of "enemies of the people" were practically ejected from the system and thereby condemned to remain on the fringes of social progress. This selection on the basis of social origin had incidentally been abandoned in the USSR since the early thirties in favor of academically based selection (although the children of the *Nomenklatura* benefited from many advantages and those who had been victims of Stalin's terror were unaffected by this change). The privilege granted to class origin no doubt varied from one country to another—in Czechoslovakia it was grafted onto old worker traditions, which guaranteed durable success beyond the Stalinist period. Nevertheless the principle was widespread. The second idea governing the educational system in the Stalin years was the close link between political education and education in general. The school was the place where the political socialization of children and adolescents was accomplished, and a significant proportion of school time as well as other activities associated with school were devoted to the creation of the "good communist," and also to verification of pupils' adhesion to the new political values. Finally, school was the place where the Russian language had to be learned. All the countries of Eastern Europe at the time required the study of Russian in their schools, and knowledge of Russian became a criterion for the continuation of schooling and social advancement. The explicit objective of the requirement of gaining mastery of Russian was to unify the communist world around the culture and the heritage of the "revolutionary people." In this forced bilingualism, the references to Russian culture as a shared and superior culture were not concealed. It went along with the preeminent role that communist political culture assigned to the USSR, whose Russian character was more and more clearly asserted. The years of the Sovietization of Eastern Europe were also the years of the Russification of all of the USSR. If the Russifying theme was less clearly asserted outside the USSR, this was because there was a time lag—the cultural revolution experienced by the satellites from 1948 to 1953 had already been accomplished in the USSR from the twenties to the forties. But the final aim was indeed the same: the Russian language was to be the vehicle of a shared political culture, communism, which in those years was identified with the history and culture of Russia.

The status of religion was no less revealing of Stalin's intentions. In all the satellites, the constitutions, following the example of the Soviet Constitution of 1936, provided for separation of church and state and for freedom of religious belief. As in the USSR, the party and social organizations were given the task of propagating atheism and fighting against religious survivals. The law imposed civil marriages everywhere and in a very general way prohibited religious instruction. However, behind these general principles growing out of profound hostility to all religion, various situations developed that reflected Soviet development during the war as well as the policies followed in the USSR in the twenties. The Soviet model was characterized by the determination, when the strength of the churches appeared insurmountable, to divide those churches and to support schismatic movements manipulated by the authorities against the church hierarchy in order in the end to discredit religion as such. On the other hand, the war had forced Stalin to make concessions to the churches, particularly where they were identified with the history of the nation and they had had a history of submission to political authority. This had long been the case for the Russian

Orthodox Church. This explains why in Poland, for example, rather than directly attacking a powerful church, a symbol of Polish national existence, the political system concentrated on undermining it, following the Soviet model and with the help of Soviet agents. In the first phase, the 1925 concordat that governed the status of the Polish church was denounced and the Polish church hierarchy had to become a supplicant of the state; moreover, it had to resolve the thorny problem of the bishoprics located in territories seized from Germany, which had to be organized and assigned bishops.[38] Although Cardinal Wyszynski, Polish primate since 1948, managed to sign a compromise agreement with the authorities in 1950, this agreement did not protect the Polish church from treatment that was as harsh as that experienced by the church in the USSR twenty years earlier: including the confiscation of church property, the arrests of priests, trials, and the prohibition of all religious instruction.[39] The persecution culminated in the arrest of Cardinal Wyszinski in September 1953.

The authorities added to persecution an attempt at demoralization by creating a progressive Catholic movement, Pax, led by an NKVD agent, Bolesław Piasecki, who established a dissident national church patterned after the "living church" created in the USSR in the twenties.[40] The strategy that for years had reduced the church to silence and bewildered believers in the USSR was not very successful in Poland, where the faithful who had always identified church and nation with one another made the imprisoned primate into a symbol of the captive nation. The situation was no more brilliant for the other Catholic Churches. In Yugoslavia, Czechoslovakia, and Hungary, the leaders—Monsignor Beran, Monsignor Stepinac, and Cardinal Mindszenty—were thrown into prison, while as in Poland, the authorities, advised by Soviet specialists in religious affairs, attempted to promote churches subject to their orders as a challenge to the authority of the hierarchy.

Soviet hostility to the Catholic Church meant that persecution against the churches was most severe in those countries in which it was best established. In this respect, the Soviet state was indeed the heir of a long Russian tradition of hostility to Catholicism. It was also anxious to weaken a church whose hierarchy depended on a supreme authority outside the state, located in a spiritual and temporal center whose importance Stalin may have scorned, although he did not completely disregard it. The famous quip, "How many divisions does the Pope have?" expresses more anxiety than genuine contempt. Stalin's anxiety in the face of an organization over which he had no control was accompanied from 1949 on by exasperation. In July 1949 in fact the Vatican excommunicated the communists, and priests could no longer give them the sacraments. There then occurred a shift in the attitudes of these governments, which simultaneously persecuted the clergy, and with a combination of persuasion and threat dissuaded the faithful from religious observances, and at the same time began the prosecution of priests who accepted the Vatican's decision and refused the sacraments to party members.

This permanent hostility toward an extraterritorial church explains the policy that was followed toward Uniates and Protestants. The Uniates, who were numerous in Rumania and in the territories Stalin had seized from Poland (Galicia) and Czechoslovakia (Sub-Carpathian Ukraine), were another religious group that the Russian tradition followed by the Soviets had always viewed with suspicion and had more or less accused of having betrayed the national religion and national traditions. Between 1948 and 1953 the same policy of repression was imposed on the Uniates within the USSR and on their brothers in Rumania. They were forced to rejoin the Orthodox Church and all recalcitrant clerics were imprisoned. Only the Orthodox Churches—national churches—escaped to a certain extent from this persecution. In Rumania and Bulgaria, despite some arrests, the status of the national churches was respected. Moreover in 1951 the Bulgarian church was elevated to a higher status within the Orthodox hierarchy. By supporting this promotion of a national church to a status of complete independence during the period of the worst antireligious repressions, the Soviet authorities revealed their intention to make political use of the churches. The patriarchate of Moscow was an agent of Soviet foreign policy, which played a doubly effective role in the postwar years. Establishing links with the Orthodox communities of Western Europe and the Middle East—in a period when the cold war limited Soviet government contacts in those countries—the patriarchate contributed significantly to the pro-Soviet and anti-American propaganda campaign waged there. It also helped to preserve links with countries that had an Orthodox tradition, thereby palliating the difficulties and isolation created by Soviet diplomacy. Thus Soviet-Yugoslav relations were maintained by the Moscow patriarchate during the break between the two governments. But until 1951 the Moscow church authorities were also isolated and criticized by the ecumenical patriarchate of Constantinople because of their subjection to the political authorities. The elevation of the Bulgarian church strengthened the position of the Soviet church in the Orthodox world and provided it with a means of dealing with obstacles to its activity.

Hostility to religion and the imposition of uniformity on diverse political cultures were thus not incompatible with different strategies whenever the interests of the USSR were at stake.

Repression as a Spectacle

The Soviet system, particularly in its Stalinist phase, presents a peculiarly perverse characteristic, the ambiguous relation between terror and legality.[41] No terrorist system had ever been so concerned with defining the law, covering itself with the law, and putting the law at the service of a terror that violated legality. The legal and the nonlegal were inextricably blended in the tragedy of the Soviet people, and the link between the two was party spirit *(partiinost')*, the supreme command of the system, which prevailed over legality *(zakonnost')* and justified the terror. Unlike other terrorist systems, which were satisfied with terrifying, jailing, or killing their opponents without worrying about including these activities within a legal system, the Soviet system fabricated a legality for the terror, so that, as Solzhenitsyn says, "where there is law, one can always find crime." In this monstrous marriage between the law and permanent illegality, the victims of that illegality, the terror, played a central role. The system could function only with their active participation. By accepting their fate and praising illegality, they gave it a legal justification, transformed the illegal into the legal, and legitimized the system as a whole. This concern to have its victims recognize and accept its positions and its excesses is in the last analysis the essence of the Soviet system, perfected by the procession of leaders of the Soviet police from Dzerzhinsky to Beria and by Stalin's great jurist, Vyshinsky, Soviet chief prosecutor.

Trials of political opponents in the early years of the Soviet state like those of the social revolutionaries in 1922 followed the classic pattern of political justice in which the accused, the defeated, defended himself and his ideas. But Stalin's trials, beginning in 1928 with the Shakhty trial, followed a totally different logic. This is what Robert Tucker among others calls the political show trial, in which the accused is really the star of a show in which he must play a precisely defined role.[42] The most important moment, the logical crux, is the confession. At that point the accused makes illegality legal and legitimizes both generalized terror and the system. In this respect, the trial has little to do with the accused; it is a privileged moment in the process of terror, in the consolidation of the terrorist system, a stage in its legitimation.

This conception of the terror and of the trials it produced was perhaps the one aspect of the Soviet model that was most thoroughly transposed onto the people's democracies. This was the means by which their Sovietization was carried out, much more than through economic or political measures, which revealed some differences.

In this rigid application of the Soviet model, the people's democracies profited from the Soviet example but also from the assistance of advisers who came from Moscow to organize a stage setting at which they were masterly and to teach their disciples how to fabricate victims.

There were three stages in the history of the terror in Eastern Europe, each one marked by purges and trials, but each stage must be differentiated from the others in order to be understood properly.

The first stage from 1947 to 1948 was characterized by the juridical and physical elimination of the communists' opponents. This was the stage of the end of the coalitions, when the losers were accused of being enemies of the revolution and were thereby doomed to disappear. There was no necessity that these people participate in their own liquidations. "Enemies of the people," "dangerous to the Revolution," they were accused of crimes that they had not committed but that were classic in this set of circumstances. They were generally accused of having become traitors for a foreign power, because their popular support remained strong enough to require the victors to justify their violence. In April 1947 the trial of the Bulgarian Agrarian leader Nicholas Petkov demonstrated the use that could be made of such trials. At that early stage, the prisons and the camps were already filled with the leaders of banned political parties, Agrarians and Socialists. Petkov, accused of having opposed the coalition on the orders of the British and the Americans, was convicted under remarkably orchestrated street pressure, recalling the circumstances surrounding the Moscow trials. Union members and demonstrators of the most diverse origins marched around the court and sent it messages demanding "death for the traitor." More, less spectacular trials followed. But the Petkov trial was enough to justify the Bulgarian government's pitiless pursuit, in the service of the revolution, of everyone it named as Petkov's accomplices. In Rumania at the same time, October 1947, the leaders of the National Peasant party, Mihalache and Maniu, were playing the same role before the court as Petkov in Bulgaria. They were convicted for having taken part in a plot concocted by American officers. Their sentences of life imprisonment—they were luckier than Petkov, who was hanged—also opened the way to an attack on all their supporters. None of these defendants had adopted a repentant attitude during their trials. But when Western governments protested against Petkov's conviction, Prime Minister Dimitrov, after the fact, produced a transcript of a confession that Petkov was said to have signed. And he asserted that had foreign states not felt called upon to intervene in internal Bulgarian affairs, perhaps despite his crimes the leader of the Agrarians might have been pardoned. Moreover, during his trial, the prosecutor had declared that "the death of the traitor would be a useful stimulus for worker productivity." In all the satellite countries, this sinister spectacle was repeated, its chosen victims those who had the greatest popularity, those who were generally capable of posing a genuine electoral challenge.

In Hungary, the trials were replaced by pure and simple terror, which was from the very beginning the work of the Soviet authorities. Citing attacks against occupying forces, General Sviridov, commander of the Soviet Army, arrested members of the Smallholders' Party and even its parliamentary representatives, and finally the party's General Secretary Béla Kovács, who was deported to the USSR and assassinated in prison. This allowed the communists to destroy his party before attacking the Socialist Party and the Catholic Party, whose leader Barankovics escaped arrest only by fleeing the country. Mikolajczyk in a similar manner saved his life by escaping from

Poland in autumn 1947; certain Czech national leaders followed his example. And in Prague, although the leaders of the Beneš government were not yet being prosecuted, the death of Jan Masaryk, by suicide or NKVD assassination, and the death from despair of Beneš took the place of more spectacular liquidations.[43]

Yugoslavia, so quick to imitate the USSR during these years, did not escape from the epidemic of trials, begun in 1946 with Mihajlović who was executed in July. Political trials proliferated in 1947 on a wide variety of charges—treason, nationalism, collaboration—but all of them bore a striking resemblance, in their contempt for the accused and their total disregard for the rights of the defense, to the repeated illegalities of the Moscow trials.

By 1948 this first wave of terror had been completed. It had simplified the political landscape by everywhere eliminating all those who did not belong to the communist parties or to the small groups they maintained within their sphere of influence, which still concealed the monolithic nature of the political system.

The second wave of purges in 1948 and 1949 took place in a different political context and with different methods. Its political backdrop was the dictatorship of the proletariat, which had triumphed throughout Eastern Europe. And the dictatorship of the proletariat in its Leninist version, far from meaning that the state dominated by the communists had been pacified, implied on the contrary "the continuation of class struggle in new forms." Moreover, Lenin had added to that definition the statement that "the state, in this phase, is a weapon of the proletariat in its class struggle."

The states of Eastern Europe, heirs of this tradition of uninterrupted struggle—which, after inspiring the liquidation of the socialists in the USSR, had led the party down the road to self-destruction—undertook in the same way to purge the communist parties of the elements that had brought about revolutionary triumph. This purge within the parties themselves was not restricted to any particular country; it spread everywhere, as though from one end to the other of socialist territory internal party treason had followed an identical logic. The great moments of this purge are so well known that it is enough simply to recall the protagonists and the locations.

In Rumania, the internal purge began in February 1948 and struck first Justice Minister Patrascanu, dismissed from his position for the "abandonment of class principles and for having joined the ranks of the bourgeoisie," according to his accuser, Gheorghiu-Dej. He was convicted and later executed in 1954. In Warsaw, Gomułka suffered a less tragic fate, since he was neither convicted nor executed. But his colleagues made an extraordinarily violent attack on his presumed motives, within the party rather than bringing him to court. His fall, which began in June 1948 with a systematic attack on his positions at the party plenum, came to a conclusion in 1951 with his exclusion from the Central Committee, which cast him out into the category of "political ghosts" or "unpersons." This exclusion was nonetheless an enviable fate in comparison to that of the Bulgarian Traicho Kostov, who had been general secretary of the clandestine Communist Party. Accused of "leftist sectarianism," and of "inadequate recognition of the historic role played by the USSR," he was however condemned to death for crimes more in conformity with the Soviet tradition. For the judges he was nothing but a common spy in the pay of the British, after having betrayed his resistance comrades during the war by selling himself to Germany. His immediate execution in December 1949 was in harmony with the general harshness of the time. The Hungarian Rajk, interior minister during the period of Sovietization of his country and leader of the party's underground struggle during the war, was treated no better. As was the case with Kostov, it suddenly appeared that behind this exemplary militant was concealed a redoubtable agent of imperialism and an accomplice of Tito. The rope used to hang him after his conviction seemed to sanction an incredible series of crimes and acts of duplicity against which the Hungarian people were promptly mobilized. The latest addition to the people's democracies, Czechoslovakia, was the last to adopt this purgative fury; but it was no more moderate than the others in its activities. In 1950 the Slovak Communist Party was decimated. At the time Clementis, deputy minister of foreign affairs, Husák, Novomeský, and many of their colleagues disappeared. The fate of these "deviationists," accused primarily of "nationalism," at least the Slovaks among them, was as dramatic as that of Rajk or Kostov. The same thing happened in Albania, where in a different context, the relations between Albania and Yugoslavia, the General Secretary of the party, Enver Hoxha, turned over to the courts "spies" who were working simultaneously for Yugoslavia and for imperialism and who had the goal of transforming Albania into a Yugoslav province. The fact that the principal spy of this type, Koci Xoxe, was interior minister and vice-premier prevented neither his conviction nor his execution.

These spectacular purges of 1948 and 1949, which presented the triumphant communist parties as arenas of conflict between honest leaders and officials who had long been corrupted, are worth careful consideration because of the new elements that they introduced into Eastern European political culture. What they contributed first of all was the Soviet model of the permanent purge with its own logic and its methods. These purges were conducted under various guiding themes, the changes in which shed light on their ultimate aims, but they oddly echoed the Stalinist purges of the thirties on the outskirts of the USSR. Stalin had then disposed of the national leaders of the federated republics who ten years earlier had led their compatriots on the path of "national communism" and had proposed to them a communist program reconciling two conflicting requirements, the desire to preserve the identity of the nation and the desire to build socialist internationalism. This was known as the Stalinist compromise between national form and socialist foundation. The 1936 purges by liquidating the representatives of national values opened the way for unification of the USSR and its Russification. This history was repeated by the second wave of purges in Eastern Europe. Stalin ordered the liquidation of all national leaders.[44] At this time he got rid of those who had joined the party and struggled for it underground and had earned their stripes as leaders without the participation of the USSR. Traicho Kostov had been one of the principal leaders of internal Bulgarian resistance during the war, while the two "historic" leaders of the party, Dimitrov and Kolarov, were in the USSR. Arrested by the Germans, Kostov long enjoyed a reputation as a pure hero, a reputation that was widespread in the early postwar years. Like him, Gomułka was a leader of the interior, who had not been exterminated by Stalin like his Polish comrades because he had been imprisoned in Poland in 1938 and had fled into the German-occupied zone in 1940. This preference for the Nazis over the USSR in 1940 clearly explains Stalin's suspicion of him and his expulsion.

Patrascanu in Rumania had also lived in his country's prisons rather than in Soviet exile, like Rajk, who had been a leader of Hungarian underground forces. Against these leaders, who had proved themselves in their own countries, in contact with the population, and whose reservations toward the USSR were unmistakable, Stalin greatly preferred those who were known as the "Muscovites," whose careers had been built in the corridors of the Comintern according to the vagaries of Stalin's favor. These numerous and docile Muscovites—Ana Pauker and Luca in Rumania, Slánský in Czechoslovakia, Ghergohiu-Dej in Rumania, Bierut in Poland—who put the communists of the interior on trial, made up the cohort of Stalinist loyalists. The elimination of national leaders had as its primary cause Stalin's natural suspicion of those who had not always depended on him, his certainty that they were more nationalist than communist, and above all, their major crime, the fear that they would not give absolute priority to the USSR. The indictments—fantastic in the mixture of crimes they alleged—like those of the Soviet trials of the thirties, mingled what was true and false in Stalin's obsessions and revealed his real purpose. The reality of what troubled him was the accusation of nationalistic deviation brought against Kostov, Gomułka, Rajk, and the Slovak leaders whose nationalism had the dual fault of ruining the unity of the Czech republic and violating the sacred principle of internationalism. Beyond the crime of nationalism, all these men were accused of an even more serious and deadly crime, which also corresponded to a constant factor in Soviet political culture. They were all accused of not granting absolute priority to the USSR in their loyalties and their programs. They were especially guilty for having thought that "the interests of Bulgaria could conflict with those of the USSR and take precedence over them." This was the criticism leveled by Gheorghiu-Dej against Kostov, whom he accused because of this heresy of having attempted to conceal Bulgarian state secrets or economic data from the Soviet authorities. The USSR was the only country to which Bulgaria could not apply the classic principles of interstate relations. This lack of confidence, this false view of the USSR had also led Clementis, according to his judges, to forget that Soviet policy was in every respect dedicated to the preservation of communism; it was from ignorance of that fundamental truth that Clementis had expressed doubts about the propriety of the Nazi-Soviet pact, while his opponents reminded him that Stalin's policies ought to have been automatically accepted and praised. As for Gomułka, he had never been able to recognize the immensity of the services the USSR had performed for his country and the cause of the revolution. In all the trials of this period, we find that the mark of infamy is represented by the expression of doubt about the USSR or by the propensity to exalt one's own country. The national communism of 1945 to 1947 that had asserted the contrary was thereby uprooted and appeared to be what it had always been in Stalin's eyes, a propaganda theme designed to influence or reassure those who wished to preserve the interests of their country while accepting the idea of profound social and political change.

But, as in the USSR in the thirties, the attack against national deviations and the underestimation of the decisive role played by the USSR in every circumstance were not sufficient themes to convince the compatriots of the principal actors in the trials. This is why, as in the USSR, the indictments were supplemented by a series of accusations of treason in the service of the external enemy. The heroes of the internal resistance, like Kostov, were accused of having betrayed their comrades to the Germans to save themselves. Rajk was convicted—it was easy to convict anyone of any crime because of the resources employed—of having been an agent of Admiral Horthy's secret service before selling himself to the Americans. In the end, all the "national" communists that the USSR had not been able to keep from such deviations seemed indeed to have long been engaged on the path of shameful agreements with all the reactionary police forces and the imperialist powers they had encountered along the way. At the end of this road, a traitor named Tito, in the ultimate betrayal, had brought all these criminal tendencies together.

The indictments were clearly based on the model that the USSR had perfected in its own trials.[45] What differentiated them was that the Eastern European trials presented a synthesis of all the offenses that had been developed from one trial to the next in Moscow. In transferring its repressive model to Warsaw, Prague, or Sofia, the USSR transferred the totality of its experiences, which made the accusations presented in 1948 and 1949 an astonishing cocktail of all imaginable offenses. But the most important aspect of the Soviet model that was transposed was the trial itself and its methods. In contrast to what had happened in 1947, the trials of the "nationalists" represented a complete political spectacle in which each person played a role and in which the accused had a central role as had been the case in the USSR in the thirties. They had to recognize their crimes themselves and thereby demonstrate the correctness of the line followed by the men in power and their legitimate right to remain in power. They were asked, in their confessions in 1948 and 1949, to give the status of objective truth to three propositions: that the USSR and Stalin embodied the interests of the Eastern European states and were alone capable of saying what those interests were; that the men in power in those states through their loyalty to the Stalinist line were on the right path, and that only they could be in the right; that the history of the war, when the parties had been divided between the men of the interior and those of Moscow, had been misunderstood. The party had not been divided; there had been only one resistance, the one in Moscow, since the others, those who were now under accusation, were paid agents of both domestic and foreign enemies. Thus was to be demonstrated the unity of the communist world around the USSR and the unity of the communist parties around those who had led them from Moscow.

As had happened in Moscow from 1936 to 1938, for these truths to be heard they had to be spoken by the accused. Public confession had always been an essential element in the Stalinist judicial-political spectacle. The Soviet police forces had long experience in imposing this kind of confession on the accused. And the dispatch of Soviet experts throughout Eastern Europe to organize the conditioning of the accused and the staging of the trials was the most widespread form of Soviet assistance to its sister states. Failures were rare. The most resounding one was at the Kostov trial. After admitting during the investigation the crimes that had been imputed to him, Kostov, like Krestinsky earlier in Moscow, recanted at the public hearing, accusing the police of having extracted his confession by torture. Like Krestinsky, he did not however escape with his life, nor did he even provoke a reaction in public opinion.

The staging of the trial itself was accompanied by a corresponding and extraordinary conditioning of public opinion, or rather a staging of public reactions. Here too the Soviet specialists merely imported the methods and the scenarios that had functioned so well at home. "Popular justice" had to be accompanied by the participation of the people in justice. Starting from this principle, the party everywhere mobilized the rank and file, who sent to the courts, to political leaders, and to newspapers telegrams and petitions signed by "the workers of a factory" or some other working group demonstrating the indignation of an honest people and demanding punishment of the criminals. Newspapers and radios carried the proceedings and they were immediately broadcast to gatherings of responsible citizens. This systematic organization of collective indignation, which bordered on hysteria, was one of the most widespread methods of socialization in those years, and it was at the same time a demonstration of the representative nature of the existing authorities, aimed at the world outside.[46]

Finally, the Soviet advisers truly "administered" the entire organization of the trials from the questioning of the accused, in which they thoroughly assisted their local colleagues, through to the setting up of the whole judicial machinery. The best known of these stage managers, a specialist in the "repression spectacle" who traveled from one people's democracy to another, was General Fyodor Balkin, about whom much information is available.

But the liquidation of the national leaders did not mark the end of this enterprise of exporting Stalinism in its extreme forms to neighboring states. A third wave of purges took place from 1951 to 1953. This time the targets of repression were none other than perfect Stalinist leaders, whose biographies and activities seemed to fulfill all the criteria of political security and loyalty that could be imagined. "Muscovites" for the most part, often having acted on behalf of the Comintern during the Spanish Civil War or in the administrative divisions of the world party of the revolution, these men were tied to Stalin by their entire personal histories. They were also tied to him by the docility with which they had lent themselves to his repressive work. Having liquidated their predecessors out of loyalty to the USSR in order to affirm its authority and its supremacy, could they not hope to profit from this choice? This had also been the hope of those who in the USSR in the thirties had accused their colleagues in the great trials and supported the thesis of Stalin's infallibility. Like these unfortunate predecessors whose fate had taught them nothing, the architects of the liquidations of Kostov, Rajk, and Gomułka were often the victims of the next purge. Hardly had the "nationalist deviationists" of the right or the left been hanged or subjected to merciless repression, when in 1951 a new series of plots was presented to popular indignation. The most spectacular victims of this new batch of accusations were the Rumanians Ana Pauker and Vasil Luca, two notorious "Muscovites" who had represented their party in Moscow during the war years, and the Rumanian Interior Minister, Teohari Georgescu.

As for the most spectacular and best organized trial of the period, this was the Slánský trial in 1952. Rudolf Slánský, general secretary of the Czech Communist Party, a notorious Muscovite totally devoted to the USSR who could hardly be suspected of nationalism and who had conscientiously helped to bring about the purges of 1948 and 1949, was arrested for treason in November 1951, convicted along with thirteen codefendants, the entire "summit" of the Czech Communist Party, and then hanged. His trial was exemplary and sheds more light than any other on the complete subjection of Czechoslovakia—both the party and state apparatus together—to Stalin. The documents put together during the Prague Spring to explain the purges demonstrate that Stalin personally decided on Slánský's arrest, that this decision was transmitted by the local Soviet adviser to Gottwald and Zápotocký, and that finally, belatedly, after the fact, the party authorities, the Central Committee and the Politburo, were informed.[47] There is no other way of understanding this destruction of communist officials whose loyalty to the USSR could not be questioned and who could not be touched by any suspicion of national deviation. No doubt we should consider two explanations, one general, the other linked to Soviet policies in the early fifties. The general explanation is that the transplantation of the Soviet model to Eastern Europe could not be partial. In his own country, Stalin had conceived of the purge as an uninterrupted process allowing him to maintain his authority by means of the repeated destruction of existing elites, the impossibility for those who were in the leading positions of power to consolidate those positions and to acquire a certain autonomy through stability in office, and the constant promotion of new officials whose loyalty to him was assured alternately by hope, gratitude, and fear. This procedure of renewal of the elites had been a very potent instrument of Stalinist power, which it had reinforced. Stalin, the sole survivor of the purges and the plots allegedly directed against him, derived from the situation an absolute authority. He appeared confronting the weaknesses of the men of his party, haloed in an infallibility that made him the rampart of the system. The same procedure repeated in the Eastern European states did not have the function in the last analysis of legitimizing the national leaders but rather of legitimizing the authority of Stalin over those national leaders, whoever they might be, and over the countries that they administered. Within a socialist territory that remained divided into juridically sovereign states, the purges had the function of assuring horizontal unity around a single leader, Stalin. In this respect, they abolished frontiers by assuring the unity of the political system and the man who embodied it for the whole of the communist world.

The charges against those who were accused in the early fifties changed. They were accused of the crime, as one might expect, of treason on behalf of Tito and the Americans. But a new charge took on great importance, Zionism or cosmopolitanism, which, similarly, expressed adhesion to other values for which Israel and the international Jewish organizations were the center. The accusations take on particular significance if we remember that a disguised anti-Semitism was simultaneously developing in the USSR and that Stalinist repression, which was returning in force, had as its pretext precisely "Zionism, linked with imperialism." In January 1953 these still only partially explicit tendencies, which had nevertheless caused deaths in the USSR and were filling the camps, found expression in the "Doctors' Plot," in which a group of doctors was accused of having conspired to decimate the party, beginning with Stalin, precisely on behalf of Zionism and imperialism. How are the developments in Eastern Europe in 1951 and 1952 to be situated in relation to the anti-Zionist orientation of the USSR? Was there a link between these developments? Did they result from the same logic?

To the internal logic of the purges, we have to add another one that was connected to the objectives of the Soviet system at the time. In the early fifties the USSR was preparing to carry out an important shift in foreign policy. After having supported Israel at its birth, Stalin had recognized that his initial calculation had been wrong, that the new state was not a privileged place for the revolution in the Middle East, and that by recognizing it he had alienated the entire Arab world. To move brutally from support of Israel to an attitude of rejection was neither thinkable nor effective. The heavy anti-Zionist machinery that Stalin set in motion in the USSR by the late forties allowed him to take preliminary steps toward this shift. But being concerned with maintaining the appearance of a great and responsible nation—the holocaust was too much present in everyone's mind to allow the USSR to adopt open anti-Zionism, much less anti-Semitism—Stalin used the Eastern European purges to undertake this revision of his political choices. The moderate-sized states of Eastern Europe, cut off from international life, could adopt irresponsible attitudes without damaging their status. And they could pave the way for the propagation of the theme of the Zionist danger, a path that the USSR would then follow beginning in the early fifties.

The principal victims of this last wave of purges were often Jewish and this was not accidental. This was the case for Ana Pauker, Rudolf Slánský, and more generally for eleven of the fourteen defendants in the Slánský trial. No doubt these were not the first purges that included Jews among the victims. But in 1952 and particularly in Czechoslovakia, as in the USSR at the same time, Jewish origin was used as an argument to demonstrate these victims' treason. A simple theme—that Jewish origin predisposed one toward cosmopolitanism and hence toward imperialism—became proof of the collusion of the accused with all the forces that threatened their countries. Soviet policy derived benefits from this because these trials demonstrated—at least, so it was claimed at the time—that the Zionist-imperialist threat was indeed primarily directed against the USSR, which established its solidarity with the dominated states, the victims of imperialism. The community of interests between the USSR and a third world that was beginning to assert itself had found its first justifications.

Although anti-Zionism and anti-Semitism were central themes of the last wave of purges of the Stalinist period, this phenomenon should not obscure another perhaps more important logic of these events. If we study the biographies of the victims of this wave, and Czechoslovakia provides the richest sample, we find another common trait. The people whom Stalin eliminated at this stage, loyal Muscovites though they had generally been, had also very often been witnesses to a dramatic and thoroughly concealed part of communist history. They were very frequently Comintern officials who had seen up close the internal struggles, shifts, and strategic mistakes of the movement. Even more often, they were former members of the International Brigades, witnesses to Stalin's tortuous choices in Spain. From the end of the war on Stalin had systematically worked to suppress all those who had seen his revolutionary activities in operation in the field; all those whom he suspected of having been contaminated by anarchist or other ideas, who had given free rein to their criticisms of that revolution that had been so strangely conducted.[48] Why finally was this last purge concentrated in a few countries—essentially Czechoslovakia and Rumania—while others, like Bulgaria and Poland, were spared? The answer is not so simple. In the case of Bulgaria, however, we can hypothesize that it largely had to do with the domestic situation. The purges had so ravaged the party there that no famous candidates were left for a new purge. The old "Muscovites" capable of succeeding the national leaders who had been eliminated were carried off by age and illness, while Stalin was eliminating their like elsewhere. Dimitrov died in July 1949, Kolarov six months later. In 1950, to replace these loyal followers, Stalin chose another Muscovite, Chervenkov, who had spent twenty years in the USSR and had returned to his country only in 1946. Hardly known by his compatriots and having enjoyed Stalin's confidence, promoted at the moment when new purges were being launched, he would have made a far from illustrious and hardly plausible defendant. He was on the other hand a general secretary of the communist party and a prime minister on whom Stalin could only pride himself. No Eastern European leader imposed the Soviet model and flawless authority so totally on his country. The perfect Stalinization of Bulgaria combined with the high degree of Russification accomplished there no doubt explain why the Zionist plots were discovered elsewhere.

The Victory of Stalinism

The trials from 1947 to 1953 were only the spectacular aspects of a state terrorism whose effects on institutions and societies were considerable. Although the transformation of mentalities is outside the scope of this book, since it is the subject of specialized works, the institutional balance sheet can be quickly drawn up. Everywhere the leading organs of the party were largely renewed, as they had been in the USSR in the thirties. Everywhere as well the communist parties were decimated and those who had been members underground or at the time of the revolution were generally replaced by a new generation of militants. The "verification" campaign organized by Gheorghiu-Dej in Rumania reduced party members from a million in 1948 to some 600,000 in 1954. In Czechoslovakia, where in 1948 with two and a half million party members, one adult out of three was a communist, the purges reduced party membership to a million and a half. In Hungary, where Rákosi was an implacable prosecutor, the purges of 1948 to 1953 caused more deaths than the Horthy regime and the party lost nearly a third of its members.[49] The same losses characterized the evolution of the East German Communist

Party, while the Bulgarian party maintained almost its entire membership and the Polish United Workers Party was more sparing of its militants. It is true that everywhere the arrival of the communists in power had been accompanied by a swelling of party membership that by 1948 had attained significant proportions. The ebb of Stalin's last years recalls the similar experience of the Soviet party in the late twenties and early thirties when purges and the determination to eliminate casual militants attracted by victory worked together.

In March 1953 just before Stalin's death the effect of these dramatic years was identical from one end of communist territory to the other. The Stalinist system of power prevailed everywhere. The party-state was governed by one man atop an entire pyramid of authorities, as Stalin ruled in the USSR. Stalin's imitators at the conclusion of the process of liquidating all their rivals were Chervenkov in Bulgaria, Gottwald in Czechoslovakia,[50] Ulbricht in the GDR,[51] Rákosi in Hungary, Bierut in Poland, Gheorghiu-Dej in Rumania, and Enver Hoxha in Albania. In rebellious Yugoslavia, Tito also held undivided power. Imitation of the Soviet model was not confined to the concentration of power and the cult of one man, nor to the purges. It led to the establishment of a Soviet-style order, that is, to a society reduced to silence with no recourse against a system foreign to its values and its tradition, a society that was shattered by the rapidity of the changes that had occurred.

The Stalinist order was also made up of new economic structures that imposed on human life, work, and the social organizations of these countries a rationality different from the one that had existed previously. This is not the place to recount the history of the economic changes, which are related to the domestic life of Eastern Europe and have been the subject of many studies. What is important, from the perspective of Soviet politics and the relations that the Stalinist state maintained with the "little brothers" of socialism, is to specify to what extent the Soviet model had been rigidly transferred into a very diversified economic and social context; also to what extent the implantation of the Soviet model was part of a global strategy of imposing uniformity on the region and organizing Soviet domination over its neighboring states.

The essential elements of the model are well known and three in number. The first was industrialization carried out at a very rapid pace in which the effort was entirely concentrated on heavy industry, and economic and human resources were mobilized to attain objectives fixed from the outset in a voluntarist fashion. The second was the accelerated collectivization of agriculture, which had as in the USSR in the thirties, a symbolic value—the disappearance of small holdings and of individualistic consciousness—but also allowed the use of agricultural revenues to support the industrial plan. Finally, there was central planning. In the adoption of this model that had produced contradictory effects in the USSR—very spectacular rates of growth combined with no less remarkable malfunctions—the East European states' room for maneuver appears to have been constantly reduced. Although the plans of the first phase from 1947 to 1949 give evidence that the leaders of the people's democracies wished to take into account national possibilities and particularities, and although they seemed concerned not to repeat the Soviet mistakes of the thirties by avoiding the adoption of a purely voluntaristic approach, from 1950 on any inclination to deviate from the single model disappeared. Moreover, this disappearance coincided with the ouster of the "national" leaders. The final result of this two-stage approach to the problem of economic change was the generalized adoption in the plans of the early fifties of the most extreme Soviet model, the first Five-Year Plan. This evolution, fostered by the purges and the permanent intervention of Soviet economic advisers—the Kostov trial had brought into the open the conflicts between these advisers and certain national officials who refused to submit to Stalin's economic demands—was also as in the USSR accelerated by international arguments. In 1950 the USSR invoked before its allies the disturbed international situation and "the war preparations" of imperialism in order to impose on them an increase in the pace of industrialization.[52]

If we note few differences in those years between the Soviet economic model and the one the satellite states had to accept, whether they wanted to or not, the reasons for these choices remain to be explained. There is no doubt that Soviet strategy was a reflection of immediate economic motives, but also of political motives. For Stalin, the justification for the pattern of development he had imposed on his allies was obviously the fact that it was convenient for the USSR. In the postwar years, which imposed on him an enormous effort of reconstruction and a near break of economic ties with the Western world, the entry of the Eastern European economies into his sphere of influence was of very great importance. From countries with advanced economies—Czechoslovakia, the GDR, and to a certain extent Poland—the USSR could derive sources of investment and strategic production. As for the other countries, although the data are still imprecise, we nevertheless know with certainty that during those years the primary beneficiary of their economic cooperation was also the USSR.[53]

But political rationality was certainly still more important in the Soviet decision to impose its economic pattern on the satellites. Stalin never placed in doubt the exemplary and universally applicable character of the model he had adopted in the thirties. He never allowed any discussion of this certainty, in which ideology and political effectiveness were combined. In the USSR in the thirties the political function of economic changes was to create a new society, cut off from its previous ways of living and working and inserted into a socio-economic context that by its novelty imposed on the society new ways of behaving and thinking.[54] It was the same concern to create a new environment and new ways of thinking for the societies of Eastern Europe that guided the choice of the development strategy in the late forties. In this case, Stalin was shaping a fragmented universe in which the satellite states had lost their regional solidarities in favor of privileged bilateral relations with the USSR. The socialist camp thereby became a constellation in which the whole system gravitated around the USSR, its point of reference. The Soviet model in the last analysis was the imposition on Eastern Europe of the system of centralism and hierarchy that in the USSR made everything radiate from the center and from the leaders of the Communist Party, that is, from Stalin; in the camp, Stalin organized the whole system around the Soviet pivot.

Stalinism in Eastern Europe as it was forged in the early fifties was thus a combination of political and economic elements whose forced adoption by countries that were hardly prepared for it transformed each country into a little USSR, each leader into a little Stalin, and unified an extraordinarily diverse region enriched by its differences, exactly as the multiethnic and multicultural Soviet state had been unified during the same period. The Soviet model thus governed in those years both the organization of each satellite and the organization of the whole of Eastern Europe.

NOTES

1.   Quoted by N. Davies, *God's Playground* (Oxford, 1981), 2:574.

2.   Ripka, *Le Coup de Prague* (Paris, 1949), 93–94.

3.   W. Gomułka, *W. walce o demokrację ludową. Artykuły i przemówienia* (The struggle for a people's democracy—articles and speeches) (Warsaw, 1947), 1:199; quoted in H. Kapur and M. Molnar, eds., *Le Nouveau communisme* (Geneva, 1978), 54.

4.   Ibid., vol. 2, quoted in Kapur and Molnar, op. cit., 55.

5.   "Our socialism will be created uniquely as a result of Hungarian history. . . . It will be socialism born on Hungarian soil and adapted to Hungary," declared Rákosi in 1946, quoted by P. Kenda and K. Pomian, *1956—Varsovie, Budapest* (Paris, 1978), 18, quoting E. Kardelj, *O narodnoj demokratiji v Jugoslaviji* (Belgrade, 1949), 8.

6.   W. Gomułka, Minutes of the plenum of May 21–22, 1945, quoted by Davies, *God's Playground*, 2:558.

7.   The text was published in the *New York Times* on February 10, 1946. The most immediate official reaction was by Churchill in a speech delivered in March 1946 who observed that an "iron curtain" had fallen on Europe. *New York Times*, March 6, 1946; Bohlen, op. cit., 216.

8.   X, "The Sources of Soviet Conduct," *Foreign Affairs* 4 (July 1947):566–82.

9.   In San Francisco, moreover, Molotov demanded from Masaryk that the Czech vote on the Polish question follow that of the USSR, Bohlen, op. cit., 214.

10.   Ripka, op. cit., 72.

11.   Ibid., 74–81.

12.   Ibid., 82.

13.   Ibid., 85.

14.   See the conversation with the Polish Foreign Affairs Minister Modzelewski in Ripka, p. 87.

15. H. Truman, *Memoirs—Years of Trial and Hope* (New York, 1958), 106.

16. A great debate later developed over the thinking behind the article by "X": R. W. Tucker and W. Watts, eds., *Beyond Containment: U.S. Foreign Policy in Transition* (Washington, 1973); Charles Gatti, "What Containment Meant," *Foreign Policy* 7 (Summer 1972):22–40; C. Ben Wright, "Mr. X and Containment," *Slavic Review* 3 (March 1976):1–31; "George Kennan Replies," Ibid., 32–33.

17. H. Ripka, *Czechoslovakia Enslaved: The Story of the Communist Coup d'Etat* (London, 1950), 56–71; *Istoriia vneshnei politiki SSSR 1945–1975*, vol. 2 (Moscow, 1975), 137–41.

18. See Ripka, op. cit., 45–46, on the attitude of Hilary Mink, Polish foreign trade minister, and for remarks by Cyrankiewicz and Modzelewski.

19. Ripka, op. cit., 49.

20. Ibid., 51; on 62 Ripka quotes Stalin's ultimatum: "If you participate in the conference, you will prove by that act that you are allowing yourself to be used as a tool against the Soviet Union. Neither the Soviet people nor the Soviet government would stand for it."

21. On the text of these constitutions see below, chapter 8.

22. Zhdanov, *Informatsionnoe soveshchanie predstavitelei nekotoryh kompartii* (Moscow, 1948), 13–49.

23. E. Varga, "Une démocratie d'un type nouveau," *Démocratie nouvelle* 9 (1947):463.

24. Bourdjalov, *Kommunist*, July 1, 1948, quoted by M. Lesage, *Les Régimes politiques de l'U.R.S.S.* (Paris, 1971), 130–31.

25. Rákosi, "La voie de notre démocratie populaire," speech of February 29, 1952, published in *Articles et Documents*, Documentation française, no. 2536, November 19, 1952.

26. Conversation of the author with Antonín Snejdárek. And E. Taborsky, *Communism in Czechoslovakia, 1948–1960* (Princeton, 1961), 101, asserts that Gottwald was sincere in his adhesion to national communism, but this affirmation goes against remarks made by Gottwald and all his behavior in the course of a long communist career.

27. V. F. Kotok, ed., *Gosudarstvennoe pravo stran narodnoi demokratii* (Moscow, 1961), 87–90.

28. *Tribuna Ludu*, October 21, 1956, quoted by P. Zinner, op. cit., 228.

29. Exchange of letters between the Central Committee of the Yugoslav Communist Party and the Central Committee of the Communist Party (Bolshevik) of the U.S.S.R., *Le Livre yougoslave* (1950), 89.

30. Ripka, op. cit., 125 and 137. The latter statement was made by a Yugoslav, repeating Soviet remarks.

31. *Pravda*, February 23, 1948.

32. See Kende and Pomian, op. cit., 25, on the traditional military and political links between Russians and Bulgarians; C. Anastasoff, *The Bulgarians* (New York, 1977), 118–120.

33. Bela Kiraly and Paul Jonas, eds., *The Hungarian Revolution in Retrospect* (Boulder, Colo., 1978), 61.

34. Seton-Watson, op. cit., 303.

35. Arthur London, *L'Aveu. Dans L'engrenage du procès de Prague* (Paris, 1968,

175, 271–72; see also E. Loebel, *Sentenced and Tried: The Stalinist Purges in Czechoslovakia* (London, 1969), 32.

36.   *The Czechoslovak Political Trials, 1950–1954* (London, 1971).

37.   Ibid., 82.

38.   On the problem of the relations between state and church in Poland, see A. Michnik, *L'Eglise et la gauche—le dialogue polonais* (Paris, 1979); P. J. Babris, *Silent Churches* (Arlington Heights, Ill., 1978); and the works of H. Stehle, *Eastern Politics of the Vatican 1912–1979* (Athens, Ohio, 1981), 263–85, and *The Independent Satellites* (New York, 1965).

39.   P. Raina, *Kardynal Wyszinski* (London, 1979).

40.   L. Blit, *The Eastern Pretender* (London, 1965); quoted by Davies, op. cit., 579.

41.   "Stalinism and Soviet Legal Culture," in R. Tucker, ed., *Stalinism* (New York, 1972), 155.

42.   R. Tucker, *The Soviet Political Mind* (New York, 1972), 49–50.

43.   On the assassination theory, see *Der Spiegel*, April 7, 1965, which accuses an officer of the security services working for the NKVD; and *Pravda*, May 8, 1968 and *Izvestia*, May 17, 1968, protesting against these "calumnies."

44.   On his personal intervention in the process, see G. H. Skilling, *Czechoslovakia's Interrupted Revolution* (Princeton, 1976), 386.

45.   Several works shed light on the mechanisms of the trials in the USSR: Pierre Broué, *Les Procès de Moscou* (Paris, 1964); Robert Conquest, *The Great Terror* (London, 1968); R. Tucker and S. Cohen, *The Great Purge Trial* (New York, 1965); Annie Kriegel, *Les Grands Procès dans les systèmes communistes* (Paris, 1972).

46.   See London, *L'Aveu*, and D. Desanti, *Les Staliniens* (Paris, 1975), 158–63.

47.   G. Skilling, quoted in Tucker, ed., *Stalinism* (New York, 1974), 274, quoting the documents of the 1968 commission of inquiry.

48.   This comes out clearly in London, *L'Aveu*.

49.   Paul Ignotus, quoted in T. Hammond, ed., *The Anatomy of Communist Takeover* (New Haven, 1975), 398.

50.   Gottwald's was an exceptional case, combining the posts of general secretary of the party and president of the republic, leaving to Zápotocký the role of prime minister.

51.   The prime minister was Grotewohl and the president Pieck; in this case, there was a division of power.

52.   R. Tucker, ed., *Stalinism*, 245. W. Brus cites the debates of a Cominform meeting in November 1949 on this point, which led to direct pressure on the communist parties. This was precisely the theme of a discussion in the Czech Communist Party in February 1950.

53.   Brzezinski, op. cit., 127, has attempted an evaluation of the profits derived by the USSR from Eastern Europe.

54.   Moshe Lewin, "The Social Background of Stalinism," in Tucker, ed., *Stalinism*, 111–37.

CONCLUSION TO PART ONE

The years from 1945 to 1953 were eight dense and tragic years in the history of Eastern Europe. They were exemplary in the breadth of the changes that took place and exceptional in the short time in which those changes occurred. While the peoples of Western Europe were nursing the wounds of war, reconstructing their societies, resuming the paths that the war had interrupted, in the center of Europe, everything was division: a break with European destiny; a break with the political culture of each nation; a break with patterns of living and working. Torn away from a fate that a long history had shaped, the peoples of Eastern and Central Europe were forcibly turned toward the Slavic world of which they had to become a part, whether they were Slavs or not, whether they accepted or rejected it. They were also forced to make total revolutions in government and society that they had not chosen to make and for which they were not prepared.

This exceptional fate, which combined foreign domination and imposed revolution, was transformed in a cataclysmic way, thereby amplifying the model that it reproduced. The USSR, which had offered its revolutionary destiny and its accomplishments as examples to the conquered peoples had taken almost a quarter of a century to give form to that model. The political revolution that emerged from the 1914–1918 war had developed into a social revolution in a discontinuous progression, sometimes leaving terrified men moments of respite. Periods of radical revolution—war communism, the frenzied collectivization and industrialization of the thirties, reconstruction—had been followed by brief phases of relaxation—NEP, the immediate postwar period—which sometimes masked the brutality of the enterprise of so absolute a transformation of these human societies. The countries of Eastern Europe were forced to imitate the Soviet model at every point, but there is one domain in which their experience diverged from the model—time and the alternation of radical and calming phases. To the quarter century devoted to change in the USSR corresponded a brief period of eight years into which the long road imposed on men, cruel and unacceptable in all that it implied of breaking with the past, had been condensed, a period one third as long. While the peoples of the USSR had had nearly a quarter century to learn to bear Stalinism or to resign themselves to it, the peoples of Eastern Europe had only a few years. Is it possible in such a short time to break men and radically transform them?

This particularity of the imposition of Stalinism on Eastern Europe was aggravated by three complementary traits that characterized the region and its relations with the USSR.

First of all, the revolutionary history of these countries, their movement into the communist system, was the product of a foreign will, of an occupation. All the appeals to Slavic solidarity or to the solidarity of the oppressed were never enough to conceal this reality. The USSR, even if it was for certain peoples at some moment a liberator, very soon through its explicit determination to transform their fates by military and political intervention assumed its true face as a dominating power. This unhappy relationship between revolution and foreign domination gave national feeling a function it did not have in the USSR and thereby transformed the Soviet model in its local variants. In the USSR, even at the most difficult moments of the social revolution, Stalin could in fact appeal to the national pride of his subjects. He assured them that constructing a new world in tears and blood was another page of their national history that they were writing. But in Eastern Europe, such an appeal to national pride was unthinkable; it came up against the primacy of the USSR and loyalty to it, elevated to the supreme national value. In his deep attachment to what was Soviet, indeed to what was Russian, Stalin could only distrust the nationalism of other peoples. Wanting to attach these peoples to the USSR through spiritual integration, if not through juridical integration, Stalin helped to create in the minds of his distant subjects an opposition between communism and nation. This opposition, which could not be expressed in the brutal times of triumphant Stalinism, burst forth as soon as Stalin was gone.

A second trait characteristic of the Stalinization of Eastern Europe resulted from the contradiction that existed between the single, unchangeable, and supposedly perfect model imposed on the entire region and the extraordinary variety of cultures, traditions, and aspirations that coexisted there. The rigidity of the model confronted with the diversity of situations made it inapplicable, or else imposed permanent violence so that particular situations would neither erode nor transform the Stalinist model.

Finally, most of the Eastern European countries had, no doubt, limited experiences of democracy and had instead authoritarian traditions favorable to the establishment of a totalitarian model. But compared to prerevolutionary Russia, the histories of the Czech, Polish, and Hungarian societies were infinitely more open to the democratic tradition. The imposition of the Stalinist model was thereby all the more traumatizing for these populations than it had been in the USSR, and the brevity of the time in which this change took place merely magnified the difficulties.

In this period that was so brief and so harsh, the Sovietized peoples were confronted with an ordeal that no other peoples had faced before them in the twentieth century, in conditions that were uniformly unfavorable. During this period they found help neither within nor outside their countries. Domestically, they could have no confidence in leaders whom they generally considered as simple servants of Soviet policy. They could not accept a program developed in Moscow and imposed by a foreign head of state whose essential justification was power.

They found no help in the outside world. The iron curtain with which Stalin wished to isolate his Europe from the rest of the world, as he had in the past isolated the USSR, was not watertight, but it could not be crossed. From beyond their borders, peoples who had until 1945 been linked to the Western world heard rumors of the reconstruction that was speeded up by the Marshall Plan and echoes of the beginnings of the economic miracle. In 1930, Stalin had offered his subjects the image of the great economic crises and consoled them for their distress by showing them the lines of the starving unemployed in other countries. In the early fifties, the West moving toward prosperity could not be used as a foil, and Soviet domination, which was intensely resented, gave the echoes of Western prosperity the aura of a lost paradise. Eight years of the march toward Stalinism had not been enough to change or eliminate the memory of lost sovereignty and abolished freedoms.

These particular conditions that surrounded the development of Eastern European Stalinism explain both the violence that went along with it and its precariousness. Because he was aware of the obstacles in his path, Stalin was merciless and impatient with the satellites. And the violence he exhibited produced striking effects. In 1953 Eastern Europe was nothing but a unified territory in which from one society to the next, from one country to the next, the same system, the same orientations, the same slogans, were perpetually repeated.

But that violence and that impatience were also sources of the precariousness of the enterprise. The Eastern European monolith, however perfect it appeared to be, concealed frustrations, hatreds, and tensions that were given particular colorations by national differences. The silence that reigned over Eastern Europe was a sign of waiting rather than resignation. In any event, it implied no acceptance. Behind the apparently so successful integration, the forces of disintegration within the monolith were present. It would take little, the death of a man, Stalin, for silence to give way to sound and fury. And thus began a new history, the history of a challenged domination, following one that had succeeded.

PART TWO

THE FRATRICIDAL EMPIRE

4

"IF I LIFT MY LITTLE FINGER, TITO WILL COLLAPSE"

In September 1947 the delegates of nine communist parties, all those in power except the Albanian party in addition to the French and Italian parties, met in a small city in Poland at some distance from Warsaw, Szklarska Poreba, to found the Cominform.[1] It was at Soviet initiative, even though the USSR called those who claimed that it intended to govern the lives of the various communist parties through this institution liars and even though the official version was that the Polish Communist Party had originated the idea.[2] In the report he presented to the conference, Zhdanov, who at the time presented himself as the "official ideologue" of the Soviet Communist Party, emphasized that the disappearance of the Comintern, necessary in its time, had left the communist parties to a disturbing isolation, bringing about the most unfortunate consequences. The result of his analysis was that the communist parties, particularly the parties in power, had an urgent need to restore close ties among one another, that a device was needed to accomplish this, and that device was the Cominform. Entrusted with organizing "exchanges of experience and the coordination of party activities on the basis of free consent,"[3] it was to have its seat in Belgrade and to publish a journal whose title Stalin himself had chosen in harmony with the concerns of the time: *For a Lasting Peace, for a People's Democracy.*

Tito had hoped for the creation of this institution as early as 1945;[4] and his efforts to promote it were rewarded by the establishment of the Cominform in his capital.[5] Belgrade thus became a center of the communism whose only leader was in Moscow. In 1948 Stalin seemed to be elevating Yugoslavia to the rank of "second big brother" of the socialist camp, a role that the Ukraine would later share with Russia within the USSR.

For most of the communist leaders meeting in Poland in late September 1948 this was a fortunate event. The majority of them were still in conflict in their countries with rival parties, socialist or not, which, though very weakened, maintained a certain prestige in the eyes of their publics. The creation of a new International, even though it was baptized an "organ of information and liaison," gave them new weight, international stature on their domestic political scenes. The event also suggested that the time for compromise with ideological opponents had passed and that the consolidation of the revolutions was imminent. Alone among the participants, Gomułka expressed his hostility to the plan without hesitation; his attitude was soon condemned as an obvious sign of his "national deviations."[6]

The Origins of the Soviet-Yugoslav Conflict

The creation of the Cominform along with the political changes that took place between 1947 and 1949 solidified the unity of the socialist camp. No doubt this unity, as Zhdanov emphasized in his introductory report, depended on equality among the parties and states.

The preoccupation with unity was all the stronger because the same socialist model had been established everywhere and the existence after September 1947 of a communist center had provided a system of reference for the whole. From this point on the socialist bloc appeared unshakable. However, the first disturbance occurred just then, and it arose from a conflict between the two countries that had appeared closest to one another in their choices and with the greatest attachment to the Cominform, the USSR and Yugoslavia.

The Cominform, which they had both wished to create, was the central theater for their confrontation. This conflict, unthinkable until the moment when it exploded, was the first of an interminable series of conflicts all of which had the same protagonist, the USSR, against successive different antagonists, and it demonstrated that the unity and equality that had been so highly praised at the birth of the Cominform had strict limits.

The Soviet-Yugoslav conflict has produced excellent studies and it is too well known to require detailed treatment here.[7] What is important is to uncover its real logic, to understand why the USSR quarreled with its most faithful ally, and how, by means of this conflict, it developed a strategy for relations with the satellite states, a strategy it was lacking before then. With the Soviet-Yugoslav conflict, in fact, the relations of the USSR with its allies left the realm of domestic politics to enter that of international relations.

In discussing the Soviet-Yugoslav conflict of 1948, many writers tend to attribute it to the incompatibility of two nationalisms and to emphasize Tito's intransigent nationalism as the principle cause of the break between the two countries. It has often been demonstrated that Tito was a communist obsessed with the national interest of his country. However, it was not so much this clash of nationalisms, understood as the opposition between national variants of communism, that was at stake in 1948 as it was the interests of Soviet foreign policy.

In 1948 Tito was still the most secure of all Soviet allies, the one who was most zealous in developing the Stalinist model in his own country. The reconstruction of the Yugoslav economy after Tito's seizure of power followed precisely the path traced earlier by Stalin in both goals and methods. There was nothing missing in the Yugoslav effort from 1945 to 1948, neither rapid industrialization emphasizing heavy industry, nor pressure on the agricultural sector to provide the capital necessary for industrial development, nor labor mobility, notably the forced exodus of peasants needed for the rapid creation of a significant working class, nor centralized planning. Like his Soviet model, through a series of purges Tito had been able to suppress all his opponents and to establish a rule of iron that Stalin would respect.[8] Like Stalin finally he demonstrated the most arrogant contempt for power sharing and held no more frequent meetings of the Central Committee of his party than his model in Moscow did during the same period.[9]

It goes without saying that there were reasons for friction between Soviets and Yugoslavs. Already during the war the USSR had shown some hesitation in supporting Tito against the government-in-exile. After the war, the USSR had attempted to develop cooperative organizations there that were nothing but disguised enterprises for economic exploitation sponsored by a nominal ally; it gave up the practice only after repeated recriminations from Tito. Incapable of infiltrating the Yugoslav Army, which had been built out of the internal resistance, Soviet leaders focused on the police and with their help tried to gain the support of superior officers.[10] In the international arena, the USSR had also demonstrated little eagerness to defend Tito's claims to Trieste, and this too provoked his bitterness. These lurking conflicts were perhaps the cause of the provocative attitude that Tito sometimes adopted toward Stalin, to mark his independence or his irritation at frequent Soviet interference in Yugoslavia. It was this provocative or proud attitude, highlighted by Djilas as an essential component of the character of his fraternal "adversary,"[11] that led Tito to proclaim in Szklarska Poreba that the Yugoslav revolution, unlike those in the other people's democracies, owed nothing to the USSR.

Despite these constant frictions and despite Tito's thundering proclamation, up to 1948 Stalin was understanding about Tito's international ambitions, or rather he thought he could combine Tito's determination to play a role in the world with the interests of Soviet foreign policy. From 1945 on Tito had been developing a grand design for the Balkans. He had at first exercised near total domination over the small state of Albania. Then he saw the advantage of placing himself at the head of a Balkan federation that would have included Bulgaria, Poland, Czechoslovakia, and Greece, where he was attempting to accelerate the revolutionary process.

Confronted with these major projects, Stalin was at first understanding, encouraging Tito to subject Albania to his authority. With his usual cynicism, Stalin mocked the Albanians who were ready to commit suicide to preserve their independence and he said that he saw no obstacle preventing Tito from "swallowing" his Albanian neighbor.[12]

On the other hand, the plan for a Balkan federation, which he at first approved, later provoked his fury and the full-scale assault he launched against Tito. This was the origin of the 1948 conflict.

During this period, the Bulgarians and the Yugoslavs reached agreement on their war disputes and signed an agreement at Bled on August 1, 1947, supplemented by the Euxinograd Treaty on November 27. These agreements organized economic and cultural cooperation, a customs union, and political consultations on problems of common interest. For Tito these agreements were merely the preliminary stages in his Balkan dream, which was designed ultimately to unite Bulgaria with Yugoslavia. He was hardly concerned with any particular forms. He was ready either to organize a federation of the two states or to incorporate Bulgaria in the Yugoslavian federation in which it would represent a seventh republic. Lying behind this plan was his hope finally to resolve to the benefit of his country the perpetual and thorny Macedonian problem. The revolution he was supporting in Greece was designed to foster Macedonian irredentism and to seize this desirable territory attracted to Yugoslavia because of its aid to Macedonian independence. The Balkan federation that would have caused the Bulgarian Macedonians to enter the Yugoslav orbit would thus have permitted the use of the argument of Macedonian unity to attract Greek Macedonia.

This grandiose plan received Stalin's support because he was aware of the inertia of reality and of the weight of history. Tito thought he would be able to extend his authority over the Balkan federation that he dreamed of. Stalin guessed that the entire plan would serve to strengthen Bulgaria. With seven million inhabitants, Bulgaria, in either variant of the Balkan dream, would be its most significant element. As a Yugoslav republic it would have much more weight than the Serbian political center and would be a pole of attraction for those who challenged Serbian hegemony, like the Croatians and the Slovenes. As an independent partner in a federation, it would be the moving force because of its ethnic cohesion and the size of its population. If the two million Macedonians joined the federation, they would be attracted to Bulgaria, carrying on the old demand of the Komitadjis of the late nineteenth century who when they shouted "Macedonia for the Macedonians" secretly thought "Macedonia for the Bulgarians."[13]

Confronting an enterprising and united Bulgaria that remembered its conflict with the Serbs and that saw its Slavic values best represented in its link with Russia, Tito's program was too detached from reality. This is why Dimitrov, a loyal follower of Stalin, willingly accepted the idea. He knew what Stalin wanted: to support the development of Bulgarian, not Yugoslav, influence in the Balkans, because Bulgaria was historically and sentimentally close to the USSR. This proximity forged by history was reinforced by geography. As a direct neighbor of the USSR, Bulgaria was easy to control and through that intermediary Stalin hoped to be able to control Yugoslavia, which was loudly proclaiming that it owed nothing to him. The plan for the Balkan federation thus contained two contrary aims, even though Stalin and Dimitrov claimed to support the Yugoslav position and Tito's interests. In this context, we can see Stalin's ideas on the use of Bulgaria in his foreign relations taking shape. Because more than any other satellite country Bulgaria was close to him, he saw it as a useful policy tool, a convenient agent for actions he could not take directly. When the plan for the Balkan federation was abandoned, the assumption by Bulgaria of the role assigned to it was delayed. But the Soviet leaders continued to think that they could use this convenient and docile neighbor.

The plan collapsed and Stalin, who had at first supported it, suddenly became furious in his condemnation because Tito had not played the game. Ambitious, always intent on expanding his sphere of influence, reassured by Stalin's support of his ideas, convinced that Stalin would grant him a role in international politics, Tito wanted to extend the Balkan federation to other countries and at a minimum to include Poland and Czechoslovakia. Perhaps he understood this as a way of getting around the Bulgarian question. Perhaps he was simply carried away by his dreams of grandeur. Stalin's reversal was sudden, taking even the loyal Dimitrov by surprise, not giving him time to abandon his federalist position. Stalin condemned the plan and forced Dimitrov to acknowledge that he had gone too far.[14] Following his usual pattern, Stalin determined to get rid of everyone who had embodied the plan that had been condemned. Although there is no ground to assert with certainty that Dimitrov's death in Moscow seventeen months later was the result of mysterious maneuvers by Stalin, the supposition, widespread in the late forties, is not totally improbable. As for Tito, Stalin tried to undermine his position and to get rid of him.[15] But this was to fail to recognize Tito's domestic strength and his capacity to foil plots. Unable to liquidate him, as he had done to all other Eastern European leaders, Stalin, in order to resolve what was still a personal conflict, inaugurated an unprecedented strategy; he made it into a conflict between socialist states.

The Confrontation: March–June 1948

The purges, which had elsewhere taken the form of the condemnation of men or groups, were to take on a particular quality for Stalin in the case of Yugoslavia, the purge of a perverse variant of communism, national betrayal.

The initial phase of the conflict from March to June 1948 reflected Stalin's confidence in his power to dominate the leaders of sister states. He was convinced as he said that all he had to do was "to lift my little finger and there will be no more Tito."[16] And when Stalin spoke of lifting his little finger against a communist leader, he was talking about the heavy artillery that little finger controlled. Stalin launched a threefold attack against Tito focused on the arena of bilateral relations that was as yet barely visible from the outside, constituting in a way a demonstration of the power of the big brother endowed with wisdom over the recalcitrant little brother. As the first attack, the first method of eliminating Tito, Stalin unleashed the advisers he had sent to Yugoslavia in an attack against Tito's authority, and their activism was strengthened by the ties that had been forged between the Soviet ambassador and some of Tito's close collaborators. The latter provided information to the USSR on the various discussions that took place within the ruling group and they were considered in Moscow as elements of a possible substitute government. Because Tito reacted immediately and opposed to these Soviet efforts a repressive organization directed against the "pro-Soviets" that was derived from Stalin's best lessons—he had been a zealous participant in the purges against his party in Moscow—[17] Stalin gave up this ineffective infiltration to launch his second bomb, the breaking off of cooperation. On March 18, 1948, without warning the USSR removed all military and civilian advisers from Yugoslavia and cut off all aid to the country. Even though the Soviet advisers in Yugoslavia had been leading a scandalously privileged existence, even though the cost of their presence was very high, and even though their political activities were close to espionage, this measure was a real trauma for Yugoslavia. At a stroke it was deprived of all assistance and all the economic resources, however unjustly costly, that cooperation had contributed. This break in cooperation made it impossible to continue the planned industrialization that had been undertaken. The USSR had been too insistent on linking the economies of its partners with the Soviet economy and had created too many ties of dependency for such a break not to have destabilizing consequences for the Yugoslav economic and political system. The agreement on the exchange of goods between the two countries signed in 1947 had further strengthened the economic links established in 1945.

Tito responded to these economic measures by an open determination to disarm Stalin's anger. He seized the opportunity offered by the anniversary of the Soviet-Yugoslav Treaty of 1945 to affirm his loyalty to the USSR. The Yugoslav press pointed out that the 1945 treaty had created indissoluble ties between the two countries and suggested that the current difficulties were largely attributable to the activities of the "imperialist and anti-democratic camp, which was fomenting war by its propaganda."

The at first conciliatory tone of a Tito who was torn by the break that he could see coming helped to convince Stalin that violence had paid and that Tito was in fact in the process of collapsing.

Following his usual pattern, he continued the assault and in a series of letters that were at first secret Stalin accused the Yugoslav Communist Party and implicitly Tito's leadership of deviations that had elsewhere been political or even physical death warrants for those to whom such messages had been sent. The eight letters and more than twenty-five thousand words of this correspondence, which was exceptionally violent both in tone and argument, is extraordinary documentary evidence of the nature of relations between these two states. [18] These letters provide a stark contrast to the muted tone of traditional diplomatic documents, particularly those of the postwar period. Neither the war, nor international conferences, nor the existence of institutions and doctrines fostering cooperation among states (like the Atlantic Charter or Cominform resolutions) changed the violence of these relations between a powerful, dominating state and a smaller neighbor, whose submission was demanded by the great power. The tone of these letters recalls the worst moments of European history.

The first letter in the series, which continued through the end of May, was dated March 27, 1948. From one letter to the next Soviet criticisms complemented one another and made up a general indictment of "Titoism"; its "anti-socialist" aspects were emphasized. Not the least interesting aspect of the letters is Stalin's conception, so completely expressed here for the first time, of the nature of relations between socialist states. The first criticism was that the Yugoslavs had false ideas about relations with the USSR and those ideas were indicative of their deviations. Did Tito complain about Soviet intervention in Yugoslav life, did he take offense when the Soviet ambassador sought information on party operations, when Soviet intelligence organizations recruited Yugoslav agents, and acted as though Yugoslavia were their own country? Stalin condemned this attitude, obviously intended to protect Yugoslav sovereignty, with such violence and contempt as to raise doubts about whether his letter was addressed to the leaders of a state with the same political system as that of the USSR. "The Yugoslav comrades do not accept criticism in the Marxist way. They react to it like provincials; they consider it an insult damaging their prestige and interfering with the ambitions of the Yugoslav leaders." And he added: "Why should we believe what Tito and Kardelj say, their repeated complaints about our military advisers? We have advisers in almost all the people's democracies and we have never received any complaints. There are problems in Yugoslavia only because they are surrounded by a hostile regime." And to strengthen his argument, Stalin added that despite all the Soviet warnings Tito was using men who were imperialist spies, like General Velebit at the Ministry of Foreign Affairs, Ambassador Leontić in London, and so on.

Everything was said in a few sentences: Tito's refusal to listen to advice and to accept necessary Soviet aid even though he had been given proof of the infiltration of his service by the "imperialists"; and the normality of that aid, accepted, requested by all the people's democracies. The Soviet message also isolated Yugoslavia from the socialist community by affirming the opposition between the countries that respected the community and its rules of operation and a corrupt Yugoslavia following its own path. Moreover, Stalin accentuated this isolation by calling the Yugoslavs "provincial." From the rank of the second big brother that they had occupied a few months earlier, they were cast into the category of "provincials," those who had neither the dimensions necessary to play a role in the communist bloc nor the understanding of what the bloc was. This was Stalin's second line of attack. The Yugoslavs were not only ill-intentioned and obstinate, they were suspected indeed guilty of belonging to the other camp. This criticism was addressed to the past, the immediate postwar period, as much as to the present and it called into question the sincerity of Yugoslavia's commitment to communism. Stalin reproached Tito with having as early as May 1945 preferred his country's interests to those of communism and with having been ready in the name of his disproportionate national ambitions to sacrifice the security of the future communist world and that of the USSR. According to the Soviets, Tito had revealed his deviations at the time in the speech he delivered in Ljubljana to glorify his performance and to assert: "We want everyone to be master in his own house. We want neither to pay others' debts nor to serve as a pawn. We want to have nothing to do with spheres of influence."

After quoting this passage, Stalin analyzed its meaning in a letter of May 14, 1948. From that moment on Tito had forgotten that it was thanks to the Red Army that his party had been able to take power in Yugoslavia. But the most serious point involved something else. What lay behind Tito's rancor, said the Soviets, was that in 1945 in order to gain control over Trieste he had wanted "the U.S.S.R. to start a war against the English and Americans; the U.S.S.R. had tried everything short of war to turn Trieste over to Yugoslavia. The Yugoslav comrades did not seem to know that after such a terrible war, we could not undertake a new one." Forgetful of the decisive role the USSR had played in the war and possessed by scandalous grudges, Tito, and this is the basis of the Soviet criticism, put Anglo-American imperialism and the first communist state in the world on the same level. The Ljubljana declaration was directed not only against the imperialists, but also against the USSR!

By raising the question of Yugoslavia's permanent anti-Sovietism, Soviet criticism pointed in two distinct directions. On the one hand, it tended to demonstrate that Yugoslavia had placed itself outside the Communist bloc. But we can also see here the determination to isolate Tito. In his letters Stalin called on the evidence of the past, on the insistence of Kardelj (recalled by the first Soviet ambassador, Sadshikov, on June 5, 1945) that the USSR consider Yugoslavia as a potential Soviet republic and the Yugoslav Communist Party as a simple national section of the Soviet Communist Party. By making public this forgotten episode that had been unknown at the time, Stalin was empha-sizing simultaneously Soviet respect for the independence of sister states, the evolution that had taken place in Yugoslavia, and Tito's personal respon-sibility. Ambassador Sadshikov's message, related in the May 14 Soviet letter, established that Kardelj was pro-Soviet in 1945 and that he was already troubled by his companion's deviations. The Soviet maneuver was thus again directed at Tito. He was the one whom Stalin wanted to isolate, to eliminate. He was certainly counting on the assumption that the Yugoslav communists would not dare to stand up to the accusation of anti-Sovietism that the letter expressed so forcefully.

He counted on it all the more—and this was his third line of attack—because anti-Sovietism and the abandonment of communism were indistin-guishable. Stalin vehemently criticized Tito for his methods of government, which were foreign, he claimed, to communist practice. He reproached him for his inordinate personal power, unconcerned with democracy, which ig-nored the party's Central Committee and the institutions of collective power and did not keep them informed of the conflict with the USSR. In short, for the Soviets everything derived from the fact that Yugoslavia was not a truly communist country but a country in which communism had been perverted by a dictator concealing behind the smokescreen of revolutionary legitimacy personal ambitions and a nationalistic and chauvinistic orientation.

If the description of Tito's personal power had not had the purpose of forcing Yugoslavia to expel him, if it had not been a maneuver to intimidate and put pressure on the Yugoslav party, it would stand as a superb anthology piece of Stalinism; Tito was criticized for having too perfectly imitated the Soviet model and for governing exactly as Stalin did. Tito did not inform the ruling institutions of the party, which in fact were functioning badly, of the conflict, just as Stalin could not inform his ruling institutions, which he never called into session.

But when Stalin raised his little finger, he obtained the opposite of the result he had expected. To the vehemence of Stalin's messages, Tito replied with measured statements expressing his sadness in the face of what he persisted in considering misunderstandings and inadequate information.

Stalin's criticisms inspired him to take wise steps, intended to forge a more coherent political system around him. Thus he gave reality to the Central Committee elected in 1940 that had never met since that date.[19] He called it into session for the first time on April 2, 1948, to discuss the attitude to be adopted toward Stalin's attacks. He also decided to hold the Fifth Party Congress as soon as possible, to bring the party together on a clear position that could be opposed to the USSR, and he debated in the Politburo, which had until then met very infrequently, on the precise language to be used in his correspondence with Stalin.[20]

While Tito was thus working to forge an internal alliance to strengthen him in his dialogue with Stalin, Stalin, aware of the maneuver, tried to prevent him from doing this by setting up his own "pressure groups" in Yugoslavia and elsewhere in the camp. It was Stalin in fact who took the initiative of making public documents that had previously been confined to the field of secret relations between political leaders. In autumn 1948 he had the texts of the Soviet messages distributed in Yugoslavia, which brought about an immediate response from the Yugoslav side: the republication of the Soviet letters accompanied by Tito's replies along with a communiqué from the Central Committee. Having failed to conquer Tito within the framework of relations at the top, Stalin tried to outmaneuver him by putting pressure on Yugoslav society. Similarly, when he realized that his direct threats had not broken Tito, he decided to change strategies and to use the Cominform to get rid of this intractable enemy definitively.

What characterized the first, concealed, phase of the Soviet-Yugoslav conflict was both the simplistic nature of Soviet objectives and the Soviet perception of the character of an intersocialist conflict. Stalin's objective was to subject Yugoslavia to the same treatment as he had the other states in the camp. After having accommodated Yugoslavia and allowed it to play its own role, Stalin grasped the difficulties of privileged treatment. These difficulties had to do with the relations between states. Left too much to itself, Yugoslavia was weakening the cohesion of the camp that Stalin wanted to be without flaws. Zhdanov's speech was clear on this point, emphasizing the two essential elements that gave vitality to the camp of "anti-imperialist and anti-fascist forces": absolute cohesion and the central, leading role of the USSR in the program; a Yugoslavia out of line, wishing to define its own role, was an element that undermined the monolith.

Moreoever, the foreign policy of the USSR and its influence on the Eastern European states could not come to terms with the preeminent role of Yugoslavia in the Balkans. Stalin was willing to assign a role to his small allies in his international strategy only if they acted in his name and if their activities increased Soviet influence. This is why Bulgaria was precious to him and Yugoslavia so difficult to use. The Soviet perception of the nature of the conflict is another interesting phenomenon of the period. Stalin saw himself as the leader of the communist world. He claimed to rule over his partners in the name of communism. This is why he spoke to Tito in the name of party duties, in the name of their shared rules, and accused Tito of behaving like a head of state, disregarding the fact that the socialist state was merely the juridical and organizational framework of the party.

Stalin's position was paradoxical and difficult to support. From 1936 on he had constantly strengthened the state. The Soviet Constitution, the one he offered as a model to sister states, was a state constitution that left little room for the party. In the May 14, 1948, letter evoking Kardelj's offer to integrate Yugoslavia into the USSR, Stalin insisted on the fact that "Yugoslavia is an independent state and the Yugoslav party an independent party." At the same time, in the name of communism and party solidarity, he criticized Yugoslav nationalism and attachment to the interests of the state. Tito on the contrary attempted to place the debate in the framework of relations between states and between state authorities in order to limit the scope of the conflict. Moreover, Djilas points out that there was a divergence of views within Yugoslavia on this point. One part of the leadership, himself, Kardelj, and Bakarić, wished to elevate the conflict, the first conflict between communist states, to a theoretical level. Tito on the contrary was determined to avoid this broadening of the debate, intent on limiting its scope.

Consciously or not, by his intransigence at this point Stalin made a breach in the ideological system on which he relied. Certain that no one would dare call into question the wisdom of the party he led, that no one would go as far as interparty conflict, he held firmly to this framework of discussion and thereby demonstrated that the Marxists' whole theory about the link between conflicts and class societies was not verified. No doubt Stalin realized the implications of his stubborn attitude. And that explains why, having been unable to defeat Tito in the framework of bilateral relations, he brought the conflict before the Cominform.

The "Internationalization" of the Conflict: June 1948

The Cominform, which until 1948 seemed to have no function beyond that of a representative body, had been informed from the very beginning of Stalin's accusations against Tito. On March 27, Stalin's first letter to Tito was addressed to all the communist parties that had participated in the September 1947 meeting. At that point, this was a step that as yet had no real significance. What was being put in place was a mechanism that had always been successful for Stalin in the interwar years. In conflicts with foreign parties, the Kremlin itself had denounced and liquidated opponents who were subjugated by definition, and the Comintern was advised as a matter of pure form. But in spring 1948 the Yugoslav reaction forced Stalin to modify his strategy. Far from accepting Soviet criticism, Tito arrested those in Yugoslavia who advocated submission to Moscow or whom he suspected of pro-Sovietism. He refused to go to Moscow to attempt to justify himself, remembering too well since he had lived through it the fate of those who innocently gave themselves up to Stalin's authority. And he proposed on April 13 that Soviet leaders come to Belgrade.[21] Confronted with his open rebellion, this reversal of positions—Stalin had never traveled for anyone; he had always had the heads of state of the great powers come to or close to the USSR—how could he, the powerful head of the socialist camp, agree to go to Belgrade? Stalin resorted to the argument of the need for intervention by the whole communist camp. He proposed that the Cominform arbitrate, and because Tito challenged the right of the other states of the camp to intervene in a dispute he wished to confine to his relations with the Soviet state, Stalin involved the brother parties in the conflict. In May 1948 the Hungarian and Czech parties demanded forcefully that the Cominform be more fully informed about the Yugoslav affair. These two countries were precisely at turning points in their own internal histories. People's democracies, in their extreme form, had been constructed later there than elsewhere. By directly involving these countries in the battle against Yugoslavia, Stalin accelerated the process of alignment. Internal hardening and suspicion of all deviations helped to accelerate the absorption of the Hungarian Social Democratic Party by the Communist Party. In Prague the communists who had been in power since February had a strong need for "mobilizing" themes. By condemning the Yugoslav heresy and the inclinations toward independence that it revealed, Stalin emphasized the essential: everything that was not a servile imitation of the USSR and acceptance of its line was criminal.

Despite Tito's refusal to debate the problem before the Cominform, Stalin called it into session in Bucharest on June 20. As one might imagine, the institution was unanimous in condemning the Yugoslavs. The Cominform resolution purely and simply removed Yugoslavia from the communist sphere, asserting that it had reverted to the condition of a very ordinary "bourgeois democracy, and an imperialist colony."[22] At the origin of this development lay a major crime, nationalism.

By striking this great blow—a solemn condemnation, reinforced by the unanimity of the communist world—Stalin, who no longer hoped to intimidate Tito, was rather trying to justify armed intervention against him. The Cominform resolution in fact cast Tito and his supporters into the outer darkness of the imperialist world, but it did not thereby assume that all of Yugoslavia had followed them in their heresy. Quite the contrary, the Cominform called on the healthy elements of the country who were still capable of saving the revolution. Did Stalin really believe in this appeal, which without doubt prefigured similar appeals to "healthy social forces," in Czechoslovakia in 1968 and in Poland in the late seventies? Or was it a means for him to establish that Yugoslavia had to be isolated by a *cordon sanitaire* to avoid spreading the plague of nationalism? The first hypothesis is certainly correct. Stalin had invested enough efforts in Yugoslavia over the years to have grounds to hope that the Yugoslav party would split, that pro-Soviet elements would be capable of mobilizing a militant movement, even one that would finally eliminate Tito. The disappointment at this stage was as great as when Stalin thought he could make Tito fall at his first gesture. Tito carried out a swift, effective, and very cruel purge of everyone he suspected of pro-Soviet tendencies. And he called an immediate meeting of the Fifth Party Congress to seek support and legitimation through a demonstration of cohesion. Before embarking on this path of national union, Tito had considered all of Stalin's possible reactions, including the hypothesis of armed intervention against Yugoslavia. The purges he had undertaken were designed not only to spoil the chances for an uprising manipulated by Moscow but especially to deprive Stalin of any pretext for coming to "restore order" in Yugoslavia. And in his calculations Tito included a factor that had until then been absent from relations between communist states, the American factor. He confided his certainty to Djilas: "The Americans are not crazy, they will not allow the Russians, in those conditions, to reach the Adriatic."[23] Despite tensions with the United States due primarily to Yugoslav support for the Greek civil war, Tito thought that his country could rely on a particular strategic situation that limited Soviet room for maneuver.

This favorable geographic and strategic situation was certainly recognized by Stalin. The USSR has always been careful not to transform a conflict between communist states into an international problem. The internationalization of intercommunist conflicts simply meant for Stalin in 1948 and for his successors later that they were the province of the entire communist camp, but that the external world had no right to examine them. Because the position of Yugoslavia could in fact provoke a real internationalization, and not in the Soviet sense, of the conflict, Stalin was prudent, confining himself to reacting with local means.

Having failed to provoke "healthy" forces to rise up against Tito beginning in the summer of 1948, Stalin deployed the whole arsenal of resources at his disposal against all of Yugoslavia and not simply against its leaders: the mobilization of the neighboring communist parties to demonstrate that the Cominform's unanimity was carried over into the political life of every communist country. The months following the condemnation of Yugoslavia were marked by a torrent of "anti-Titoism" in the press of the communist states and in popular demonstrations organized everywhere.[24] In this connection, the Cominform's condemnation inaugurated a collective process of intimidation of recalcitrant states that enjoyed a continued existence in the post-Stalin period.

But these demonstrations of the unanimity of the camp were only the visible part of Stalin's reprisals. Yugoslavia, which could not be conquered, became the object of concrete persecutions systematically organized by the USSR. Following the example of the big brother, the socialist countries broke all economic ties with Belgrade, and the USSR imposed a blockade that was all the more dramatic because the country depended on its allies and because the Western world, still not convinced of the reality of the crisis, at first refused all assistance. The notion of a "false crisis," of a scenario designed to deceive the West while the cold war demanded vigilance, had a certain success. This Western blindness to the seriousness of the break was repeated some years later when the Sino-Soviet conflict broke out. Deprived of all external help, excluded from all the collective institutions to which it had

belonged, Yugoslavia had to make its way alone in order to survive economically and politically. The unexpected result of Stalin's maneuvers was to
force Tito to find an alternative to the Soviet model. Self-management,
limitation of the party's role to the ideological and political realm, the search
for a social democracy—these themes announced at the Yugoslav Sixth Party
Congress in 1952 were undoubtedly the results of the break. For the first
time, the communist party even decided to change its name to indicate
clearly its independence.[25] But Stalin was not content with orchestrating
insults against "the traitor and assassin" of Belgrade nor with asphyxiating
the Yugoslav economy; he also tried to destroy it politically by taking
advantage of the means afforded by the geography and the ethnic structure of
the country. The neighboring states, from the USSR to Albania, undertook a
policy of harrassment, border incidents, and provocations showing that
Stalin had not given up the notion of provoking an internal uprising or
disorders and that he held in reserve the possibility of using force. The most
classic of these border threats were simply military maneuvers that were
stepped up at the time and provoked a protest by Yugoslavia to the U.N. in
1951.[26] More spectacular were the terrorist activities undertaken on Yugoslav
territory by agents of neighboring states, particularly Bulgaria and Albania.
The terrorists organized assassination attempts and local battles that the
Yugoslavs feared would lead to large-scale reprisals. Indications given by the
Yugoslavs show that border harrassment was carefully organized, that the
USSR never openly took part in it, holding itself out as an arbiter, and that a
division of labor was worked out between the states specializing in terrorist
activities (Bulgaria was the center of this kind of action) and espionage, which
fell to special services in Hungary and Rumania. It appears, moreover, that
the Rumanians set up a center in Temesvár designed to train agents in
methods of stirring up their compatriots who had been repatriated to
Yugoslavia.[27] For multiethnic Yugoslavia, these provocations during the
period of isolation presented a considerable danger. The decentralization
policy that Tito launched in 1951 was a response to these attempts to break
up his country.

It is appropriate to note that the Cominform's unanimity concealed many
differences and that Stalin was never able to involve all his allies in his anti-
Yugoslav crusade. If we analyze in detail the daily harrassments that
Yugoslavia suffered, we note that two countries did not answer the call,
Czechoslovakia and Poland. No doubt having no common borders with
Yugoslavia they could not participate in the campaign of infiltrating terrorists
and spies that mobilized the countries bordering on Yugoslavia. And Czechoslovakia compensated for this absence in the field by vigorous denunciation of
"Titoism" in line with other countries. Poland, on the contrary, at this early
point revealed its singularity. Although it had been unable to abstain from
voting on the Cominform resolution, its leaders demonstrated extreme moderation in their criticism of "national communism." At the plenum of the

Central Committee held in June 1948, at the moment when the Cominform was condemning Yugoslavia, Gomułka promoted the Polish communist tradition. Three months later at the September plenum he had to recant and admit that he had underestimated the debt owed by Polish communism to the USSR. But, ejected from his position by Bierut, he was never tried or turned over to the Soviet police as his counterparts in the other people's democracies had been. In the tragic period, tragic for all the people's democracies, of purges that followed the Soviet-Yugoslav crisis, the absence of high-level purges in Poland was already an indication of the sympathy with which the Polish communists regarded national communism.[28]

But the economic blockade, the border provocations, the constant slander, and the anti-Tito hysteria unleashed by Stalin against Yugoslavia could not conceal two realities: Stalin's failure (his first failure in a confrontation with a communist state leader), and his prudence. Stalin did not go beyond the stage of threats and provocations and he did not transform a serious political conflict into an armed conflict. Tito's confidence in an eventual American response to military intervention on Yugoslav territory never received the slightest confirmation. If Stalin drew back from such a decision it was because of his own analysis of the disadvantages and the risks of armed conflict, not because he was stopped from outside. And this prudence was all the more remarkable because Yugoslavia, surrounded by four states submissive to Stalin, was vulnerable on four sides. In 1950 the situation changed, and the time when Stalin could take initiatives had passed. Yugoslavia undertook a reconciliation with the Western world that assured it, if not of protection, at least of a less solitary position in the world.

*   *   *

Soviet policy in the conflict with Yugoslavia remains puzzling. Why was such a powerful country, indifferent to international opinion, unable to bring down a smaller and infinitely weaker state? If there was a constant element in the three phases of this confrontation (the Soviet attempt to intimidate Tito, the "international" intimidation, and reprisals), it was the Soviet inability to make Tito give in, to find effective responses to Yugoslav determination. This Soviet patience is more understandable if one considers the unprecedented nature of the situation. When he said at the beginning of the crisis that he had only to lift his little finger to make Tito give in, Stalin was relying on his earlier experiences, all the past confrontations he had had with foreign communist parties. None had resisted. But this was precisely the unprecedented nature of the conflict. Up to that point, the USSR or the Comintern had confronted parties cut off from power, leaders without real political support in their countries. These parties or leaders, because they did not hold power, because they were persecuted or at best a minority presence at home, had only one source of support to defend their claim to accede to power, the international communist movement, that is in the last analysis the

USSR. At the outset they depended totally on the Soviet Union. It was therefore easy to influence such parties or officials who owed everything to Moscow and to the communist movement, who were nothing without their support, and for whom Stalin's anathema meant the loss of all legitimacy.

For the first time in the quarter-century of the history of communism, Stalin was confronted with a party in power proclaiming the interests of a state and a nation and relying on their support. Tito's legitimacy, which he forcefully claimed, was domestic.[29] It depended on the theory of "socialism in one country" that the USSR had invented for itself, had refused to extend to other countries, and about which Tito said: "Stalin and Lenin declared that it was possible to construct socialism in one country. I can say that that was entirely possible in Yugoslavia."[30]

The difference of these perceptions of the relations of the USSR with its allies, in Moscow and Belgrade, explain why Stalin throughout the crisis persisted in setting himself in the classic framework of relations between parties in which in his eyes the USSR, and the Cominform, maintained their authority. Tito, for his part relying on the reality that he tirelessly described—socialism in one country, Yugoslavia—arrived at the opposite conclusion; embodied by different states, socialism was a merely domestic phenomenon, peculiar to each state, and it could not become a factor in relations between states. At the most, the shared ideology should create particular understandings and the respect of one state for another; but it could play no role in the conception of national interest.

This gap between the positions of Stalin and Tito shaped the whole development of the conflict. Stalin could not manipulate the Yugoslav leadership or impose his will on Tito and the Yugoslav Communist Party because they all occupied solid positions. For them, Stalin's maneuvers amounted to pure and simple interference in their affairs, like the intervention by the Cominform and its condemnation. The Cominform followed the earlier pattern of the Comintern, making unappealable judgments on the parties within its sphere and excluding or changing them at will. Excluded from the Cominform, Tito did not lose power since he did not owe power to the Cominform. By rejecting the Cominform's arbitration and asking Stalin to come to Belgrade to debate, Tito clearly indicated that his party could not be identified with the Yugoslav state, that it was a component part of the state, and not the opposite.

By acting in this way, Tito brought to light the real nature of relations between the USSR and its satellites and he destroyed the fiction behind which it was concealed that Stalin wanted to preserve at any cost. The reality was that Soviet power favored the interests of the Soviet state in its relations with fraternal parties and sister states. The fiction was that internationalism, that is, the interests of the avant-garde, of communism, was the basis for all decisions and choices in the USSR. Tito was not in fact challenging the reality of relations among communist states. He was simply demanding that

that reality be extended to his country, that the interests of Yugoslavia be taken into account. In a certain sense, without saying so, the USSR accepted the validity of this demand for recognition of the primacy of relations between states. In the last phase of the conflict, after the condemnation by the Cominform, when it began to persecute Yugoslavia, to deprive it of the means of existence, to threaten its borders, it was indeed attacking the Yugoslav state. Unable to break Tito, Stalin reacted in the end in a way that was not unprecedented either, along the lines of what could be called a paranoid response. He took the position of denying a fact that he could not control and he became defensive. By denying Yugoslav communism, he thought he had done away with the problem. At the same time, he proclaimed that the Yugoslav deviation, "Titoism," posed a moral threat to the entire communist system, and he took advantage of the situation to reinforce constraints, to purge, to bring others into line, but also to undertake a process of integration. The Comecon was created in 1949 at the height of the crisis to become the framework for economic integration of a political space that had been made totally uniform.

From his political defeat by Tito, Stalin derived an argument to strengthen his dominance over all the other satellites, to construct a perfect monolith, to recreate on the scale of the whole camp the prewar besieged citadel.

But by denying the very existence of Yugoslav communism and by strengthening the terror, Stalin gained nothing at bottom. The problem that had disoriented him by its novelty, exasperated him by its intractability, was still there. Because Stalin had been unable to make the Soviet-Yugoslav conflict into a victory, it demonstrated that there could be conflicts between communist states. It also demonstrated that the camp, held together by a single ideology, by the victory of the working class, was not sheltered from contradictions.

The conflict with Tito shattered two myths at once: the omnipotence of Stalin and the communist family. In 1917 Lenin had believed that the Russian Revolution was laying the groundwork for a world of revolutions, a family of pacified peoples, liberated from their national antagonisms. The first conflict between communist states demonstrated that this was only a dream, and that there were Atreides even in the communist universe. By excluding Yugoslavia from the communist family, Stalin was attempting to evade that troubling reality. His death spared him from a cruel disillusionment. The Yugoslavs had merely opened a path, the path of conflict, that over the years became more and more crowded.

NOTES

1. On the Cominform, see E. Reale, *Nascita del Kominform* (Milan, 1958), published in French under the title *Avec Duclos au banc des accusés*; L. Mercou, *Le*

Kominform (Paris, n.d.); and his article about the Cominform's structures after the break in *Die Tat* of Zurich, May 11, 1949.

2.   A. Zhdanov, *Informatsionnoe soveshchanie predstavitelei nekotoryh kompartii* (Moscow, 1948), 13–49; the French version, *Sur la situation internationale*, a report presented at the conference of representatives of some communist parties in Poland in late September 1947, *Pour une paix durable, pour une démocratie populaire* 1 (Oct.–Nov. 1947); the brochure reproducing Zhdanov's report contained twenty-eight pages and two documents as appendices and was published in Paris in December 1947.

3.   The resolution on the exchange of experiences and the coordination of parties represented at the conference is appended to the text noted in the previous footnote.

4.   Vladimir Dedijer, *Tito parle* (Paris, 1953), 292.

5.   On this point Zbigniew Brzezinski, *The Soviet Bloc* (Cambridge, Mass., 1960), 63, sets out the advantages and disadvantages for Yugoslavia and the USSR.

6.   On Gomułka's hostility, see E. Reale, *Nascita del Kominform* (Milan, 1958), 35; on the criticism of Gomułka on this point, see *Pravda*, September 9, 1948.

7.   See particularly the documents published in R. Bass and E. Narbury, eds., *The Soviet-Yugoslav Controversy, 1948–1958: A Documentary Record* (New York, 1968); *Echange de lettres entre le Comité central du Parti communiste de Yougoslavie et le Comité Central du Parti communiste bolchévik de l'U.R.S.S.* (Paris, 1950).

8.   Milovan Djilas, *Tito, mon ami, mon ennemi* (Paris, 1980), 44–45, 107, 125–133.

9.   Ibid., 124.

10.   Ibid., 48. Djilas says that the Soviet secret services had agents in Tito's own entourage.

11.   Ibid., 48–49.

12.   Milovan Djilas, *Conversations avec Staline* (Paris, 1962).

13.   The Turks gave the name Komitadjis to two groups established in the late nineteenth century, the Macedonian Revolutionary Organization set up in 1893 and the Macedonian High Committee, close to the Bulgarian court.

14.   *Pravda*, January 28, 1948.

15.   This episode is remarkably well recounted by A. Ulam, *Titoism and Cominform* (Cambridge, Mass., 1952), 112–13.

16.   This remark was reported by Khrushchev in 1956; Stalin's general views about Tito and the relations between the two men are made especially clear in Milovan Djilas, *Conversations avec Staline* (Paris, 1962).

17.   Hebrans, one of Stalin's "agents" in the Yugoslav Communist Party, hanged himself or was hanged in his cell. On the development of Tito's terror, see Djilas, *Tito, mon ami*, 124.

18.   On April 11, 1948, *Politika* published an editorial commemorating the third anniversary of the Soviet-Yugoslav treaty.

19.   Djilas, *Tito, mon ami*, 124.

20.   Ibid., 52, 124–25; for the date of the meeting, 131.

21.   Vladimir Dedijer, *Tito parle*, 313.

22.   The Russian text of the resolution was published in *Kommunist*, no. 11 (July 1948), 3ff.

23.   Djilas, *Tito, mon ami*, 191.

24. "The Clique of Tito, Kardelj, Djilas, and Ranković" became a common expression throughout the camp; see, for example, the article published by Laszlo Brankov in *Szabad Nep* on October 31, 1948, entitled "The leaders of the Yugoslav Communist Party in the shameful role of imperialist agents," translated by La Documentation française, *Articles et Documents*, No. 1408, November 24, 1948; see also numbers 359 and 1404 of the same publication.

25. In 1952 at the Sixth Party Congress the name was changed to the League of Yugoslav Communists.

26. See the relatively complete summary of incidents in an article by S. Milosavliević, "Stalin's policy of hypocrisy and aggression," *Borba*, October 5, 1952, translated in *Articles et Documents*, No. 2518.

27. Ibid.

28. This is what R. Wraga called at the time "the pacification of Polish communism" in his article, "Pacifikacja Polskiego Komunizmu," *Kultura* no. 9/26 (1948), 5–12. I owe this interpretation of the Polish attitude to R. Wraga, who had the kindness to translate his article into English for me and to comment on his views.

29. See for example the Ljubljana speech of November 17, 1948, translated in *Articles et Documents*, No. 1408, November 24, 1948.

30. Vladimir Dedijer, *Tito Speaks* (London, 1953), 188.

5

NATIONAL "VOICES" IN THE COMMUNIST CHORUS

Stalin died on March 5, 1953. Few events in this century have had more serious consequences, at least where the terrifying shadow of his power was spread. For Eastern Europe, the death of the man who had imposed revolutionary order and Soviet domination on the region opened up a period of change during which at certain moments absolutely everything seemed possible: the destruction of the political system; the reconquest of national independence; shifting out of the Soviet orbit. Nineteen fifty-three saw the beginning of a process of destabilization and diversification in the communist world, a time of growing divergences. The monophonic chorus of 1945 to 1953 was gradually replaced by a confused ensemble in which discordant voices became ever more audible. This break in the unity created by Stalin was provoked by his successors. They later tried to manage the change in order to find a new definition of communism for several countries.

Berlin 1953: The First Clash

In the legacy bequeathed by Stalin his heirs found a monolithic socialist camp in which, as in the USSR, a pall of silence and fear played the role of consensus. As in the USSR, men were moved by habit and constraint; but it was clear that the system had no vitality. Soviet leaders vaguely realized that they would also have to bring about change in this area, not to weaken their authority but to preserve it on a long-term basis. In the difficult period of the transition from Stalin's absolute authority to that of heirs still unsure of their power, the only intuition shared by all the potential successors was that the Stalinist system could not survive without Stalin, that they had to come to terms with a changed world.

In 1953 this intuition affected both the domestic and the foreign policy of the USSR and therefore the policy that its satellites had to follow. On every level, political, economic, intellectual, the months following Stalin's death gave rise to initiatives designed to bring about a certain thaw. There were the partial amnesties of March 28, 1953, the liberation of those involved in the "Doctors' Plot" on April 4, a lowering of prices in the spring of 1953, repeated gestures in favor of the peasants, the insistence on the necessity of thinking about consumer goods and hence about personal needs and not only about the needs of heavy industry. This new form of speech contrasting with Stalinist rigor was accompanied by international overtures, at least one of which provoked great hope in Eastern Europe.[1] On June 8, 1953, Austria, which had been partially occupied by Soviet troops since 1945, was the beneficiary of an unexpected measure, one that remained unique.[2] Interzonal Soviet control was removed and the sending of an ambassador announced; the peace treaty that until then the USSR had tied to a solution of the German problem was detached from that problem (it was signed in May 1954); and from this moment on it seemed that Austria could hope to recover its independence. No doubt it had enjoyed exceptional treatment from 1945 on since communism had not been imposed on it and moreover the USSR had treated it as a liberated country, not as an enemy. But neither Poland nor Czechoslovakia had been among the enemies, and this had not prevented the USSR from imposing on them political systems patterned after its own. In 1953, at a time when the Soviet leaders were feeling their way, when publicly expressed dissension about foreign policy choices indicated a certain fragility in the USSR confronted with the succession problem, the hopes born in Austria suggested that the situation of 1945 was perhaps not frozen. It was this hope, this perception of wavering on the part of the USSR, of obvious opposition between the supporters of controlled change and the supporters of no change at all, that provoked the first disturbances in the Eastern European system, the Berlin riots. But this crisis also provided the opportunity for the Soviet leadership, divided as it may have been, to clarify its views on the future of the communist world and to indicate the limits of its possible accommodations.

The workers' riots that erupted in East Berlin on June 17, 1953, and which moved from a limited demonstration at the outset to a generalized popular uprising, had as their origin the weakening of constraints inside the USSR and the gap between the policy of openness of the Malenkov group and the persistent Stalinism of the leaders of the GDR.[3] While the prisons in Moscow were gradually being opened and Malenkov was concerning himself with the difficulties of daily life, in the GDR Ulbricht increased prices and work requirements and expelled and threatened prosecution of important political officials. No doubt a number of these measures traced back to 1952—the peak of the curve of terror in the communist world—but instead of being interrupted by Stalin's death, they continued. Furthermore, because economic policy—the forced Soviet model—provoked population flights to the West, the East German government punished everyone who directly or indirectly challenged this untenable economic policy with taxes and the refusal to provide ration cards. "Enemies of the people" flourished in East Germany in the spring of 1953, even while the notion was disappearing in Moscow. The USSR was aware of the dangers of this attachment to a policy that had been abandoned elsewhere. This was evidenced by the arrival in the GDR of a new high commissioner, V. S. Semionov, who attempted to bring his German interlocutors back to the path of reason. The June 17 uprising confirmed the fears of the Soviet leadership; but it was not taken unawares, as the rapidity of its reaction reveals. The Soviet military commander launched a tank assault against the insurgents and drowned the uprising in blood. The cost in human lives was very high, estimated at nearly five hundred dead.[4]

Soviet determination deserves both emphasis and explanation. In the summer of 1953, the Berlin riot was only the most spectacular expression of the agitation that was growing throughout Eastern Europe at the time, an agitation that had as a backdrop economic deterioration due to the imposition of Soviet structures. Forced collectivization and a badly prepared and too rapid industrialization were provoking the same failures as they had in the USSR. At the moment when changes were observable in Moscow and a new kind of speech could be heard there, in the monolithic space of Eastern Europe the peoples rose up against the continuation of these policies. In Czechoslovakia, factory workers went on strike, and demonstrators attacked public buildings in Pilsen. In Hungary popular discontent was more muffled but nonetheless perceptible. The USSR was caught in a contradiction. On the one hand, it wanted to accommodate the political leaders put in place by Stalin and protected by him whose loyalty to Moscow was total and who had a visceral attachment to Stalinist methods of exercising power. On the other hand, it saw discontented and frustrated populations, hostile to their leaders and to Soviet constraints. Should it support these populations and thereby in Eastern Europe as well as in the Soviet Union attempt to establish a new social contract based more on individual interests than on terror? Or should it continue to support the leaders whose domestic unpopularity could not erase their devotion to Moscow? Either solution involved the danger of shattering the system. Caution and the advice to make accommodations everywhere in the months following Stalin's death were unable either to overcome the obstinacy of Ulbricht and the other imitators of Stalin or to slow the rise of discontent and—most important, indeed essential—public expression of that discontent. And the inability of Soviet leaders to carry out policies with one clear choice, vaguely perceived in the people's democracies, merely increased tensions. The Berlin explosion and the very disturbing general context put an end to these hesitations. By using tanks against the insurgents the Soviet authorities clearly demonstrated their conception of change. Although they wished to adjust the political and economic system in order to provide a more peaceful basis for its relations with its subjects, individuals and nations, they had no intention of changing the nature of the system. If changes were to be made, they would be the result of a decision made from above. In no event could they arise from debate in the street or from popular pressure. The Leninist concept of the relation between society and political system remained intact. Society was the object of a history shaped by the system. The first crisis of the empire gave the group in power in Moscow the opportunity to take hold of itself and to define its intentions. It also provided the opportunity to define the nature of relations within the communist world. The USSR was the center of the system; possible changes and their direction were decided there. If the chorus of communist states produced wrong notes, the chorus leader had the task of correcting them.

The Berlin crisis clarified the Soviet conception of the thaw. It also clarified to a certain extent the debate within the USSR. It is important to note that the tank attack was conducted without hesitation and that more than thirty years later that decision has never been the subject of criticism in the USSR. The suppression of the revolt, however harsh it may have been, was historically perceived as indispensable; for official history, the rebels were "fascists."[5] The debate that took place in Moscow over the responsibility for this crisis, which had profoundly shaken Eastern Europe in 1953, was very important. When the day of reckoning arrived, Beria was accused of having provoked the disorder by appealing to the national feelings of the peoples of Eastern Europe (as well as those of the USSR); he was accused of having wanted thereby to develop his own "clientèle" in order to seize power.[6] The impulse to seek support in a national clientèle after Stalin's death was undeniable.[7] Did this imply that Beria alone was responsible through the concessions he favored and his conciliatory stance for the weakening of power in Berlin? Although he was denounced after his death for having carried out a personal policy, all the evidence suggests that the intent to impose on the Stalinist leaders of Eastern Europe political conformity with the post-Stalinist USSR was not promoted by Beria alone and that a part of the group in power shared that orientation.[8]

Once calm returned to Berlin, the attention of Soviet leaders was for a time directed toward the succession within the Soviet Union. Until Malenkov was deposed on February 8, 1955, domestic problems took priority. But hardly had Malenkov been removed when the Khrushchev-Bulganin team began to take international initiatives. At that point the evolution of Eastern Europe speeded up and the atmosphere of violent or muffled crisis of 1953–54 was followed by a more relaxed atmosphere marked by the hope for important changes.

Khrushchev-Tito: Dialogue of Equals

In the torrent of events that were at that time profoundly changing the international situation, two deserve particular mention because they had a lasting effect on relations within the socialist camp: the reconciliation with Tito and the creation of the Warsaw Pact. Occurring in the course of a few weeks in May 1955, these events indicate the complex character of Soviet intentions and decisions for the future of the communist world. The desire of the new ruling group to relieve tensions and to present the peaceful side of the USSR was obvious. This was true in the USSR itself, where Malenkov's downfall opened the way for new political practices. For the first time in Soviet history, a leader left power without having been accused of treason, tried, or excluded from political society. Malenkov remained a member of the highest institutions in the system and his continued presence in party organizations, after he had been eliminated from the government, seemed to indicate to the world that the USSR had changed. In this context, the signature of the Soviet-Austrian treaty should also be noted, the conclusion of a shift that had begun at Stalin's death that seemed to confirm the fact that the USSR agreed to a questioning of its position of 1945.

Did the Soviet-Yugoslav reconciliation, which the USSR wanted and for which it alone paid the price, fit in logically with this evolution? The facts are too well-known to require detailed description, but the meaning of this reconciliation is worth recalling.

When he came to Belgrade on May 26, 1955, to erase the dispute of 1948, Khrushchev intended to give his journey and his gesture a precise meaning. As secretary of the Soviet Communist Party, he came in the name of his party to make peace with a fraternal party. His mission was to proclaim that past arguments had been forgotten, to restore links between communist parties, and to demonstrate that party solidarity was more important than arguments between states. To attain these goals, Khrushchev was ready to acknowledge that the USSR had made mistakes; the confession was all the easier because the guilty party had already been designated. Beria, condemned by his peers in 1953, had been accused of having been a spy in "the pay of the imperialists." It was easy to connect his influence, the interests of imperialism, and the break that had occurred between the two socialist countries.[9] This confession had the virtue of minimizing conflict between communist parties, reducing it to the dimensions of a conspiracy in which internal and external enemies in concert had managed to destroy the natural solidarity of the communist world. But Tito rejected, if not this simple explanation, at least its implicit consequences: the return to a specific pattern of relations between states adhering to the same ideology, that is, to privileged relations between parties, ignoring the particular interests of the states or overriding them. As a price for the restoration of peace, Tito received from Khrushchev a formal recognition of the orthodoxy of his party; above all, he imposed the statement in the final communiqué of June 2, 1955, that new principles would govern Soviet-Yugoslav relations.[10] The USSR had to agree as Tito demanded that relations between the two countries be definitively placed on the level of relations between states. Ideology, even though it was shared, became a matter for each state and created no particular link between them. The consequence of this shift from specifically communist international relations to traditional ones was the recognition of Yugoslavia's independence in all areas. That independence was total, thanks to the principle of noninterference in the internal affairs of others, a principle explicitly set out in the final communiqué at Tito's insistence. Independence in the definition of socialism: Yugoslavia was free in its domestic choices, free to adapt socialism to its own interests, its political and social tradition, and its needs. The national road became a royal road, no longer a deviation. A second consequence of Soviet concessions was the recognition of Yugoslav equality. Free to make its own choices, Yugoslavia was the equal of the USSR. By recognizing its right not to rejoin the socialist camp from which Stalin had excluded it, by recognizing the fact that a country could be genuinely socialist without submitting itself to Soviet judgment and the Soviet model and without agreeing to integrate itself into the bloc led by the USSR, Khrushchev acknowledged that the progress of communism could take place in a context of equality among states and of recognition of their absolute sovereignty. Thus it was the USSR that made all the concessions in 1955 to a Tito who was unshakable in his refusal to compromise with his interlocutors. What he gained was considerable for his country, namely, peace with the USSR and its allies, but also considerable for the other socialist states. If the national road was legitimate, if a socialist country was free to make its own choices, in the name of what principle would the USSR limit this revision to Yugoslavia? We can glimpse the future disturbances implicit in the Belgrade agreement. And we should ask what explains Khrushchev's concessions. Had the USSR so profoundly changed that it was ready to destroy the monolith and replace it with a constellation of self-determined states? Did the Leninist centralism that had prevailed in Berlin in June 1953 no longer exist?

An attentive examination of this privileged moment—the high point of the Soviet thaw—shows that events in Belgrade had more to do with Khrushchev's improvisation and with political conflicts within the USSR than with a really innovative design. In his memoirs Khrushchev explained how he came to this acceptance of Tito's demands. Even if his account is to be treated cautiously, with respect both to the authenticity of the text[11] and to the problem of special pleading, it nevertheless sheds invaluable light on these events.[12] In the general context of a foreign policy of openness to the external world, the ruling group was divided. One of the most consistent opponents of this policy was Molotov, Stalin's minister of foreign affairs since

1939 who remained in that position until 1956. When the problems of the communist world were reconsidered in the light of the violent or latent crises that were affecting it, the divisions were accentuated. [13] A commission presided over by Shepilov, Molotov's future and very ephemeral successor at Foreign Affairs, was established to determine "the nature of present-day economic social, and political structures in Yugoslavia."[14] The commission reported, writes Khrushchev, that "nothing justified considering Yugoslavia to be a capitalist state."

Once Yugoslavia was recognized as worthy of being numbered among the socialist countries, the reasons for the break provoked by Stalin disappeared and with them all the elements contrary to a policy of reconciliation. [15]

We can see how Khrushchev's international preoccupations and internal problems interacted. In his march to power, foreign policy was a means of imposing himself. His adversaries—guided by Suslov, with Molotov among them—held to certain Stalinist choices, which encouraged Khrushchev to dissociate himself from them. No doubt, he genuinely recognized the need for a normalization of intersocialist relations. But this innovative position also reinforced him in the succession struggle. Khrushchev found himself from the outset caught in a crossfire. The conservatives were opposed to any reconciliation with a country that, according to Suslov, was no longer socialist. [16] But on the other side, Tito seemed no more inclined to compromise. Khrushchev writes that he chose to lead a delegation to Belgrade rather than summoning Tito to Moscow because he sensed Tito's reservations and the need to take the first steps. These were far from negligible, because Tito's views on the conflict that Soviet citizens had previously known only in the truncated and insulting version of its leaders had already been published in Moscow. [17] Here too Khrushchev took the initiative and tried to create an irreversible situation. The Soviet delegation that went to Belgrade was indicative of the debate within the USSR. Led by Khrushchev, it was made up of Bulganin, head of the government, Mikoyan, and Shepilov. The minister of foreign affairs, Molotov, was excluded. Surrounded by men who were close to him or who, like Mikoyan, were ready to accept every shift, Khrushchev was in a better position to make the concessions that the obvious hostility of the Yugoslavs toward the USSR imposed on him. [18]

Having gone so far as to have undertaken the journey and having published Tito's positions, Khrushchev could hardly return to Moscow with an admission of failure. His adversaries would then have easily triumphed and denounced the weakness of his initiatives. The extent of his concessions to Tito can thus be attributed to this internal pressure, which condemned him to succeed in Belgrade or to admit that he had been wrong in his positive evaluation of Titoism. Reconciliation on the basis of the Yugoslav demands was thus a calculated risk, like many others Khrushchev took later, designed to strengthen his political position. On his return, Khrushchev was confronted with vehement criticism from Molotov and Suslov, who never accepted the reconciliation.[19] But the return to peace within the socialist camp seemed at the time to be the tangible result of the Belgrade meeting. The seeds of future crises that Khrushchev's concessions would foster were not yet visible. Khrushchev could thus assert that he had won, that he had strengthened socialist cohesion and rectified the disaster of 1948. For the moment, he was the one who scored points. Soviet-Yugoslav relations seemed to be on an even keel and the following year Tito made a triumphal journey to the USSR.

Soviet tolerance toward Yugoslavia in 1955 does not, however, provide a complete account of Moscow's attitude toward the socialist states. It had as a counterpart an almost contemporaneous event, the establishment of the Warsaw Pact on May 14, 1955. No doubt in this initial period the pact appeared more as a political expression directed against NATO and against the possibility of German rearmament than as an institution whose later usefulness had been weighed. The stationing of Soviet troops in several Eastern European countries had not yet been challenged and Moscow had no need to establish a system to justify that continuing occupation. But because the problem of German rearmament had already been posed and because the countries bordering on Germany that might be targets of territorial demands were alarmed, the Warsaw Pact was greeted without hostility. In the calm situation of 1955, the Warsaw Pact was not seen as a dangerous creation nor as a supplementary stage in the domination of Eastern Europe. In May 1955 the restoration of Austrian sovereignty, confirmed by treaty, and Tito's triumph occupied everyone's attention.

The Twentieth Congress: The Search for a New Imperial Order

For the Eastern European world, the ideological and political revisions of the Twentieth Congress of the Soviet Communist Party held in February 1956 had decisive importance. Everything about the congress affected their future, from the break with Stalinism to the new conceptions of international life proposed by Khrushchev. In fact everything in the congress explicitly or implicitly condemned the domination that had been imposed on those countries.

In 1947, the cold war, the Stalinist definition of an implacable world in which communism and capitalism were pitiless opponents, had served as a justification for the USSR to organize itself and to organize the Eastern European empire into a fortified camp. The external peril was the explanation given for the stiffening of the system and for the imposition of satellite status. The new definition of international relations that dominated the Twentieth Congress took apart both that Manichean vision of the world and the alignments that it legitimized.

For Khrushchev, the spokesman of the Soviet Communist Party, the world had changed and what henceforth determined the international balance was the existence of a strong and expanding socialist camp no longer afraid of a declining imperialism.[20] From this observation of communist victories—to which Khrushchev added the rise of a third element between two irremediably hostile blocs, the decolonized countries or those struggling to become so—Khrushchev drew the conclusion that peaceful coexistence was now possible. It was the strength of the communist world that led him to agree that the two worlds could live together in peace because this would irreversibly lead to the general propagation of communism.[21] It went without saying that living together did not mean reconciliation.

Contrary to the ideas that were later prevalent in the Western world, neither Khrushchev nor any of his companions or successors even suggested that the evolution of the two wholes, communism and capitalism, could converge in the same direction. But the relatively long period of peaceful coexistence permitted the prediction of changed relations between the two systems.[22] Openness could take the place of isolation and favor a form of peaceful evolution toward communism. This was the second major innovation of this new theory, the one that opened the greatest number of perspectives for the socialist world. Because the world was not as dangerous as it had been and because communism was sure of itself, vigilance and strict alignments were less indispensable. To follow the ineluctable path of revolution, each country could adopt its own patterns, taking account of its own traditions and preferences.[23] Thus the national road for which Yugoslavia had obtained recognition a year earlier was codified. This national road also allowed the adaptation of the construction of socialism to the conditions of each people. The choice also implied equality among socialist states, established in Soviet-Yugoslav relations since the Belgrade declaration, which in 1956 became a central principle of intersocialist relations.

Khrushchev's initiatives in Belgrade led a year later to a new theory of revolution in several countries. It was an attractive theory because in addition to equality among states and the freedom to choose the path to follow, it suggested that revolutionary change could take place peacefully within the framework of legal institutions. No doubt on this last point the revision carried out by the Soviet Communist Party was hardly convincing, because the example offered of revolution through the "parliamentary path" was that of Czechoslovakia in 1948.[24] To propose the "Prague Coup" as an illustration of legal revolution was to cast doubt on the entire argument. But these extreme aspects of the official report presented by Khrushchev to the congress were to some extent obscured by a still more radical break with Stalinism, which deeply affected the people's democracies, the secret speech. The rejection of Stalinism that was its foundation implied first of all the rejection of Stalin's work, that is, for Eastern Europe, its forced Sovietization.

No doubt the speech was prudent on many points, careful not to disturb the existing order. With respect to Eastern Europe, it contained precise condemnations in two areas: the break with Yugoslavia and the liquidation of the Polish Communist Party in 1938. If the reconciliation with Belgrade made the passage in the secret speech devoted to the 1948 break hardly explosive, the same thing was not true of the details provided on the destruction of the Polish Communist Party.

One of the justifications for the authority that Moscow had arrogated to itself in Eastern Europe was the weakness or nonexistence of local communist parties. Their elites, decimated by Stalin in the late thirties, had given way to leaders dependent on Moscow, terrified at the idea of suffering the fate of their predecessors for whom the most complete and blind adhesion to all aspects of the USSR took the place of a program. In the general purge of communist leaders between the wars, the only survivor was the "father of all communists," Stalin. But once the secret speech admitted that Stalin had not been the wise and infallible leader and that all his activity from 1934 on had been a series of tragic errors, how could his authority over the other parties be justified? This question took on particular significance in Poland. The secret speech explained that Stalin had completely unjustly suppressed the Polish Communist Party. At a stroke, everything was restored to Poland: its communist party, the certainty that it had its own communist tradition that could be invoked in support of the life of the nation, and the certainty of having been criminally forced to make certain choices. Even though the secret speech tended to place the weight of the crimes committed on Stalin alone and was intended to have the function of exonerating the communist party for those crimes, of assuring its own legitimacy liberated from Stalinism, its effect was entirely different. It was the Soviet Communist Party and the USSR as a whole as guide and model for the communist states that were disqualified. But also this indictment disqualified the groups in power, products of Stalin's policies. The national roads began with the liquidation of the groups in power and their programs throughout Eastern Europe.

The precautions taken to limit distribution of the secret speech to the leadership alone of the communist parties of the sister states were soon overcome. Khrushchev noted delicately that in Poland the disorder caused by the death of Bierut explained why the speech circulated "among Polish comrades hostile to the Soviet Union, who used the speech for their own ends and had it duplicated."[25] This is a quick and superficial treatment of the profound reactions, sometimes anti-Russian and not only anti-Soviet, provoked by this explosive text. For the question that it posed was indeed the central one of the legitimacy of the system set up by the USSR, of the legitimacy of satellization, of the legitimacy of the existing leaders. The events that marked the end of 1956 in Poland and Hungary demonstrated that those problems had been clearly understood.

Warsaw and Budapest: Two Variants of the Thaw

Following the Twentieth Congress all those in power in Eastern Europe were confronted with an urgent problem: what consequences should the Soviet leadership's change in direction have for their method of government? Disciples of Stalin, considered by their compatriots as representatives of the USSR, the leaders of the satellite states had little room to maneuver. Could the regimes established by authoritarian methods in each country adapt to the "new course" without doing damage to the existing authorities? Could Stalin, whose giant statue dominated every capital, whose name, constantly repeated as an incantation, lent support to every policy that was followed and took the place of ideology, be removed from the collective consciousness or denounced for his mistakes? If one attacked the Stalinist cult of personality, how could one legitimize the disciples of the cult and the authority they had exercised in each of the countries following the model established by Stalin? These were all questions that the "little Stalins" wished to avoid, but Soviet pressure forced them to take them into account.

In Moscow, Khrushchev, who had been identified with de-Stalinization by the secret speech, remained in conflict with those who were troubled by a blow struck against the cohesion of the system and against the legitimacy of the communist party.[26] In order to defeat those who challenged his choice he had to move rapidly down the path of de-Stalinization. Throwing caution to the winds as he had done with Tito was the only policy that allowed him to gain over his adversaries. And he had to seize this territory quickly because a coalition of all those who were threatened by de-Stalinization was taking shape against him—the conservatives of Eastern Europe. In fact, a few months later they succeeded in having the party's Central Committee, concerned with the preservation of its authority, accept a resolution on the personality cult that represented a substantial backward step. The resolution was remarkable in its insistence on the "historic virtues of Stalin which offset his personal mistakes."[27] The heavy machinery of the party thus quickly leaned toward conservatism and this internal development that expressed the deep political division among those in power weighed on the choices made by the leaders of the sister states.

In these conditions, de-Stalinization was slow and marked by the will to retain all existing power. Prudence was the dominant characteristic of the Stalinist leaders, whose authority was still considerable, and the secrecy surrounding Khrushchev's speech fostered its preservation. Thus in the GDR Ulbricht, having carried out a few symbolic gestures, a muffled and partial critique of Stalin, a few rehabilitations, decided that de-Stalinization, useful of course, but dangerous, required time and caution; and with that he ended the debate. The memory of the 1953 riots and their repression was sufficiently alive for everyone to encourage those in power to support this waiting game. Stalinism remained solidly established in Germany. The same prudence inspired the Czech leadership in 1956. No doubt some gestures had to be made following the Twentieth Congress to avoid confronting a momentarily triumphant Soviet leadership. This concern to accommodate Khrushchev led Novotný to an attitude that was apparently open to change but that at bottom preserved all of the Stalinist system. Speaking to a hastily convened meeting of the Central Committee following the Twentieth Congress, Novotný summarized the secret speech, dismissed the minister of defense, and expressed regret over the haste with which Slánský and Clementis had been executed. Moreover, his conclusion was simple. The person really guilty for all these excesses was Beria, who had frequently betrayed and gone beyond the orders he had received. Novotný thus very cleverly appeared to align himself with Khrushchev and also to a great extent exonerated Stalin for the excesses of the "personality cult." Since Beria had never served as a model or a source of legitimacy, everything that justified Novotný's power remained essentially untouched. In Bucharest, Gheorghiu-Dej not only preserved his authority but revoked some of the concessions he had made to the principle of collegial leadership and resumed the place he had temporarily abandoned at the head of the party. De-Stalinization was interpreted in Rumania as a call to increase power that had been held since 1945 with Stalin's help. This strengthening of existing power was also after a brief period of hesitation and retreat chosen by Enver Hoxha in Albania. Although he stimulated a debate on de-Stalinization in April 1956, he almost immediately reversed course and returned to the practice of dictatorship and political arrests. Only one country appeared to conform to the changes suggested in Moscow: Bulgaria. Close to the USSR in 1956 as it had been in 1945, Bulgaria was remarkable for the rapidity with which it followed all the turnings of Moscow's policies. Chervenkov, a loyal disciple of the Soviet leadership, gave up the position he held at the head of the government; but the party was still led by one of his close collaborators, Zhivkov. Thus stability and change were generally reconciled in these decisions that preserved the essential, continuity in the leadership of the party.

The few new men who appeared—Stoica, who became prime minister of Rumania, and Yugov, prime minister of Bulgaria—served to reassure Moscow. They seemed to establish that the message of the Twentieth Congress had been heard. Collegial leadership and the separation of party power from government power were put in place. The excessive power of one man that had led to the "cult of personality" was no longer acceptable. It hardly mattered that this division of labor was not extended to all countries, that Novotný in Prague for example continued to embody Stalinism. The general concern in Eastern Europe was to control the course of change and its effects, to avoid anything that might seriously challenge past choices. The Soviet-Yugoslav reconciliation had already suggested the advisability of downplaying the heavily exploited argument concerning the "Titoist danger" and of glossing over the fact that many leaders had been liquidated on the pretext that they were "Titoist agents." Tito's triumphal tour of the USSR in the spring of 1956 brutally raised the question of the fate of those who had been condemned for Titoism in neighboring countries. Rather than openly confronting these purges, the Eastern European leaders preferred silence or limiting their self-criticism to the denunciation of Beria. Their refusal to take steps toward democratization helped them to maintain this deathly silence. On the other hand, more or less firmly they proclaimed their intention to "return to Leninism" or to strengthen it. They made a few limited economic changes—plans were often revised to take more account of light industry and agriculture—but they refused to touch the essential matters, economic and social structures and the party's authority.

Why did this de-Stalinization, everywhere timid, barely expressed, and immediately limited, give way in Hungary and Poland to tumultous attempts to change basic structures, that were even more radical than the model offered by Moscow? The events of October 1956 in Poland and Hungary make up an indissoluble whole: they are the thread of a common history in which only the last stages diverged. Although at the time the more dramatic character of events in Budapest attracted more attention than the Polish crisis, later developments in Poland have tended to blur the importance of the Hungarian October and have made us forget that it was a complete break with the socialist system there that led to many later changes. Hence, while attempting to focus on the essential points of both crises, the events in Budapest occupy a privileged position here. Later developments justify this choice. It is impossible to separate the two crises because, being contemporaneous, they provided reciprocal support for one another. But, following François Fejtö, we may begin with Poland, because, as he has pointed out, "the Hungarian insurrection began in Poland."[28]

In Poland, in contrast to the situation that prevailed elsewhere in Eastern Europe, Stalin's death had had very sudden consequences.[29] As early as October 1953 the Polish party slowed down its collectivization campaign. A year later in late 1954 the Ministry of Security, a symbol of repression, was abolished and its director, Stanisław Radkiewicz, dismissed.[30] Gomułka and those who had been purged with him were freed. Finally, censorship was relaxed to the point that the *Poem for Adults* by Adam Ważyk was published in July 1955. Describing all the aspects of everyday life that made the Polish citizen's existence a daily hell, the poet concluded:

> We should demand on this earth . . .
> Truth, a paradise of freedom . . .
> We should demand it from the Party.[31]

Although these criticisms and demands remained modest, the mere appearance of such a text before the Twentieth Congress, in the Poland in which Marshal Rokossowski embodied the presence of the USSR, represented a quasi-revolution. No doubt there had been frequent criticisms of daily life in communist countries. But these criticisms had been directed against scapegoats and it was the party that orchestrated or used them. In 1955 the criticism arose in the name of an unhappy society and was addressed to the party. This episode provided a foretaste of later developments in Poland, the constantly increasing gap that still separated the party from the society twenty years later.

However, this de-Stalinizing path was not the only reality in Polish life in the years preceding the Twentieth Congress. The party was tolerant in some respects, not in others, and its attitude toward the Church at the time was particularly harsh.[32] Cardinal Wyszinski, who proclaimed from the pulpit the necessity to separate Caesar's realm from the realm of God, was arrested in September 1953 and the government tried to mobilize the clergy against him.[33] But despite the pressure, the number of priests who agreed to break with him remained small, while a majority, followed by many parishioners, began to come together in his name in silent rejection of a policy that was already outmoded. From 1953 to 1956 an underground development took place in Poland, and the Twentieth Congress brought its effects to the surface. For Poland, the Twentieth Congress was not only a Soviet event; it had internally the immediate consequence of a change of leadership. The Polish first secretary, Bolesław Bierut, died in Moscow as the congress came to an end. It hardly matters whether he died from natural causes or suicide; the event was in any case providential.[34] It permitted the immediate replacement of the man who had embodied Stalinism. His successor, Ochab, named in the presence of Khrushchev who had rushed to Warsaw to control a troubling situation, was able to appear as a man who was freer from the Stalinist past, even though he had been a major Stalinist figure; and he took full advantage of that freedom.[35] Caught between those who wanted to move away from the Soviet model and those who wanted to maintain its essential elements to save their positions, Ochab, with the help of Prime Minister Cyrankiewicz, managed to follow a policy of moderate and controlled liberalization.

The Poznań riots of June 1956 changed the nature of the situation in a way that alarmed Moscow. The workers of the Zipso factory paraded with banners that proclaimed not only "bread and freedom," but also "Russians go home."[36] The Soviet leadership could not consider with indifference an uprising that fit into a sequence with similar events, all made possible by the death of Stalin. After the East Berlin workers rose in 1953, after the convict uprising against Soviet power in the Siberian labor camp of Kingir that lasted for forty-two days in April and May 1954, the Poznań uprising suggested that a groundswell of protest had taken hold of the population from one end to the other of Soviet territory, a movement that repression could not hold in check. The Polish government sent in tanks under the authority of the Ministry of the Interior and the militia, decreed a state of siege, and restored order at a cost of fifty dead and many wounded.[37] The speed and effectiveness of the reaction could not conceal disturbing realities. First of all, a local uprising about limited questions had quickly turned into a national and anti-Russian conflict. The insurgents had proclaimed their hostility to Big Brother and had devastated police and party headquarters, the symbols of the political system established by the USSR. Moreover, the behavior of the army was troubling. Soldiers could not be used against the insurgents because they immediately fraternized with one another. Two months later on August 26 a million Poles who had come together at Częstochowa turned their pilgrimage into another demonstration of solidarity, in favor of the imprisoned prelate of course, but more generally in support of their will to freedom. How could calm be brought to a country whose agitation was so troubling to Moscow?[38] From that point on, the Soviet leadership determined that the inability of the Polish authorities to control domestic disorder meant that the Soviets had to intervene more directly. The Central Committee of the Polish United Workers' Party (the Polish communist party) met in Warsaw a few days later in the presence of a Soviet delegation including Marshal Zhukov, which was a troubling sign. Bulganin, the head of the Soviet government, offered "advice" and proposed to help Poland. But the Soviet defense minister, Zhukov, embodied the alternative that had already been used in Berlin—Soviet military intervention.

In Moscow as well there was no doubt dispute about the most appropriate solution to the growing disorder. Khrushchev called on Tito, multiplying bilateral meetings with him in order to try to work out a variable model of national socialism to gain his support with the satellite countries, especially with those who were breaking with Stalinism. At this point Tito argued vigorously that the USSR should encourage all its satellites to renew their ruling groups and to get rid of unrepentant Stalinists. Soviet perplexity affected the attitude of the Polish leaders and explains the time that elapsed before innovative decisions were made. Ochab and Cyrankiewicz were already convinced that they should assume leadership of the movement that was developing around them, at the risk of being overwhelmed, as they had been at Poznań. But the ambiguous advice of the Soviet delegation heavily affected their ability to decide. It was not until October that they admitted that only one man could resolve the crisis, Gomułka. Freed from prison and present at the meeting of the Central Committee, he was engaged in many political activities that had restored him to public life even before any decision on this point had been made at the top. At the conclusion of difficult and obscure negotiations, and after having been asked to participate in the government in order to legitimize it, Gomułka presented his demands. He intended to assume supreme authority in the party and demanded that conservative elements be expelled from the Politburo, especially Marshal Rokossowski, the minister of defense and veritable representative of the USSR. For the Stalinists of the party, there was only one solution, Soviet intervention, and Marshall Rokossowski took steps to create the conditions for that intervention. For Moscow, it was indispensable to recapture the initiative if they were not, as Gomułka's demands indicated, to see Poland rise up against the USSR in an expression of intransigent nationalism. Gomułka, saved from the 1938 Stalinist purge by his imprisonment in his own country, had never been a sure man in the eyes of the Soviet leadership. Even though Khrushchev in 1956 was seeking new leaders for the satellites in order to reinforce his positions, Gomułka's nationalism, his choice by a new ruling group carried out within Poland, and the popular ferment all made Gomułka unacceptable to him. And to get out of this difficulty, the USSR, in search of new solutions, resorted to the most traditional methods. On October 17 the Soviet ambassador transmitted to the Polish leaders an invitation to come to Moscow for discussions. Was the scenario of 1938, whose conclusion had been Stalin's liquidation of the Polish Communist Party, going to be repeated? Armed with this memory, with the example of Tito who always refused discussions with his Soviet counterparts outside Yugoslav territory, and with the argument of "various roads to socialism," the Polish Politburo rejected the invitation, arguing that a Central Committee meeting to elect its new leaders was scheduled for October 19.

While Stalin had retreated in the face of Tito's determination in 1948, in 1956 Khrushchev stood firm and undertook a test of strength. In the month of October 1956, in contrast to a triumphant Stalin who had dominated the satellites and had been able to isolate Yugoslavia, Khrushchev felt the ground shifting under his feet. Hungary had been experiencing problems for three years and the agitation developing there was following the rhythm of the Polish changes. In Moscow moreover Khrushchev was on the defensive; his adversaries remained vigilant. He was being accused of having provoked the nationalist awakening in Poland by his desire for change. His future depended on his ability to resolve the crisis. On October 19, at the moment when the plenum of the Central Committee opened, a Soviet delegation that was neither invited nor expected arrived in Warsaw. Khrushchev was not alone, and he was even under surveillance, since he was accompanied by two opponents of his positions who embodied an attachment to authoritarian solutions, Molotov and Kaganovich. Clearly the two opposing tendencies in the USSR on the limits of de-Stalinization were side by side, ready to decide in the field not only the fate of Poland but also their own conflict. As in Berlin in 1953, internal Soviet antagonisms were having a substantial effect on local decisions. The Poles were also under surveillance, indeed under a direct threat, since the Soviet delegation included several generals. At the same time, Soviet troop movements indicated that the tense faces of the Soviet leaders were not expressions of a weakened will. Soviet units in Silesia in Eastern Germany were moving toward Poland. Warships were cruising off Gdańsk. Even more seriously, within Poland, Marshal Rokossowski, who was still defense minister, had units of the Polish Army carry out maneuvers in the direction of Warsaw.[39] The vise was tightening and it was all the more threatening because the USSR had very cleverly raised the specter of a confrontation between Poles. What the fraternizations of Poznań had been unable to accomplish seemed to be attained by the preparations of Marshal Rokossowski, who was staking his career on the event. Civil war, tragic in any circumstances, would mean for a people that had been so often divided, and that had been preserved only by a sense of unity, ultimate destruction.

The Polish reaction, which was quick and remarkably cool, proved to be effective. Ochab stepped down in favor of Gomułka, hastily coopted onto the Central Committee and presented as a candidate for the position of first secretary. Invested with the confidence of the entire party united behind him, it was as a representative of his party—not of the people—that Gomułka met Khrushchev for a very long discussion in which he was persuasive. His argument was simple. It corresponded to the wishes of a hesitant and divided Soviet leadership, uncertain about the risks of a military operation. Gomułka presented himself for what he was in fact, a convinced communist, aware of international realities and Soviet demands. He asked for his country only the right to choose, domestically, the paths most in harmony with Polish tradition and its possibilities in order to move toward socialism. In return for this recognition of a Polish road restricted to the domestic sphere, Gomułka guaranteed the maintenance of a Leninist political system, that is, one dominated by the party and functioning according to the rules of democratic centralism. Above all he guaranteed Polish loyalty to the communist world and its adhesion to a foreign policy defined by the USSR. What Gomułka asked for was thus much less than the version of a national road negotiated by Tito in Belgrade and even less than the egalitarian theses of the Twentieth Congress. As a realist, he demanded only what he knew his adversaries could grant him. And he was not indignant when Khrushchev vehemently reproached him for coming to power through an arrangement that had not previously been negotiated in Moscow. Khrushchev unambiguously set out an argument that would become standard: Moscow had to control all the decisions of the fraternal parties. Equality had to be understood in this context. That too was in the end accepted by Gomułka. Appointed without Moscow having been consulted, he could very well later agree to recognize that his colleagues had been wrong in taking such liberties.

Extremely conciliatory on the essentials of the system and the maintenance of the alliance with the USSR, Gomułka had pleaded his cause all the better because he had also used military blackmail. If he were forced to give in, he said to Khrushchev, the Polish people would remember its long tradition of resistance. It would fight against the Soviet army; and Polish units or even spontaneous commandos would attack East Germany, endangering the entire Soviet defense system in Eastern Europe.[40] Did Khrushchev believe this threat? Although it is impossible to answer on the basis of the available documents, one can nevertheless assert that like all Soviets he knew from historical experience that Gomułka's threats were plausible. The courage of the Poles was never in doubt in the USSR. In any event, Khrushchev could only find this hypothesis convenient. It allowed him to impose his views on his colleagues and to return to Moscow with the benefit of a crisis calmly resolved. He could argue that the concessions made to Gomułka had avoided a bloody crisis in Poland and a weakening of the entire Soviet military system. And the peaceful solution of the Polish question, when Khrushchev returned to Moscow, was all the more urgent because the Polish example was wreaking havoc in Budapest. The agreement reached in Warsaw arrived at a propitious moment. It contained enough guarantees for the USSR to later be offered as a model for other countries. The return of Rokossowski to the USSR, a necessary concession, apparently freed the Polish Army from the direct Soviet control that had until then been exercised by the defense minister. But the existence of the Warsaw Pact opened the way to other forms of control, as the future would abundantly show. The attention of the USSR and that of the world as well then turned toward Budapest, where the picture was much more gloomy.[41]

Like Poland, Hungary had been infected by Stalin's death and the virus of change as early as 1953. But, unlike Poland, Hungary took some rather radical turns, very early bringing about a situation of conflict between two opposed camps. In 1953 the initiative for change in Hungary came from the USSR. Confronted with a completely Stalinist and pro-Soviet Hungarian leadership, Stalin's successors imposed on the Hungarian Communist Party a division of power, the replacement of Rákosi in the government, and the adoption of more flexible policies. The Soviet choice fell on Imre Nagy, whose orthodoxy was guaranteed by his past in the Comintern. Power was divided as in the USSR between Nagy, who had been won over to a position favoring liberalization, and Rákosi, who remained at the head of the party and was hostile to innovation. This division of tasks between two men with opposing views obviously reflected, once again, the division that existed in Moscow. Quite naturally, the attitudes of the two irreconcilable adversaries conformed to the opposing views of their protectors, and Rákosi did not hesitate to go to Moscow in search of support against Nagy, whom he accused of having succumbed to nationalism. Moscow hesitated between the two, but it quickly appeared that the Hungarian "new course" was going beyond acceptable limits. Collective farms were being depopulated, central planning was being challenged, and above all intellectual agitation was turning into political criticism and going beyond, from the Soviet point of view, the normal framework of discussion within the party.

In 1955 Malenkov's fall marked a retreat from the liberalizing position. It had as a consequence the fall of Nagy, who was accused of rightist deviation. He was expelled from the Politburo and replaced in the government by his predecessor, Rákosi. This was a return to the old methods of the Comintern and Stalin in which the USSR arrogated to itself the right to make authoritarian decisions about the direction and leadership of foreign parties. But the period of shared power in Budapest had borne fruit. Nagy came out of it with the halo of a national hero; and his compatriots were no longer willing to accept a return to a past attributable to Soviet interference and to domestic turnings in the USSR. The rise of national consciousness in Hungary at the end of the period of anesthesia caused by the tragedies of the war took place very quickly and irreversibly.

The struggle between Nagy and Rákosi between 1953 and 1955 and the Soviet intervention in favor of Rákosi in 1955 raised the question of how Hungary might have developed if the episode had not taken place. In part because Rákosi relied on a political apparatus whose weakness he was aware of although he claimed to be defending it, the rivalry between him and Nagy led to a break between that apparatus and national and liberal forces. No doubt Rákosi could not have taken the lead in the movement for renovation. The Rajk trial, still present in everyone's memory, and his own personality cult made this kind of conversion impossible for him. Nor did circumstances help him to play the role played in Poland by Ochab. From the outset "liberal" developments in Hungary tended to take place outside the party, not to be led or channeled by it as in Poland. It was thus predictable that developments in Hungary would turn out to be less acceptable to the USSR than similar ones in Poland. Furthermore, the example of Yugoslavia aggravated the situation. Since 1945 opposition to Soviet leadership there had constantly been assimilated to opposition to communism itself and had become an article of faith. But Tito's rehabilitation in 1955 and the confession of Stalin's mistakes had pointed up the relativity of the dogma. Nagy's promotion and his attitude brought back to the surface the contradictions that the unity of the communist world had until then resolved.

These circumstances made Rákosi's situation during his second reign practically impossible. Incapable of adapting to the circumstances, he could imagine no response but repression. The USSR decided to intervene again, but this time against Rákosi. The memory of Poznań was too fresh for the Soviet leaders to risk another explosion. But their intervention, although it tended to restore calm, did not go so far as to restore the Nagy experiment. In 1954 Voroshilov had gone to Budapest to try to reconcile Nagy and Rákosi, whose conflict was leading to a break. In July 1956, Suslov and Mikoyan went to Budapest, repeating the 1954 trip, to look for a solution to the conflict between Rákosi and an exasperated Hungary.[42] But as always the USSR treated the problems of its allies in the perspective of its own conflicts. Suslov was not very inclined toward compromise, as he had shown in his attitude to Yugoslavia, while Mikoyan advocated adaptation in all circumstances. This team pulling in opposite directions could only give the Hungarian solution an ambiguous, contradictory, and therefore ineffective character. Even if they had wanted to promote a popular political leader, as Nagy was at the time, they did not dare to. The solution imposed was a compromise between conservative positions and the desire for change. To satisfy the former, they replaced Rákosi, who was in the way, with Gerö, his right-hand man. To satisfy the supporters of innovation, they showered Gerö with counsels of moderation and reform and with financial aid.[43] No doubt Gerö followed in part the program that had been laid out for him. He held a national funeral service for Rajk and restored to public life a number of those who had been excluded by Rákosi or who had been eliminated in the Stalinist period. But it was rather late to attempt moderate reforms, as Rajk's burial on October 6 demonstrated. On that day, the ceremony planned by Gerö, that is, by the party, was transformed by the crowd (more than three hundred thousand people assembled) into a popular demonstration against the regime's arbitrary powers.[44] The party's decisions were thus overwhelmed by the streets.

Suslov and Mikoyan were doubly mistaken when they thought they had found a solution that could ease the tension of the situation. The choice of Gerö was inept. He was too tied to the past and to Stalinism to be able to present himself as a new man. Imposed by the Soviets, his very presence in power indicated that decisions about Hungarian political life were still made in Moscow, something the Hungarians no longer accepted. Mikoyan and Suslov like all Soviet leaders had evaluated the mood of the Hungarian people by the measure of popular reactions in the USSR, where with rare exceptions passive acceptance of party decisions prevailed. The Moscow leadership was ignorant of or underestimated the extent of political developments and the proliferation of national political tendencies in Hungary since 1953, their explosion into varied demands, and the maturation of ideas. Mikoyan and Suslov correctly perceived the need for placing Hungary on the path of serious reforms. They did not know and no one in Moscow yet knew that the Hungarian people wished to take control of their own fate and that they had already rejected permanent Soviet intervention and even the absolute authority of their own leaders. Finally, the Hungarians at that moment—when the Budapest crowd acclaimed the memory of Rajk—had their eyes fixed on Poland and drew lessons from the events that were taking place there.[45] Gomułka's return to power on October 19 and his victorious dialogue with Khrushchev could have convinced the Hungarians that confronted with a spreading crisis in the satellites the USSR was being forced to compromise. What had been accepted in Poland, a Polish choice, a Polish road, should be accepted in Hungary. But the USSR reacted brutally to the revolution that broke out in Hungary, breaking without apparent hesitation a movement that had brought a whole nation together. This was to pose political and ideological problems with long-term effects on the communist community in the broadest sense, states and parties together.

The growing agitation in Hungary during the days when Poland's fate was being decided explains why the USSR both temporized and attempted to influence events. But when the insurrection began on October 23 and the insurgents acclaimed Nagy and demanded his return to power (he had been accepted back in the party on October 14), the USSR was confronted with an urgent and ineluctable choice. To treat Hungary like Poland, to give in, would be to grant a further concession to Poland and to do nothing about a disturbing process. The second Budapest demonstration, which like the one on October 6 brought together more than three hundred thousand people, had its point of departure in the desire to demonstrate Hungarian solidarity with the Polish movement. Giving in to the demonstrators would swell the size of the "front" in Budapest and Warsaw that continued to draw strength from events taking place in both countries and might revitalize the Polish movement that had just been contained. Moreover, the USSR was not in the habit of giving in to street demonstrations. Lenin's old hatred of popular spontaneity still governed his successors, who knew how one could manipulate organized groups and were particularly distrustful of anything that escaped from organization. Against the crowd that toppled Stalin's statue, Gerö was without power, and the USSR hesitated momentarily. For once the initiative was not with Moscow. Panic-stricken by the revolution that was sweeping away the whole system, the Hungarian party or what remained of it gave in to popular pressure and recalled Imre Nagy to the government. The Hungarian leaders, Imre Nagy among them, then called on the USSR to help put down the demonstrations. From this moment on the USSR acted in an uneven way but without interruption. The appeal for aid sent to it on the night of October 23 led to military intervention by a limited number of troops, which provoked opposition from Yugoslavia and Poland.[46] This first intervention reflected above all Soviet perplexity. The troops were insufficient and ill-prepared to confront a revolution involving a whole people. Clearly Moscow thought that only conventional political questions were at issue. Once again Suslov and Mikoyan were dispatched to Budapest on October 24 to find solutions.[47] They forced the removal of Gerö, replaced him with Kádár, and installed a new Soviet ambassador, Yuri Andropov, who had earlier demonstrated some cleverness in Carelia.[48] It was at this point that the difficulties involved in these Soviet choices appeared most clearly. The two men who had been put in power were, in principle, acceptable to the

Hungarian people. Nagy, who had just been recalled, was popular and Kadar had a reputation of integrity. Chosen or accepted by Moscow, they had its confidence. So what explains the intervention that provoked a stiffening of the popular resistance, the spread of fighting, and undisguised anti-Sovietism? Against whom was the military intervention that began on October 24 directed? How could it be justified? Khrushchev provides a response in his *Memoirs* that is not very convincing.[49] The "counterrevolution" that he described, according to him, threatened the whole country with bloody conflict. This amounts to not paying sufficient attention to the realities of those tragic days in Hungary. But his explanation has the particular virtue of suggesting that the Soviet leadership did not understand the deleterious effect that its intervention had on the evolution of events. It could not have failed to destroy thoroughly the confidence of the masses in the newly installed government or else to have pushed the government into the arms of the masses, cutting it off from Moscow. Perhaps because they finally became aware of this dilemma, the Soviet leaders eagerly signed the cease-fire of October 28, proclaiming that the counterrevolution had come to an end.[50] The next day the team of Suslov and Mikoyan, who had been anointed as experts on Hungary, again landed in Budapest and concluded their expedition with a declaration "of friendship between the USSR and the other socialist states" that clearly provided for "nonintervention in the domestic affairs of each country."[51]

However at the moment when this declaration was being worked out the Hungarian situation changed radically both domestically and internationally. Domestically, the political reforms set in motion by Nagy and approved or at least tolerated by Moscow were having immediate consequences. The Hungarian regime was evolving, the single party had on October 27 given way to a coalition in which the democratic parties participated, councils were being formed in factories, and Nagy was negotiating with delegations from revolutionary organizations that had no link to the party. Such changes, such an obvious break with the Soviet model, had never existed before, since neither Poland nor Yugoslavia had ever escaped from the party's authority. Nevertheless up until October 30 the Soviets focused more on resolving the Hungarian problem than on its heterodox aspects, even though they were aware of these developments. The moderation of the Soviet press on this point up to October 30 and the tone of the statement that concluded the trip by Mikoyan and Suslov all indicated that Moscow wished to avoid a confrontation.

How was the move made in a few days from this moderation, a still limited police operation, to a brutal military repression of the Hungarian October? There is no doubt that the sudden shift of the preceding days, particularly in the international realm, explains the change. The Hungarian revolution that Moscow thought it could tame with substantial concessions, which Nagy had even attempted to channel by opening his government to ever more various forces, had a dynamic that escaped from all programs of containment and that nothing could stop. The revolution had rejected the established political system, the authority of the party, and communism. Soviet policy, expressed through Nagy's reforms, consisted in pretending to ignore this rejection while accepting it in reality. First of all the USSR closed its eyes to the changes in the political system that were rapidly developing, concerned only to preserve appearances. This was a triumph of jargon, but reversed. The talk was of communism and the one-party state, while nothing of the kind any longer existed in Hungary. But the persistence of jargon and appearances was a trap that was to close around Imre Nagy. Because he claimed that he was remaining within the system that had been only slightly modified, he could not fully carry out his enterprise to establish a new government and a new party that could hold in check the popular forces that had unanimously rejected the existing government and party. At the same time, Imre Nagy sensed that the society had gone too far to accept this restraint of the revolution, this preservation, if only in appearance, of some elements of the people's democracy. This domestic choice, which gradually deprived him of popular support—the Hungarian people were being swept forward by an irresistible movement—forced him to replace his lost support in another domain, that of foreign policy. This explains why Nagy so clearly posed the problem of the real independence of his country, demanding the departure of Soviet troops stationed on its territory, then announcing on October 31 that Hungary would withdraw from the Warsaw Pact, and finally on November 1 announcing that it wanted to be a neutral state. Nagy was no doubt aware of the dangers of the Soviet reaction, and to protect against it he simultaneously offered to renegotiate the relations of a neutral Hungary with the USSR and asked the United Nations for the protection of Hungarian neutrality by the four great powers. By internationalizing the Hungarian problem, Nagy hoped to restore the presence of the Western powers in the region and to take away from the USSR the initiative for making decisions concerning the states that had been situated in its camp since 1945. It was a unique moment in the postwar history of Eastern Europe in which the system that had prevailed since 1945 seemed to be on the point of being abolished. The common responsibility of the great war allies that had been supposed to govern the region in order to restore it to normal political life, something that Stalin had stubbornly refused to recognize, was again invoked. Stalin's successors who had been so hesitant until then were convinced that a brutal reaction was necessary or else the course of European history would be reversed. It was necessary to break the Hungarian attempt to ruin the Warsaw Pact. Acceptance of Hungary's exit from the pact implied that the pact was not a definitive structure for the socialist states. The irreversibility of the revolution derived from that fact. All the progress that had been accomplished by the USSR during the preceding ten years—the establishment of the satellite system, the extension of the revolution—was in the process of collapsing. Nor was it a negligible argument that this collapse was about to take place in a strategically vital location on the Austrian border in a country that was opening itself to the opposing system and that could therefore no longer be either controlled or intimdated. The USSR was losing control over a satellite in a much more dramatic way than had been the case with Poland, because the communist regime was being violently rejected by society and Hungary from the outset had placed itself under international protection by appealing to the United Nations.

The decision made in Moscow matched the perceived danger. The limited military intervention of October 24 was followed on November 4 by a very large-scale military intervention, which General Béla Király who participated in the events said was a war, and he added: "I do not have the slightest doubt that after November 1 the USSR was at war with the socialist democratic state of Hungary. The Soviet Union has the dubious privilege of being the first socialist state in history to have made war against another socialist state."[52]

There is no doubt that the USSR saw very clearly that what it was undertaking in Hungary beginning on November 1, 1956, was not an armed intervention of the same character as those it had launched against Berlin in 1953 or against the Hungarian insurgents on October 24. This explains the international efforts carried out at the same time by those in power in Moscow throughout the socialist camp. While Soviet leaders had previously maneuvered in their tanks without seeking the approval of any of their partners, in late October 1956 before the final assault they put forth an intense diplomatic effort in order to ensure the communist world's blessings on the intervention. For the first time in the history of intercommunist relations, Moscow appeared to be concerned with the opinions of other states in the communist world and called for their agreement. This was an unprecedented event that merits consideration. The entire Politburo was mobilized for an extraordinary shuttle between capitals.[53] While Mao sent Lin Shaochi to Moscow for consultation, Khrushchev, Molotov, and Malenkov conducted discussions near the Soviet-Polish border with a delegation led by Gomułka and Cyrankiewicz; then Khrushchev and Malenkov went to Bucharest to meet Gheorghiu-Dej, who was troubled by his own position and was therefore ready to support Soviet plans.[54] In Bucharest there were also meetings of the Soviet delegation with a Czech delegation led by Novotný and one from Bulgaria headed by Zhivkov. Finally, Khrushchev and Malenkov went in search of Tito's support. A consensus emerged from this feverish activity: "The leaders of the sister states were unanimous: we had to act and act quickly," writes Khrushchev.[55]

The support no doubt came with some qualifications. Tito especially, who was disturbed by the now uncontrollable course of events in Budapest, was still restrained by deep sympathy for Nagy and for an experiment in which he saw many characteristics of the Yugoslav model. His reticent support for the interventionist argument was clarified after the collapse of the Nagy regime when he offered Nagy temporary asylum, which poisoned his future relations with the USSR.[56]

While Yugoslavia was reserved, other countries, more concerned with their own internal order, even offered to help the USSR in its military effort against Hungary. This was clearly the case for Czechoslavakia, Rumania, and Bulgaria, where for various reasons hostility toward Hungary was very deep rooted.[57]

But even while it was negotiating for this support from the sister states and sending more troops toward Hungarian territory, the USSR continued to negotiate on the spot with Nagy and to promise him a tolerant attitude.

The delayed publication by the Soviet press of the declaration worked out during the last visit by Suslov and Mikoyan to Budapest left open the hope that Moscow would negotiate the withdrawal of its troops.[58] Did the declaration not state: "The Soviet government is prepared to undertake appropriate negotiations with the Hungarian government and the other Warsaw Pact governments on the question of the presence of Soviet troops on Hungarian territory."?

Because he was troubled by these contradictory elements—peaceful statements and troop movements—Nagy made several appeals to the Soviet ambassador, Andropov, who was prodigal with reassuring statements, assuring him that the reported troop movements involved nothing but relief forces. The role that Yuri Andropov played in Budapest at the time is far from negligible. He helped to maintain Nagy's illusions about a possible reconciliation with the USSR while the mechanism that would crush the Hungarian revolution was put in place.[59] The size of this military machine led by Marshall Koniev and the preparation of a political replacement—János Kádár opportunely disappeared from Budapest at war to be restored to power by the Soviet Army on November 4—all suggest that these actions were not improvised on November 1 but rather that Soviet policy had been constantly following a dual path, both negotiations and preparation for violent action. The second intervention was not the product of a dramatic improvisation but the application of a radical policy that the Soviet leaders had had in readiness for several years. There is no doubt that this ambivalent policy reflected debates within the Soviet leadership, the existence of two orientations. The radicalization of the Hungarian revolution from October 30 on signified the collapse of Khrushchev's position and also indicated the dangers and limits of de-Stalinization, while opening the way to those who like Suslov and Molotov had always been disturbed by the vagaries of the Eastern European states after 1953. This does not mean that Khrushchev by himself would have acted otherwise. But since the Twentieth Congress he had linked his name and his political fate to a reformist line, and his rivals were fighting him on this line and its consequences. He devoted so much energy to his trips to other communist states in late October in order to secure their agreement to intervention because he had to avoid the accusation of weakness in the face of the uncontrolled situation that had developed; and from that moment on he was as determined as his adversaries to liquidate the Hungarian revolution. Khrushchev also remained deeply attached to the classic Soviet model. He was a communist, not the "gravedigger" of communism. The reforms with which he had gradually become identified were in his eyes the most certain ways to improve and revitalize the communist system, not paths toward its annihilation. For this reason, after November 1 the Soviet leadership was no doubt unanimous about the solution to the Hungarian crisis, and it also relied on a relatively unanimous perception of the danger this crisis posed for the entire system among its allies in the communist world.

With the crisis resolved through violence and bloodshed, we must attempt to understand the sources of Soviet conduct in several essential respects. First of all, why did the USSR that had tolerated the Polish October crush the Hungarian October? What was the real meaning of that October that brought to Eastern Europe both immense hope and immense despair? Was the direction of the communist world changed by these events? Or in the last analysis had the November intervention restored the old order? A preliminary observation should first be made about the methods of Soviet foreign policy in 1956. In April of that year, the Cominform, which was in fact moribund, had been suppressed and its dissolution, offered as a pledge to Yugoslavia, left the USSR as the sole judge of Eastern European crises. Even though the Cominform had in the past been nothing but a tool in Stalin's hands, it had nevertheless been a convenient screen for intervention in the life of other socialist states. Deprived of this screen, the USSR had to declare its "interventionism" at the very moment when—in the Belgrade declaration of 1955 and the Twentieth Congress in 1956—it had proclaimed that the fundamental principle of intersocialist relations was respect for the sovereignty of others and noninterference in their affairs. And it repeated this commitment in the October 30, 1956, declaration on the Hungarian situation. To get out of this uncomfortable situation, Moscow called on the verbal support of the other communist states and the constant trips by Khrushchev and Malenkov demonstrated its determination to commit its allies to its actions, even if it was later necessary to compensate for this support by making concessions to those allies. But the approbation that communist leaders gave to intervention in Hungary should not conceal the essential reality. In 1956 the USSR, which had officially repudiated the Cominform and its methods of action, had nevertheless not given up the classic methods of Stalinism. To resolve political difficulties, Stalin's successors did as he had always done: they forced a change in personnel. The appointment of Ochab and the persistence of hostility toward Gomułka, the appointments of Rákosi and Gerö, the authoritarian summoning of the Polish Politburo to Moscow with the obvious purpose of intimidating it, perhaps even of sequestering it, all of these certainly belonged to the arsenal of Stalinist methods.

But what was new on the other hand was the pragmatism that generally characterized the practices of the post-Stalin period. When Mikoyan and Suslov went to Budapest for the first time in October 1956 it was less to intimidate than to understand. When Gerö was appointed, it was not simply because he was considered a sure man but because the Soviets were looking for a leader who was capable of succeeding where Rakosi had failed, capable of reforming by making the party the engine of reform. Despite the profound differences that separated the two men, it was clear that for Moscow the appointment of Gerö in Budapest was the equivalent of the recognition of Gomułka in Warsaw. Both were charged with accomplishing a single task—to reform the system without breaking it. This is the key to the later differences in treatment of the two countries. Why allow the situation to develop in Poland, why destroy it violently in Hungary, when at a given moment developments in both countries seemed to be moving identically toward a point of no return? And why the difference when military intervention was considered in both countries?

The cause can be found in the domestic situations of the two countries and in their very different processes of de-Stalinization.

In Poland, the USSR had to confront a process of change over which the party was able to take control from beginning to end. There is no doubt that this de-Stalinization was radical, but it had not gone outside the system. The Polish party, aware both of the extent of the popular movement and of its dangers, was able to take a place in that movement and at the crucial moment turn over its leadership to a man who appeared to be a victim of Stalinism and of the existing leadership, Gomułka. Symbol of the national struggle, supported by the entire party, truly embodying the consensus of the country, Gomułka was in turn able to make a choice among fundamental objectives in order to preserve them. For this country that had been suppressed three times in the course of its history, the principal objective was clearly internal cohesion, the guarantee of domestic sovereignty. To preserve this domestic sovereignty, that is, the Polish road around which Polish society could be organized, Polish leaders were ready to grant to the USSR what it most ardently desired: the maintenance of Poland within the socialist camp, guaranteed by both the maintenance of the socialist regime domestically and the continuance of Poland in the Warsaw Pact for external policy. Given this price, the USSR could close its eyes to the way that Polish leaders conceived of their national path toward socialism.

Two elements had a decisive effect on Polish developments that were obscured by the traditional clichés about the country. There is first the role played by Ochab. It is customary to credit Gomulka and Cardinal Wyszinski for Polish progress, to assert that their prestige and their powerful personalities were an extraordinary stroke of luck for their country. But it is clear that this luck could not have been exploited if Ochab, the man in power when the popular movement broke out, had not at the outset been capable of stepping aside for Gomulka and supporting his successor with all his strength, thereby securing the unity of the party behind him. History usually forgets the losers and thinks that the winners shaped the course of events. In the case of Poland, Ochab, the man who was defeated in October, was probably the man who prevented the victory from later turning into a tragedy.

The second element that needs to be emphasized since it also contradicts traditional views is the extraordinary political realism demonstrated by the Poles. It is customary to characterize the Poles in an entirely different way, to emphasize their romanticism, their inclination for sacrifice and for desperate struggle. But during this terrible and threatening month of October, romanticism was notably absent from Poland. Every step taken by Polish leaders was characterized by extraordinary realism, which was also reflected in popular attitudes. When Hungary was invaded, the Poles could not fail to experience painfully a battle that evoked a tragic memory for them, the Warsaw uprising of 1944.[60] This memory and the natural sympathy of the Poles for the Hungarians, coupled with their awareness of the influence of the Polish October on events in Hungary should in principle, even disregarding any kind of romanticism, have provoked reactions of solidarity in Poland. However, Poland—the people and the leaders united—made no false moves. In this connection we must quote the bitter and lucid judgment of this "realist" choice made by the poet Adam Ważyk: "We were used to being the conscience of history; today, *raison d'état* requires our silence."[61]

While the USSR could not help but be reassured about Warsaw, its judgment of the Hungarian situation was entirely different. Developments there had daily become more disturbing. Before October, the group in power had been incapable of carrying out de-Stalinization and of ensuring the unity of a party divided between Stalinists and victims of Stalinism. As a consequence of this division, the reforms demanded by the rank and file could only be popular if they were carried out outside the party. This also meant that Hungarian leaders, whoever they might be, in order not to be suspected of allegiance to the USSR and to a party identified with Moscow, had to carry out popular demands to the end and in doing so had to go against their thorough knowledge of the general situation, the necessity for alliance with the USSR and for Soviet agreement with any change. Popular demands required not a modification of the system but a break. To make himself heard by the society, to bridge the gap that separated him from it, Imre Nagy had to make concessions that did not correspond to the norms of orthodox Leninism. He could not restore parliamentary democracy and remain in the Warsaw Pact, which was open only to communist states. In the last analysis what occurred in Hungary in October 1956 can only be characterized as a revolution, the first revolution that had taken place in Eastern Europe in decades. It hardly matters that Moscow took refuge behind the convenient explanation of a counterrevolution stirred up by NATO.[62] As Hugh Seton-Watson clearly points out:

The events in Hungary in the last week of October 1956 were a *revolution*, in the conditions that have been described (a revolution is a violent action aimed at overthrowing an entire system of political and social powers, and replacing it with something new). What followed was a *war* between two armies of unequal strength. . . . What followed defeat in the war was a counterrevolution . . . (a counterrevolution is a violent action aimed at overthrowing a political and social order established by a revolution, and restoring the political and social order that existed before the revolution).[63]

The USSR had already been confronted with challenges to its model by Yugoslavia and Poland, to its authority and determination to include all communist states within a single organization, by Yugoslavia, and with riots in Germany. But it had never anticipated revolution anywhere. Yugoslavia, whose example no doubt encouraged those who aspired to greater independence from Moscow, did not on the other hand offer any particular attraction for the supporters of pluralism. Hungary was an exception, an independent force. But if its attempt at liberation was tolerated, it could become a perfect reference for all those who were still kept from extreme demands by realism and who faced by a demonstration of Soviet weakness would no longer hesitate to make demands for complete independence. Hungarian developments thus required from the USSR—to the extent that it considered the progress of the revolutions it had organized as the norm—a merciless act to halt them. This was all the more necessary because, as Seton-Watson correctly argues, the Hungarian revolution was victorious.[64] Seton-Watson's argument is all the more significant because he also points out that the success of the revolution was not only the destruction of the existing system, but the creation of a new political order; a new social order could, of course, not be constructed in such a short time. Now the Leninist conception of revolution is essentially political. All of Lenin's thought points to the primacy of the political. Loyal to Leninism, his successors had always favored political over social and economic considerations. And although they had been and were still able to accommodate social and economic reforms, secondary in relation to the political field, the overthrow of the political order meant for them the end of revolution as they understood it. They launched a war, not an intervention, because for them only war was a response to such an absolute defeat; only war could reverse the course of events and transform defeat into victory. This reaffirmed the old link between war and revolution whose importance Lenin had pointed out.

We have to ask further why the Hungarian party was incapable of taking the measure of these events, of the Soviet analysis, and of the foreseeable consequences. Why were its leaders unable to act in the Polish manner, following the path that they had shown led to success? The explanation must first of all be looked for in the history of the countries themselves and of their communist parties. Polish communism had a long past. Poland itself had a long history of independence that had been trampled on and of struggles to reconquer it. This is why at the moment of crisis Poles of all factions were so careful to preserve their sovereignty by clearly defining its terms and limits. They knew that their fate depended on the USSR and on it alone, that it would be resolved in the dialogue between Moscow and Warsaw, and that by recognizing that dependence on the USSR Poland had already partially won the difficult negotiations. The Polish communists had drawn the lessons from the long history that was their legacy, while the Hungarians, less used to Russia's ambitions, thought they could deal with that country as they did with other powers and look for external alliances to support their cause; that was something the USSR could not accept. Dialogue, or confrontation, among communist states represented a special domain of international relations. No doubt before 1956 no one in the communist universe had imagined that there could be a confrontation among communist states. The Soviet response to this new state of affairs, which was entirely empirical, would later have to be given theoretical justification. But at the moment when confrontations among communist states were discovered, Poland was cleverer than Hungary in recognizing the rules of the game.

It was true, and this is the final point worth mentioning, that Poland was forced to act prudently because it had no precedent to which to refer. For Hungary, on the contrary, the Polish precedent—Soviet troops leaving the outskirts of Warsaw at Gomułka's command—was very encouraging. And the Hungarians, more romantic in this case than the Poles, began to dream. Why should they not receive the treatment granted to neighboring Austria a few months earlier? Why could they not establish relations with the USSR comparable to Soviet-Finnish relations? Why, finally, would they be refused Finnish status, the free choice of government in return for benevolent neutrality toward the USSR? In this dream the Hungarians failed to take into account the conditions under which and the moments when Finland had been granted that status and noncommunist Austria had been liberated by Soviet troops. For different situations there were different solutions; this had been understood in Warsaw but not in Budapest.

A Conflict without Thaw: Rumania

After the 1948 break with Tito, the USSR had experienced a period of absolute calm in its relations with its allies. The authoritarian and bloody imposition of Stalin's control over Eastern Europe was the basis for this *pax sovietica*. Similarly, the war in Hungary opened the way for a new era of apparent harmony. This time the methods were different, and the USSR chose to appease its allies with a policy of concessions and encouragements of national choices. The USSR adopted the same attitude everywhere modeled on the November 1956 agreement with Poland. It reduced its economic pressure on its allies, forgave debts, and granted long-term loans in order to encourage profound economic reforms. The stationing of Soviet troops in other countries became an element of the Warsaw Pact, no longer a situation left over from the war, and the USSR agreed in principle to discuss their movements. This agreement, negotiated with Poland, was applied with particular fervor in Hungary where the USSR had to overcome the bitterness of a broken people. To reach this goal, the USSR gave János Kádár, who had returned in the wake of Soviet tanks, considerable latitude in carrying out reforms, which allowed him not only to restore the economy but also to relax political constraints.

This pacified climate in the communist world was, however, short-lived; and the clouds came from a part of Eastern Europe where until then loyalty to Moscow had seemed unshakeable, Rumania.

The USSR had complete confidence in their Rumanian ally for many reasons. It had been accommodatingly welcomed there in 1956. Gheorghiu-Dej, while suspect to Khrushchev because of his Stalinist zeal, had been able to remain in power and strengthen his authority.[65] By the end of the fifties Rumania was declaring ambitions and political attitudes not in conformity with the general orientation of Soviet policy. But Gheorghiu-Dej benefited at the time both from the Soviet Union's internal struggles and from Khrushchev's desire to establish solidly the policy of peaceful coexistence with the West. In this domestic and international context, which preoccupied the Soviet leaders, Gheorghiu-Dej managed to win success for particular arguments. On the domestic level he resolutely turned his back on all reform policies and set himself with those in the Kremlin who were challenging Khrushchev's reformism; with the Chinese leadership as well, he maintained that orthodoxy and political rigor were inseparable in a communist state. Although the defeat of the Soviet conservatives in the "anti-party" crisis in July 1957 undermined this argument in the USSR, Gheorghiu-Dej's position was already strong enough for him to obtain the international concessions he had asked from Moscow. Rumania wanted a withdrawal of Soviet troops. This was a demand that Bucharest had presented to Khrushchev shortly after Stalin's death,[66] and it had been all the more effective because the man who presented it, Emile Bodnaras, Rumanian defense minister, was an old communist who had held Soviet citizenship before the war; trained in Moscow, he had been one of the architects of the revolutionary manipulation practiced from 1945 to 1947. The fact that he became spokesman for the Rumanian desire for international independence was not something that could be ignored.[67] In 1958, when Khrushchev had gotten rid of the anti-party group and could apply his domestic policies, he launched a series of major reforms that implied a certain reduction in military spending. He then agreed to withdraw Soviet troops from Rumania, which now found itself in the same position as Czechoslovakia and Bulgaria. This decision, never completely explained, was connected first of all with an economic concern. Khrushchev himself had said: "Support of a division abroad, on the territory of another socialist country, costs twice as much as support of the same division on our own territory. We have to reduce the cost of our armed forces, abroad as well as at home."[68] Given the fact that in 1958 Rumania was guiltier of the rigor of its system than of any innovative characteristics, the risks of the withdrawal were not great. Rumania could even become, since it presented all the external signs of independence from Moscow, a bridge toward the Eastern Mediterranean countries, members of NATO. Although in many respects Rumanian conduct of foreign policy, for this was the ground Gheorghiu-Dej had chosen on which to define a national communism, diverged from that of the USSR, these differences were not very alarming for Moscow. No doubt Rumania had authorized emigration to Israel when the USSR had not decided to do so, and it undertook a resumption of commercial relations with the West that had been broken off at Stalin's direction. But in this instance Rumania was only anticipating a Soviet change in direction, and there are many examples of Soviet shifts having been preceded, or indeed tested, by other countries of the bloc. In 1962, on the other hand, Rumania openly rebelled against Soviet policy.[69]

At the Twenty-First and Twenty-Second Congresses, Khrushchev had established as his country's goal "to catch up with and surpass the United States." It was an extravagant and unrealistic program that brushed aside both the economic backwardness of the USSR and the difficulties of the socialist world as a whole. To attempt to reach the goal it was necessary to mobilize all the resources of the USSR, and also all those of its allies. The fifteenth session of Comecon that was held in Warsaw in December 1961 had to adopt under Soviet pressure a text ratifying "the principles of the socialist international division of labor." These principles quite obviously contradicted Rumania's major industrialization program contained in the six-year plan adopted at the Third Congress of the Rumanian Communist Party in June 1960. The Soviet leaders could not have been unaware that their program was irreconcilable with Rumanian plans and that it presupposed their prior abandonment. This is another example of the hasty and ill-considered character of many of the decisions made by Nikita Khrushchev when he imposed his views, and his colleagues would criticize him for this "subjectivism" when they overthrew him. Khrushchev had attended the Third Congress of the Rumanian Communist Party and had not reacted to the presentation of such an ambitious plan, which implied the mobilization of all Rumanian capacities in order to succeed. The Rumanians had every right to consider his silence equivalent to agreement. When the charter of the "socialist division of labor," so harmful to Rumanian interests, was presented, nothing had been done in Moscow to prepare for it and to win over to it a partner that had until then been a loyal ally. In June 1962, when the Comecon held its meeting in Moscow, the Rumanians rebelled and flatly refused any program of supranational planning. Moreover, because they felt their economic independence threatened, they associated with it a policy of international independence, turning toward the West and toward China, whose break with Moscow was on the point of being consummated. From defense of its economic interests, the Rumanian government in fact quickly moved on to demonstrations of complete independence in foreign policy. Wherever the USSR adopted a position, Rumania followed the opposite path: in the Sino-Soviet conflict in 1964 when Bucharest proposed to mediate and pretended to consider the two causes equally good, delivering a lecture on morality and good conduct to Moscow as well as to Peking (in the declaration of the Rumanian Central Committee of April 22, 1964);[70] in its relations with West Germany, which grew closer, leading to official recognition in 1967; finally, in the same year during the Six-Day War, by taking a position in favor of Israel while the USSR supported the Arab cause and denounced Israel as an aggressor. Everywhere Bucharest vigorously asserted that adhesion to the same political system did not compel international alignment but authorized each country to choose the foreign policy that suited it. Finally, Rumania did not hold back from posing the thorny problem of Bessarabia, which it had lost in 1945, and it gave its undisguised demands particular emphasis as the twentieth anniversary of the annexation approached.[71]

It was Soviet calm in the face of the rise of Rumanian hostility that was the noteworthy response. Up until 1964, far from reacting, the USSR appeared to accept Rumanian objections and to give in to them.[72] The arrival of the Brezhnev-Kosygin-Podgorny group to power in October 1964 confirmed the desire of Khrushchev's successors not to poison relations with Bucharest. Confronted with a legacy that included many dark spots—a backward economy and a revolt of managers domestically; the loss of prestige over the Cuban crisis of 1962 and the open conflict with China in the foreign relations sphere—Khrushchev's successors avoided wherever they could increasing their difficulties. In the case of Rumania their good faith was obvious. They believed all the more in the possibility of using their personal prestige and their critique of Khrushchev's "subjectivism" to normalize relations with Bucharest because at the same time the Rumanian leader disappeared from the political scene. In March 1965 the death of Gheorghiu-Dej brought Nicolae Ceauşescu to power. Could there not be an understanding with this bureaucrat, the prototype of a new generation of communists attached to their power and to effective rule? But it quickly became apparent that Ceauşescu was going to pursue his predecessor's independent line and to maintain the same rigor domestically. Moscow had counted on a reversal of Rumanian priorities that would at least temporarily have concentrated Ceauşescu's attention on domestic development. This hope was quickly disappointed, and a succession of declarations flatly antagonistic to the USSR reopened the hostilities.[73] From then on Moscow replied to Bucharest's attacks and its "misconduct" with similar virulence.[74] The open hostility of Moscow was expressed by criticism of the Rumanian regime and by indirect statements calling into question Rumanian claims to Transylvania, but the polemic never went beyond these verbal reactions. Although the USSR considered the Rumanian rebellion unpleasant, it is obvious that it attributed to it only minor importance in the hierarchy of problems posed by the communist states.[75] And this leads to the following question: For the USSR, what distinguishes a minor case from a serious conflict? Where is the threshold located that transforms venial insubordination into intolerable rebellion?

The Rumanian attitude in the sixties was characterized by the fact that its demands were eminently national. Moreover, that attitude was expressed by the party apparatus with no interference from society and it allowed the party apparatus to legitimate the permanent constraints it exercised over the society. No doubt all conflicts in Eastern Europe since 1948 have had a national character. Within the framework of the Eastern Europe that had been shaped by the war, all of these states tended to search for the road to a certain autonomy. But none of the intersocialist conflicts that marked those years had had such a pronounced national character, for nowhere as much as in Bucharest were demands as clearly expressed in terms of the interests and the freedom of action of the national state.

Moreover Rumania was being assisted by the internal evolution of the USSR. When Rumanian leaders—Gheorghiu-Dej in April 1964 and especially Ceauşescu in 1967—demonstrated more and more forcefully their conception of Rumanian sovereignty, the Soviet authorities had already changed their views on the desirable evolution of the political systems of Eastern Europe. Even before he was deposed, Khrushchev, exposed to the contradictions of his policies and the hostility of his peers, had abandoned all hope of pursuing a thaw. In 1964 he had already been obliged to make concessions to the conservative mood and taking refuge in foreign policy he left the field open for his opponents. The end of the thaw was already predictable at that moment. His successors, brought to power by all the discontents that his numerous and contradictory initiatives had provoked in the party, but also in the society—more sensitive to incoherence and failure than to intentions—were above all conscious of the destabilization engendered by the thaw. Without returning to Stalinism, they chose to emphasize the authoritarian character of the system and rigorous orthodoxy, except in the economic realm where, as they knew, effectiveness required reforms. But on the political level, and this was the essential level for them, the hour for reformism had passed. In this respect, Rumania was above suspicion. Ceauşescu offered the best example of untouched party authority that no one in his country could challenge. What Khrushchev's successors aimed to restore Ceauşescu had maintained. Thus, in consideration of this exemplary domestic policy, it is understandable that the Soviets would respond with irritated patience to international skirmishes that moreover placed nothing in danger.

But although rebellious Rumania was not really dangerous, its attitudes contained the seeds of much more troubling choices in other contexts and pushed to other extremes. In asserting so clearly that each communist party and not only each state endowed with a socialist regime was free to define the national interest in its own way and that national interest and the interests of socialism were the same (and not that the general interest of socialism defined the contours of the national interest), Ceaucescu was very close to formulating the decisive question: Is it possible to turn away from Soviet norms—and not only from Soviet foreign policy—without thereby "betraying socialism"? This was the question that Czechoslovakia, so calm up to that point, would raise in 1968.

Prague 1968: The "Interrupted Revolution"

The "Prague Spring" took place twelve years after the Hungarian revolution in a country that in 1956 had shown little sympathy for what was happening in Budapest.[76] Enclosed in a persistent Stalinism, Czechoslovakia had reacted to the 1956 crisis with a hardening of domestic constraints, while in most Eastern European countries the years following 1956 were marked by a desire to reform. The 1960 Czechoslovak constitution clearly expressed a concern with faithfulness to the Soviet model, which was uncertain itself in Moscow but was understood in a conservative manner in Prague. This constitution, which asserted that the stage of people's democracy had been completed, insisted on the leading role of the party in the life of the state and the nation. Nearly two decades in advance it announced Brezhnev's concept of the state as that was to be inscribed in all the constitutions of the late seventies. No doubt Novotný, hanging on to his power, sensed the necessity to adapt to the denunciations of Stalin's crimes and to a certain increase in flexibility in the conduct of the economy. But he did so hesitantly, delaying by half-measures constantly called into question and always counterbalanced with authoritarian decisions. This chaotic pattern, which after 1963 gave way to unmistakable signs of flexibility, continued to provoke both impatience and frustration, and could have no beneficial effects on economic blockages nor could it above all appease Slovakia, which continued to feel dominated by the Czechs. The 1960 Constitution further reinforced Slovak discontent by limiting the powers of Bratislava. In 1967 all the difficulties that had accumulated over the years led to an attack on the regime and its failures by the Fourth Congress of Writers. This explosion, which took place against the backdrop of the Six-Day War and the alignment of Czechoslovakia with the USSR, while popular feelings favored Israel against the Arabs, epitomizes the general criticism of the writers of all aspects of party policy, foreign and domestic. The agitation following the congress and party divisions over the line that should be followed to deal with the crisis led to Novotný's fall and his replacement by Alexander Dubček in January 1968 as the head of the party.

With the arrival in power of this Slovak, trained in the USSR and from a national group that had suggested in 1945 joining Slovakia to the USSR, who seemed to be the best guarantee for a policy acceptable to Moscow,[77] Czechoslovakia was to undertake an experiment that would permanently ruin the friendship that Czechs and Slovaks had certainly felt for their Soviet "big brother." The eight months of the Prague Spring are too well known and too complex to be summarized here. But the view the USSR had of it is worth explaining.

Dubček's reforms were aimed at modifying the system without attacking it. The April 1968 program contained many general ideas about the way of bringing forth "a new model for socialist society," but it in no way undermined the existing system, even though in Moscow there began to be some concern that Czechoslovakia would become a "weak link" in the system because of the blows that had been struck against the party's authority.[78]

During the first three months of change in Prague, the USSR reacted with some uncertainty. News in the Soviet press was relatively scanty and the situation did not come out clearly. The leaders oscillated between expressions of sympathy for Czechoslovakia and moderate warnings.[79]

After the April plenum of the Czech Communist Party, when the Action Program was adopted, to the contrary the tone gradually changed in Moscow and it is possible then to detect growing worry and a desire to control developments in Prague. Before that point the Soviet leaders had asserted that what was happening in Czechoslovakia was a purely internal matter ("Eto vashe delo"—It's your affair), said Brezhnev to Novotný who was trying to win him to his cause).[80] After that point, they made it a problem for the socialist camp. The USSR undertook a series of consultations and visits within the communist world that amounted to a policy of systematic pressure against the group in power in Prague. On May 4 Dubček was in Moscow;

although at the time precise information about the purpose of this brief visit was scarce,[81] when the crisis was resolved by violence, it turned out that Dubček had been summoned to be denounced even at that early stage.[82] At almost the same moment, Marshall Koniev, whose troops had played a decisive role in 1956 in Budapest, was in Prague to celebrate Soviet-Czech friendship. And a few days later, Marshall Grechko, minister of defense, also came to Prague for the same reason along with Prime Minister Kosygin. At the same time, the Soviet press was devoting a good deal of space to declarations from military leaders, pleading for "vigilance and socialist cohesion in a dangerous international situation."[83]

It was clear that Czechoslovakia was being treated as suspect. This was evidenced by the summoning to Moscow on May 8, in this context of constant travel, of the secretaries of the communist parties of the bloc. Although such a summit was not unusual in the practices of the communist world, what was unusual was the absence of Czechoslovakia. Rumania, which had openly been playing the role of rebel since 1967, was normally absent from such meetings, but Czechoslovakia, until then so loyal to socialist internationalism, was on the contrary a pillar of such meetings. Its absence was particularly remarkable in view of the agenda, which included "the urgent problems of the communist world and the workers' movement."[84] The theme of the solidarity of the socialist world and of the deviations that threatened its cohesion was aired almost daily in the Soviet newspapers. The summit of May 8 was indeed already a preliminary mobilization of the allies to develop a response to the "errant ways" of the Prague Spring. This mobilization was not futile because the press in these allied countries followed *Pravda's* lead. The closest alignment with Soviet positions was demonstrated in Poland and the GDR; but Hungary still held back and presented in the newspapers the sense of being interested in developments in Prague.[85]

While in Moscow the fraternal parties were being mobilized and criticism was proliferating, in Prague the movement was accelerating and positions were being radicalized under external pressures added to internal tensions. The plenum of the Czech Communist Party, held at the end of May, while not lacking in friendly and reassuring statements about the USSR, took positions on two points that hardened Soviet reactions.[86] The plenum took a position against any "constraining model applicable to all socialist countries," thereby emphasizing the party's desire to bring out of the Prague Spring a "socialism with a human face." It also decided, despite many hesitations, to call for an extraordinary Party Congress.[87] In the increasingly passionate atmosphere of Prague during the preparations for the congress, measures like the abolition of censorship in June provoked a rise in protest from conservative elements of the party and in reaction a determination on the part of the innovative faction to define the program of change more clearly. The Manifesto of Two Thousand Words published in several Czech newspapers on June 27 was the work of this innovative faction.[88] Its authors wanted to build a bridge to public opinion to obtain its support for the democratization in progress against the blockages it was experiencing. The program of associating society with change, of having it participate in debates at all levels was without any doubt in harmony with the traditional vision of democracy; but it was totally opposed to the Soviet conception of the relations between government and society. It is thus hardly surprising that in the face of these various Czech movements—a specific program of socialism, an extraordinary congress called to approve these innovations, a society called upon to become an element in political decision making—the USSR thought that Czechoslovakia was calling the whole socialist system into question. The violence of the Soviet response and the level at which it was expressed from this time on contrasted with the relative moderation of the preceding months. The Soviet Politburo delegated several of its members to challenge forcefully the idea that there were more or less likable forms of socialism. From Leonid Brezhnev, who attacked those "who are hiding behind a pseudo-socialist disguise," under a "mask of national forms," to undermine and "soften socialism,"[89] to Pyotr Shelest, first secretary of the Ukrainian Communist Party and member of the Politburo, who denounced the "speechmakers fabricating abstract and confused models of socialism, humanism, and democracy," who were in the last analysis nothing but "opportunists who had been won over to petty bourgeois ideas,"[90] all the attacks were violent. The criticisms often led to a barely veiled threat, when their authors, like the head of the Soviet government Kosygin, recalled that as members of the Warsaw Pact the USSR and Czechoslovakia had imperative duties inscribed in the logic of the pact from which they could not escape.[91] The critiques by Soviet leaders and the alarmist articles in the press were reinforced—here the threat was clearer—by Warsaw Pact maneuvers that took place on Czech territory in late June and whose size was greater than had been initially planned. The maneuvers were significant and the withdrawal was very late, not beginning until July 13 and slowed down for various reasons.[92]

Against this background of already violent criticism of the particular "deviations" of Czechoslovakia (the counterrevolutionary character of the Two Thousand Words, the threat weighing on the whole Warsaw Pact) and of military movements, a summit of Communist Party leaders of the pact was held in Warsaw on July 14. The Czech party was neither invited nor even informed.[93] Excluded from the Warsaw meeting, it received on the other hand a letter of admonition explaining to it why the communist world was forced to interfere in developments over which the Czech party was losing all control. The party was asked to react urgently, with the promise of support from the fraternal parties.[94]

For Moscow, the decisive phase began at this moment, when Soviet will came up against a not less clearly proclaimed will. In place of self-criticism or an evasive answer to the remarks of the five parties, the Czech party replied that while it was aware of the possible dangers of the experiment in democratization it was in control of the process.

For the USSR, everything about the Czech attitude was intolerable. The condemnation of the experiment was to be developed out of the summits, conferences, and conversations organized by the Soviet leaders during the months preceding the invasion. This marathon began with the bilateral Soviet-Czech meeting in Čierna nad Tisou on July 29, where the Soviet Politburo confronted the Czech Politburo, to which had been added General Svoboda. The bilateral conferences of Čierna nad Tisou continued the next day in Bratislava, where the Soviet delegation was joined by delegations from the four other parties loyal to Moscow.[95] This extension of the Čierna conference was the result of intense Soviet pressure. The USSR, which had accepted a bilateral meeting to satisfy Czech demands for explanations, was anxious to return to a plenary meeting of the members of the Warsaw Pact. Since the conflict had begun to appear as serious as the previous great crises of the socialist world, the USSR had become determined to set a trap for Prague, a confrontation with the pact as a whole. For the Soviet leadership it was important not to repeat the duels of the years 1948 and 1956, not to present itself as a great power oppressing a smaller state, but as the older brother of a community of equals. This strategy, which was set in place at the Warsaw summit, was applied continuously until the end, despite Dubček's efforts to escape from this process of collective condemnation.

In Bratislava, the communist conclave managed to produce a declaration prepared by the USSR.[96] This text repeated the great principles on which the socialist community is based—equality, respect for sovereignty and national independence, territorial integrity, mutual fraternal aid and solidarity—but at the same time it made explicit the conditions under which the security and progress of the socialist community could be assured. Behind the well-known phraseology of egalitarian relations and mutual aid, the conditions under which the pressure of all could be exercised against the sovereignty of rebellious states began to be perceptible.[97] This text however seemed to suggest that an agreement had been reached, and that political debate had replaced threats. This illusion was strengthened by the intervention in the Moscow-Prague conflict (a bilateral conflict not really disguised by the broadening of the conferences) of various participants, concerned either with helping Prague or with strengthening the pact's arguments.[98] Outbursts in the Soviet press then increased, throwing a shadow over the apparent consensus.[99] To the open political pressure thus brought to bear on Czechoslovakia was added, and this was the most serious, military pressure.

The extended maneuvers that had surrounded the Warsaw summit were in this respect only a warning. The time necessary for the evacuation of foreign troops was in fact so extended that they never completely left the country during the entire crisis. A provocation, picked up by the Soviet press, allowed this state of affairs to be perpetuated. While the evacuation of the troops who had come for the July maneuvers was in progress, *Pravda* announced the discovery in Bohemia near the German border of American plans preparing for an intervention in Eastern Europe. The discovery of an arms cache added to the credibility of the documents that were quoted.[100] Despite American denials and protests from the Czech authorities, the USSR immediately came to the conclusion that these discoveries justified a military reaction. The reaction came in two forms; the prolonged presence of some troops in Czechoslovakia and the proliferation of maneuvers on the western border of the USSR, in the GDR, and in Poland, that lasted until mid-August. There is no doubt that this permanent sound of boots explains why the Czechs finally raised in clear terms the question of foreign troop movements on their territory. The initiative, moreover, lay with the USSR. From the beginning of the Prague Spring, using the pretext of new international conditions, they had been calling for the stationing of a Warsaw Pact unit in Czechoslovakia.[101] Confronted with the Czechs' refusal to accept these troops and with their reluctance to agree to significant maneuvers on their territory at the time, the Soviet leaders reacted immediately. They had at first agreed to the principle of maneuvers being limited to command exercises; then they took advantage of the aggravation of the crisis to organize the very large-scale maneuvers of June and July and to limit the evacuation of troops. This explains why at the very moment when the Warsaw summit was meeting, General Prchlík, head of the Department of State Administration in the Central Committee of the Czech Communist Party, in a celebrated press conference, called into question the whole balance of national relations within the pact. Violently criticizing the privileged role of the USSR in the integrated command, the overwhelmingly dominant position of its military leaders, and the conditions under which troops were stationed and maneuvers conducted on the territories of the various states, he was in fact asking for a complete revision of the pact.[102]

There could be no doubt about the Soviet response. There was too great a distance between the Soviet high command's desire to station troops permanently on Czech territory and General Prchlík's demands for "egalitarian revision" to permit the slightest illusion. And in the heated atmosphere of the summer of 1968, Czech demands could only in return increase Soviet pressures. While the joint maneuvers of the USSR and its allies were taking place on the borders in late July and early August, Czechoslovakia was preparing for maneuvers that were scheduled to take place in central and western Bohemia on August 21 and 22 in the presence of allied observers. That would remove Czech troops from the borders and would open the way for troops from the pact.[103] It is clear that the USSR had carefully prepared the coup of August 21, 1986.

The intervention got under way during the night of August 20 and it involved significant forces, now evaluated at a half-million men, under the authority of General Pavlovsky.[104] Within thirty-six hours, Warsaw Pact armies controlled all of Czech territory. The speed and effectiveness of this intervention, the obvious surprise of Czech leaders, their lack of preparation while everything should have prepared them for the event—not only the threats, the incessant military maneuvers, but also the warnings issued by Soviet dissidents like General Grigorenko[105]—immediately pose a question. How can such lack of foresight be explained? Was it naïveté or the sense that the battle was lost before it began? Gordon Skilling, relying on varied sources, points out that a considerable part of the responsibility can be attributed to the infiltration of Czech intelligence services by the USSR.[106] In any event, the Czech leaders' choice when confronted with the invasion was the contrary of those made by the Yugoslavs and Hungarians in the past. General Svoboda, commander in chief of the Czech armed forces, in agreement with the party presidium ordered the people and the army not to resist. The army was confined to barracks and the population asked to adopt a passive and dignified stance. There is no doubt that the country's leaders, aware of their weakness and isolation and of the general hostility of neighboring states, thought that any resistance would have been suicidal. And perhaps they still hoped that their passive attitude would convince the USSR that Czechoslovakia had not left the path of socialism; in any case, they thought they were thereby depriving the intervention of any justification.

Although the USSR and its allies had no difficulty in carrying out their military program of the suppression of the Czech experiment and even provided a brilliant demonstration of their military capacities, things turned out entirely otherwise for the political side of the operation, which was the most important.

Unlike Hungary, which had broken its ties with the socialist camp by denouncing the Warsaw treaty and returning to a multiparty system that allowed the elimination of those responsible for such a shift, Czechoslovakia at the dawn of August 21 was led by a communist party and by political leaders who called themselves communists. It was unthinkable purely and simply to overthrow them by means of military operation; they had to be opposed by another legitimacy from within, which would justify the military intervention and the ensuing political changes.

The political scenario was simple. It had worked in Georgia in 1921 and would reappear later in Afghanistan. It consisted of invoking an appeal for help by a party threatened with counterrevolution to which the socialist "brothers" would respond. This was the meaning of the communiqué published by Tass on August 21.[107] The communiqué asserted that Warsaw Pact troops had responded to an appeal launched by party and state leaders so that they might oppose counterrevolutionary activities that threatened socialism.

Pravda immediately published a text by unidentified politicians, and thus from the beginning of the invasion the explanation of the situation that the USSR intended to offer was available: The political system was divided between a "minority group of right-wing opportunists" led by Dubček, which was opposed by the "healthy core" of the party.[108] This description of the Czech situation was intended to allow the installation of a pro-Soviet government, whose leader was initially supposed to be Alois Indra. This plan was supposed to unfold following stages that were different from those that were finally adopted. The conservatives were supposed to provoke an internal crisis, delay the Party Congress, and call for aid from the allies. Thus, coup d'état and external intervention would have coincided. But this operation turned out to be unworkable because of the cohesion of the party, even though the Soviet ambassador to Czechoslovakia, Chervonenko, assisted in the hours following the intervention by General Pavlovsky and by KGB representatives, engaged in intense activity to intimidate the members of the Central Committee and win them over to this scenario.[109] Unable to form a presentable government—the small group of aspirants, Indra, Bil'ak, and the like were unable to win over the Central Committee—the Soviet government had to resort to an unsatisfying and paradoxical solution, negotiations with Dubček and his colleagues. At the time of the invasion the governing group had been abducted and imprisoned in Soviet territory. At first, General Svoboda, who had come from Prague, was considered the only possible negotiating partner. He was the one whom Leonid Brezhnev attempted to convince of the need to form a new government and to lend his support to it. Confronted with Svoboda's opposition to this plan and his insistence that the leaders imprisoned in the USSR be associated with the discussions, Brezhnev gave way. This produced the astonishing spectacle of a negotiation about the future of Czechoslovakia carried on by men who had already failed to reach an understanding in Čierna nad Tisou: on the Soviet side, Brezhnev, Suslov, Kosygin, and Podgorny; on the Czech side, Dubček, Smrkovský, Černík, and Svoboda.[110] If we remember that the three principal Czech negotiators had moved without transition from the Soviet prison where they had been confined after their abduction to the negotiating table, we can have some sense of the political difficulties that the Soviet leaders had to deal with. The final communiqué, which emphasized the representative character of the negotiators (nineteen Czech participants confronting the entire Soviet Politburo, reinforced by the defense and foreign affairs ministers), was in general conciliatory, far from crisis and intervention.[111] Affirming that equality and sovereignty were the fundamental principles of Soviet-Czech cooperation, the text suggested that the troops that had come into Czechoslovakia would have to keep out of internal political affairs and would leave the country as soon as the situation had returned to normal.

Reading this text and the list of Czech leaders present, it is difficult to reconcile it with a state of war and with the treatment accorded a few days earlier to the Czechs and Slovaks who were present. The communiqué is more comprehensible in light of the secret protocol that accompanied it, specifying Soviet demands.[112] The agreement reached in Moscow allowed the Dubček group to remain in place for a year; the party, whose Fourteenth Congress would be obliterated from official history, changed its governing bodies by including both those who had been elected at the clandestine conference and conservative elements supported by the USSR. A strange cohabitation characterized Czech political life for a few months longer. Pro-Soviets and reformers lived side by side; day after day Dubček and Svoboda rubbed elbows with the country's real authorities, the Soviet ambassador and his collaborators. A silent population was constantly confronted with the occupation forces. These were ambiguous months during which no one would understand the meaning of the juxtaposition of blatant occupation and an appearance of autonomous political life; no one would know why the occupiers had to be accepted silently and without resisting; no one would ask the principal question: What is the truth, a compromise that preserves the essentials, or an ultimatum accepted out of despair? In 1969 "normalization" put an end to this numbing transition and plunged an entire people into a darkness like the one it had experienced thirty years earlier.

The Soviet-Czech crisis of 1968 is infinitely more difficult to follow than the crises of 1956 because, spread out over several months, it revealed Soviet attitudes that were less coherent than those evidenced in the earlier, briefer crises. If we look carefully at the Kremlin's reactions and initiatives from January to August 1968 we can discern unchanging elements but also some very clear breaks. From the moment the plenary assembly of the Czech Communist Party had proclaimed its intention to remove socialism from the Stalinist orbit, the Soviet leadership, followed by several leaders of fraternal parties, adopted a critical and anxious position. This anxiety was reinforced by Czech leaders during the preparatory meeting for a world conference of communist parties held in Budapest in February 1968. While Mikhail Suslov, representing the USSR, argued very forcefully in favor of greater unity within the communist movement and for the adoption of a common resolution—a program of action imposed on all parties—the spokesman of the Czech Communist Party, Vladimir Kúcký, seemed without joining their camp to be adopting the arguments of the Yugoslav and Rumanian "dissidents." To the unitary argument of the USSR he opposed an appeal for the recognition of differences; he also supported the reintegration of those who had been excluded and those who were absent. The Rumanians, who were hostile to Suslov's position, made a conspicuous departure from the conference, and the representative from Czechoslovakia seemed to take on their role.[113] In the face of these developments, which seemed to be leading Czechoslovakia down the path that Yugoslavia had followed in the past and that Rumania was following in the present, Dubček's statements of friendship toward the USSR carried little weight. From February 1968 on the USSR had been considering the risks to communist solidarity posed by the changes in Prague and had been urging the fraternal parties to share its concern. This preoccupation, expressed before any criticism of Czech ideas about "socialism with a human face," remained constant in the USSR. In response, the leaders of the Czech Communist Party constantly repeated in the bilateral and multilateral meetings forced on them by the USSR the same themes. The movement that had started in January was intended only to rid communism of its Stalinist excrescences. Undertaken by the party, this revision remained under its control and would not be affected by deviations of the right or the left. The experiment of "socialism with a human face" was limited to domestic politics and would have no effect on Czechoslovakia's international commitments. Dubček thus seemed to be inspired by earlier conflicts in the socialist camp, to be relying on their lessons, and to be placing himself in the line of the declaration of October 30, 1956, as a kind of protection. However, the USSR, revealing another constant aspect of its attitude, immediately noticed that the situation in 1968 differed from the one that existed in 1956; Moscow thereby implicitly dismissed the idea that the declaration of October 1956 could be used as a normative document for contemporary intersocialist relations.

The October 30, 1956, declaration defined the nature of the relations of the USSR with the other socialist states and was thus placed in a bilateral framework, but the Czech crisis of 1968 was located in a multilateral framework. The USSR did not present itself as Czechoslovakia's privileged negotiating partner, as the leader of the system, but took refuge behind the system's collective institution, the Warsaw Pact. There is no doubt that this was nothing but a tactical maneuver. The Czech crisis was taken over by the USSR and it was a crisis in Soviet-Czech relations. But from January to August 1968 Soviet strategy was characterized by the deliberate design of the USSR to transform a crisis that it was confronting and attempting to resolve into a problem for the socialist bloc. Although there were bilateral meetings—and Czechoslovakia, not wanting to be caught in the trap that had caught Tito twenty years before, insisted on its determination to have face-to-face dialogues with leaders in the USSR—Brezhnev took pains to emphasize that these bilateral meetings were normal for Warsaw Pact countries, but that essential questions would be decided in the major multilateral summits of Dresden and Bratislava. The Warsaw meeting of May 1968, without Czech participation, clearly expressed the Soviet plan. Like the Cominform in the past, the general meetings were veritable tribunals called on to apply discipline and collective rules on countries that were guilty of deviation. Thus although the bloc had not come to an agreement to recreate common norms, the USSR accomplished the same thing in practice.

Moreover, the declaration of October 30, 1956, specified that the principles of sovereignty and noninterference were established at the heart of intersocialist relations. In its relations with Czechoslovakia in 1968, the USSR constantly reiterated that these principles governed relations between two countries of the system, notably the relations that it maintained with sister states. But at the same time it outlined the limits of this notion of sovereignty. The Warsaw Pact, a collective body, the center of agreement, had the responsibility to preserve communist regimes. Whenever these regimes were in danger the notion of sovereignty lost all meaning, since the sovereignty in question was that of states for which the principles of communism made up the framework for development. On several occasions, the USSR gave concrete indications of its conception of the limits of sovereignty precisely by appealing to those who could challenge it, Czechs who disagreed with their government. Two examples will illustrate the point: The Soviet press—at the very moment when the bilateral meeting demanded by the Czechs was taking place at Čierna nad Tisou—published a letter from workers in a Prague factory addressed to "our Soviet friends" and requesting their presence to ensure the safety of socialism and of those who like the signatories felt threatened by the current deviations.[114] The supposed call for help, which was invoked at the time of the intervention, fits into the same logic. In the end, it hardly matters whether these letters were or were not written and sent to Soviet leaders. What does matter is the communitarian logic that, based on a restrictive interpretation of sovereignty, justified in advance in Soviet eyes all later military actions.

A final point is connected to these two. During most of the crisis, at least from May onward, the USSR used the threat of military intervention. By linking together domestic developments in Czechoslovakia, their consequences and international repercussions, and the responsibility of the Warsaw Pact, the USSR generally left little room for autonomous action or independent initiatives by the Prague leaders. During the entire crisis, they were treated if not as adversaries at least as dangerously irresponsible, and that led to the conclusion that the community had to guard against them with every resource, including military force. In this connection, although the intervention of August 21 was surprising in the light of the consensus reached at Bratislava, it was not a total surprise. It is clear that the military option was present throughout the process.

In the context of the constant elements in the Soviet attitude, two breaks in these event-filled months are difficult to explain in rational terms.

Toward the end of May 1968 after three months of unbridled criticism, the USSR suddenly seemed to calm down and take note in a limited and not very detailed way of decisions made in Prague, like the calling of the Fourteenth Congress. Even more, the statements made by Czech leaders on the solidarity between the two countries were given prominence, as though to emphasize that that aspect of things was more important than the recent difficulties.[115] But immediately after this brief lull, the tone sharpened again and emphasis was again placed on the internal deviations and the revisionism of the Czech Communist Party. To denounce these deviations, many members of the Politburo and of the Soviet Academy of Sciences were mobilized. The most spectacular polemic was carrried out by the academician Konstantinov who attacked Czech developments in theoretical terms asserting that Leninism was the real target of the Prague revisionists. This was a crime of lèse-majesté that the USSR could never allow to be committed.[116] In this climate of renewed violence came the Warsaw meeting and the letter of the five to the Czech party, whose text, it is important to point out, was widely disseminated in the Soviet press while the Czech party's answer disappeared from sight. Thus Prague seemed to have accepted the indictment. An even more remarkable lull seemed to set in early in August during the summits at Čierna nad Tisou and Bratislava. The communiqué published after the meeting between Brezhnev and Dubček evoked the atmosphere "of complete frankness, sincerity, and mutual understanding" that had surrounded the summit. Moreover, the Bratislava declaration could be considered a charter for solidarity among the countries of the pact, co-signed by Czechoslovakia, which thus seemed to be reintegrated into the family circle. The August 21 coup resounded in a context of relative optimism, all the more so because the troops still remaining in Czechoslovakia after the maneuvers had been withdrawn.

Several questions are raised by the continuity of the political and military threats weighing on Czechoslovakia and the breaks in the hostility demonstrated by the USSR. Why did the USSR invade Czechoslovakia? Was that end to the Prague Spring part of the Soviet plan from the beginning or was it the result of decisions made during the course of the crisis? Finally, why did the invasion occur on August 21 when an agreement appeared to have been reached at Bratislava? In the last analysis, what was the value of that agreement? Was it a ruse designed to prepare the invasion effectively and to take Dubček by surprise, or a failed agreement?

To uncover the causes of the invasion, we have to pose the question in more precise terms and ask whether the USSR considered the Czechoslovak affair dangerous to the extent that it concluded that no compromise could be reached; that only pure and simple suppression of such an experiment was imaginable. There is hardly any doubt that for many reasons the Soviet leaders held this to be certain. It was unacceptable to them to see an alternative model opposed to the model of socialism they offered and embodied. To be sure, since 1956 Poland had followed a national road with the agreement of the USSR; and as early as 1955 Khrushchev had explicitly admitted that Belgrade had similar rights. But by 1968 Khrushchev's successors had in many respects long been convinced that he had opened dangerous breaches in a system whose solidity depended on coherence and immobility. The variants of socialism were among the breaches that urgently needed closing. The Soviet conception of a viable political system had become exceedingly clear by the time the Prague Spring began. It included the affirmation of the leading role of the party, the solidity of political structures, and an eminent position for the principle of democratic centralism. Moscow thought that these elements in some cases were being attenuated to the point of disappearance by the course of events in Czechoslovakia. The fact that the conception of "socialism with a human face" that gradually came out of the Prague Spring was incompatible with a return to Leninist conservatism, which was being carried out at the same time in the USSR, was indisputable. These opposite developments were aggravated by the manner in which the Czech program was presented and by Dubček's incorrect and to some extent naive perception of Soviet behavior. To present the developments occurring in Czechoslovakia as a search for "democratic socialism" or a "socialism with a human face" was to suggest that the socialism existing until then was neither.[117] Not only were Soviet concepts roughly treated but also the pride of the "first socialist state in history," just as that pride had suffered harsh blows after the Čierna and Bratislava meetings, which were hailed in Czechoslovakia, in Eastern Europe (particularly in Albania and Rumania), and in the western world as a "Czech triumph" and a "Soviet defeat."[118] While Poland had always before the mid-seventies contrived to accommodate its powerful neighbor by emphasizing that it was in no way deviating from the model that was offered to it, the leaders of the Prague Spring, careful to reassure the USSR on the future of the alliance, were less concerned to affirm their loyalty to the Leninist political model. The Prague Spring offered both the example of a concrete search for a national communist path and a theoretical justification for that path, since it was described in terms that were supposed to be new and attractive, like "democratic" and "human." This was not only to insist on the pluralism that was possible in the conceptions of institutional communism but also to cast the Soviet model into the realm of imperfection and backwardness. The singleness of the model and its perfection were challenged simultaneously.

It is indisputable that Dubček, inexperienced in leading the state and carrying on intersocialist relations, failed to perceive what was important to the USSR. First of all, he thought of the situation of 1968 in the light of the events of 1956, when the USSR had been particularly anxious about loyalty to the Warsaw Pact. But in 1968 what was supremely important to the USSR was the unity of communism expressed by adhesion to one model and by recognition of its authority. Those elements were particularly important for Moscow in 1968 precisely because they were being challenged. Since 1956 Soviet primacy had been denounced by China; it would never again be accepted by Yugoslavia; it had been rejected by Rumania and Albania. With the exception of Rumania, all the rebellious states also criticized the political model that the USSR offered them and thereby no longer recognized its authority. Moreover, in 1968 the USSR was also confronted with a rapid evolution of the European socialist camp, of which Rumania was an extreme example but not the only one. This evolution was assisted by the Western policy of building bridges with the socialist states and affirming their right to autonomous existence. Dubček misperceived the impact of this context. He was convinced that by affirming his country's loyalty to the alliance he would earn the right to reform the domestic system. Beyond this anachronistic perception of Soviet demands, we must also take into account his lack of experience in dealing with the political world. Dubček had hoped by using conciliatory language to convince his adversaries of his good faith. Because he was aware of a certain division within the Soviet political leadership about the proper solutions to the Czech problem, he had hoped by his temperate attitude to gain their confidence, but this was totally refused. Relying on understanding, he paid no attention to the warnings he received to negotiate in terms of strength. He thought it wise to respond to threats with conciliatory gestures, instead of following Tito's example by answering threatening statements with equally harsh responses, placing himself in the same realm of military retaliation. Clearly Dubček never seriously considered the possibility of invasion, hoping by his confidence in the myth of fraternal relations to disarm his opponents and to block them from recourse to military means. This was a dangerous misconception of the elements that underlay the Politburo's decisions.

If we examine the behavior of the Kremlin from January to August 1968, we are led to accept the argument of Skilling and Jiří Valenta according to which the possibility of military intervention was always considered as one means, although not the only one, of dealing with the Czech crisis.[119] The division within the Soviet leadership on the appropriateness of using this means cannot be doubted, and there are many signs that the debates were lengthy. But as soon as Moscow decided that the Prague experiment posed genuine and unavoidable dangers to the whole system, it was clear that the military argument had gained new strength. The USSR had always asserted that military force should be used on every occasion against a political or military threat. And beyond the fears that the Soviet leaders felt for Czechoslovakia itself and for the risks of contagion in certain other socialist states, they were also alarmed about their own citizens. In the Ukraine, in fact, the Czech affair almost became a domestic matter when it brought about a reawakening of the nationalist movement in the Prešov region of eastern Czechoslovakia, populated by Ukrainians, related to those who had been absorbed by the USSR in 1945.[120] This "Ukrainianization" of the Prague Spring on the borders of Soviet Ukraine, although it delighted the Ukrainians of the USSR, was particularly troubling for Moscow, always alarmed by any resurgence of Ukrainian nationalism. Although it is difficult to evaluate the precise weight of the Ukrainian "danger" in the hardening of the Soviet attitude toward Prague, it is impossible to deny that this factor had some effect. In the Soviet debate, the voices of leaders of Ukrainian origin, Podgorny and Pyotr Shelest (the leader of the Ukrainian Communist Party), were loud in their insistence that the troubling effects of the Czech crisis on the Ukraine could not be ignored.[121] Nor was it a matter of indifference that the chief Soviet military leader, Marshal Grechko, and the Soviet Ambassador to Prague, S. Chervonenko, were Ukrainians. Aware of the frustrations of their compatriots, probably careful not to be accused of national deviations, the Ukrainians of the Soviet "establishment" were the most ardent defenders of the military argument.[122] At Čierna nad Tisou, as we know, the Soviet delegation called on Shelest's testimony to accuse the Czechs of engaging in separatist propaganda in the Sub-Carpathian Ukraine.[123] Confronted with a risk of internal contagion, the Soviet leaders (whatever their internal divisions)[124] adopted the argument for intervention at a moment that most historians still hesitate to identify, some point between August 6 and August 17.[125] What should be noted is that on August 6 General Shtemenko was appointed commander-in-chief of the Warsaw Pact forces and that this promotion of a man who had been tied to Stalin and who had admired him, although it may not have meant the immediate setting in motion of the war machine, seemed freighted with implicit threats.[126]

Whatever the developments in Prague may have been, whatever Dubček's concessions or blunders, in the last analysis, the fate of the Prague Spring was decided in Moscow, in the Politburo, by weighing a multitude of Soviet domestic factors and elements affecting the interests of the USSR. The "elder brother" felt himself alone responsible for the fate of his turbulent sibling.

*   *   *

The fifteen years from 1953 to 1968 were a profoundly contradictory period. On the one hand, Stalinism disappeared with Stalin. But on the other hand, the inclinations of the peoples subjected by Stalin to reject Stalinism were in every case broken. That the means used to accomplish this were various matters less than the characteristic common to all the crises, Moscow's refusal to allow the peoples of Eastern Europe to follow the paths that seemed most fitted to their traditions and to the wishes of the populations. These decisive years began with the intervention of tanks in East Berlin, continued with the crushing of the Hungarian revolution, and ended with the annihilation of the Prague Spring. They were to be sure placed under the sign of renewal, but that renewal was always accompanied in the background by the noise of rolling tanks and rumbling cannons. This strange and tragic period, torn between the wildest hopes and the deepest despair, when everything seemed possible and then, suddenly, all possibilities were destroyed by naked force, transformed Eastern Europe into an unstable zone in which each country, one after another, was seized by the flames of national passion. The "revolutionary spark" struck by the USSR in 1945 had produced this unexpected result and its promoters had to change themselves into firefighters. But hardly had they put out one fire when another was lit. Or else, as the example of Poland shows, the fire never ceased to burn because the coals remained lit beneath the ashes.

NOTES

1.   Speech by Malenkov, *Izvestia*, March 16, 1953; in Eisenhower's declaration of April 16, 1953, the agreement with Austria was one of the necessary conditions for change in the international arena, according to a comment in *Pravda*, April 25, 1953.

2.   Molotov openly showed his disagreement with the policy of openness; Chester E. Bohlen, *Witness to History—1929–1960* (New York, 1973), 380–81.

3.   The riots have been very well analyzed in S. Brant, *The East German Rising of 17th June 1953* (London, 1955).

4.   Phillip Windsor, *City on Leave: A History of Berlin* (New York, 1964), 154, quoted by M. Heller and A. Nekrich, *L'Utopie au pouvoir* (Paris, 1982), 435; L. Nagy, *Démocraties populaires* (Paris, 1968), 159.

5.   Heller and Nekrich, *L'Utopie au pouvoir*, 437.

6.   *Izvestia*, December 17 and 24, 1953, published these accusations against Beria.

7.   See the excellent work by Charles H. Fairbanks, Jr., "National Cadres as a Force in the Soviet System: The Evidence of Beria's Career, 1949–1953," in J. Azrael, ed., *Soviet Nationality Policies and Practices* (New York, 1978), 144–89, particularly 162ff.

8.   R. Fritsch-Bournazel, *L'U.R.S.S. et les Allemagnes* (Paris, 1978), 75, suggests that the fact that Ambassador Semonov was not dismissed after the riots even though he too had advocated relaxation of constraints in Berlin, indicates that Beria was not isolated. She also notes that in *Izvestia* on March 10, 1967, Khrushchev accused Malenkov of having supported Beria in this policy.

9.   André Fontaine, *Histoire de la guerre froide* (2 vols., Paris 1966–67), 2:222.

10.   See Khrushchev's statement in *Pravda*, May 10, 1955, and the June 2 communiqué, *Pravda*, June 3, 1955.

11.   Robert Tucker in a letter to the author in 1976 said that these memories have an authentic "ring."

12.   Khrushchev, *Souvenirs* (Paris, 1970), 355–72.

13.   Ibid., 358.

14.   Ibid., 359.

15.   Ibid., 359.

16.   Ibid., 358.

17.   *Pravda*, March 9 and 12, 1955.

18.   Khrushchev, op. cit., 361.

19.   Molotov criticized it in the July plenum, *Pravda*, July 16, 1955.

20.   *Dvadsatyi s'ezd Kommunisticheskoi Partii Sovetskogo Soiuza* (Moscow, 1956), 1:20–42.

21.   Ibid., 20–21.

22.   Ibid.

23.   Ibid., 38–40.

24.   Ibid., 39.

25.   Khrushchev, op. cit., 333.

26.   Ibid.

27.   Central Committee resolution, June 30, 1956, quoted by Heller and Nekrich, op. cit., p. 443.

28.   François Fejtö, *Budapest, 1956* (Paris, 1969), 15.

29.   The narrative of events in Poland presented here is based on P. E. Zinner, ed., *National Communism and Popular Revolt in Eastern Europe: A Selection of Documents on Events in Poland and Hungary, February–November 1956* (New York, 1956); Francois Fejtö, *Histoire des démocraties populaires* (Paris, 1952), vol. 2; A. Bromkl, *Poland's Politics: Idealism vs. Realism* (Cambridge, Mass., 1967); G. Sakwa, "The Polish October," *Polish Review* 23, 3(1978):62–78.

30.   N. Davies, *God's Playground*, 2 vols. (Oxford, 1981), 2:582.

31.   Quoted from Davies, op. cit., 582–83.

32.   H. Stehle, *Eastern Politics of the Vatican, 1917–1979* (Athens, Ohio, 1981).

33.   A. Michnik, *L'Eglise et la gauche—le dialogue polonais* (Paris, 1979), quoted in *Problems of Communism* 31 (Jan.–Feb. 1982):7.

34.   Davies, op. cit., 583, argues for suicide; Adam Ulam, op. cit., 578, concludes that he died from a heart attack.

35.   A. Ulam, op. cit., 578.

36.   Davies, op. cit., 584.

37.   More than 50 dead and 500 seriously wounded according to *Nowa Kultura*, October 20, 1957.

38.   *Pravda*, July 4 and 16, 1956, referred to the existence of a counterrevolutionary plot in Poland.

39.   Davies, op. cit., 585.

40.   Ibid. Khrushchev in his *Memoirs*, 399–400, is quite silent on this episode and suggests that the Polish situation was very easily settled.

41.   For Hungary, see Zimmer, op. cit.; Zimmer, *Revolution in Hungary* (New York, 1962); François Fejtö, *Budapest 1956* (Brussels, 1982); W. Brus, P. Kenda, and Z. Mlynar, *Processus de normalisation en Europe centrale soviétisee*, (Cologne, 1983); Kiraly and Jonas, eds., *The Hungarian Revolution of 1956 in Retrospect* (Boulder, Colo., 1978).

42.   On Mikoyan's mission, see *Pravda*, October 5, 1956.

43.   François Fejtö, *Budapest 1956* (Paris, 1966), 73, notes this opposition.

44.   Ibid., 75.

45.   Many writers, among them Fejtö, op. cit., 15, and Adam Bromke, "Poland," in Kiraly and Jonas, op. cit., 90, quite correctly point out that in a central Europe divided by many oppositions among peoples, the Hungarians and the Poles represent an exception in their lasting friendship, which was always preserved, even when, as Bromke notes, they were at war with one another.

46.   Zbigniew Brzezinski, *The Soviet Bloc* (Cambridge, Mass., 1960), 225.

47. *Pravda*, October 25, 1956.

48. *Pravda*, October 31, 1956.

49. Khrushchev, *Memoirs*, 396.

50. *Pravda*, October 28, 1956.

51. *Pravda*, October 31, 1956.

52. Kiraly and Jonas, op. cit., 59.

53. Khrushchev, op. cit., 339–400.

54. Fischer-Galati, in Kiraly and Jonas, op. cit., 97.

55. Khrushchev, op. cit., 400.

56. Kiraly and Jonas, op. cit., 109–11.

57. Khrushchev, op. cit., 400, and Paul Zimmer, in Kiraly and Jonas, op. cit., 116, on Czechoslovakia. See also O. Hick, "Czechoslovakia—Stable Satellite," *Problems of Communism* 7 (Sept.–Oct. 1958):32–39.

58. It appeared in *Pravda* on October 31, 1956 at a time when the Hungarian command was informed of troop movements at the border.

59. Heltai, in Kiraly and Jonas, op. cit., 53.

60. Bromke, in Kiraly and Jonas, op. cit., 91.

61. Ibid. This text was published in *Nowa Kultura*, November 25, 1956.

62. Khrushchev, op. cit., 396, repeating all the themes of Soviet criticism of November 1956.

63. Kiraly and Jonas, op. cit., 1–2.

64. Ibid., 2. "The entire fortress, apparently invincible, had collapsed in a few days."

65. As early as 1954 Khrushchev thought of replacing him as he did with the leaders of other countries. S. Fischer-Galati, *The New Rumania: From People's Democracy to Socialist Republic* (Cambridge, Mass., 1967), 45–60.

66. Khrushchev, op. cit., 480.

67. Khrushchev emphasizes precisely the confidence that the USSR had in Bodnaras for the biographical reasons indicated. He also points out that one of Bodnaras's arguments was that the attachment of Rumanian communities to the existing political system, far from requiring the support of Soviet troops, would be strengthened by their departure. Khrushchev admits that he was shaken by this discussion, ibid., 481–82.

68. Ibid., 492.

69. Rumanian developments described here are based on B. Cioranescu, "Revirement politique," in *Aspects des relations russo-roumaines* (Paris, 1967), 227–39; D. Floyd, *Rumania: Russia's Dissident Ally* (New York, 1965), particularly 70ff; S. Fischer-Galati, in Kiraly and Jonas, op. cit. 98, and *The Socialist Republic of Rumania* (Baltimore, 1969); J. M. Montias, *Economic Development in Communist Rumania* (Cambridge, Mass., 1967), particularly 187 and 220.

70. The Rumanian text of what was a veritable declaration of independence was published in *Scinteia*, April 23, 1964; for an English translation, see W. E. Griffith, *Sino-Soviet Relations* (Cambridge, Mass., 1967), 269ff.

71. G. Cioranescu, op. cit., 237–39.

72. At the Comecon meeting in July 1963 the USSR implicitly recognized Rumania's freedom to preserve its plan and to reject any supranational planning.

73. In the declaration published to celebrate the forty-fifth anniversary of the

Rumanian Communist Party, Ceauşescu proclaimed among other things that military pacts were anachronistic and that the USSR ought to respect its neighbors, at the risk of seeing a revival of legitimate demands. This was an obvious allusion to territorial problems. The declaration was published in *Scinteia* on May 8, 1966.

74.   The tone of these reactions is clearly demonstrated in an article in *Pravda* on February 6, 1967 commenting on Rumanian recognition of West Germany.

75.   See the excellent article by G. Haupt, "La genèse du conflit soviéto-roumain," *Revue française de science politique* 8, no. 4 (August 1980).

76.   I borrow both the title of this section and the summary of events from the indispensable study by G. H. Skilling, *Czechoslovakia's Interrupted Revolution* (Princeton, 1976); see also G. Golan, *Reform Rule in Czechoslovakia: The Dubček Era 1968–1969* (Cambridge, Mass, 1973); V. Kusin, ed., *The Czechoslovak Reform Movement 1968* (London, 1973); J. Pelikan, *The Secret Vysočany Congress—Proceedings and Documents of the Extraordinary XIV Congress of the Communist Party of Czechoslovakia* (London, 1971); J. Valenta, *Soviet Intervention in Czechoslovakia—1968* (Baltimore, 1979).

77.   *Pravda,* January 30, 1968, provided a very favorable account of Dubček's visit to Moscow.

78.   *Pravda,* April 23, 1968; see the article by Zagladin in *Pravda,* April 29, 1968.

79.   Thus, for example, during the celebration of the anniversary of the "Prague Coup," Brezhnev, who had come to the Czech capital, praised in his speech the virtues of the country and its "internationalist socialism." *Pravda,* February 23, 1968. The same newspaper had reprinted a long article by Dubček on February 21.

80.   Quoted by J. Valenta, op. cit., 29, following testimony by Smrkovský in Valenta's presence.

81.   *Pravda* reported on it on May 5, 6, and 7, 1968.

82.   *Pravda,* on August 22, 1968, stated that during this visit, Dubček had already recognized the dangers of his policies and committed himself to rectifying them.

83.   See the article by Marshal Yakubovsky, commander in chief of the Warsaw Pact, in *Pravda,* May 14, 1968, and Gromyko's warnings in *Pravda,* June 28, 1968.

84.   *Pravda,* May 9, 1968, and the article by Kolesnichenko commenting on the summit in *Pravda,* May 12, 1968.

85.   "We should note that during Kadar's visit to Moscow in July, Brezhnev became pressing and emphasized the dangers of the Czech crisis and the necessary solidarity among party chiefs of the Pact." G. Skilling, op. cit., 250. See *Pravda,* July 4, 1968.

86.   G. Skilling, op. cit., 251–60.

87.   Notes of conversations that the author had with Jiří Hájek in Prague in September 1969.

88.   Alexandrov, in *Pravda,* July 11, 1968, called it "counterrevolutionary."

89.   *Pravda,* July 4, 1968.

90.   *Pravda,* July 6, 1968.

91.   *Pravda,* July 16, 1968. *Krasnaia Zvezda,* on July 12, 1968, emphasized like Kosygin, but evoking the pact as an alliance, that the common duty of socialist states was to be vigilant.

92. G. Skilling, op. cit., 254.

93. See *Pravda*, July 16, 1968, for the communiqué about the Warsaw meeting.

94. The text of the letter appeared in *Pravda*, July 18, 1968, and *Kommunist*, July 1968, 3–10.

95. *Pravda*, August 2, 1968. G. Skilling, op. cit., 304, notes that the conference has been little mentioned, and he has published Smrkovský's notes on Soviet demands as an appendix, 882–83. After the invasion, *Pravda*, August 22, 1968, asserted that the Czechs were in agreement with the Soviets at Čierna, but that they went back on their word.

96. Published in *Pravda*, August 7. See the commentaries on the conference in *Pravda*, August 6 and 8.

97. G. Skilling, op. cit., 308, notes a subtle distinction in the formulation. "Respect" (of sovereignty) is expressed in Russian by *uvajenie* (moral respect), in Czech by *zachování* (preservation).

98. Fitting into this category were Waldeck Rochet's proposals for a discussion of the problem in a large meeting of European communist parties; *L'Humanité*, May 18, 1970, published the minutes of Waldeck Rochet's meeting with Dubček. János Kádár played the role of an intermediary between the two opponents during a visit to Moscow in July, *Pravda*, July 4, 1968, and in Karlovy Vary in the middle of August, *Pravda*, August 17, 1968.

99. The themes of Soviet attacks can be divided into three groups: 1) the criteria of a Leninist party—by definition those that developments in Prague had rejected. See for example Radionov, in *Pravda*, July 30 and August 9, 1968; Zhukov, in *Pravda*, July 26, 1968, called the "democratic socialism" demanded by Czechoslovakia a "social-democratic slogan leading to an anti-socialist and anti-Marxist political system."; 2) Czechoslovakia had "betrayed" the Bratislava agreements. See for example the article by Zhukov in *Pravda*, August 16, 1968; 3) The link between the activities of the "Czech deviationists" and German "revanchism." *Pravda*, July 22, 23, and 26, 1968.

100. *Pravda*, July 19, 1968.

101. See the article by General Yakubovsky in *Krasnaia Zvezda*, June 22, 1968; G. Skilling, op. cit., 635, writes that Soviet demands amounted to the stationing of ten to twenty thousand men.

102. *Pravda*, July 16, 1968. See the analysis of this event in Kusin, op. cit., 44ff.

103. G. Skilling, op. cit., 713.

104. On the various estimates and their sources, the best summary is in ibid., 713.

105. Grigorenko, *Mémoires* (Paris, 1980), 561–64.

106. Skilling, op. cit., 714. In a conversation with Jiří Hájek in Prague in September 1969 the author asked this question and did not receive a different answer.

107. *Pravda*, August 22, 1968, published the text of this "appeal," which supported the communiqué published by Tass on the 21st. On the authenticity of the appeal, see Skilling, op. cit., 716, who points out that in August 1968 all members of the Czech party, even the most conservative, asserted that they had not participated in the appeal. Skilling reminds us that in December 1970 the argument of the appeal was taken up by a plenum of the Czech party but that, although the text that was

supposed to have forty signatures on it was invoked by Bil'ak who claimed to have it in his possession, no one has ever seen it. Jiří Pelikan also maintains that it never existed. This was also the thesis of Antonín Snejdárek.

108.   *Pravda* editorial, August 22, 1968.

109.   See the well documented analysis by Jiri Valenta, op. cit., 148–54; Skilling, op. cit., 716–17, R. Lowenthal, "Sparrow in the Cage," *Problems of Communism* (Nov.–Dec. 1968):2–28. Antonín Snejdárek has fully confirmed this analysis, which can also be found in Pavel Tigrid, *Why Dubček Fell* (London, 1971), 113–35.

110.   Valenta, op. cit., 151.

111.   *Pravda*, August 28, 1968.

112.   The text has been published in several variants. On these variants, see Skilling, op. cit., 799–800.

113.   *Pravda*, February 22, 1968.

114.   *Pravda*, July 30, 1968.

115.   *Pravda*, June 8 and 17, 1968.

116.   For the Konstantinov-Císář polemic see *Pravda*, June 14 and 24, 1968.

117.   The April action program used the term "new model of socialist democracy," while the expression "socialism with a human face" appeared for the first time in late July 1968. Skilling, op. cit., 827.

118.   Valenta, op. cit., 157, who thinks that this blow to Soviet pride after Bratislava may have helped push the Soviet leaders to intervene.

119.   G. Skilling, op. cit., 719; Valenta, op. cit., 159. See also M. Lowenthal, loc. cit., 14, and the contribution of V. Aspaturian to W. Zartman, ed., *Czechoslovakia: Intervention and Impact* (New York, 1970), 15–46.

120.   G. Hodruett and P. Potichnij, *The Ukraine and the Czechoslovak Crisis* (Canberra, 1970), especially 70–91.

121.   Ibid., 80–84.

122.   At the time of his fall, Shelest was in fact accused of having promoted Ukrainian nationalism. See Y. Bilinsky in J. Azrael, ed., *Soviet Nationality Policies and Practices* (New York, 1978), 106.

123.   Testimony by Smrkovský, quoted by Skilling, op. cit., 882.

124.   Valenta, op. cit., 140–45, thinks that a group hostile to intervention gathered around Suslov, Kosygin, and Ponomarev and that the criticism of the conciliatory approach to the problem (*Soglashatel'skii podkhod, Pravda*, editorial, August 22, 1968) was aimed at this group. Brezhnev, who leaned toward intervention, apparently achieved a consensus in the Politburo after long debates.

125.   For Valenta, op. cit., 145, the struggle within the Politburo began on August 10 and led to agreement on intervention on August 17. The same pattern is seen by Lowenthal, loc. cit., 21, and Skilling, op. cit., 723.

126.   V. Suvorov, in *The Liberators: Inside the Soviet Army* (London, 1971), which contains a fascinating report on the behavior of Soviet troops in Czechoslovakia, suggests that one of the reasons for delaying the operation was to allow the harvest in the Ukraine to be completed, 153–54. See also *Krasnaia Zvezda*, August 6, 1968.

6

THE ART OF KETMAN

In *The Captive Mind*, Czeslaw Milosz writes that Poland adapted to Stalinism by practicing the art of Ketman that in feudal Persia allowed men to protect their lives or careers through concealment, hypocritical speech, duplicity, and deception. Gobineau noted in this connection that there was not a single true Muslim in Persia. And Milosz adds, there are very few true communists in Poland.[1]

In the fratricidal history of the socialist family, the development of Poland fully illustrates this penetrating judgment of his compatriots by Milosz. In the succession of crises that have periodically shaken Eastern Europe violently or beneath the surface, since 1953, those that occurred in Poland were remarkable in several respects. First, they were frequent; second, they occurred at shorter and shorter intervals; third, on the occasion of each crisis, the USSR seemed to push back the limits of what it had elsewhere considered "intolerable"; finally, at the end of each crisis, the system seemed incapable of choosing a clear solution, reformist as in Hungary, or conservative as in Czechoslovakia. Could this oscillation between contradictory choices, which periodically cost those in power another confrontation, last indefinitely?

Between the "Polish Road" and Sovietization: Perpetual Failure

Since 1956 Poland has experienced four crises in succession, four groups in power, and four failures for the government. The stages on this peculiar road are the landmarks of the last two decades: 1968, 1970, 1975–76, 1980.[2] And yet the period immediately following the 1956 crisis, a crisis which the communist party weathered because it had the wisdom to control the popular movement, had been promising.

Gomułka, who was brought to power by the party whose absolute authority he affirmed, was also an embodiment of the national spirit. The reforms in which he involved his country permanently changed the Polish system; agriculture was essentially decollectivized; the Polish church, gathered around the primate, Cardinal Wyszinski, was established as a coherent and autonomous social body confronting the state; and Polish intellectuals asserted their critical vocation. Since 1956, the socialist state, all powerful, incapable of adapting to a civil society that would moderate and influence it, has been forced to live with that civil society. This is the very essence of the Polish model.

For twelve years from 1956 to 1968 the "Polish road" seemed able to weld together the society and the political system and to give Gomułka a genuine legitimacy based on social consensus. In reality, the consensus that had existed since 1956 and the homage to the man who had embodied a certain resistance to the USSR began to weaken in the mid-sixties, because Gomułka gradually became satisfied with maintaining the system instead of continuing to reform it.

In March 1968 the explosion came from intellectual circles and was provoked by a hardening of government policy in cultural matters. The movement remained limited in its effects because the intellectuals were isolated; the working class ignored their uprising. But the regime was deeply shaken. It was able to measure the extent of social disenchantment in the rebellious universities. Two years later in 1970 the crisis of the consensus broke out in the part of society that had remained silent in 1968. The working class, in the Baltic ports first of all, rebelled against a rise in food prices. This social rejection, confirming economic failure after a critique of his political retreat, provoked Gomułka's fall. In fourteen years the hero of 1956 had lost all his popularity and all his legitimacy. Only the peasantry remained quiescent, because it remembered that it owed the return to private farming to Gomułka.

His successor, Edward Gierek, had in his turn to seek a compromise with society, and like Gomułka he at first enjoyed general support. His policies tended to try to cure all past faults, economic failures, political hardening, and the isolation of Poland. Workers' wages were increased; the peasants were relieved of forced deliveries to the state that they experienced as a form of servitude, and the state no longer bought their production at ridiculously low prices. For the rebellious intellectuals of 1968, censorship was softened and the borders partially opened. The state invested and incurred foreign debt.

The Polish "model" that thus emerged in 1970 was not so much political as economic. But freedom was gained from rapid economic progress and from modernization that drew support from Western aid. Finally, the Church openly presented itself as a spokesman for society. This mixture of purely economic reformism, of a search for a moderate social consensus, and of political firmness, was successful at the beginning. For a time Gierek seemed to have succeeded in gaining popular confidence through economic progress and by restoring the authority of the party. And as always strong national feeling served as the glue for the Polish experiment. But a few years were enough to show that the economic model had succeeded no better than had political liberalism.

By the middle of the seventies, the consensus sought by Gierek came apart over a dual crisis, political in late 1975, economic in 1976. In 1975, Gierek's regime, like Gomułka's a few years earlier, suddenly turned away from the reforming spirit that had won it the confidence of the social body. The first indication of the change was the reform of the constitution. The amendments adopted limited internal freedoms and the freedom of the Polish state. As in 1968, intellectuals and students mobilized against the amendments, thereby indicating to the regime that the truce had come to an end. As in 1968, their rebellion was solitary; the rest of the social body did not follow them. At this point we should emphasize that Gierek was not at liberty to avoid this constitutional reform. The USSR had imposed it on all its allies. Détente, which allowed Western capital to flow into Eastern Europe and produced movements on both sides of the ideological border and a certain relaxation of constraints, had an underside. Moscow feared that the opening to the West would bring about a weakening of the system and it reacted by tightening the controls. The Helsinki Conference, at which the USSR accepted the principles set out in the "third basket"—the free circulation of people and ideas, at least the Western world hoped it had won this concession—was a very important turning point in the history of the communist political system. For Moscow all the concessions, even the agreement on the "third basket," were justified, since the conference sanctioned the postwar European order, the division of Europe. But as soon as this confirmation of its objectives had been achieved, Moscow set about negating its own concessions. The new constitutions, various pieces of legislation, and an unmistakable harshness toward everyone who attempted to take advantage of the Helsinki provisions were the ways in which Moscow fulfilled its commitments and responded to Western illusions. It was in this context of the general hardening of the system that, repeating the 1970 crisis when Gomułka fell from power, the 1976 crisis took place.

The crisis of June 1976, though it began with economic realities, helped to change the political situation of Poland. As in 1970 the detonator was purely economic. The rise in food prices decreed on June 24, 1976, provoked violent reactions from the workers. Ursus and Radom were the scenes of the strongest demonstrations but the movement spread to several industrial centers. The government reacted in a disorganized and contradictory manner, revealing its confusion. It persecuted the workers who had participated in these events (with prison terms, physical abuse, the loss of jobs), but it also recognized as early as June 25 that it was incapable of imposing the price rises it had decided on. Finally, it tried to have the Church calm the working class.

Out of these contradictions, a new situation was born. The intellectuals, active opponents of the state in the constitutional crisis, who until then had been distant from the workers, mobilized to defend them.[3] The KOR (Workers' Defense Committee) was established for that purpose. At the same time the Polish Church spoke out in favor of the workers. From that moment on the Polish leaders who had been installed in 1970 found themselves in a situation as precarious as that of Gomułka in the late sixties. The economic model was producing vacillation; the society was united in a severe critique of the leaders who had revealed their uncertainties. On the eve of the crisis of the summer of 1980, the balance sheet for the last quarter century in Poland was ambiguous. The "Polish model" had failed in its two successive variants (political liberalism, economic success); concessions made to society in the course of various crises had for the most part been maintained, but at the same time they had been "nibbled" away, which reduced their effectiveness and created frustrations. This was particularly clear in the case of the peasantry. The decollectivization of the greater part of agriculture, although it was maintained, had not been compensated for by increased productivity, because the state had constantly attempted to call that concession into question by placing obstacles in the way of the private sector (by priorities granted to state farms, weak agricultural prices). Even if the peasantry in 1979 and 1980 was not a troublesome sector of society, it nevertheless did not support a government that it distrusted; and its low productivity weighed heavily on the economic life of the country. Although aware of this problem, the Warsaw government had done nothing to resolve it. Since the constitutional crisis of 1976, the Polish government had generally taken refuge in immobility instead of acting to forestall mounting discontent. The 1980 crisis was only the consequence of problems that had accumulated since then, while the political system that came up against them had not changed but had succeeded in unifying the whole society against it. Economic failure and political powerlessness, combined with a social movement that clearly expressed its discontent, were the decisive elements that brought about Gierek's fall. He had been used up much more quickly than Gomułka. His fall opened up a period of crisis that was infinitely more serious than that of 1970.

As in 1956, and in contrast to 1970, the crisis of 1980 reintroduced the USSR into the Polish arena. A concealed witness, but carrying considerable influence over the course of events, the USSR decided very quickly that the Poland of 1980 was not the Poland of 1956 or 1970 and that what was happening there, like the events in Budapest in 1956 and Prague in 1968, concerned the whole socialist community and not Poland alone. What explains this break in the Soviet Union's relative tolerance of its turbulent neighbor? Was it a change in the nature of the Polish crisis or a change in Soviet policy?

Solidarity: The Time of Compromise

The course of events in Poland sheds light on the Soviet attitude. The strikes that broke out in Poland in July 1980 seemed at first to be repeating the agitation of 1976 and the Soviet leaders left Gierek the task of finding the least costly solutions. The confidence in which Gierek was held in Moscow is obvious from reading the communiqué that concluded his traditional summer visit to Brezhnev on the shores of the Black Sea. The Brezhnev-Gierek conversations in late July involved no threatening summons to impose a political line decided on in Moscow.[4] It was only at the end of August, when it became clear that Gierek was out of his depth and when he had to negotiate with Solidarity, whose organization he had been unable to prevent, that the Soviet position changed. On August 31, 1980, the day the Gdańsk agreements were signed, the Soviet press for the first time used the word "strike" to characterize the events in Poland, a sign of disarray and considerable displeasure.[5] We must remember that this term was hardly ever used to characterize events in communist countries. By definition, strikes were confined to the capitalist world, where conflicts of that sort could take place. In the space of forty-eight hours, the analysis was refined and, although the Gdańsk agreements were barely mentioned, *Pravda* published an article under the signature of Petrov, that is, authorized by the Central Committee, which was an extremely troubled and threatening commentary on the Polish situation.[6] This collective article emphasized the fact that the affair was not purely Polish; it had an international dimension. What had happened in Poland, explained the Kremlin, and exactly what that was remained vague, was not the result of popular action but of a manipulation by elements hostile to socialism whose active agents were foreign to the Polish people. Petrov clearly identified them: they were the "imperialist" circles, Western press organizations, and finally Polish émigrés determined to destroy the Polish system. In this very violent attack against the workers' movement, *Pravda* nevertheless took pains to keep its distance. It was careful in fact to refer to an article in *Tribuna Ludu* and thus to emphasize that the USSR was in no way involved in the affair. Nevertheless, the authors of the article thought it appropriate to recall that the geo-strategic position of Poland was very important. The reactions of the Soviet press show that Moscow was attacking the Polish government for its lack of ability, but the agreements reached with Solidarity were not being condemned. Gierek's inability to control events was what counted, and that explains the repeated insistence on necessary replacements in the leadership.[7] The fact that Kania, who had participated in the

Gdańsk agreements, replaced Gierek indicates that for the Soviet leaders Gierek's failure had condemned him and that they hoped for more cleverness on the part of his replacement in restoring the authority of the party, which had been seriously undermined in the negotiations with Solidarity.

During the three months following the Gdańsk agreements, the USSR remained as far as possible apart from the Polish crisis. It left to Kania the possibility of establishing himself as the one responsible for the decisions that were being made and thereby of finding the road to a national consensus that allowed for the peaceful resolution of earlier crises. It is clear that in September 1980 the Kremlin thought that Kania, like Gomułka in 1956 and Gierek in 1970, would be able to offer to his compatriots plans that were attractive enough to appease them. This hope for a Polish solution to the crisis appears in the official attitude adopted by Moscow until December. Everything was set in motion to support Kania, to ensure his legitimacy, and not to ruffle Polish feelings. Kania was supported with confident statements: "We are sure that the Polish people, under the direction of the party, will be able to triumph over the difficulties it is experiencing today," said Leonid Brezhnev, congratulating him on his rise to power.[8] He reiterated this confidence in the Polish party when Kania went to Moscow with the President of the Council of Ministers, Pinkowski, in late October for consultations on the eve of the meeting scheduled between Pinkowski and representatives of Solidarity. There the confrontation on the status of the union would threaten the delicate balance negotiated in Gdańsk.[9] There is no doubt that the conversations in Moscow contributed to the about-face of the Polish leaders, to their determination to revise the commitments they had made. This open support for Kania's hesitant policies was accompanied by economic support. By early September a Polish economic mission had negotiated a loan in Moscow. The head of the delegation, Jagelski, vice president of the Council of Ministers, was received not only by Brezhnev but also by Suslov and several other political and not merely economic members of the Soviet leadership.[10]

What was remarkable during these first months of the crisis was the attention given to all the Polish visitors. All were received by the principal Soviet leaders and all were greeted with confident declarations.

Moscow was certainly mobilized at the time by the effort to legitimate the group in power. Support for the Polish party and endless repetitions of the statement that it was capable of confronting the situation was only one aspect of Soviet speeches on the subject. The other side was the treatment of the crisis itself. Here too Soviet prudence was remarkable. All commentaries were determined to ignore the gulf that existed between the Polish government and Polish society, first of all by ignoring Solidarity, whose name was mentioned for the first time in the USSR two months after the Gdańsk agreements and very rarely repeated thereafter.[11] The image that the Soviet press gave of the Polish situation was in general pleasant. On the one hand was a working class united with its leaders, with confidence in them; on the other, "outside agitators, imperialists, emigrés," determined to undermine the Polish social order.[12] For the USSR, the problem thus lay outside the borders of Poland, which justified both support for Kania and his concessions to Solidarity and the vigilance that the socialist community had to demonstrate, for that was another aspect of the Soviet attitude during this period. Beneath the support lurked the threats; threats from the neighboring states, principally Czechoslovakia and the GDR, where the press was much more violent about events in Poland, offering an interesting counterpoint to Soviet moderation; military threats as well when the press frequently referred to the maneuvers taking place on Polish territory.[13] Generally speaking, the USSR increased press reports about military activities and the vigilance that the army had to maintain.

Whom did the USSR wish to intimidate with these sometimes contradictory attitudes? Were the two languages—tolerant in Moscow, more brutal in Prague and East Berlin—the result of divergent positions between one capital and another or of a subtle division of labor? It is reasonable to adopt all these hypotheses simultaneously, to think that the USSR wanted both to strengthen Kania by supporting him and to defuse the crisis by ignoring Solidarity; but also to threaten Solidarity and to urge Kania to greater firmness through those threats, or at least to place him in a better negotiating position with Solidarity. We must above all recognize that the Soviet leadership was itself divided over the analysis of the crisis and the solutions that should be adopted. Different attitudes, variations in time and space, were as much the reflection of divergences of views within the Kremlin as of a well-orchestrated division of labor.

A second period in the crisis—considering it from the perspective of the opposition between Moscow and Poland, not in terms of an analysis of events in Poland—began in December and continued up to Kania's fall from power. This period was probably the most dangerous, the one during which the USSR was closest to intervening directly.

After a period when the tone of Soviet statements was relatively moderate, everything seemed to change suddenly. Press commentary became more incisive, more directly linked to events. Meetings between Soviet and Polish leaders took on the appearance of imperious commands rather than demonstrations of support. Military threats became more definite. In its commentary, the Soviet press began to accuse not only foreign provocations but also forces hostile to socialism within Poland. In the way in which it was explained, the Polish crisis was moving from the foreign to the domestic sphere. "Anti-Soviet and antisocialist" (the two terms were beginning to blend) activities were being produced by "antisocialist elements" determined to "destabilize the political system." And this evolution (at this point the analysis took a very troubling turn) was compared to developments in Czechoslovakia in 1968.[14] Many commentators insisted on the extent of the dangers that the continuing crisis posed for Poland, on the attacks against its sovereignty because of "foreign interference" (Zbigniew Brzezinski and Western radio stations headed the list of foreign actors), on the weakening of its defense capabilities, and on the risks of a general collapse of the system. In the face of what was more and more frequently being identified as "counterrevolutionary threats," the tools for restoration were also more clearly defined. Soviet-Polish cooperation was to guarantee Polish sovereignty; the same thing was to be accomplished by the cooperation of the whole camp.[15] The meeting of party leaders and heads of state of the member countries of the Warsaw Pact on December 5 allowed simultaneously for the expression of confidence in the Polish people and their leaders and for the statement that they could "be assured of the fraternal solidarity and support of the Pact's member countries."[16]

Quotations of this kind could be endlessly repeated. They all pointed in the same direction; they indicated that Soviet confidence was gradually giving way to genuine skepticism about the usefulness of concessions that were bringing about growing demands and increased assurance in Poland and not demobilization of the workers.

There is no doubt that the ideological weakness of the Polish United Workers Party made an impression on the Soviet leaders. It was to remedy this weakness that they sent their experts in "ideological work" to Warsaw and attempted to check the backsliding they had observed in the area of public debate.[17] The development of the debate in Poland—on the rights of Solidarity, on the five-day week—the general participation of the society in the debate and the government's inability to maintain control over popular turmoil were all seen by Moscow as signs of the slow disintegration of the party. In the growing number of conversations between Soviet and Polish leaders, there constantly recurred the theme of the party's ability to keep itself from being overwhelmed by Solidarity's demands and to maintain the initiative over concessions.[18] Until late January, Soviet concern was focused on the manner of making concessions, but with the question of the five-day week, the criticism shifted to a more fundamental question: Was the policy of concessions of any use?

The January 31, 1981, agreement between the Polish government and Solidarity on this question, reached in an atmosphere of proliferating strikes ("the battle for free Saturdays"), certainly struck a blow against Soviet "patience." The concrete demands, like the five-day week, presented by Solidarity were seen by Moscow as pretexts for creating "chaos" and for pursuing a "systematically counterrevolutionary" policy. Solidarity, which had been practically ignored in the preceding period in the USSR, had changed roles. The free labor union had become the tool of a foreign plot aimed at putting an end to the communist regime; it had also become a rival to the Polish Workers'

Party, from which it was attempting to seize the monopoly of power.[19] This change of theme was important. It indicated in the first place that the USSR no longer thought that Solidarity could be neutralized by ignoring it or that it could be coopted by compromises that would have satisfied some of its demands. By seeing it both as a potential political party, determined to divert the existing party's power in its direction, and as a tool for foreign counter-revolutionary activities, Soviet commentaries clearly indicated that the time of illusions had passed in Moscow. There would be no more compromises tending to neutralize the free trade union. In the end, Solidarity was con-demned to death, even though the Soviet leaders still had no clear views on how that would be accomplished. On the other hand, their attitude on another point was clear: compromise was useless. Although in the first phase the argument that could be labelled conciliatory, which tended to resolve the Polish crisis by immediate concessions, had prevailed—Kania was expected to find in Warsaw the proper balance between concessions and firmness—by early 1981 the opposite argument had become dominant. The meaning of Soviet commentaries was clear because they all led to the same conclusion: the concessions had helped only Solidarity and had weakened the party. This led implicitly to another conclusion: Kania had not been able to fulfill his contract; another leader had to be found in order to prevent the Polish problem from going beyond its borders. Two new phenomena helped to increase Soviet doubts about the policy Kania had been following: the problem of the press and the extension of the union movement to rural areas. The fact that Solidarity wanted to negotiate for access to the media was totally contrary to the logic of the Soviet model and could make Solidarity's gains difficult to call into question later.[20] Because this problem arose at the time when Solidarity was also trying to establish the movement in the countryside, and because, to reach its objectives, which were continuously developing in new areas, a strike had become the pressure tactic that preceded every discussion, Moscow began to think that another solution was neces-sary.[21]

A peaceful solution from within, or a restoration of order imposed from outside? A very thorough study of the movements of the Soviet Army during the course of these months has led an American writer, R. Anderson, to conclude that on two occasions, in December 1980 and March 1981, the USSR was ready to resolve the Polish problem by force.[22] According to Anderson, the first crucial moment occurred around December 5 at the summit meeting of the Warsaw Pact we have already mentioned, and he suggests that the essential reason for the abandonment of this plan was the more than negative attitude of the troops that had been assembled for an intervention. Comparing evidence from the West with indications in the Soviet press,[23] Anderson concludes that the Soviet Army's lack of prepara-tion for an immediate campaign was a serious enough problem to have led to the postponement of military action and to many disciplinary actions being taken at the upper levels of the military hierarchy. It is no doubt legitimate to wonder about the extent to which rumors about an imminent intervention, based on indisputable measures recalling reservists, were also designed to impress the Polish authorities and the Polish people. A short time later a conversation between Marshal Kulikov, the leader of Warsaw Pact forces, and Kania might in fact have strengthened the impression that military leaders from the Soviet Union or from other Warsaw Pact countries were developing increasing interest in the evolution of the situation in Poland.

According to Anderson, the second "hot" moment in military terms occurred in March 1981. In this case, his analysis conforms to the reports and warnings of the American government, which noted increased mobilization and troop movements in regions near Poland.[24]

It is true that at that point, too, there were numerous criticisms in the USSR about the Soviet Army's lack of preparation. The commander-in-chief, Marshal Ogarkov, in particular launched a long diatribe against the excessive slowness of mobilization exercises and the perpetual inadequacy of links between the army and civilian authorities.[25]

We must again consider the causes of this sudden military agitation and the reality of the threats of intervention. Considering civilian and military events together it is clear that as in December troop movements coincided with a summit in which the USSR expressed its impatience. On March 4, 1981, a summit meeting between Polish and Soviet leaders was held in Moscow. This was the second meeting of the kind since Kania had come to power, but many signs indicated a decline in Soviet confidence. While the summit of October 30, 1980, was clearly designed to strengthen Kania's position and to indicate Soviet support for him, the March meeting had all the trappings of a trial. The report of the meeting is very revealing.[26] First of all, there was the unusual size of the Soviet delegation, made up of seven representatives. Brezhnev was accompanied by leaders of all the international sectors of government (Gromyko, minister of foreign affairs, and Rusakov, the party secretariat official, in charge of relations with communist parties in power); the minister of defense (Ustinov); and also by Andropov and Suslov. Finally, the government was represented by Tikhonov. The Polish affair had mobilized everyone in the USSR who was responsible for overseeing party matters, ideology, and security, not to mention experts on the problems of foreign countries. Their concern was not only to treat the problem as a domestic one; the absence of economic experts who had participated in many negotiations with the Poles in the first phase demonstrated that the focus of the discussion was the political and military situation.[27] Another significant fact about the composition of the Soviet delegation is that it was identical to the one that had participated in the Warsaw Pact summit in December 1980 in Moscow. This suggested that a "crisis cabinet" concerned with the Polish situation had been set up in Moscow.

Confronting this crisis cabinet, the Polish delegation contained only four members. Kania and General Jaruzelski, the recently named head of the government, were accompanied by a member of the Politburo and a secretary of the Central Committee, and they appeared as criminal defendants. Moreover, the communiqué explained that they had come "to provide information about the situation in the country and the measures taken to overcome the threat weighing on the conquests of socialism."

Even though the communiqué in the usual terminology spoke of a "friendly meeting," it contained passages heavy with meaning. The crisis could lead to "a change in the balance of world forces and weaken the socialist community and the entire international communist movement."[28] The impression of *déjà vu* was further accentuated when the Soviet delegation explained that along with the other fraternal states it was ready to "supply and would supply all the support needed to socialist Poland and to the Polish communists in their continuing effort to rectify the situation fundamentally."

At the same time, the atmosphere in Poland was tense. Crises and power struggles followed one after the other and culminated in the confrontations in Bydgoszcz, a logical conclusion to the growing agitation in the peasants' world.[29] To calm the strikers who during these tense weeks had been loudly proclaiming their demands from one work place to another, Wałęsa, generally supported by the ecclesiastical authorities, was negotiating on two sides, for the workers to return to work and for the government to satisfy the workers' demands. And in every case the authorities gave way in order to avoid the paralysis of the country. It was this constant retreat by the government and the intensification of demands that explain Moscow's apprehensions and its desire to demand an accounting and a commitment to firmness from the Polish delegation summoned on March 4. Were these circumstances enough to make a plan for intervention plausible? Did they justify the rapid mobilization, so visible that the American government was troubled by it?

It is tempting to adopt another explanation, one more in conformity with the circumstances, which were tense to be sure, but which had not yet created anything irreversible in Poland; in conformity as well with the ambiguous, but in no way dramatic, tone of the March 5 communiqué. Wasn't the noise of boots on Polish borders designed to go along with a serious warning? The March 4 summit clearly explained that, for the USSR, "the Polish communists have the means and the opportunity to reverse the course of events."

The Brezhnev group said everything in this communiqué: that the course of events was scandalous but that it could still be reversed, and that the Polish communists ought to be able to accomplish this. Behind this advice in the form of a warning, wasn't the military threat contained in the communiqué and confirmed by the mobilization measures intended to strengthen the fervor of the Polish leaders? To convince them that Soviet patience had limits? And also to convince the outside world that if it encouraged Solidarity too openly, it would bear the responsibility for the Soviet reaction? This determination to use military pressure to force the Polish leaders to act or to provide them with ammunition for their domestic arguments was confirmed by the frequent trips that Soviet military leaders, using a wide variety of pretexts, made to Warsaw. As in Czechoslovakia in 1968, every few weeks a member of the Soviet military command would come to question the Polish leaders about the situation. Thus a few scant days after the Moscow summit, Marshall Kulikov, leading the "Soyuz 81" maneuvers met with Kania and General Jaruzelski.[30] This continual mixing of political and military concerns pointed much more toward intimidation than to actual preparations for an invasion. It seemed to suggest to the Polish leaders that it would be dangerous to neglect the role of the military in the Soviet decision-making process, dangerous to believe that they blindly followed the Politburo and accepted its decisions and its version of events.

It can readily be agreed that the Soviet leadership contained members who favored a military solution—Anderson thinks that Kirilenko was the leader of this faction, opposed by Brezhnev who was intent on negotiations. That this debate led them in December and again in March while nothing had been decided in Poland to prepare for an invasion, which extraneous factors like delays in mobilization slowed up, is less plausible. In March, many courses of action remained available, particularly a change in Polish leadership.

The Rise of the "Strong Man"

Coinciding with the Moscow summit and the troop movements, the change of prime minister in Warsaw showed that the Soviet leadership was largely relying on internal means to recapture the territory that the Polish Communist Party was losing daily. When Kania came to power in October 1980, according to information published abroad he had enough time to carry out a policy based on flexibility, which demanded much more time than repressive measures.[31] However, because in the course of a few months Kania demonstrated the dangers of the negotiations that were to open, he had to share the responsibilities of power with the man who by the spring seemed to be the strong man that Kania was unable to be. In February, a few days before the Moscow summit, General Jaruzelski became prime minister. His promotion, which the West greeted with indifference, was on the contrary hailed in Moscow as a turning point in a more and more confused situation. The official reaction was immediate from the Soviet government, but also from

Leonid Brezhnev.[32] More important than the traditional congratulations was the sudden change in the nature of Soviet commentaries.[33] Violent criticisms of strikes and anarchic movements were replaced by measured consideration of the effects of the appointment of a new prime minister. In the appeal he made to his compatriots before the parliament and the eighth plenum of the Central Committee, Jaruzelski asserted his determination to end disorder. This appeal, designed to forestall strikes for three months, was for Moscow a serious attempt to return to a normal situation. The Soviet press emphasized the lassitude of the Polish people and the economic cost of the strikes and concluded that the truce proposed by the new prime minister had come at an opportune moment to reassure a society that was adrift. The target for Soviet attacks shifted. It was no longer so much Solidarity that was attacked—as though a negotiating partner for General Jaruzelski were being preserved—as the "antisocialist forces determined to destroy the system." These forces were "grouped together in the KOR," which was according to the Soviet press "only the emanation of circles foreign to Poland."[34] This concern to give its chance to a strengthened leadership group, which had expressed firm positions during the Eighth Plenum, inspired the Soviet attitude and that of its most anti-Polish allies, East Germany and Czechoslovakia, for nearly two months. It was a reprieve of which Kania tried to take advantage to reassure the neighboring states, which he visited to explain his new ten-point program designed to restore calm and to put Poland back to work. It was a brief respite, even though the virulent press campaigns that had marked the early months of 1981 seemed to have been abandoned. The efforts of Polish leaders, which were both calming and authoritarian, had as a backdrop the long "Soyuz 81" maneuvers, which demonstrated for nearly three weeks that the Warsaw Pact armies were ready to answer any appeal from Poland. Once again the context was one of constant intimidation, which added a troubling echo to Soviet declarations of confidence in the Polish leadership's capacity for action.[35] Still more disturbing in the expressions of support for the group in power in Warsaw was the suggestion of the need to call on ill-defined political forces. Until spring 1981 the Polish United Workers' Party was designated as the natural instrument for a return to order. Later the Soviet press expressed its confidence in "the communists, the laborers, the working class,"[36] a broad definition that in many respects recalled the definition of "healthy forces" frequently used in Prague in 1968.

It is true that the Polish Communist Party, which Kania continued to head, exhibited unusual signs of weakness, and Moscow quickly realized that the process of disintegration was progressing within the party. When preparations for the extraordinary congress of the PUWP got under way with Kania offering assurances that it would usefully demonstrate the vitality of the party, Soviet commentators insisted on the presence "of revisionist elements within the party who want to force it to reform."[37] More lucid than Kania, the Soviet leaders anticipated what polls being conducted at the time in Poland would show. A dual shift was taking place. Polish society was falling entirely into Solidarity's camp, with 90 percent of its members expressing support for the union organization.[38] And this shift was openly taking place at the expense of the party, whose growing degree of isolation was shown by the polls (32 percent of those surveyed expressed confidence in the PUWP in May 1981).[39]

This recognition of the isolation of the party in society explains why the congress of the PUWP was subjected to the pressure of a great number of its officials who were concerned to adapt to this new situation, to cooperate with Solidarity, to welcome its members, and to establish as a principle that there was no incompatibility in belonging to both organizations. This development brought about a veritable hemorrhage of party militants toward Solidarity. It is easy to see how this development affecting a communist party, its structures, its organization, and its fundamental rules, was considered unacceptable in the USSR. The Soviet party had sent a letter to the PUWP on June 5 imploring it to "mobilize all the healthy social forces."[40] It appears from all the documents published at the time that after the congress the USSR no longer thought that these healthy forces were located in the Communist Party, which was rapidly deviating from its original model. While the PUWP had demonstrated its inability to find within itself a response to the crisis, Solidarity was increasingly asserting itself as the center for political initiatives and for a new definition of the system. Solidarity's congress, held from September 5 to 10 and again from September 26 to October 7, gave the free trade union everything that the PUWP had lost a few weeks earlier: a legitimate leadership, statutes, and a program that was political as well as economic and social. At this point, legitimacy and the claim to organize the life of the country were transferred from the party to Solidarity. The objectives of the program approved by the Solidarity congress indicate the union's movement toward a political vocation. Several points in this program deserve particular consideration, since they came to the attention of the Soviet leaders and explain their anxiety and their final decision.[41] First was the range that Solidarity gave to its influence: "This movement . . . has in the course of the past year won over all sectors of the world of work: workers and peasants, intellectuals and artisans."

This extended definition of Solidarity's audience, including to begin with those who were supposed to be the pillars of the Polish Communist Party, corresponded to a clear determination to establish the legitimacy of the union by its identification with the society as a whole and to occupy the field as representative of all social groups. Solidarity left no room for the Communist Party. Competition between organizations representing society, which the Leninist model had always rejected, had come to an end in Poland in a divorce between party and society and by the society's adhesion to an organization over which the party had no control.

On this point, Solidarity's program rejected any ambiguity. It did not present the union as an appendix to the party, as a social organization that would in the end accept the party's authority, but as a "mass organization of workers, a force . . . capable of constructing a just Poland for all," hence as an autonomous force emanating from society and bringing it together.

Solidarity's program was clear not only in its definition of the union's representative function, but perhaps even clearer when it challenged the right of one organization, without a social consensus, to speak in the name of society:

Democracy is not the power of a group that places itself above society, which grants itself the right to identify society's needs and to represent its interests. Society must be able to speak aloud, to express the diversity of social and political ideas, to assure to everyone a just share in the material and spiritual goods of the country. . . . Our objective is a self-managed Poland.[42]

And the program's authors added: "We consider pluralism indispensable to political life." These few formulations expressed everything; everything indicated that the Polish "revolution" had been carried out.

There was nothing in common between these clearly articulated objectives and the Soviet conception of the socialist state. No compromise was possible. Of course, it was still only a program and Polish political life continued in a framework of institutions antithetical to it. But Polish institutions had the Communist Party as guarantor, and the party had become spineless. It negotiated endlessly with Solidarity, which in fact did not recognize any social legitimacy in the party; it hesitated over the attitude to adopt when its militants by joining Solidarity demonstrated that party spirit (*partiinost'*) had lost all meaning for them. The summer of 1981 solidified both the extraordinary success of Solidarity and the moral and organizational collapse of the PUWP, which no longer dared invoke the fundamental principles of every communist party: primacy and the monopoly of power.

Could this situation, which had never had an equivalent anywhere, last for long? A specialist on Poland, G. Mink, comments on the question:

No one would have believed it before August 1980: the vise of the Yalta agreements could be loosened by the will of an entire people acting without delegating, at any point, the responsibility for changing its rulers. The *tour de force* was to operate simultaneously with a Soviet-style political system and the mechanisms of autonomous social representation, unions understood as transmission belts for the party and unions totally separated from the state apparatus. Real social connections were established by the unions in that incarnation. While appearances were kept up, it can be said that, beginning in the summer of 1980, the limits of the possible have been expanded in Poland for what is now an already extraordinarily long period. In this particular instance, Poland has become the laboratory in which future transformations of the countries of the Soviet bloc will be tested.[43]

Seen from Warsaw, the reasoning was impeccable. But this was to forget that for nearly forty years everything had been decided in Moscow. It was also to forget that the problem of the USSR was not so much to preserve a mythical Yalta agreement as to ensure that political systems modeled on its own were everywhere untouchable, thereby guaranteeing the continuous integration of states and peoples within its empire. Moreover this Soviet obsession did not escape the author of that enthusiastic praise of Solidarity's conquests. A few months later, summing up the five hundred days of the Polish revolution, he admitted that "what has happened in Poland is certainly not generalizable to other Soviet-style societies."[44]

This is why the USSR never accepted the "concurrent operation" of its system with other mechanisms. Competition between ideas or organizations was precisely the one element that the communist system could not accept, for competition meant choice while communism implied the end of choice, since it was the final and irreversible stage of human history. The USSR, that is, the various communist parties, could come to terms with all social forces and all ideas that were not located on their terrain. They came to terms with churches, with nationalism, and with all kinds of movements that could not lay claim to the exclusive representation of the world of work. The drama of Solidarity arose because it was an alternative to the communist party, following the same logic. It was a revolutionary force.

Since that was the case, and since the Polish Communist Party was incapable of stifling its opponent, the USSR had to find another means to resolve the Polish problem. In the circumstances, resolution meant the suppression of Solidarity as a socially representative organization and the restoration of the traditional order. The operation had in other places and at other times been given the well-known name "normalization."[45] It is important to note the vocabulary that was used. The Soviet term for normalization was *szdorovlenie*, or return to health. Once the two related notions of "healthy forces" and "return to health" had been invoked in the USSR, this in turn implicitly suggested a reversal of the situation, a radical change, and the idea of "assistance" to this process.

While an irreversible revolutionary process was developing in Poland—for it had passed the point of no return, even if the prudence of the Poles led them to avoid explicit expressions of their revolution—the USSR undertook the exploration of a "normalizing" solution.

In appearance, nothing had changed in the Soviet attitude and the respite allowed to Kania to restore order was still in effect. Soviets and Poles continued to debate about economic cooperation.[46] The Soviet Communist

Party sent a delegation to the extraordinary congress of the PUWP and it was full of calls for vigilance and hopes for quick "normalization."[47] Soviet leaders came to Warsaw to meet their Polish friends.[48] And on August 15 Kania undertook the traditional pilgrimage for summer talks in the Crimea with Brezhnev.[49] No doubt during these conversations on the shores of the Black Sea an interesting signal was given to Polish communists by the presence of General Jaruzelski alongside Kania. The communiqué published at the conclusion of the conversations, although it concentrated on the well-known themes of cooperation and solidarity between the two countries, was interesting because of its insistence on the "patriotic" and "national" aspects of the struggle that had to be conducted in Poland against the forces of disintegration. It was less the Polish Communist Party that was being summoned to vigilance and action than "patriotic forces, in the name of national salvation and salvation of the fatherland."[50]

The emphasis on what the nation had to accomplish suggested both Soviet skepticism about the possibility of using the Polish Communist Party in the immediate circumstances as a framework for the process of stabilization and psychological preparation for a subsequent stage, the promotion of the army as guarantor of the national interest.

It seems in fact that at this point, while attention in Poland was focused on preparations for the Solidarity congress, the USSR slightly shifted its reactions and its activities. The Polish crisis began to be presented more as the product of a Western attempt at subversion than as a confrontation between Polish government and Polish society, whatever the level of "sickness" in that society.[51] No doubt this shift from a direct attack on Solidarity to an attack on the "foreign friends of the KOR" was not confined to the summer of 1981. The Soviet press had constantly oscillated between two ways of treating the Polish problem. Sometimes it minimized the domestic aspects in order to emphasize international responsibilities. Sometimes on the contrary it provided minutely detailed descriptions of the work of domestic subversion. But in the context of the summer of 1981, many elements came together to suggest that the USSR wanted to give priority to the dangers threatening *all* of Poland, government and society together, which implied a national, rather than a communist mobilization.

The military machinery of the Warsaw Pact also seemed to have been set in motion in reaction to repeated statements about the general security of the socialist system, threatened by events in Poland and by foreign interference in Poland.[52]

The Warsaw Pact then became the framework for intense activity. On August 9 a meeting was held in Warsaw among Marshal Kulikov, General Shcheglov (Warsaw Pact forces ambassador to Poland), General Jaruzelski, and the commander-in-chief of Polish forces, General Sawicki. The purpose of the meeting was to inform Warsaw Pact officials about the fighting capabilities of the Polish Army, which was supposed to be "a strong link" in the common defense system.[53] The meeting echoed the anxieties that had often been expressed in Moscow about the dangers that the Polish crisis posed for the country's defensive capacity and hence for the safety of the entire common defense system.

The Soviet Army was not left out of the debate. From September 4 to 12 while the first phase of the Solidarity congress was taking place, the Soviet Army and Navy were engaged in the large-scale Zapad-81 maneuvers, led by the Defense Minister, Marshal Ustinov. These maneuvers took place precisely on Polish borders with the Baltic republics and Byelorussia.

All the defense ministers of Warsaw Pact countries as well as those of non-European socialist countries associated with Comecon were asked to attend this giant exercise designed to "perfect joint concentration and action of troops and weapons."[54] For the Polish defense minister, this demonstration of force and readiness must have had a particularly disturbing character, capable of erasing the memory of the mobilization difficulties of earlier months about which the Soviet press had been very vocal.

Hardly had the maneuvers come to an end when the Soviet ambassador to Warsaw brought a message to the Polish leaders, Kania and Jaruzelski, from the "Soviet leadership." The message transmitted by Aristov was an order addressed to the Polish government to put an end to an intolerable situation: the activity of counterrevolutionary forces at the Solidarity congress, which were undermining the system and attacking the USSR and Soviet-Polish relations.[55]

The message was clear: it identified the crime and the source of the plot. Solidarity was the guilty party, at best infiltrated by counterrevolutionary forces, at worst totally identified with those forces. And the Solidarity congress whose second phase was to begin a few days later was denounced as an opportunity for subversive forces to express themselves. The inability of the leaders to resist Solidarity's pressures—the law on workers' rights was adopted by the Polish parliament, the Sejm, on September 25, 1981—and the resumption of the Solidarity congress definitively sealed Kania's fate. And everything indicates that his replacement was already ready. Jaruzelski, who had been asked to replace Kania in October 1981,[56] had for months been participating in all the meetings with Soviet leaders; he had been associated with all of Kania's activities; his move to the forefront seemed to consolidate rather than anticipate what was to follow, the December coup. In the overheated Poland of 1981 the cleverness of these Soviet tactics lay in their gradual development of a domestic solution that allowed the leader in place at the appropriate moment to carry out his *coup d'état* as a logical step in the process of the restoration of order that had begun with his appointment. General Jaruzelski was in fact able to demobilize Solidarity and to mollify its distrust by placing himself at first in continuity with the actions he had participated in for months. Continuity and effectiveness seemed at the beginning to be the reasons for his rise to power. And he gave a certain strength to this illusion on November 4 by proposing a tripartite discussion among the three active forces in Polish political life in 1981: Solidarity, the party, and the Church. Everything helped to foster the illusion in Warsaw that the USSR had agreed to remain aloof from the debate.

A New Formula: Self-Normalization

However, if we look at events more closely and change the focus from Warsaw to the community of communist states, we are led to a totally different conclusion. There were feverish cooperation and constant contacts between Jaruzelski and the authorities of the Warsaw Pact. On November 25 the new head of the PUWP met the commander-in-chief of the Warsaw Pact forces, Marshal Kulikov, and the meeting had more of the character of a report to a superior than of a purely diplomatic visit.[57] Between the day that General Jaruzelski acceded to the leadership of the PUWP and the *coup d'état* there were no fewer than three meetings of the pact along with this meeting with Marshal Kulikov, which was of course closely connected with the activities of the alliance under the direction of the USSR. Indeed, the Military Council of the pact's armed forces met from October 27 to 30, presided over by its commander-in-chief, Kulikov.[58]

In early December, the foreign ministers of the pact met in Bucharest,[59] while the Committee of Defense Ministers was meeting in the Soviet capital.[60] This series of meetings was certainly not an unprecedented phenomenon in the annals of the pact, whose various committees met regularly. But their temporal proximity was oddly reminiscent of the summer of 1968. However, in contrast to 1968, these feverish meetings did not lead to a military expedition. The coup came from a direction that Solidarity had not anticipated, from the head of the party, who proclaimed a state of war during the night of December 12, 1981. Addressing his compatriots, General Jaruzelski justified his action by saying that in the face of the rising anarchy, there was no other way to avoid intervention by the communist states. This appeal to national unity against a threat that had not been carried out and the denunciation of an anarchist enterprise were not exactly what the USSR considered justifications for the *coup d'état*, although General Jaruzelski's speech was widely published.[61]

According to the Soviet leaders, who presented their views in a statement of the Tass news agency, what was happening in Poland was an internal matter. The state of war was a "healthy," natural response to a twofold danger: a counterrevolutionary enterprise and an enterprise threatening the national independence of Poland by preventing it from being a veritable ally of the Warsaw Pact. In the last analysis the Tass statement placed more emphasis on the security of the whole alliance, threatened by the internal condition of Poland, than on anarchy. It also stressed "Soviet-Polish relations, the cornerstone of the interests of the Polish state," more than the concrete arrangements of the state of war.[62]

This analysis corresponds thoroughly to the general attitude adopted by the USSR toward the military coup and the government that came out of it. This is not the place to follow the process of normalization step by step. It is, however, useful to see how the USSR attempted to orient the normalization of Poland. Any restoration of the order that had existed before this kind of confrontation presupposed that the USSR would appear, whether or not it openly took part in the normalization, as the big brother who guided and protected. And at this stage, protection was above all economic; for the process of calming a broken population involved compensations, immediately tangible progress in the economic sphere.[63]

As soon as the state of war was proclaimed, the Polish government turned to its allies. It invoked the economic disaster created in Poland by the joint activity of counterrevolutionaries and imperialists to ask for their help in its enterprise of political, but also economic, reconstruction. The Polish leaders visited all the capitals of the sister states to obtain increased exchanges in conditions suitable for Poland. The needs of Poland described by these envoys were immense and multifarious: loans, raw materials (especially chemical fertilizers and seeds), spare parts, and industrial plant. It was logical that the big brother was first on the list of Comecon states to respond to Polish requests. The trade agreement, signed in Moscow on January 6, 1982, by the Soviet and Polish commerce ministers, Patolichev and Nestorowicz, established a trade program for 1982 that was substantial but less than what was needed. The USSR offered a loan of two billion seven hundred million rubles designed to cover Poland's trade deficit with the Soviet Union and to finance Polish purchases in the USSR in 1982.[64] No doubt this Soviet aid would contribute to the resolution of some urgent problems of the Polish economy. But its limits cannot be ignored. Soviet deliveries of raw materials were inadequate to restore industrial production that had been virtually paralyzed by chronic shortages of materials and spare parts and by administrative failures, not to mention the lack of productive spirit among the workers themselves. Nor were Soviet loans able to resolve the problem of the Polish debt to the West, which reached an intolerable level in 1981–1982. Moreover, Soviet aid was limited by the burdens the USSR was carrying throughout Eastern Europe, which were reaching considerable proportions. Nor did the other Comecon countries have unlimited means to contribute to Polish recovery, considering their own needs. And any attempt by the USSR to impose on them a planned program of exchanges within the framework of Comecon posed the strong risk of provoking new tensions, which was the last thing Moscow needed. Thus, despite the speed with which the USSR granted supplementary loans to Poland immediately after the proclamation of the state of war, the "economic card" as a tool for normalization was not easy for Moscow to play.[65] The deterioration of the Soviet economy, the collapse of the Polish economy, and the extent of the needs of a country as populous as Poland made Hungarian-style solutions difficult.

This explains why Soviet efforts were largely directed toward the political aspects of normalization and why the USSR seemed to count on firmness rather than concessions. This choice became clear in the conversations General Jaruzelski had with Soviet leaders in 1982 that defined the objectives of normalization and the position of the Soviet government toward normalization and the position of the Soviet government toward the government that had come out of the December 13 coup.

Two important meetings produced an outline of the bases of a policy encouraged by Moscow: one in Moscow in March and one in the Crimea in August.

General Jaruzelski's visit to Moscow on March 1 and 2, 1982, took place in the context of a series of crisis summits in which in turbulent phases the leaders of Eastern European countries were literally taken in hand by the big brother. This was reflected in the composition of the Soviet delegation, which for the third time included the "crisis cabinet" that had followed the Polish affair from the beginning. Six delegates already known to Kania were present: Brezhnev, Gromyko, Andropov, Ustinov, Tikhonov, and Rusakov. The seventh, Suslov, had died, and it was natural that he be replaced in this informal body by the man who had already succeeded him in many functions, Chernenko.[66]

Confronting this assembly of recognized specialists in the Polish question, the delegation from Warsaw seemed quite weak and inexperienced. General Jaruzelski was not accompanied by important leaders who had some authority in the Kremlin. In fact the Polish Politburo seemed to be absent from the scene, and General Jaruzelski, who had concentrated power in his hands, also appeared to want to embody all legitimacy. In this connection, the Soviet position was not without interest. Although Leonid Brezhnev affirmed that the USSR fully supported General Jaruzelski, his sympathy for a military regime was seriously qualified. In the speech he delivered, Brezhnev, who was head of state as well as general secretary of the party, presented himself primarily as responsible for the interests of the communist parties. He clearly emphasized that for the USSR authority in Poland belonged to the Communist Party and he praised his guest's intention to restore the role of the party as soon as possible.

Moreover Brezhnev was very clear in his views on the way to restore order. "It is normal," he said, "that the party rid Poland of everything that is foreign to the nature of socialism." After him, Leonid Zamiatin took up more or less the same idea by pointing out that although the counterrevolution in Poland had experienced a serious setback, it was still far from being defeated. The meaning of the message was precise: at the point that Poland had reached

no compromise was possible with the social forces that had expressed themselves during the "five hundred days of Solidarity." General Jaruzelski was in
power to normalize, not to hesitate and negotiate. Where the procrastination
of Gierek and Kania had failed, the USSR confirmed that the same hesitant
path was closed to their successor. His mission was to restore, not the old
order in its totality, but the conditions in which the party could begin again
to exist and to exercise its power.

The summer conversations in the Crimea confirmed Moscow's attitude
and its directives. Jaruzelski met Brezhnev there for the second time that year
on August 16. Accompanying Brezhnev were his foreign minister, Gromyko,
Konstantin Chernenko, and an assistant, A. Blatov. Confronting his interlocutors—the same ones who had met him in the Crimea in July 1981—
Jaruzelski was accompanied by J. Czyrek,[67] a member of the Politburo and an
ardent supporter of an understanding with the USSR.[68]

The statements made during this meeting echo those made in the Kremlin
meeting. But the warmth of the earlier meeting was absent. There is no
doubt that the Kremlin's more severe attitude—indicated by a comparison
between the two communiqués—was attributable to annoyance at the slow
pace of normalization. "Resolution of the crisis is slowed down by the
existence of a clandestine counterrevolution." The fact that responsibility for
this latent and continuing crisis was primarily attributed to the United States
is of little importance in this connection; the essential point is that the work of
the restoration of order was obviously considered too slow and weak. In the
light of this criticism, it is even easier to understand the statement made
about the party. As in March, the role of the party, its legitimacy, and the
need to strengthen it were repeated with remarkable insistence. Moreover, the
communiqué at no point gave the slightest hint that the party was not the
dominant power in Poland. It was as though the gulf separating the collapse
of the party in autumn 1981 from a normalized situation had already been
bridged. For the Soviet leaders, and this was reiterated from one summit to
another, power in Poland belonged to the party and military power was only
a parenthesis, an instrument designed to palliate the momentary weakness of
the PUWP. By this time, all criticism of the party leadership—neither Gierek
nor Kania was mentioned by name—and all allusions to mistakes made by
the party had disappeared from Soviet commentaries. To legitimize the
party's return to power and to place all the work of the restoration of order
under its auspices, it was necessary to establish that it had always been right.
The frequent visits of PUWP members to Moscow after the proclamation of
the state of war also allowed the Soviet leadership to emphasize the fact that
the Polish Communist Party existed and that it counted.[69] When Brezhnev
was replaced by Andropov, he adopted the same attitude in the conversations
he had with Jaruzelski who had come to participate in the jubilee ceremonies
of the Soviet state.[70]

The Soviet attitude was thus characterized by continuity in the Polish crisis and in normalization. For the USSR, what counted above all was that the Polish system with the party holding a monopoly of power survive or be restored. Then why did it choose a military solution, even in the short run? Why did it discard the possibility of intervention and let the Polish Army act, though its capacity to deal with Solidarity had not been demonstrated? What results did the USSR hope to attain in the last analysis?

The first point that needs to be made, harsh as it may be, is that the "normalization" that Poland had avoided in 1956 was unavoidable in 1980. This was the case for several reasons, all of which equally doomed Solidarity's hopes. First of all, the crisis created by Solidarity in the summer of 1980 was a crisis of the political system, the conclusion of which could be either the defeat of Solidarity or the transformation of the Polish Soviet system, that is, its disappearance. Although this system could deal with adjustments, as had occurred in Poland after 1956, it could not without ceasing to be itself allow those adjustments to affect its essential element, power. In this system power belonged to the party, and there was no possibility of sharing or competition. Moreover, the notion of power encompassed not only political institutions but all aspects of the organization of social life.

An article published in the USSR early in the crisis sheds light on the Soviet attitude on this point. As was often the case in the USSR, burning questions of the moment were addressed by a historical reference. Analyzing the Tenth Congress of the Bolshevik Party of 1921, which was marked by a violent conflict over the roles of unions and of the Communist Party, *Pravda* opportunely reminded its readers of Lenin's thinking, which was still the orthodox line. The Tenth Congress had concluded that unions had to be subordinated to the party. Only "opportunistic" elements according to *Pravda* had at the time argued for a separation of party and unions and for an autonomous role for the unions.[71]

The first mistake of Solidarity's leaders, or their illusion was that by transposing the compromise established between church and state in 1956, they hoped to separate the union sphere from the political sphere, or, more precisely, they hoped to define a properly *political* domain having to do with institutions, which would have freed an area outside politics for social initiatives. By doing this, Solidarity had forgotten that in the Soviet system *everything was political*, and that society was inseparable from political authority precisely because the myth of the identification between party and society conferred legitimacy on the entire system.

The leaders of the movement, no doubt aware that they were carrying out a *revolution*, hoped that several factors would restrain Soviet reactions. First among them was international pressure. Aware of international sensitivity to the Polish cause—ever since Marx it had been repeated that support for Poland was a sign of a democratic or revolutionary attitude—they hoped that the USSR would be more affected by world opinion than it had been in Budapest and Prague. They also relied on phenomena that did not exist in

1956 and 1968: a Polish Pope and Soviet power that was said to be bogged down in Afghanistan.

Relying on these undoubted elements in Soviet calculations, and also on their own strengths—a large population, unshakeable courage, and a strategic position that would make a confrontation with the USSR formidable—Polish union leaders acted at the limits of the possible, thinking that the only plausible form a Soviet reaction could take would be an invasion, the difficulties of which they knew only too well.

Soviet strategy helped a great deal to foster these calculations and it is worth considering. From the outset of the Polish crisis, the USSR coupled its warnings with the implicit threat of a military intervention that constantly hung over Poland. At times troop movements and mobilization measures substantiated the notion that intervention was imminent. Moscow thus constantly destabilized Polish public opinion, provoking in turn both intensely emotional and mobilizing reactions and their contrary. These repeated crises necessarily had a wearying effect; above all, they finally convinced the leaders of the Polish movement of the futility of mobilizing against other forms of normalization. Their lack of preparation for General Jaruzelski's coup is largely attributable to this fixing of their attention solely on their borders. International public opinion was similarly subjected to psychological manipulation, moving it from anxiety to relief and back again. This concentration of world attention on the possibility of intervention both gradually diminished the general interest in Poland's fate and helped to make any other solution appear relatively acceptable. The state of war declared on December 13 was generally perceived as a lesser evil than the intervention of Warsaw Pact troops. And the permanent threat of such an intervention gave General Jaruzelski an argument—no doubt weak but accepted in part in the West— that an internal police operation was better than an invasion. However specious it may have been, the argument enabled the West to avoid questions about the reaction it should have to the coup organized in Moscow. The myth of noninterference was strengthened by the myth of unavoidable intervention.

This leads to the question of whether the USSR really considered intervening. It is obvious that there was a debate within the USSR as there was in relation to Czechoslovakia in 1968 over the surest means of putting an end to the problem of Solidarity. It is more than probable that the possibility of armed intervention was considered by Soviet leaders, should all other solutions fail. What is on the other hand doubtful is that at any particular point they had thought that they had exhausted alternatives. In contrast to what had happened in Hungary, the Soviet leaders were not confronted with a violent rejection of the party. The society was uninterested in it and had turned toward different structures of authority, but it was perfectly tolerant of the existence of the party and party leaders. The habit of concealment—

the art of Ketman—had suddenly given way to sincerity. In contrast to what had happened in Czechoslovakia, the party did not come together around a Dubček but allowed successive leaders, Kania and Jaruzelski, to be imposed on it. With the society's indifference toward the party and the party's indifference toward its leaders, the USSR maintained enough room to maneuver so that it could place men of its choosing at the head of the party. At first, the problem lay in the party's inability to reduce Solidarity's demands, and to remedy this, the USSR imposed changes in the party leadership. In a second stage, when the party had collapsed from within, another solution had to be found; this was the replacement of the party by the army, provisionally granted a governing role. But the role assigned to General Jaruzelski should not be interpreted as a shift of the communist system toward a military system. In Soviet strategy in 1981 the army was a tool for the restoration of order, a substitute for a faltering party and it was intended that it be withdrawn once the party had reestablished itself. This provisional substitution of military for political power had the advantage of possessing the effectiveness of a military intervention for which the party was not prepared. It also had the advantage of leaving the party removed from the process of normalization. Eventually, when it had been reconstructed, the party would be able to present itself as the representative of a legal order and as such more acceptable than a military order. The future party was thus exonerated from the two faults of having destroyed the Solidarity experiment and of having acted as the representative of the will of the socialist community, that is, of the USSR, against the will of Polish society. Soviet strategy had thus learned the lessons of past experiences—Budapest where only the USSR appeared as the invader and Prague where the intervention of the Warsaw Pact forces provoked a scandal—and developed a novel approach, self-intervention, thanks to highly developed military integration, within the Warsaw Pact.

The solution adopted in Poland in 1981 had moreover already been explored for Czechoslovakia in 1968. But at that time, the USSR had been unable to find the actors for such a scenario in the Czech Army, which was still insufficiently integrated. The prominent position given to General Jaruzelski several months before the proclamation of a state of war indicated that the proliferation of crises in Eastern Europe is not the only aspect of the evolution of the region in recent years. The progress of integration is the other side of the coin, and it is just as significant.

NOTES

1.   I have taken these remarks from the remarkable work by Norman Davies, *God's Playground: A History of Poland*, 2:578. See Milosz, *The Captive Mind*, 2nd ed. (New York, 1981), 54ff.

2. On the Polish crises from 1960 to 1970, see Davies, vol. 2; F. Claudin, *L'Opposition dans les pays du socialisme réel* (Paris, 1983), 263, 325; J. Staniszki, *Pologne: La Révolution autolimitée* (Paris, 1982); Nicolas Bēthell, *Gomulka* (London, 1963).

3. A. Korbonski, "Poland," in Rakowska-Harmstone and Gyorgy, eds., *Communism in Eastern Europe* (Bloomington, 1979), 37–71; Korbonski, *Politics of Socialist Agriculture in Poland, 1945–1960* (New York, 1965).

4. *Sovetskaia Rossia*, August 1, 1980.

5. *Pravda*, August 31, 1980.

6. *Pravda*, September 1, 1980.

7. *Izvestia*, August 26, 1980; *Pravda*, August 28, 1980.

8. *Pravda*, September 8, 1980.

9. *Pravda*, October 30 and 31, 1980.

10. *Izvestia*, September 12 and 13, 1980.

11. *Literaturnaia Gazeta*, October 31, 1980.

12. See, for example, *Pravda*, October 31, 1980.

13. *Izvestia*, November 11, 1980.

14. *Pravda*, November 30, 1980. Commentaries in *Pravda* were indirect; they relied on an article in *Rudé Právo* that strengthened their threatening tone, since *Pravda* was suggesting that it was reflecting the general anxiety of the socialist camp. *Pravda*, October 7, 1980. The same remarks had already been made by Honecker. And the theme was repeated in *Literaturnaia Gazeta*, December 3, 1980.

15. *Krasnaia Zvezda*, December 6, 1980.

16. *Izvestia*, December 6, 1980.

17. On the Zamiatin mission to Warsaw from January 13 to 20, 1981, see *Pravda*, January 21, 1981.

18. *Pravda*, December 27, 1980 (meetings between Brezhnev and Czyrek); *Izvestia*, January 15, 1981 (economic discussions).

19. *Pravda*, February 3, 1981; *Izvestia*, February 4, 1981, explained that Solidarity's activities were applying antisocialist directives from the West, particularly from Radio Free Europe.

20. *Pravda*, February 1, 1981.

21. *Izvestia*, February 3, 1981.

22. R. D. Anderson, Jr., "Soviet Decision Making and Poland," *Problems of Communism* (March–April 1982): 22–37.

23. *Washington Post*, February 13, 1981; *Krasnaia Zvezda*, January 7, 1981, quoted by Anderson, op. cit., 32.

24. *New York Times*, March 27, 1981.

25. N. Ogarkov, *Kommunist*, 10 (July 1981): 80–91.

26. *Pravda*, March 5, 1981.

27. Economic problems were, however, also on the agenda; see the article in *Pravda*, February 20, 1981.

28. Anderson, op. cit., 30, 34–36.

29. *Pravda*, March 27, 1981.

30. *Pravda*, March 19, 1981.

31. Anderson, op. cit., 36, quoting the *New York Times*, November 24, 1980: "Various reports indicate that at their October 30 meeting, Mr. Brezhnev told Mr. Kania that the USSR would give the Polish leadership until summer to restore order."

32. *Izvestia*, February 13, 1981.

33. *Pravda* and *Izvestia*, February 17, 1981.

34. *Literaturnaia Gazeta*, February 18, 1981; *Krasnaia Zvezda*, February 18, 1981. *Izvestia*, on March 28, 1981, called the KOR not only an "antisocialist" organization but also an "anti-Polish" one.

35. *Pravda*, April 8, 1981.

36. *Pravda*, March 8, 1981.

37. *Pravda*, April 26, 1981.

38. *Polacy 80: Wyniki badań ankietowych* (Warsaw, 1981), 20, quoted by D. W. Paul and M. D. Simon, "Poland and Czechoslovakia," *Problems of Communism* (Sept.–Oct. 1981): 36.

39. *Spoleczne Zaufanie dla instytucji politicznych, spolecznych i administracynych* (Warsaw, 1981), 2, quoted by Paul and Simon, op. cit., 37.

40. *Pravda*, June 12, 1981.

41. "Program N.S.Z.Z. Solidarnosc uchuvalony przez i krajowy ziazel delegatoro," *Tygodnik Solidarnosc*, 29 (Warsaw, October 16, 1981). Quotations are taken from the translation published by La Documentation française, *Problèmes politiques et sociaux*, March 12, 1982, 14–20.

42. Ibid.

43. G. Mink and J. Y. Patel, preface to the dossier "Interrogations polonaises," published by La Documentation française, *Problèmes politiques et sociaux*, June 19, 1981, 3.

44. G. Mink, "Pologne, l'an II de la revolution," *Universalia 1982*, *Problèmes politiques et sociaux*, March 12, 1982, 4.

45. The notion and processes of normalization are the subject of research by the group led by Zdeněk Mlynář. It has already produced a very stimulating work: Brus, Kenda, Mlynar, *Processus de "normalisation" en Europe centrale soviétisée*, 55.

46. *Izvestia*, June 5, 1981.

47. *Pravda*, July 14 and 15, 1981.

48. Gromyko met the entire ruling group from July 3 to 5, *Pravda*, July 4 and 6, 1981.

49. *Pravda*, August 15 and 16, 1981.

50. *Pravda*, August 16, 1981.

51. *Izvestia*, August 2, 1981, accused West Germany of being the center of a vast enterprise of subversion in Poland. *Pravda*, August 25, 1981, widely publicized a speech by the Polish interior minister on the same theme.

52. See, for example, the article devoted to the twenty-sixth anniversary of the Warsaw Pact, *Zyćie Warszawy*, May 14, 1981: "The Warsaw Pact guarantees our national sovereignty . . . The history of every country, every nation, includes good and bad moments, troubled periods. In these periods, national sovereignty, border security, and the fact that the existence of the state depends on sure and tested guarantees, are all particularly important. The Warsaw Pact protects those conquests that are for Poland a *raison d'état.*"

53. *Pravda*, August 10, 1981.

54. *Krasnaia Zvezda*, August 14 and September 9 and 13, 1981.

55. *Pravda*, September 19, 1981.

56. See Brezhnev's message of congratulation, *Izvestia*, October 20, 1981.

57. *Izvestia*, November 26, 1981.

58. *Pravda*, October 31, 1981.

59. *Izvestia*, December 2 and 3, 1981; *Pravda*, December 3, 1981.

60. *Krasnaia Zvezda*, November 27 and December 4, 1981; *Izvestia*, February 5, 1982.

61. *Pravda*, December 14, 1981, immediately announced the essentials of the measures taken by the Military Council of National Salvation and published Jaruzelski's speech.

62. *Izvestia*, December 15, 1981.

63. Pierre Kende and W. Brus, *Processus de normalisation en Europe centrale soviétisée*, 8 and 45, very correctly emphasize the role of economic aid and economic recovery in the process of normalization.

64. *Izvestia*, January 8, 1982.

65. These Soviet hesitations appeared in discussions on the reorientation of Poland's economic relations toward the Comecon countries that took place between Baibakov and Jaruzelski in Warsaw in December 1982, *Izvestia*, December 13, 1982. The same theme (increased cooperation with the East, less dependence on the West) had been debated in the Talyzin-Jaruzelski discussions during the twenty-fourth session of the Soviet-Polish Commission for Economic, Scientific and Technical Cooperation that met in Warsaw in April 1982, *Pravda*, April 11, 1982.

66. *Pravda*, March 2 and 3, 1982; *Izvestia*, March 2, 1982.

67. *Pravda*, August 17, 1982.

68. See the positions of Czyrek during his journey to Moscow in January 1982, *Pravda*, January 11, 12, and 13, 1982.

69. In addition to Joseph Czyrek's visit already noted, we should mention the April visit to Moscow of a PUWP delegation led by A. Orzechowski, *Pravda*, April 2, 1982.

70. *Pravda*, December 24, 1982.

71. *Pravda*, March 8, 1981.

CONCLUSION TO PART TWO

BEYOND NORMALIZATION: "ENLIGHTENED TOLERANCE"?

Thirty years separate Stalin's USSR from that of Andropov. Thirty years of a developed power and an empire that had increased its territory. But also thirty years filled with events that had "troubled the bloc." The family of nations put together by the USSR had been continuously divided, had quarreled, and war had entered the bloc as an almost normal means of settling conflicts. In the succession of crises that affected almost all the countries of the bloc, the cause of conflict—despite differences in the manner of their expression—was always the same. By imposing its model on its allies, by asserting that it was the only one and that communism meant precisely the adoption of this unique model, the USSR had created an unstable universe in which material aspirations and the wish to follow a path in conformity with the tradition of each people increasingly came into conflict with the communist idea. Soviet style revolution, a melting pot of populations, had given rise to anti-Soviet revolutions identified with popular freedom.

But these thirty years of fratricidal struggle had also been thirty years of the restoration of order, of normalization. From one crisis to the next, the USSR had imposed a return to its unifying conceptions, the reintegration of the rebels into a bloc affected only superficially by those crises. The Soviet political system and its representatives in each country of the bloc had in the last analysis demonstrated a remarkable capacity to detect, in the various demonstrations of disagreement, the essentially unacceptable elements: rejection of the party's monopoly of power and the movement toward pluralism. Whenever "real socialism" was threatened by pluralist tendencies, the Soviet system was always mobilized to preserve or restore the original system. Depending on the depth and nature of these repeated crises of the system, this mobilization took the form of latent resistence to change or of normalization.

The experience of these thirty years and the violent conflicts, military or not, by which they were marked leads to two conclusions. Conflict is a permanent phenomenon of communism in all its institutional forms in Europe or in Asia. But the USSR at least until now has always been able to respond to conflict and to maintain its conception of communism. As Zdeněk

Mlynář notes in his theoretical discussion of normalization, for the last thirty years the USSR has developed a scenario for normalization adaptable to completely different situations and conditions. Thus, normalization did not always have the same meaning everywhere, even though the general strategy was the same and the result achieved was uniform: it suppressed or masked for a time the permanent crises of the bloc.[1]

This Soviet strategy of normalization generally developed in two phases (Zdeněk Mlynář sees three), found, with variations, in every country. The first phase was that of the violence that broke down the dissident movement and broke those party members or opposition figures who embodied an alternative to the Soviet model. This phase was characterized by an extensive use of violence, the restoration of a terrorist order, no doubt less widespread and frightening than the one Stalin had established, but an order that, in an attenuated way, perpetuated the main features of Stalinism. The target was society as a whole, which had to be convinced of the necessity for a return to order by means of exemplary terrorist measures. Examples were made of the most politically active elements of the society (intellectuals, party officials, or leaders of Solidarity, according to the circumstances), those who had led the movement. But this process was designed less to punish its victims than to create in the society as a whole the kind of disarray and passivity that would favor the restoration of "real socialism." Trials, jailings, and frequent harassment were often limited measures to retard the development of awareness and social mobilization and in the last analysis to block the formation of a civil society.

The second phase was that of reconstruction, the elaboration of a social contract on the basis of material values. To a morally broken and desperate society the political system offered the satisfaction of its material needs, economic progress, and everyday security. In this phase, the political system was to receive the help of the whole socialist community, and reconstruction depended on this general mobilization of resources, symbol of a solidarity that legitimated the violence of the first period and the collective efforts of the second. The system also made concessions relating to organization and to economic rights. The "national road," which was the goal sought in every crisis, could be resurrected in an atrophied form reduced to the economic sphere in order to increase the likelihood of success for reconstruction efforts.

In short, the Soviet system proposed that a humiliated and desperate society accept a limited contract. In exchange for a freedom that was forbidden, out of reach, it offered to restore a degree of prosperity. If it was capable of providing these material compensations quickly, if the economic success was striking, the system could hope that a certain consensus would develop in the society that would stabilize it around these concrete advantages.

No doubt, economic success—assuming that it could be achieved—was not a sufficient condition for this limited consensus. Kádár's success in

Hungary, Husák's failure in Czechoslovakia, and the general hostility to Jaruzelski in Poland indicate that many factors were involved: the initial situation, the personalities of those directing the normalization, and the historical and cultural context. In this connection, the attitude of intellectuals, of those who articulated social reactions, was a factor of almost decisive importance. If it is easy to reduce an entire society to despair and thereby to make it into a malleable entity, it is more difficult to prompt intellectuals to a denial that would destroy their reason for existence. This is why intellectuals were the immediate targets of repressive measures and also of attempts at corruption. And their attitudes from one country to another largely depended on the political culture that had shaped them.

It is these profound differences affecting the process of normalization and its results that explain how, despite the violence, the period of reconstruction was characterized by many, sometimes surprising, concessions. Normalization in each country, because it was designed to recreate a consensus—no doubt limited—followed a distinct path, seeking support in each society from those elements that would foster the consensus. In Poland, while agitation and rebellion persisted, the military regime took the risk of compromising with the Church and allowing the Polish Pope to return to his country because the entire history and political culture of Poland revealed that there was no other means by which the possible and difficult consensus could be achieved.

Normalization as it has been carried out for thirty years has had the single function of maintaining a homogeneous, monolithic system against repeated attempts to replace it with pluralism. To achieve this end every means was acceptable. In particular, after the repressive phase, every force that could be used to achieve consensus and the restoration of social peace found a place within this strategy. The party's monopoly and control were reestablished and the appearance of normal life according to the wishes of the majority could be restored because the means for controlling it were again in place.

In the course of the last thirty years the leaders of the USSR have replaced the enlightened despotism of past centuries with a strategy that one would like to characterize as enlightened tolerance. For such a strategy to succeed, many conditions must be met, especially a tricky use of time. The time of the defeat of revolutions, the time devoted to blows against society, the time of violence must be very brief. And the time between defeat and the offer of tangible results offered as compensation to the society must also be brief. People have to be quickly discouraged and quickly convinced. On the other hand, the time for forging the new consensus is necessarily longer. It involves the realization of the realities, of the irreversibility of normalization, as Pierre Kende has correctly pointed out.[2] It is only afterward that a new social contract can be constructed, giving assurances to the political system established during the phase of violence. Every system thus needs several years to prove itself and to determine whether normalization has been internalized by the population or has definitively failed. Because every situation is different, because every population follows its own path, the USSR cannot rely only on normalization through "controlled violence." While the world has had its eyes fixed on these spectacular processes of reconstruction of the system, the USSR has on the fringes of these crises been carrying out a deeper process of the construction of an integrated communist society.

NOTES

1.   W. Brus, P. Kende, and Z Mlynar, *Processus de "normalisation" en Europe centrale soviétisée* (SL, 1983).
2.   Ibid., 7.

PART THREE

THE EMPIRE OF THE JANISSARIES

7

BIG BROTHER

"The experience of the solution of the national question in the Soviet Union is considered by communists not only as an example of the brotherly friendship of peoples within the framework of a single multinational state, but also as the foundation of the socialist conception of relations among nations in general."[1]

This declaration by a secretary of the Polish United Workers' Party echoes the position maintained by the USSR since 1945 that the Soviet model is exemplary because there is no other that can lay claim to the heritage of Marx and Lenin, and because there is no other that has resolved the problem of the peaceful coexistence of different peoples.[2]

Behind this apparently simple proposition, important ideological changes lie concealed. On the first argument—the exemplary nature of the Soviet model—the position of the USSR has hardly varied, while on its application to relations among socialist nations, the Soviet position has on the other hand registered considerable changes. Domestic experience, that of a multiethnic state in which the nations had a preestablished tradition of common life because of the imperial past, could not immediately be transposed to the organization of sovereign nations that had lived within the framework of state sovereignty during the period between the wars. Once the immediate postwar period had passed, when moral disarray and material destruction relegated reflection about relations among nations, expressed at the time in terms of power relations, to the background, the USSR undertook the task of defining them. In the Stalinist period, this reflection was limited, confined within the simple framework of relations between blocs. Within each bloc, the unity of states—unity of organization and behavior—should prevail. Yugoslavia's expulsion from the Cominform was logical in this Manichean perspective. Unable to force it into line, Stalin had to resign himself to the choice of rupture and rejection. But the end of Stalinism, the entry of the USSR onto the international stage and its militancy in favor of national liberation movements again placed on the agenda the problem of the nation and hence of the relations among nations of the same system. Once a socialist camp made up of sovereign nations existed, it was necessary to define the nature of relations within this camp and thus to define the nature of the entire camp. This reflection varied following changes within the USSR and the crises that shattered the socialist camp. It makes up the political framework that the USSR has imposed on the system as a whole and is thus not a negligible element in its evolution. The ideology of the relations among socialist nations is both an instrument for the legitimation of the authority that the USSR has arrogated to itself over the other states of the camp and the vision that the leaders of the fraternal countries have of their national fate. This ideology, the world view of the elites of the socialist world, has helped to shape a horizontal socialist space where responsibilities are carried out and within which the officials of the *Nomenklatura* of the whole system live. It is here that the link between domestic policies and external attitudes is established, and the national and the international converge.

Diversity and Equality: A Pedagogy of Internationalism, 1956 to 1968

After the stifling and rigid alignment of Stalinism, the post-Stalin years, expressed first of all in ideology, had the effect of opening for the countries of the region possibilities for action and different relations in the world. We will not reconsider the themes developed by the Twentieth Congress and the opening it created for a diversity of experiences. What is important here were the effects of that diversity, which was for a time accepted in Moscow. Indeed, the USSR did not merely say that one could follow different paths to socialism. In the mid-fifties it rehabilitated in its ideological system national values and the national interest. And it asserted that the national state was the framework within which these values were best developed and protected. On dissolving the Cominform on April 17, 1956, the USSR was able to justify the measure, as it did when the Comintern was dissolved in 1943, by saying seriously that it had achieved its historical mission. Even though this ritual formula accompanied the 1956 decision,[3] the essential points were the recognition of different roads toward socialism and the insistence on the "particularities and national conditions of each country" and on the "national aspirations and interests" that should guide the actions of each communist party. The change in the title of what had been the journal of the Cominform from *For Lasting Peace, For People's Democracy* to *Problems of Peace and Socialism*, by eliminating the term "people's democracy,"[4] also gave a strong indication of the desire not to favor a single socialist model. Once the crises of 1956 were over, the recognition of the right to diversity had domestic consequences that are well known, but it also had international consequences. The declaration of October 30, 1956, intended to put an end to the Hungarian crisis, provided the basis for various forms of action by the different states. It accomplished this by asserting that "the socialist nations can construct their relations only on the principles of complete equality of rights, respect for territorial integrity, for political independence, and for sovereignty, and non-interference in one another's affairs," by recognizing that in Stalinist policies "pure and simple mistakes had been made, particularly in relations among socialist countries; these violations and these mistakes have reduced the reach of the principles of equality of rights in relations among socialist countries." Moreover, by asserting that "the historic decisions of the Twentieth Congress have created the conditions for a strengthening of friendship and cooperation among socialist states on the unshakeable foundation of the total sovereignty of each state," the USSR was saluting a universe of equals, not of satellites irresistibly drawn to the center. All the measures designed to demonstrate this equality—the withdrawal of Soviet advisers from every country and especially state-to-state discussions on whether Soviet troops would remain on national territories—gave this declaration a scope that the states of the camp took seriously. The "socialist camp" that replaced the bloc was defined as a group of states linked by ideological solidarity, by a single vision of peace and prosperity, but devoid of constraints. The behavior of the allies of the USSR was thereby immediately changed. Because they were recognized as individual states with the vocation of defining and defending their own state interests, the states of Eastern Europe opened themselves to the outer world, as the USSR was doing in the same period. Taking advantage of the momentary tolerance of the USSR but also of its increased commitments in the world that partially diverted its attention from its partners, the socialist states carried on significant international activities between 1956 and 1968. They joined a large number of international organizations, increased bilateral ties, particularly economic and cultural ties, with the noncommunist countries of Europe and thereby fully assumed sovereign positions in the international community of states. Their involvements were not always identical with that of the USSR and these differences helped to give them an international dimension. Thus, during these years, in the framework of organizations affiliated with the United Nations, while the USSR did not belong to the Food and Agriculture Organization, all the Eastern European states did. The GATT, from which the USSR was absent, accepted Czechoslovakia, Rumania, Poland, and Yugoslavia.[5] A careful study of the affiliations of communist states with international organizations in 1965 shows that, while the USSR belonged to thirty-eight, it was outdistanced by Rumania, Poland, and Czechoslovakia, who at the time generally carried on an extraordinary amount of foreign activities and maintained personnel and missions abroad that, considering the relative size of the states, indicated an interest greater than that of the USSR.[6] Thus, in 1963–64, while the USSR had 1345 diplomats in foreign posts, Czechoslovakia had 422. We could multiply examples, all of which indicate that these countries wanted to go outside the socialist environment to reestablish themselves in international life as independent states and not as members of a community. Two socialist states broke records in this progression toward international independence: Yugoslavia, which because of its leading role in the nonaligned movement occupied a unique position that the Soviet Union could not challenge in the realm of relations among states; and Rumania, whose demonstrations of independence were numerous at the time. Not only did Rumania have a foreign policy distinct from and sometimes contrary to that of the USSR (in the Arab-Israeli Six-Day War, for example), but also Ceauşescu did not hesitate to assert that international conflicts were largely the work of the two great imperialisms, resolving their opposition on the backs of medium-sized states. By calling a plague on both houses, the Rumanian head of state carried heresy to its extreme, since he suggested that there were no attitudes specific to the socialist states, and that international relations were dominated only by power relations.[7]

No doubt the USSR suffered no loss by this sensational entry of its allies onto the international stage. Although Rumania was opposed to it, the other states were in general close to its positions and their actions often allowed it to diversify its activities, indeed to use these handy intermediaries for steps it did not wish to take openly. Thus for example the first deliveries of arms to Egypt in 1955 were carried out through the intermediary of Czechoslovakia.[8] But the use by the USSR of its allies' activities, the fact that in many organizations Bulgaria acted as a stand-in for the USSR, the support it received from the states in its camp on votes at the United Nations, and the various restrictions imposed on the sister states' freedom of maneuver should not be allowed to conceal the change that took place in the status of these states between 1956 and 1968. Because they had an international existence, they became equals in the socialist camp and developed arguments on the basis of this equality to support their independence in making domestic choices.

The USSR had few arguments to oppose to this evolution. It had offered theoretical propositions that emphasized the importance of the national interest and sovereignty and had attempted to establish the socialist camp on the basis of this collection of national interests, hoping that equality would give rise to a new feeling of kinship.

The Soviet ideological choice in this period took place within two contexts. As a champion of independence on the international stage, the USSR had to stop presenting itself as the leader of a satellized universe. The Stalinist monolith led from Moscow was not an attractive example for the countries that the USSR was then attempting to win over and to bring into the realm of the nonaligned states and whose independence it claimed to guarantee. Because it was convinced of the importance of the third world in the international relations between the great powers, because it thought that the struggle for power was being played out in the third world and not in Europe, the USSR had to loosen the vise that held the Stalinist monolith together and revise its model of relations among nations. A domestic consideration accompanied these international concerns. For Stalin's successors, the model for relations among nations that had been developed in the USSR had unquestionable validity. The mistake in Eastern Europe, they recognized during the 1956 revolution, was to have rushed the process and to have imposed on the countries occupied or liberated in 1945 a forced uniformity, forgetting their specific characters and particular situations. Stalin repeated in Eastern Europe in 1945 the move toward uniformity that he had undertaken in the USSR in 1922. Prevented by Lenin from forcing the nations to integrate themselves too quickly into a unified whole,[9] he returned to his plan in the USSR of the thirties and especially in the Eastern Europe of 1945. After 1956, his successors, in order to defuse the rancor and frustration that Stalinist precipitation had created, attempted to revive the Leninist idea of a transitional stage during which the equality of nations would be an education for internationalism.[10] The slogan of a "return to Leninism" that covers the period of de-Stalinization was unquestionably at the heart of this restoration of relative equality in relations among socialist states. For a few years the socialist camp that had succeeded the compact bloc of satellites of 1948 was based on this conception of fraternity among equal states in which, following Orwell, the USSR was "more equal than others." It used the egalitarian myth to set up structures of cooperation—the Warsaw Pact, Comecon—in which it immediately took on the predominant role. But during those years in which diversity was recognized, the activity of these institutions remained weak and their place in the ultimate program of integration barely perceptible.

Limited Sovereignty: 1968 to 1976

Diversity led to discord and failure. As soon as they recognized the disintegrating effects and not the anticipated "rapprochement" of the diversity accepted in 1956, Soviet leaders reacted, immediately renounced the theory of "many roads for the development of socialism," and began to encourage uniformity. In this case the ideological shift followed events rather than preceding them. In Warsaw and Budapest in 1956 the insurgents had been encouraged to follow different paths because they had drawn the lessons from the Belgrade agreement and the Twentieth Congress, while in 1968 the USSR had no theoretical justification to support the invasion of Czechoslovakia. The Czech Communist Party was solidly supported by the entire theoretical arsenal that the USSR had provided it, and it took inspiration from the examples of the divergent paths followed by Poland, Rumania, and

Yugoslavia. Confronted with this revolution, the USSR chose to cut to the quick and to suppress it by force, in contradiction to the whole egalitarian system that had been so constantly affirmed. But immediately afterward, it placed the relations among socialist nations into a new framework in order to avoid the recurrence of similar crises. The theoretical development of inter-socialist relations in the years following the invasion of Czechoslovakia was much more than an *a posteriori* program of justification for a coup. Begun in fact under the compulsion to explain and justify this reaction this developed ideology was later designed to define the political program of the USSR in Eastern Europe and to provide it with clear legitimacy and a clear direction.

The first definition of what has wrongly been called the Brezhnev doc-trine was produced in the days following the invasion. *Pravda*, in its first editorial on the subject, pointed out that the defense of socialism in Czecho-slovakia "was not only an internal matter for the people of that country, but it was also a matter of defending the positions of world socialism."[11]

The editorialist of *Izvestia* added to this explanation a more developed analysis of the function of the camp's collective institutions.[12] Challenging the notion that there had been an intervention, a term that was judged inappropriate to describe a natural dynamic, *Izvestia* pointed out that "The Warsaw Pact does not have as its only function the defense of the borders and territories of the signatory states. The Pact was signed to defend socialism, in response to the creation of the aggressive military bloc of NATO."

This was the very first appearance in a published text of the recognition of the *internal* function of the Warsaw Pact, directed toward the allies of the USSR, not toward its enemies. Until then the argument that it was a means of defense against an organized imperialist bloc had been the only one officially recognized.

These circumstantial arguments had already been hinted at in the various documents and declarations that the Prague Spring had prompted from the USSR and its allies. But they had never appeared in the form of clear principles contradicting the egalitarian principles of the preceding period. Because the contradiction was flagrant, and because the Yugoslavs and Rumanians argued that it was scandalous, the Soviet leaders undertook the task of harmonizing the principles of 1956 with the intervention of 1968. This task was encrusted to a specialist in Marxism, Professor Kovalev, who wrote a long article developing what would later be called the theory of "limited sovereignty."[13] In this article, which incidentally does not use the expression, Professor Kovalev contrasted real sovereignty with the abstract approach to sovereignty and self-determination, independent of social relations. Sov-ereignty was a concept linked to the entire history of the development of the socialist world; there was no doubt that it implied free choice of the path to be followed, but within the framework of socialism and its interests. Once a socialist state had started down a path that threatened its domestic orientation and more broadly the interests of socialism and of the socialist camp, sovereignty no longer had any meaning. And the right to self-determination was also contained within this precise ideological framework. Socialism gave that right its reality, while "neutralist" temptations destroyed the community of socialist states and threatened its interests. Sovereignty thus had a concrete content that had to be taken into account: it was socialism, for which all communist states were responsible. This notion of sovereignty was also adopted by Leonid Brezhnev, who, speaking to the Polish communists, said that respect for the sovereignty of states was the organizing principle of relations among them; but he also said that the duty to preserve the socialism of a state, threatened from within or outside, was an integral part of this conception of sovereignty.[14]

These hasty formulations, reactions to criticism provoked by the intervention from communist states and communist parties, were developed in the early seventies into a more coherent theory of international relations within the socialist world. It is easy to understand why Soviet analysis was directed less to the ideological community than to the international community. At the time the Soviet leadership was engaged in intense international activities with significant stakes. Negotiations with West Germany were finally about to normalize the situation of Eastern Europe and to lead to the conference on European security that the USSR had long been asking for. For Moscow, this conference had an appeal and a necessity that the myth of Yalta has long obscured. Because all the arrangements of 1945 were provisional and because there had been no peace treaty with Germany giving these arrangements permanent status through a general agreement, in theory everything was subject to revision. In this progression toward legal consolidation of the postwar European situation and its division, the USSR was aware that it was in an ambiguous position. It was less a question of the Czech intervention, which would not prevent the development of détente, than of the possible effects of détente on the coherence of the socialist world. Was it possible simultaneously to push for a major European negotiation and to maintain the conception of a unified socialist camp occupying a particular position and obeying particular rules? In the early seventies, the USSR wanted to gain international recognition, based on universally accepted principles of international relations, of its domination over Eastern Europe. Was it possible to confirm this domination through the general rules of international law and to avoid turning those rules—of unlimited sovereignty and self-determination of peoples—against the USSR?

This preoccupation was at the heart of the theory of intersocialist relations that the USSR developed between 1970 and 1976. It was a rather complete theory, attempting to respond in advance to all the problems that could arise in the socialist camp. The question was no longer to justify past intervention but to erect a protective barrier against future erosion of the socialist universe.

This new theory of relations among socialist states was made up of several elements. In the first place, the Soviet theory attempted to demonstrate that the particular, unique character of relations among socialist states, the existence of a "socialist space" in international relations, created particular forms of solidarity, a specifically socialist foreign policy, and connections of a unique character specific to the system between domestic and foreign policy.[15] One writer described these new conditions of international life in these terms: "The scope and intensity of the coordination of foreign policies within the socialist community, the degree of unity, and therefore of effectiveness, of its international actions, is without precedent in the history of world politics. Socialism has not only brought to international life new norms and new principles. . . ."[16]

This particularly socialist space of international relations derived first of all from the fact that the socialist system in order to satisfy the interests of its components needed to develop as "a unique entity."[17]

The specificity and uniqueness of the socialist space meant that links of a new kind were created among states, links unknown to the nonsocialist world, the abandonment of which would be a serious historical regression. Socialist internationalism, about which "Lenin said that it was a decisive element in the establishment of communist states," was the basic principle on which the Eastern European community was founded. The legitimacy of actions taken by the Brezhnev leadership to develop the meaning of socialist internationalism—in the Czech affair, for example—was thus based on Lenin's teaching.[18] It is significant that in order to define the place of socialist internationalism among the duties of the socialist community in whose name the intervention in Czechoslovakia had been carried out, not only did Soviet writers refer to Lenin, but they also used the term *zakonomernost'*, that is, in conformity with law. Thus, what was involved was an absolute law of the socialist community. The Soviet theory developed the idea that the socialist realm, "a new category in international relations,"[19] had been consolidated precisely because of and not in spite of an active struggle carried on by the entire socialist community to defend the system's achievements. In other words, the use of military force was from the beginning one of the privileged means for ensuring and extending these victories: through the efforts of the Red Army in the first stage, through bilateral treaties in the second stage, through the Warsaw Pact in the third stage. This new community had found its fundamental content first of all in "political and military assistance."[20]

This definition of a socialist internationalism inseparable from the very existence of the socialist world is very important for the light it sheds on Soviet concerns during this period. The first concern was to present the Czech intervention as an example of this theory. Far from trying to erase the episode, Soviet leaders constantly came back to it. Every text devoted to the definition of the socialist world insisted on the exemplary character of the

Czech crisis and of the demonstration of socialist internationalism that brought it to an end. Husák returned to the question at the Fourteenth Congress of the Czech Communist Party,[21] and alluded to it at the Twenty-fourth Congress of the Soviet Communist Party. This determination not to "bury" the Czech affair was misperceived and misunderstood in the Western world, which saw in Soviet insistence on the subject only the desire for self-justification and the need for reconciliation with the communist parties that had been shaken by the violence. But the Soviet attitude in the early seventies was entirely different from this presumed wish to justify itself. Soviet explanation were not governed by the recent past but by the near future. The USSR defined the nature of the socialist community in order to place itself in a strong position for future all-European negotiations. It wanted these negotiations to give it international recognition and not to dilute it in a Europe with vague ideological borders. This explains the Soviet desire to approach these negotiations with a clear position, having asserted that there was a specific socialist space in Europe whose fundamental law and duty was socialist internationalism. And the example of Czechoslovakia was invoked to support this argument. In the negotiations that were about to take place, the USSR intended to approach its negotiating partners on precise grounds, that is, taking into account the Czech intervention and not despite that intervention. The USSR cannot be criticized for having concealed its approach to European relations on this point. Everything was very carefully explained, not only the nature and the obligations of the socialist community, but also the particular character of the states that made up that community. The leading role of the communist party in the socialist state was also, with reference made to Lenin, an objective law—*zakonomernost'*—that could not be changed. Although the leading role of the party did not exclude the development of other social organizations, "like unions, soviets, cooperatives, youth and sport groups, and so on," it was "the party that exercised the leading influence on all activities of social life."[22] It was emphasized that this leading role of the party was necessary "to guarantee the unshakeable political and ideological unity of the whole society."[23]

By locating the leading role of the party within this general philosophy of the socialist state and of the whole community welded together by the duty of internationalism, by locating the unions in the interminable cohort of organizations guided by the party on the same level as sports associations, were the Soviet leaders not establishing in advance the judgment they would make of the Polish experience at the end of the decade? Against this definition of the socialist state, of its characteristics and limits, applicable to all, no one could take refuge in the notion of sovereignty, for that notion was part of the ideological mechanism set up at the time. The Soviet theory developed the idea of a new sovereignty, linked to revolutionary achievements, a popular sovereignty that, far from being in conflict with socialist internationalism, was inseparable from it.[24] The strength of the socialist system and of the socialist state thus lay in this harmonious conjunction of national and international interests, which class society has never succeeded in reconciling.

From the idea of a "limited sovereignty," hastily articulated immediately after the Czech invasion in order to give the Warsaw Pact armies a reason for having broken the rules inscribed in the 1956 declaration, to this new definition of intersocialist relations much territory had been covered. What can be discerned from declarations and documents produced toward the end of the decade is that the definition of the socialist camp propounded in 1956 was out of date, and that the continuous progress of the socialist system in both domestic and foreign spheres—the Warsaw Pact functioned as an integrating institution—had invalidated definitions of sovereignty associated with the phase of transition between the old order and the socialist order. This notion of a link between the continuous progress of socialism within each state and the development of relations among socialist states is very important. It contradicts international law, which bases relations among states on permanent principles, defined in a fixed manner within an unchanging context. Sovereignty, the inviolability of borders, noninterference are concepts whose meaning is considered unaffected by space and time. On the other hand, and this notion was important for the period following the Helsinki conference, the USSR was already suggesting that in the socialist sphere concepts had a variable content, developing according to the rhythm of the progress of socialism. There was no doubt that the socialist states were sovereign. But the content of their sovereignty in 1970 was not what it had been in 1956. And the equality that had governed their relations was soon to take on a new twist. Intervention in Czechoslovakia had in the end two consequences. In the immediate term, it allowed the USSR to put an end to an experiment that Moscow could not accept. But in the longer term it allowed the beginning of a revision of the principles governing relations among socialist states. Once again it would be wrong and dangerous for an understanding of Soviet conduct to imagine that the USSR developed this theoretical arsenal to justify, *a posteriori*, an intervention that incidentally did nothing to slow the progress of détente. The Czech crisis was an opportunity for the USSR to carry out a revision of relations within the bloc that had already been begun concretely with the Warsaw Pact. The extensive activities of this institution in the mid-sixties demonstrate clearly that the norms of intersocialist relations were already in the process of being transformed. After the Czech crisis, the USSR had a good reason to conform theory to practice.

The Soviet Model of Reconciliation of Nations

The summer of 1975 represented a decisive moment in the history of the relations of the USSR with "its" Europe. The Helsinki conference brought it confirmation after three decades of the territorial acquisitions of the Second World War and of its sphere of influence in Eastern Europe.[25] Although it is now fashionable to consider that little that was new came out of the final act signed by thirty-five powers in Helsinki, and that so much noise and so many meetings to set out general principles and the desire to bring about more sincerity and cooperation in Europe had few practical consequences, this is to forget two aspects of the final act, two extremes of the document. First of all by subscribing to the inviolability of European borders, the international community deliberately closed its eyes to the ambiguity of the principle and to the fate of the populations located within the Soviet sphere since the war. The ambiguity of the principle was linked to the document's lack of precision. International relations have been full of similar misunderstandings that have had tragic consequences. While the text accepted by the West was indeed centered on this inviolability, the text relied on by the socialist world used the term "untouchability." In one case, borders could not be changed by force; in the other, they could not in any event be changed. In the eyes of the USSR this misunderstanding perpetuated the inclusion within Soviet space of the Baltic states, Bessarabia, and the Sub-Carpathian Ukraine, as well as the division of Germany and the territorial changes in Poland. It meant that the socialist territories could not be changed. The other element affecting the relations of the USSR with its allies was the "third basket" (human rights provisions), about which debates had been very bitter and which committed all signatories to accepting the common principles of the free circulation of people and ideas. By signing this charter—particularly the third basket—the USSR and the Eastern European states accepted political concepts shared by all the signatories and accepted rules of political organization and activity that had not until then been present in the socialist camp; more generally they joined an international community that had adopted stable principles, defined in the preamble to the final act, whose most important elements were respect for state sovereignty, noninterference in others' affairs, and the renunciation of violence as a means to settle problems of international relations. Acceptance of the Helsinki principles thus placed the USSR in an unprecedented and contradictory situation. On the one hand, these principles satisfied longstanding efforts to consolidate the European order that had come out of the war—which the USSR had changed for its benefit by institutionalizing the *de facto* division of Germany—while on the other it destroyed the thesis of a specific socialist space with its own norms of behavior. In this new international context that it had adhered to along with all its allies, could the USSR continue to maintain the thesis of socialist internationalism governing the domestic life of the various socialist states? This difficulty was immediately perceived by the inhabitants of the USSR and the East European countries. The two years following the signature of the final act of Helsinki were marked by an extraordinary proliferation of movements designed to change conditions under the protection of measures accepted by the USSR. The committees for the application of the Helsinki agreements created in the USSR sometimes called for the application of the third basket, and sometimes in the national republics emphasized sovereignty and the right to self-determination. Charter 77 in Czechoslovakia was perhaps the most spectacular, but it was not the only application of the Helsinki principles.[26]

Confronted with these changes, which simultaneously supported and challenged its conquests, the USSR could not persist in relying on principles developed in the early seventies that were hardly compatible with the Helsinki principles, as was revealed at the time by "rank and file" initiatives.

It was urgent to define once again the framework for the existence of the socialist states. The USSR carried this out in three areas: international life, the Soviet model, and definition of the socialist community. In these three areas, although the basic reasoning was not always new, the arguments were, and they lent some strength to the whole theory. The occasion for explaining these points was the Soviet Constitution adopted in October 1977 to commemorate the sixtieth anniversary of the revolution. If we recall that this new constitution had been in process or on the agenda since 1961 and that no one in the USSR, after such a long period of silence, believed in it, it seems clear that the coincidence of its adoption with the sixtieth anniversary of the revolution was rather fortuitous and in any event secondary. On the other hand, the document appeared at the appropriate point to close the gaps opened in the domestic and international Soviet system by the policy of détente and by Helsinki. The document was a response to a series of problems that tended to weaken the system.

The first important theme was the definition of international life and of the articulation between generally accepted norms—codified in the Helsinki final act—and the socialist states' system of reference. The constitution resolved the difficulty within which its Western negotiators had naively thought they could trap the USSR by forcing it to subscribe to a general code of good conduct. While Helsinki changed the USSR into an ordinary state and contained its relations with other socialist states within this general framework, the 1977 Constitution demolished this fragile construction and restored socialist specificity. It restored the notion of a "specific socialist space" that fell outside general international norms.

The 1977 Constitution—the fundamental law of the USSR, which superseded every other document—left no ambiguity about the extremely important problem of the particular nature of intersocialist relations. Unlike earlier constitutions, the fundamental law of 1977 included a section devoted to international relations, and the organization of this article sheds light on its logic. Article 29 repeated in their totality the ten points of the final act of Helsinki, which thus acquired, according to a writer in the theoretical journal of the Academy of Sciences, "for the first time, and in one country alone . . . constitutional validity."[27]

The USSR thus reconciled its fundamental principles with those of Helsinki and placed what followed under the sign of an international consensus on *its* ideas. While Article 28 described the field of international relations primarily in classic terms, the constitution nevertheless divided this domain into three zones: relations with countries with different social systems where general principles applied; relations with developing countries where the USSR had a special duty of aid and support; finally, and especially, relations in the sphere of intersocialist relations. Article 30, devoted to this problem, made the architecture of the whole document explicit: "The USSR, as an integral part of the world socialist system and the socialist community, develops friendship, cooperation, and friendly mutual aid with the socialist countries, on the basis of socialist internationalism, and it actively participates in economic integration and in the international socialist division of labor."[28]

Commenting on this passage, the writer already quoted emphasized the fact that it gave to the policy of the USSR and the sister states a specific socialist dimension that was thereby consolidated.[29]

All the commentaries published in the USSR on the 1977 Constitution emphasized the importance of this international conception. "Real socialism actively affects world development, with its experience and its example of a new kind of international relations."[30] This new kind of relations was basd on "the development of the dictatorship of the national proletariat into an international formation."[31]

Following the promulgation of this constitutional document, the leaders of the socialist community in turn emphasized the realities for which the document presented a theoretical framework, rather than the theory itself. Leonid Brezhnev hailed both the document and the developments behind it as reflections of an unprecedented situation.

"The socialist community," he said, "is a union of an entirely new kind. It is not simply based on the community of interests of a group of states, but it is a family of fraternal peoples, led by Marxist-Leninist parties, welded together by the same conception of existence. . . . This union is supported by an exceptional unity in theory and practice."[32]

It was also pointed out that this community of a new kind had an "international content . . . that it operated with reference to a defined international totality, objectively opposed to the capitalist world and to the old forms of relations between nations and states."[33]

It would be difficult to be more explicit, and it would be possible to fill an entire book with similar quotations, but that would serve no purpose. The fact remains that in the constitution and in commentaries on it both in learned journals and by many leaders of socialist countries,[34] there was presented a certain number of definitions of the socialist domain, of its specificity, of its fundamental incompatibility with the rest of the international sphere, and of the unity of conceptions, of choices, and of tendencies that were its objective norms.[35] The essential point was the affirmation of the dual character of international society and international life: the world contained a socialist space and space that was not socialist. And the USSR, like its allies, had a dual nature. They were states like other states when they acted within the framework of nonsocialist space; they were different, specific states, acting according to their own principles, when they acted within socialist space. Neither the framework within which the socialist countries were developing nor the essential principle that governed that framework, socialist internationalism, were subject to discussion. On this point, the USSR had carried out a substantial effort of clarification addressed simultaneously to the "fraternal nations" and to the Western world. In the conferences following Helsinki, the USSR, concerned with avoiding demands that it did not wish to consider, very clearly expressed its notion of what was appropriate for international discussion and what was not. Anything having to do with socialist internationalism was not a subject for discussion in meetings involving states of both social systems. In reconstructing a bipolar universe, the USSR intended to close off its camp, to protect it from the infection of external ideas and interventions, and at the same time not to lose the benefit of the dialogue that had been begun in Helsinki.

The second no less important aspect of this revision of the organizing principles of the socialist world had to do with the Soviet model. While the universal validity of the Soviet state model and the duty of sister states to imitate it were principles that had varied little since 1945, in 1977 the USSR crossed a new frontier in the imposition of its example on Eastern Europe. From that point on what it offered as a model for the sister states was not simply the party-state, but, at a second stage, the multiethnic community.

The USSR had always asserted that it represented a perfect and unique example of the solution to national conflicts. The Soviet state "combines harmoniously sovereignty of the Soviet national republic and sovereignty of the multinational state,"[36] according to the president of the Soviet of Nationalities of the Supreme Soviet, writing in 1970, who it cannot be denied had some competence to deal with this delicate subject.

From this initial observation, he drew a conclusion that is at the center of all subsequent Soviet theory: "The experience of the friendship of peoples in the USSR forms the invaluable basis for the construction of socialism in the sovereign countries of the socialist community, united to us by the great internationalist fraternity."[37]

Several essential ideas emerge from this statement and they have been constantly reiterated since then. The Soviet federation, as a mode of organization of the relations among sovereign states, is a universal example. The organization of the socialist community created in 1945 should reproduce the Soviet system. The relations of Eastern Europe—a community of states of a new kind—with the USSR were to be constructed according to the model of the relations of the peoples of the USSR with the majority nationality, the Russian people. This kind of reasoning implied that the Soviet empire was made up of two groups. The first was the USSR, whose center was the Russian state and the Russian people, which was the older brother of this family of peoples and states. The second group was the socialist community as a whole, whose central axis was the USSR, which became in turn the older brother of the Eastern European world. It was the older brother because it had opened the path to revolution, because it had been able to pioneer cultivation of the harsh soil on which socialism was built. The common definition of the USSR during these years—a large family in which the older brother supported and guided the younger ones by his example and his wisdom—was thus extended to the socialist world, which was in turn defined as a family. And conflicts within this framework of fraternal relations were reduced to the comforting level of "family matters,"[38] which as everyone knows are resolved domestically, not in public.

This general definition of the socialist community, the extension of the Soviet federation to a part of Europe, reproducing its balances and its logic, was supplemented after 1977 by a more precise definition of the state and of the medium-term objectives of the USSR and hence of its appendages.

The 1977 Constitution and its accompanying commentaries defined the USSR—at the stage of "developed socialism" and then of "real socialism"[39]—as a new historical community, the framework of a new human community, the "Soviet people," which transcended social and national differences.[40]

It is important to pay close attention to current conceptions of the evolution of the Soviet people because they are applicable, as we have seen, to the development of Eastern Europe. For years the general scheme for the development of peoples was seen in three stages—independent growth, mutually beneficial alliances, fusion into one[41]—but this radical conception, which had provoked many disturbances in the USSR, had later been modified.

The notion of the "Soviet people, a new historical community," was the product of the association of nations (*sblizhenie*), understood in a different way from the way it had been understood in the sixties. Whereas Khrushchev's view of the coming together of the nations was of a stage at which all national characteristics weakened, inevitably leading to fusion, later definitions of the phenomenon had an entirely different content involving both the continuation of national differences and "the consolidation of common views and uniform patterns of behavior."[42]

The Twenty-Sixth Congress of the Soviet Communist Party in 1981 confirmed this conception—closer to Soviet reality than the voluntarist theories of Khrushchev—in which there was undoubtedly a dual dynamic at work. Aims were very forcefully expressed, and at the same time the political system tended to impose a single pattern of behavior on different societies.

Because the Soviet political system had for years been attempting to impose a common consciousness on different peoples by denying their cultural and historical differences, by asserting that those differences were in the process of disappearing, it had provoked defensive reflexes that had developed national passions. It now accepted these differences and their continued existence and had decided that rapprochement could be brought about on the basis of common political values, a common political program, and networks of political and economic interdependence.[43] This development emphasized the integration of the system and of the elites that kept it in operation, and it left room for feelings of national identification on the part of peoples and individuals.[44] In keeping with the Soviet Constitution as a whole, whose logic was that of the system, the conception of the new historical community, the Soviet people, was a "systemic" rather than organic or historical conception.[45]

The principal statement by Yuri Andropov on the question confirmed in the terminology that he used that he had no intention of innovating in this area but rather that he had adopted the line that had been followed since 1977.[46] For Andropov too the time of illusion had passed; it was on the basis of a totality of administrative and political structures and of cooperative procedures that rapprochement, a key word in his public pronouncements, would give strength to the Soviet people. Although Andropov used the word "fusion," he did this only once,[47] evoking a distant goal carefully described as far in the future and preceded by many obstacles. On the other hand, the word "rapprochement" was used constantly. Andropov in particular in speaking of the USSR insisted on the role of the Russian people: "Without its inexhaustible fraternal assistance no accomplishments would have been possible"; similarly, he pointed to "the unique importance," in this process of rapprochement, "of the Russian language."[48]

It is probably unnecessary to note that Andropov also adopted the theory that the socialist community occupied a particular sphere of international life.[49]

The development of these ideas in the USSR was not confined to a particular group. This development began under Brezhnev and was taken up by Andropov because in the mind of the leaders it was a means of shaping the mental universe of the communist societies, of imposing a common language that was an indispensable means for going beyond the conflicts and problems of the past thirty years.

From the USSR to Eastern Europe: A Single Political Space

The conception of national relations within the USSR was to be completely transposed to Eastern Europe. For several years now Moscow has not been content with praising the excellence of the Soviet model and asserting its universal validity. All descriptions and projections of the future of Eastern Europe have been constructed precisely according to the Soviet model. This tendency was already visible at the Twenty-Fifth Congress in 1976 at which the general secretary's report asserted that "the process of gradual rapprochement among the socialist countries now seems to be a law (*zakonomernost'*).[50]

The fact that the term "rapprochement" of nations, which defined the process of development within the USSR, was being transposed and used systematically to describe the course of events in Eastern Europe clearly indicates that the region was for the USSR an extension of the federated republics.[51]

We can see how the USSR thought of the future of Eastern Europe. It proposed an ideological model with the dual objective of offering to the integrated elites a solid conceptual framework, closed off from external influences, and of legitimizing all the actions and pressures that would foster the progress of an Eastern European space adapted to this definition. Eastern Europe like the Soviet federation at the end of a common history already four decades old was a new community, a "historical category" of a new kind,[52] for which the only precedent was the Soviet federation. The historical community of the socialist countries was not different from the Soviet community, it was its extension, gradually restoring the unity of the revolutionary space proclaimed by Marx and Lenin that had been delayed by the failure of the 1917 revolutions. This community was developing according to objective laws in a dynamic way so that its permanent progress was certain. Once the community existed, it could only like the USSR move forward on the path of rapprochement and "unity" (which was not the same as fusion).[53]

It goes without saying that this socialist community, like the Soviet federation, had its own requirements—the safeguarding of the system—and its own international system created "from new principles of international law previously unknown." This new international law was by definition superior to the common law, since it had come from the movement from democratic to socialist norms, hence from the progress of history.[54] When this kind of argument was developed by the holder of the chair of international relations of the University of Moscow, it was easy to see that it, and the process it described, had a normative character.

We can thus see an ideological vise closing around the Eastern Europe empire. National paths that had for a time been accepted—but which had been justified by the concern not to hasten an inevitable process—were now replaced by a single and uniform framework in which national states were maintained while the community and homogeneity of values and patterns of behavior were moved forward. And the more rapprochement within this community was emphasized, the more this Europe guided by its exemplary brother had to distance itself from the other Europe from which it was separated by everything—fundamental principles and systems of organization.

Was this ideological system that legitimized policies, this mental framework designed to shape social behavior, a pure intellectual aberration? Or was it rooted in concrete structures? Several recent works provide precise answers to this question, and they favor the second hypothesis.

Not only was the rapprochement of the socialist countries a historical law, the same qualification applied to its methods, covering three areas: a growing resemblance of domestic structures, a common attitude toward the external world, and the development of organic structures and links. From all of this was supposed to emerge an indestructible international "entity."[55]

These elements conditioning the progress toward the unity of the socialist countries were not the products of popular spontaneity. They developed because of the initiatives and the determined activities of communist parties. Their role in this decisive historical stage was more important than ever before. It was up to the communist party to educate the society, to make it aware of what was at stake, to protect it against the threats that such a program inevitably provoked.[56] The leading and exclusive role of the party in this context was affirmed much more clearly than it had been earlier. And it was defined in relation to the community framework, rather than to the classic norms of international relations on which the USSR places so much emphasis today. The leading role of the party and the socialist community of a new kind formed an indissoluble whole. In this context, how could a political experiment that reduced the role of the party, as in Poland, be accepted by Moscow?

The central role of communist parties at this historical stage had a corollary, flowing from the ideas already developed: "The Soviet Communist Party and the Soviet state constantly consider that one of their central tasks is to struggle to strengthen the unity of the socialist countries, for their friendship and cooperation, and for the coordination of their activities."[57]

*   *   *

The architecture of the European socialist community—the USSR and the Eastern European states—was well defined by the early eighties: rapprochement leading to unity; constantly progressing cooperation; uniformity in systems and patterns of behavior; and constant references to a common program. The definition of this community was unquestionably very different from the Stalinist "colonial" universe, from the more diversified universe of the Khrushchev period, and from the empire based on a totally pragmatic authority in the years following the invasion of Czechoslovakia. It demonstrated among the leaders of the USSR a sharper sense of the realities, a concern to adapt their ideology to particular situations, and perhaps greater self-assurance. From this evolution of ideas that has been going on for more than a quarter of a century a few elements emerge, sketched out from one stage to the next, which clearly attained dominance in the early eighties.

In the first place, it is worth emphasizing the importance attributed by the USSR to the definition of the system. This ideological impulse, amusing to adherents of political realism, is nonetheless very important. The Soviet system of domination no doubt relies on force, but it relies even more on the force of its ideas. It is an ideocratic system, as Alain Besançon has so eloquently described it, and it permanently resorts to ideology and locates its behavior within an ideological framework. It is thus of some interest in evaluating the effectiveness of its ideas to note that by the early eighties the Soviet ideological system defined its empire in a much more complete and coherent way than it had in the past.

The second element to be noted is that the thinking that followed the suppression of the Prague Spring very extensively emphasized the importance of processes and methods of integration. While in early periods, under Stalin as well as Khrushchev, the conception of intersocialist relations was relatively static, thereafter a dynamic vision came to the fore. Integration by various means was conceived of as a veritable race against the centrifugal tendencies at work in Eastern Europe.

In the third place, by examining the terminology used in these developments we can observe the significant changes in the Soviet conception of relations within the socialist world. After Stalin's death, the principle of the equality of states and of a fraternal system—brothers are by definition equals—was constantly reaffirmed. At the same time we see the appearance of different terms limiting the scope of equality and fraternity. The 1977 Constitution and all its accompanying commentaries gave a place of honor to a term that until then had been little used in documents of this kind: socialist countries, instead of states. This terminological shift was not accidental. The notion of country was broader than that of state, including the party, social and national forces, all the groups that could come into existence. This meant that the current principles organizing the socialist community did not apply only to states and that within each state, no group, not even Polish civil society, could escape from these principles or could set itself against the state in the name of different principles. The socialist space of a new kind encompassed the entire state and also all components of society.[58]

Finally, the predominant role of the USSR, which had long been obscured by the emphasis on equality and the notion of a "socialist family," was now asserted. In the community of a new kind inspired by this model, the people that remained exemplary (the Russian people for the family of Soviet peoples, the Soviet people for the extended family of the Eastern European peoples) resumed its primary place. The "elder brother" whose supremacy had been assured by Stalin returned to honor in the USSR of the eighties, despite the thirty years that separated the present from the Stalin era and the ideas he had supported.

GUIDE FOR THE USE OF "LITTLE BROTHERS"

What is Socialist internationalism?

"It is the realization of slogans in reality: freedom, independence, equality of all nations; their right to self-determination and the creation of their own state order; the guarantee of a really free development of nations according to the path they have chosen.

"It is the establishment in relations among nations of sincere friendship, confidence, mutual understanding, and mutual aid.

"It is the gradual and logical liquidation of economic and cultural inequality among nations, disinterested aid to less developed nations from those more developed.

"It is broad development of cooperation, of relations in the realms of the economy, science and technology, culture and art, all of social life.

"It is unfailing solidarity in defense of socialist conquests, of the international positions of socialism, a common struggle in the anti-imperialist struggle, for the solution of all the major international problems.

"It is the harmonious combination of the national and international interests of the socialist countries, by placing the common interests of the whole socialist system in the forefront, along with the world revolutionary process.

"It is finally the union of the socialist states and peoples in the new historical community—fraternity, socialist friendship, which creates the most favorable conditions for unity of action in the solution of the central problems of the contemporary world.

"Socialist internationalism, according to the general secretary of the Central Committee of the Soviet Communist Party, is an immense responsibility for the fate of socialism, and not only in his country but in the entire world. It is an immense respect for the national and historical particularities of the development of each country, and the absolute determination to help others."

Source: K. Sonder, "Mezhdunarodnyi soiuz novogo tipa" (An international union of a new kind), *Kommunist Sovetskoi Latvii* (Nov. 1977): 47–48.

NOTES

1. *Sovetskii Soiuz i sovremennyi mir* (Prague, 1972), 126.

2. These arguments were widely made on the occasion of the fiftieth anniversary of the October Revolution. See for example the statements published in *Pravda*, June 25, 1967; Timofeev, "Mezhdunarodnoe znachenie okt'iabr'skoi revoliutsii i sovremennaia ideologicheskaia bor'ba," *Voprosy istorii K.P.S.S.*, 6 (June 1967): 7–9.

3. *Pravda*, April 18, 1956, commenting on the decision.

4. The Cominform's journal was published in Bucharest. It was resurrected in 1956 under the title *Problems of Peace and Socialism*.

5. Noted by V. Aspaturian in T. Rakowska-Harmstone and A. Gyorgy, eds., *Communism in Eastern Europe* (Bloomington, 1979), 14.

6. Ibid., 12.

7. N. Ceauşescu, *Romania pe drumul desavirsicii constructei socialiste* (Bucharest, 1968), 342–43, quoted in M. Shafir, *Rumanian Policy in the Middle East, 1967–1972* (Jerusalem, 1974), 12.

8. H. Carrère d'Encausse, *La Politique soviétique au Moyen-Orient, 1955–1975*, (Paris, 1976), 17–40.

9. H. Carrère d'Encausse, *Bolchévisme et nation. Des débats théoriques à la consolidation d'un état multinational* (Paris, 1986), chapter 2.

10. Lenin, *Polnoe Sobranie Sochinenii* 5th ed. vol. 45, 211–13.

11. *Pravda*, August 22, 1968.

12. Kudriavtsev, in *Izvestia*, August 25, 1968.

13. *Pravda*, September 25, 1968.

14. *Pravda*, November 13, 1968.

15. See P. Alampiev, "V. I. Lenin i sotrudnichestvo sotsialisticheskih natsii," *MEIMO* (Jan. 1970): 3–13; V. Razmerov, "Sotsialisticheskie mezhdunarodnye otnosheniia," *MEIMO* 12 (Dec. 1974): 3–14.

16. Razmerov, 12.

17. I. V. Dedinskii, "International'nye interessy i sotsialisticheskoe gosudarstvo," *Voprosy Filosofii* (Oct. 1973): 67.

18. E. T. Usenko, "Sotrudnichestvo stran-chlenov S.E.V. i sotsialisticheskii internationalizm," *Sovetskoe Gosudarstvo i Pravo* (April 1970): 82.

19. N. V. Chernogolovkin, "Zashchita sotsializma—Krovnoe delo sotsialisticheskogo gosudarstva," *Sovetskoe Gosudarstvo i Pravo* (Sept. 1971): 8.

20. Ibid.; I. P. Blishchenko, *Vneshnie funktsii sotsialisticheskogo gosudarstva* (Moscow 1970), 33–35.

21. Husák's remarks were published in *Pravda*, May 26, 1981. This was, of course, the "official" Fourteenth Congress, since the clandestine congress of August 1968 had been suppressed from the history of the Czech Communist Party.

22. V. V. Pletkovskii, "Partia—rukovodiashchaia sila sotsialisticheskogo gosudarstva," *Sovetskoe Gosudarstvo i Pravo* 8 (August 1970): 12.

23. L. I. Brezhnev, *Piat'desiat let velikih pobed sotsializma*, (Moscow 1967), 67.

24. G. T. Chernobel, "Kontseptsiia narodnogo suvereniteta," *Sovetskoe Gosudarstvo i Pravo* (Aug. 1970): 30–37, especially 36.

25. On the origin of the conference, it is helpful to consult A. Fontaine, *Un seul lit pour deux rêves* (Paris, 1981), 243–44 and 384–86.

26.   On the significance of Charter 77 see the excellent work by G. H. Skilling, *Charter 77 and Human Rights in Czechoslovakia* (London, 1981).

27.   B. Topornin, "Osnovnoi zakon strany sovetov i ego mezhdunarodnoe znachenie" (The fundamental law of the Soviet nation and its international meaning), *MEIMO* 4 (April 1978): 13; see also the editorial on the constitution, *MEIMO* 8 (August 1977) 12, which also discusses Article 30.

28.   In proposed amendments in 1977, the idea of "inscribing" the duty of Soviet armed forces to defend socialism in the socialist countries was offered as a complement to Article 31. *Krasnaia Zvezda*, August 21 and 25, 1977.

29.   B. Topornin, loc. cit., 12.

30.   "60 let SSSR: Po puti sotsializma, mira, internatsionalisma," *MEIMO* (Dec. 1982) 11 (Sixty years of Soviet life: On the path of socialism, peace, and internationalism).

31.   Ibid. Here the author referred to Lenin, *Polnoe Sobranie Sochinenii*, 41: 165.

32.   L. I. Brezhnev, *Mir sotsializma—torzhestvo velikih idei* (The world of socialism—triumph of great ideas) (Moscow, 1978), 508–9.

33.   I. Novopachin, "Ukreplenie sploshchnosti stran sotsializma—Glavnoe napravlenie vneshnei politiki KPSS" (Strengthening the unity of the socialist countries, principal direction of the Soviet Communist Party's policy), *MEIMO* 1 (Jan. 1980): 3–14.

34.   See, for example, the declaration of János Kádár quoted in an editorial in *MEIMO* (Feb. 1982): 6.

35.   This theme of common interests and activities has been subjected to methodological analysis. V. I. Zuev, *Mirovaia sistema sotsializma: ekonomicheskie i politicheskie aspekty* (The world system of socialism—economic and political aspects) (Moscow, 1975). A bibliography of recent Soviet works devoted to the specificity of intersocialist relations can be found in L. N. Nezhinski, "Aktual'nye problemy edinstva stran sotsialisticheskogo sodruzhestva v osveshchenii sovremennoi sovetskoi istoriografii" (Current problems of the unity of the countries of the socialist community in the light of contemporary Soviet historiography, *Novaia i Noveishaia Istoriia* 2 (Mar. 1980): 5–7.

36.   I. I. Paletskis, "V. I. Lenin i velikoe sodruzhestvo natsii" (Lenin and the great friendship among nations), *Sovetskoe Gosudarstvo i Pravo* 4 (Apr. 1970): 18.

37.   Ibid.

38.   The expression was used by Leonid Brezhnev in 1967.

39.   B. Ponomarev, "Real'nyi sotsializm i ego mezhdunarodnoe znachenie" (Real socialism and its international meaning), *Kommunist*, February 1979, 17.

40.   Art. 70, §2 of the 1977 Constitution.

41.   See H. Carrère d'Encausse, *Decline of an Empire* (New York, 1980). A very well-documented study of this problem is E. I. Burkhanova, *Natsional'nyi vopros i natsional'nye otnosheniia v SSSR* (The National question and national relations in the U.S.S.R.) (Dushanbe, 1976).

42.   SSSR—*Velikoe sodruzhestvo narodov-brat'ev* (The U.S.S.R., a great community of fraternal peoples) (Moscow 1972).

43.   *Pravda*, Feb. 12, 1982.

44.   R. Sharleth, "The New Soviet Constitution," *Problems of Communism* 31 (Sept.–Oct. 1977): 7ff.

45. S. Kaltakhshian, *Pravda*, Oct. 2, 1981, 2–3; this was a long theoretical article in which the term "systematic" was used by the author.

46. Speech of December 21, 1982, *Kommunist* 1 (Jan. 1983): 3–16.

47. Ibid., 6.

48. Ibid.

49. Ibid., 10.

50. *Materialy XXV s'ezda KPSS* (Materials from the Twenty-Fifth Congress of the Soviet Communist Party), (Moscow, 1976), 6.

51. A. A. Trebkov, "Vneshne—politicheskoe sotrudnichestvo sotsialisticheskih gosudarstv: sushtnost'osnovnye cherty" (International cooperation among socialist states: content and fundamental aspects), *Sovetskoe Gosudarstvo i Pravo* 7 (July 1976): 36.

52. L. N. Nezhinski, *loc. cit.*, 13.

53. I. S. Novopashin, ed., *Mezhdunarodnye otnosheniia novogo tipa: voprosy teorii i praktiki razvitiia mirovoi sistemy sotsializma* (International relations of a new kind: problems of theory and practice in the development of the world socialist system) (Moscow, 1978), 43.

54. I. I. Il'inskii, "Mezhdunarodnoe znachenie opyta sovetskogo gosudarstva" (The international significance of the experience of the Soviet state), *Sovetskoe Gosudarstvo i Pravo* (1977): 118.

55. I. S. Novopashin, *Sotsialisticheskie mezhdunarodnye otnosheniia kak sistema* (Socialist International Relations as a System) (Moscow, 1978), 33.

56. Editorial in *MEIMO*, Feb. 1981, 6.

57. Novopashin, loc. cit., 4.

58. This shift has been very clearly explained by M. Lesage, *La Constitution de l'U.R.S.S.*, *texte et commentaire*, published by La Documentation française (Paris, 1978), 40.

8

THE SOCIALIST FAMILY

"The last ten years have been marked by great development and by an enrichment of the cooperation among the countries of the socialist community. This cooperation is a powerful means for accelerating the development of each of the fraternal countries. It is also, for all of us, the guarantee of continued progress in a difficult and troubled world." This declaration by Leonid Brezhnev in 1980 corresponds clearly to the evolution that the USSR had imposed on its camp from the time of the intervention in Czechoslovakia.[1] Since 1968 all forms of cooperation had been revised, consolidated, and extended.

The notion of a development that corresponded to objective laws had also been applied to cooperation; and these laws, according to a Soviet writer, demand:

ever increasing rapprochement of fraternal nations by the multiplication of common elements in the various spheres of the internal life of the societies, and the strengthening of international and inter-state collaboration of these states; by a process of adaptation and transformation of political, economic, and social structures making these systems progress toward new historical frontiers.[2]

This was indeed what was happening: the transformation of the relations of the USSR with the sister states; the transformation of the nature of those states to put an end to antagonisms and tensions. In its way the USSR was organizing the socialist family. It imposed its views in a variety of areas that in theory did not infringe on the juridical sovereignty of the states or the independence of the nations; but in practice, constantly extending the scope of common life and common practices, it gradually but ineluctably emptied sovereignty of its real content. The areas that were the focus of the Soviet Union's most constant efforts were those involving the general framework of interstate relations, by means of bilateral treaties; the framework of social organization, by means of constitutions; the development of the societies, by means of economic integration; and the development of domestic political life, by means of the multiplication of bilateral contacts.

The particular characteristic of this system that has been developed spectacularly since 1968 is that the socialist family is first of all established on a solid bilateral basis. Big brother solidly backed by an ideological system legitimizing his authority has continuously worked to organize the common life of the family on the basis of a network of laws radiating out from him in all directions and returning to him. He has constantly consolidated his power and has prevented coalitions from taking shape outside or against him that would weaken his authority. The principle of democratic centralism also presided over the development of the socialist family.

Bilateral Treaties: "Positive Pactomania"

Since the first treaty of this kind goes back to 1943, the first steps toward the most central elements of the system were the bilateral treaties linking the USSR with each socialist state. The USSR has signed so many treaties with its allies that some observers attribute this proliferation of documents to pure "pactomania."[3]

However, a first effect of these treaties that were different from all others made by the USSR was precisely that they helped to define a socialist space outside international space governed "by a new kind of international relations."[4] It is not an accident that the recent "Soviet law on the international agreements of the USSR" focused on this problem and explained its importance and specificity.

Since the war the USSR has signed treaties with all of its allies and it is important to understand their general meaning and certain differences among them.[5]

All these treaties were constructed on the same model and were generally entitled "Treaty of Friendship, Cooperation, and Mutual Aid between the USSR and . . ." In the wording of this initial definition of the treaties there are now no differences from one treaty to another, although variations did exist in the past taking account of the different state of relations between the USSR and its partners. The first treaties with Poland and Czechoslovakia, signed in the midst of the war, evoked "friendship, mutual aid, and cooperation after the war." The different formulations of the series of treaties signed with the GDR also reflected variations in the tone of relations between the USSR and that country. The 1955 treaty, signed after the USSR had recognized the GDR as an independent country in 1949 was quite simply entitled "treaty on the relations between the USSR and the GDR,"[6] which was in comparison to the other treaties signed after 1943 extremely dry. On the other hand, in the second treaty in 1964 the complete formulation was used. In general, in their first form from 1945 to 1949 these treaties were signed for

Bilateral Treaties Signed by the USSR		
Country	*Date*	*Remarks*
Bulgaria[a]	March 18, 1948 May 12, 1967	———— Validity: 20 years
Hungary[b]	February 18, 1948 September 7, 1967	———— Validity: 20 years
Poland[c]	April 21, 1945 April 8, 1965	———— Validity: 20 years
German Democratic Republic[d]	September 20, 1955 June 12, 1964 October 7, 1975	———— Validity: 25 years
Rumania[e]	February 4, 1948 July 7, 1970	———— Validity: 20 years
Czechoslovakia[f]	December 12, 1943 November 27, 1963 May 6, 1970	———— Validity: 20 years
Yugoslavia[g]	April 11, 1945	———— Validity: 20 years Treaty denounced in 1949

[a] Bulgaria, 1948: *Sbornik*, 13:15–16; 1967: *Sbornik*, 25: 35–37.
[b] Hungary, 1948; *Sbornik*, 13:17–19; 1967: *Sbornik*, 25: 38–40.
[c] Poland, 1945: *Sbornik*, 21–24; 1965: *Sbornik*, 14:39–40.
[d] GDR, 1955: *Sbornik*, 17–18: 17–19; 1964: *Sbornik*, 23:39–41; 1975: *Sbornik*, 31:44–47.
[e] Rumania, 1948: *Sbornik*, 13:20–22; 1970: *Sbornik*, 26:37–39.
[f] Czechoslovakia, 1943: *Sbornik*, 11:28–31; 1960: *Sbornik*, 23:43–44; 1970: *Sbornik*, 26: 41–43.
[g] The 1945 treaty with Yugoslavia was published in *Pravda*, April 12, 1945.

twenty years and contained an automatic renewal clause for periods of five years. However, when they expired, instead of simply renewing them the USSR set in motion a second wave of treaties, much more elaborate and also set for twenty years, also with a renewal clause. Although it is impossible to determine Soviet intentions from the texts of this second series of treaties that is due to expire in the late eighties, the latest treaty signed with the GDR nevertheless suggests certain governing outlines. The provisions considerably extend the time of the treaty's validity from twenty to twenty-five years and the automatic renewal clause provides for successive periods of ten years.[7] This change is important and leads to the conclusion that either the USSR prefers not to reopen the problem of renegotiating bilateral treaties too often or has turned toward treaties of indefinite duration. The content of these treaties is also very interesting in its architecture and in the differences in provisions from one treaty to another.

In general, all the treaties of the first wave set forth the bases for relatively unconstrained cooperation between the signatories. Starting from a declaration of friendship and of common interests to defend, these documents considered three kinds of questions. They provided for common defense and military assistance in the event of aggression from Germany or any other country operating in concert with Germany. They imposed on the signatories a commitment not to participate "in a coalition or an alliance, or in any other enterprise" directed against the other signatory. Finally, they provided for growing cooperation in the economic and cultural spheres. Including the solemn commitment to respect the independence and sovereignty of others and not to interfere in their internal affairs, these treaties finally appeared to be relatively innocent, even though they had already imposed limits on the foreign policies of the signatories. There were more particular provisions in two treaties of the period. An ancillary agreement to the Soviet-Czech treaty of 1943 decided the fate of the Sub-Carpathian Ukraine, that is, the treaty transferred it to the USSR; and in the Soviet-German treaty of 1955, signed according to the preamble "in awareness of the new situation created by the operation of the 1954 Paris agreements," Article 4 stipulated that Soviet troops would remain stationed in the GDR.[8]

The second wave of treaties, signed in the mid-sixties and still in force, deserves more careful attention. The first thing that has to be said is that for three countries, the GDR, Rumania, and Czechoslovakia, the normal time period was not respected. The 1955 treaty with the GDR was to remain in force "until the restoration of German unity, or else until the point at which the signatories decided to abrogate or change it" (Article 6). Although the second hypothesis governed the new version in 1964, the duration of the treaty was set for twenty years and renewable for ten (and not for periods of ten years), according to Article 10. By 1975 a new Soviet-GDR treaty had been signed. Changes were made in the duration and renewal provisions of the treaty. More important, the 1975 treaty provided for a complete change in the nature of the relations between the two states. In 1964 there had been no concrete clause for defense, particularly military defense, in case of an attack on either of the countries (Article 5: "The other party will provide immediate assistance," with no indication of its nature), while in 1975, Article 8 of the treaty contained a mutual assistance clause "including military means." From 1955 to 1964 the GDR had moved into the ranks of the allies, even though it was still somewhat affected by bad memories of the war. In 1975 it was elevated to the rank of a complete ally. And while the preceding treaties had contained clauses referring to the restoration of German unity (in the preambles of the treaties of 1955 and 1964), this clause disappeared in 1975, since the treaty was signed a few months after the Helsinki agreements. The case of Rumania is just as remarkable. The Soviet-Rumanian treaty was signed two-and-a-half years after the expected date—while all other treaties were renewed a few months in advance—and this delay clearly revealed Rumanian resistance to any commitment to the USSR, a resistance that had been exacerbated by the Czech affair. However, and we will return to this point, Rumania had to accept the same conditions as the other, more docile states. Czechoslovakia, which signed a treaty of the new kind in the second wave and was thus "up to date" until 1983, finally signed a third treaty in 1970, taking account of normalization. This obviously leads to the question of the content of the treaty that was to be signed by Poland in 1985. Would it show traces of the 1980 crisis?

It was above all the content of the treaties of this second wave that had changed from their counterparts negotiated twenty years earlier. Four elements were decisive in this respect. All the treaties were "based on the unshakeable principles of socialist internationalism";[9] all the treaties affirmed the commitment of the signatories "to respect unfailingly the obligations deriving from the Warsaw Pact";[10] all the treaties including the one with Rumania in 1970 included a clause concerning military defense in case of aggression against one of the parties;[11] all the treaties, finally, emphasized the necessity of the compatibility of international commitments with the treaty of friendship with the USSR (which took priority), thus defining a hierarchy of obligations not present in the treaties of the first phase.

Careful comparison of the treaties nevertheless reveals some curious differences, and one can finally glimpse the classification that the USSR was using in its system of alliances, revealing sometimes a hierarchy of problems, sometimes a set of priorities. To evaluate these differences more clearly it is interesting to introduce into the comparison the Soviet-Finnish treaty, because Finland represented a model that many Eastern European countries dreamed of imitating.

The USSR signed a treaty with Finland in 1948 and has renewed it twice.[12] The initial treaty provided for a duration of ten years, automatically renewable for five-year periods. The two protocols of renewal simply continued the treaty for twenty years in 1955 as well as in 1970.

If one may wonder about the haste made in establishing these protocols, we must recognize that the content of the 1948 treaty was unchanged and resembled the treaties signed by the USSR with the socialist states in the late forties, including the formulation of the title of the treaty as one of "friendship, cooperation, and mutual aid."

But the Soviet-Finnish treaty explains at the outset that it "takes account of Finland's wish to remain apart from the contradictions between the great powers."[13] This recognition of Finnish neutrality involved very great prudence in the definition of the conditions for mutual assistance in case of aggression. Although "in case of extreme necessity," Soviet assistance to Finland was provided for, the term "military" was absent from this stipulation and it was stipulated that this kind of assistance had to be based on a previous understanding at the moment at which the problem arose (Article 1). The only two obligations actually imposed on Finland (aside from the vague threat that the USSR could be put in danger from Finish territory) were the prohibition against joining alliances against the USSR (Article 4) and the commitment to "consultations in case of a specific threat of aggression." (Article 2).

Very curiously, the country whose commitments to the USSR were closest to those of Finland was not Rumania, so attached to its independence, but Poland. Perhaps because of the long tradition of hostility between Poland and the USSR, after the usual salute to the principles of socialist internationalism, the treaty of 1965 evoked in exceptionally warm terms "the eternal and indestructible friendship between the two countries."[14] But beyond the mutual defense clause, "by all means including military means," the treaty was surprisingly vague about Poland's obligations. There was no mention of the compatibility of this commitment with other international commitments and with respect to foreign policy the treaty stipulated that the "signatories would agree and would consult on the most important questions concerning them."[15] The treaty made it clear that one of the gravest risk factors in Europe was the security of Poland's western border.

Bulgaria, Rumania, and Hungary made up a second group of allies with more precise obligations than those of Poland, although there were differences among them. The treaty with Rumania did set forth that it had the aim of developing cooperation between the two countries, but the term "many-sided," found in the other treaties, was avoided in this one; similarly, the treaty provided for consultation between the two countries on international problems "with the aim of reaching common positions," which is rather vague, like the text as a whole. For the two other treaties, cooperation was to be "many-sided" and consultations were accompanied by the obligation "to reach common positions" in the case of Bulgaria,[16] while the Soviet-Hungarian treaty provided that its signatories "would act on the basis of a common position, defined with reference to their mutual interests."[17] In all the treaties the prohibition against entering into agreements in contradiction with the agreements signed with the USSR was expressly set out.

At the top of the hierarchy of bilateral alliances was Czechoslovakia, preceded by the GDR. Quite obviously Czechoslovakia was paying for the Prague Spring with harsher constraints than those imposed on neighboring states. In this case, socialist internationalism, always evoked but never explained, was defined by the meaning that had been given to it on August 21, 1968. The preamble to the treaty explained in fact that "support for and strengthening and defense of the conquests of socialism realized by the heroic efforts and the abnegation of each people are the common duty of the socialist countries."[18] This obligation experienced by Czechoslovakia in 1968 was repeated in Article 5 of the treaty, which explained that the contracting parties "will take all measures necessary for the defense of socialist conquests."[19] Foreign policy was also more restricted than in other treaties because besides the obligations to consult and to reach a common position was added an obligation of information-sharing absent from the other treaties.[20] As in the case of Poland the treaty with Czechoslovakia stipulated that the signatories were linked by eternal and indestructible friendship. This was also the case with Rumania and Bulgaria, but it was not so with Hungary whose friendship with the USSR was merely eternal, nor with the GDR with which the USSR had "formed a close, fraternal alliance, based on Marxism-Leninism and socialist internationalism." Thus, what linked all the other countries to the USSR, friendship, with various qualifications, was absent from relations between the USSR and the GDR, between which the links were purely ideological. The difference is not insignificant. If one goes beyond the initial lack of warmth, one recognizes that the contractual ties based on attachment to the same principles here reached a level unknown in the other treaties. The text naturally included the obligation of defense of all members of the socialist community,[21] extended cooperation to areas like ideology that were generally left out, and gave much space to the coordination of planning and to economic specialization. Finally, and here the text was closely tied to the German situation, Article 6 of the treaty was given over to an affirmation of the unchangeability of the borders that resulted from the Second World War, whether the borders be those between Warsaw Pact states or those between the two Germanies. The use of a complex vocabulary—unchangeable borders and inviolable borders—suggests that the signatories of the treaty reserved the right to decide where and when border adjustments could be made and in what situations borders had to be considered unchangeable.[22]

This hierarchy of treaties and the development discernible in relation to them over the course of time are full of implications. They reveal several preoccupations in this construction patiently pursued by the USSR. There was first constant attention paid to the countries of "the northern flank." This was where the treaties were most precise and restrictive, except for Poland. But in that case it was clear that at the date the friendship treaty was signed, 1965, the USSR was still intent on accommodating Poland and on erasing by adhering to a "Polish road" the memories of hostility that history had produced. During this period, Poland could justifiably imagine that it was like Finland or that it was developing in that direction. These concessions to its fierce nationalism were all the more acceptable to the USSR because Poland had no borders outside the Warsaw Pact, and surrounded by Soviet allies and Pact members it could not make much use of its current status as tending toward neutrality. And the USSR could on the other hand by such concessions to Polish national feeling hope to calm tension in this territory that was so important for its whole military system. The history of the late sixties and the early seventies having shown that this calculation was false, the USSR, as we shall see, corrected by other means the gaps that had been left in the bilateral treaty of 1965.

The countries of the "southern flank," on the other hand, enjoyed if not a greater autonomy at least clauses less visibly affecting their sovereignty, even if Rumania had had to accept conditions that it had always challenged, and if in the case of Bulgaria the text contained cooperation clauses that were so extensive as to seem to be a preparation for integrating the country into the USSR.

Whatever the degree of constraint in these treaties, they had two virtues for the USSR. The links they created covered diverse areas and could supplement any system of alliances. These treaties, which gave evidence of the existence of a socialist space and of a community of interests recognized bilaterally, made the USSR the arbiter of all decisions. Finally, because they had to be periodically renewed the treaties could be adapted to developing situations and new difficulties. A comparative reading, both temporal and spatial, of the texts demonstrates that the USSR constantly used them to respond to crises in the system, to erect safeguards, and to accelerate the process of intervention in the lives of the states and of their integration.

Just as "positive neutralism" had been for the USSR a powerful way to cause third world countries to move from neutralism to a nonalignment that Cuba undertook to manage for the benefit of the USSR, so this "pactomania," however apparently innocent, played a very "positive" role in the development of the Soviet program of integration of its camp.

The Constitutions: Alignment through Law

Commenting on the meaning of the term "rapprochement," one of the most celebrated Soviet political writers, Shahnazarov, emphasized that the term does not refer only to many exchanges creating "proximity" but to the formation of an "internal affinity," particularly in the political realm.[23] The institutions and the domestic law of these states as defined by their norms of development are important means for creating this affinity. This explains the attention paid by the USSR in the mid-seventies to constitutional revision, which had the aim of aligning all the constitutions on a single model. During the conference of communist parties in Moscow in 1965, Leonid Brezhnev had suggested that the time for more thorough reflection on law and on the conception of the state and of power had come.[24]

The result of this suggestion was a remarkable burst of constitutional activity giving birth to new fundamental laws in Bulgaria in 1971 and

Hungary in 1972 and revised ones in Poland in 1976, the GDR in 1974, and Rumania in 1975.[25] Contrary to what might have been expected, the new Soviet Constitution did not come before the revisions of the other constitutions, but came as the capstone to the edifice. It is obvious that all the texts had the same inspiration and that the Soviet Constitution, even though it came later, was nevertheless their implicit model. Moreover this comes out in the analyses of the various constitutions carried out in the USSR.[26] Soviet writers simultaneously point to "the kinship and unity" of the constitutions as the product of a constant interpenetration of ideas and influences, and reject the idea of a "standardization" of social states.[27] Although the diversity of solutions to particular historical or sociological problems is obvious, "the fundamental principles governing the organization of socialist systems are the same everywhere."[28] These remarks of G. Shahnazarov were accompanied by an invaluable analysis of what was fundamental in the revisions: the role of the party and the principles of foreign policy.[29]

This was in fact the reason for the intense juridical activity of the mid-seventies. The crises of the system had showed the USSR the two directions constantly taken by the rebels from one stage to the next: a new definition of the political system that weakened the communist party; or else a determination to rejoin the international community by denying the specificity of the socialist community and the privileged ties that united its members. The new constitutions and the constitutional revisions responded to these challenges by imposing on each state and each society strict principles in these two areas. Everywhere the principle, until then badly expressed, of the leading role of the communist party was set out clearly. Everywhere principles guiding the foreign policy of the states were introduced, defining it on the basis of socialist internationalism and the fact that the states belonged to the socialist world. However, there are many differences among these constitutions reflecting Soviet attitudes toward and demands on the various countries. Among the "model" constitutions from the Soviet point of view are those of the GDR and Bulgaria. The constitution of the GDR adopted without nuances the most orthodox positions. It affirmed "the leading role of the working class and of its Marxist-Leninist party" (Article 1); "the perpetual and irrevocable alliance with the Union of Soviet Socialist Republics. This close and fraternal alliance . . . the GDR is an inseparable part of the socialist community of states. Loyal to the principles of socialist internationalism, it contributes . . . to the mutual assistance of all the states of the socialist community" (Article 6); "in the interest of the preservation of the peace and security of the socialist state, the People's National Army maintains close and fraternal relations with the armies of the Soviet Union and the other socialist states" (Article 7, §2).[30]

In other terms and under different conditions in its new constitution of 1971 Bulgaria demonstrated equal warmth for the USSR and for the socialist family. The preamble evoked the war and "the decisive aid of the liberating Soviet army," and it affirmed that the citizens of the People's Republic of Bulgaria "depended on cooperation and mutual assistance with the Soviet Union and the other countries of the socialist community . . . to strengthen and extend the indissoluble alliance, friendship, and total cooperation with the USSR and the other fraternal socialist countries." Following the preamble, Article 3 stated that the state was "to develop and consolidate friendship, cooperation, and mutual assistance with the USSR and the other socialist states," and Article 5 set forth as fundamental principles of the political system "national sovereignty, the unity of power, democratic centralism, legality, and socialist internationalism."[31] It is noteworthy that sovereignty and socialist internationalism appear in the same sentence, which clearly expresses both the content and the limits of sovereignty. It is not surprising that a country so attached to the USSR and to its principles should so bluntly affirm that "the leading force in society and the state is the Bulgarian Communist Party" (Article 1, §2). Nor is it surprising that the constitutions of these two countries were the most often and the most favorably discussed by the Soviet leaders.[32]

Czechoslovakia, in the most recent variants of its constitution, comes close to the warm feelings and orthodox propositions expressed in the fundamental laws of the GDR and Bulgaria.[33] The preamble states that the country is moving toward communism "hand in hand with our great ally, the fraternal Soviet Union, and with all the other fraternal countries of the world socialist system, of which our country is a solid link." And, in the body of the text, there is this affirmation: "The Czechoslovak Socialist Republic is a part of the world socialist system." (Article 1, §3).

If Czechoslovakia can advance toward communism, "this is with the friendly assistance of the USSR and the other countries" (Article 14, §2). It goes without saying that "the leading force of society and the state" is the communist party (Article 4). Broken in 1968, Czechoslovakia had learned the lessons of its defeat and the total alignment with the Soviet model found in the constitution is nothing but a reflection of the slow agony of a people.

Along with these good pupils, the socialist family also included more reticent figures, those slower to respond to the unifying program. Hungary acknowledged much more sketchily and in a purely formulaic way the "friendly assistance" of the USSR in postwar reconstruction (in the preamble) and said that as "part of the world socialist organization, it would develop and strengthen its friendship with the socialist countries; it would attempt to cooperate with all the nations of the world" (Article 5, §2). Although the communist party was presented as "the leading force of society" (Article 3), this formula was unable to conceal the rather imprecise character of Hungarian commitments to the socialist community. There was no reference to socialist internationalism in the text, the USSR was given little space, the socialist community was dissolved in the vague formulation regarding the "world socialist organization," and Hungary intended to direct its efforts of cooperation toward all other countries as well as toward this group. This document, which was thoroughly developed in other respects, indicated that Hungary intended to devote itself to its own development while affirming a general loyalty to the system. And this attitude was in conformity with the path that has been followed by Hungary since October 1956; it was also in conformity with the unstated "concordat" agreed to between Moscow and Budapest. In return for a forced alignment that it never questioned and for real loyalty to the alliance, not forcefully expressed, Hungary could in the last analysis develop according to its own pattern.[34]

The case of Poland was enormously more difficult. The repetition of crises there and the broadening of Polish aspirations led the USSR to the determination to surround Poland with dikes designed to control the constant groundswells taking place in the country. But once again Poland was exceptional in every respect. The USSR knew that it had to proceed with caution; it also knew that the geographic position of Poland was a permanent phenomenon that justified in the last analysis patience in Moscow. The "battle" of Polish constitutional amendments in 1975–76 reflected Moscow's perpetual oscillation between annoyance leading to a desire to accelerate the course of events and retreats designed to avoid confrontation. The adjustments made to the 1952 Constitution were both derisory and important.[35] The amendments dealt with the role of the party and the definition of the alliance. On the first point, the PUWP was defined as "the leading political force in the society," a definition analogous to the one adopted by Hungary and more limited than those of Bulgaria and the GDR, since the party was not linked to the state. Moreover—and this is a semantic distinction that Soviet commentary emphasized—the Polish terminology further attenuated the function of the party, since the term used to define it meant "guiding role" not "leading role".[36] The Polish Constitution recognized the existence of two other political parties— the Unified Peasant Party and the Democratic Party, both integrated into the United National Front (Article 3, §2);[37] it also recognized, and this is a unique case, that the Church had particular rights (Article 82, §§1 and 2), while all the other constitutions merely referred to freedom of conscience. The polemics about the constitutional amendments were concerned with the definition of relations with the USSR. Article 6, after having enumerated (§1) the fundamental principles of Polish politics: sovereignty, independence, security, and the wish for peace and cooperation among nations, explained in a second paragraph that Poland "was aligned with the tradition of solidarity, with the forces of freedom and progress, and that it strengthened friendship and cooperation with the USSR and the other socialist states." This formulation included no formal references to socialist internationalism and it was no more than moderate in its definition of friendship with the USSR.[38] The most striking term in it is "alignment," and it was over this term that Polish intellectuals had fought; it was here that Soviet theoreticians and theoretical organizations had reintroduced the notion of internationalism.[39] Finally, it was on this point that the Soviet leaders had the sense that they were rectifying the weaknesses of the bilateral friendship treaty of 1956. Compared to the formulations of that treaty, the constitution did indeed represent a higher degree of commitment by Poland to the USSR. This development becomes obvious from a comparison of commentaries on the Polish Constitution with ones on the Hungarian Constitution, about which a Moscow writer could find nothing better to say than: "This document defines the relations of the Hungarian People's Republic with the other states of the socialist community."[40] It is true that even by twisting the meaning of the Hungarian fundamental law it would be impossible to find the slightest reference to principles of socialist internationalism, while the Polish formulation lends itself to the support of such principles.

Comparison of the Polish Constitution with the Constitution of Rumania, the perpetual "Lone Ranger," is even more instructive and more clearly explains the reactions of Polish intellectuals. The Rumanian Constitution is the only one that sets forth its principles at the outset: Rumania is a socialist republic. "The Socialist Republic of Rumania is a sovereign, independent, and united state of the working people of cities and villages; its territory is inalienable and indivisible" (Article 1). This declaration of principles with no preamble or reference to any friendship clearly reflects the "Rumanian path" in which loyalty to the most rigid and orthodox system went along with an extremely touchy sense of independence. The role of the party was presented in a particular form: "The leading political power in the society is the Rumanian Communist Party" (Article 3)

Although the constitution never mentioned the USSR, it was nevertheless careful not to cut connections with the socialist community. The article dealing with this question mirrored the Rumanian position in the Warsaw Pact: "inside outside." Article 14 states: "The Socialist Republic of Rumania maintains and guarantees friendly relations and fraternal cooperation with the socialist states in the spirit of socialist internationalism, develops relations and collaboration with countries having different political systems. . . ." This article is exceptional in three respects: because it treats socialist states as a group without giving the USSR a special place (the community is made up of equals); because it defines Rumanian perspectives "in the spirit" of socialist internationalism, which leaves substantial room for maneuver; and finally because it places relations with the community of socialist states exactly on the same level as relations with states with different systems. By putting everything in a single sentence with no textual breaks, the Rumanian jurists had destroyed the thesis of a socialist space within the realm of international relations and of the specific characteristics of socialist international relations.[41] There was an enormous gulf between the GDR and Rumania. And the Soviet effort toward alignment was particularly assiduous and demanding in the priority zone of the "iron triangle." Rumania retained the right to affirm its independence. Loyalty to the domestic political model in no way suffered from this. And Soviet tolerance for these international deviations was designed to simplify relations with this southern flank country that might one day play an important role in Soviet ambitions. For the states bordering on the southern flank, like Greece, the freedom of maneuver in the international realm enjoyed by Rumania might be an argument to justify neutralism. Rumania was for the time being a model for the eastern Mediterranean states that might be tempted by neutralism.

Vertical Integration

Bilateral treaties and uniform constitutions were certainly not the only means the USSR used to bring the little brothers closer to the Kremlin. The treaties and constitutions provided a framework for rapprochement and fostered a process of integration that often followed less viable paths and nevertheless gradually changed the political life of every state. This process of change was made up of bilateral contacts, institutional or not, that developed very rapidly after 1968 and have established between the USSR and its sister states many links, common practices, and a common life whose meaning and scope it is important to understand. These contacts took place in every area, but the most important were those that linked communist parties and states. Suslov frequently emphasized the ideological function of bilateral relations between communist parties, which, he said, when they were institutionalized at every level allowed for agreement and unity in points of view and actions.[42]

What Suslov called the ideological function was the coordination by the parties of all sectors of state activity—political, cultural, economic, military—the broad lines of which were defined by the communist party. In Moscow a department of the Central Committee—the department of liaison with communist parties in power—led by Konstantin Rusakov had the special task of organizing this kind of contact, which was in the end an exceptional means of integration.

It is difficult to imagine without following them day by day the quantity of interparty contacts coordinated by the Soviet Communist Party, all of which constantly drew the system toward its center of gravity, Moscow. A simple survey of Soviet press reports of intercommunist meetings leads to the observation that there were a minimum of a thousand bilateral meetings between the Soviet Communist Party and the sister parties in power in the course of five years in the late sixties.[43]

The most spectacular aspect of this process is well known, the annual meetings in the Crimea in July and August between the general secretary of the Soviet Communist Party and his Eastern European counterparts. This tradition was established in the wake of the Czech crisis and has been scrupulously respected since then. If we take the years 1980 and 1981 as examples we can see a veritable ballet of communist leaders dancing around Brezhnev. In 1980 this round of summits on the shores of the Black Sea opened with a meeting between Brezhnev and Kádár on July 24 that laid the groundwork for a five-year plan for an increase in Soviet-Hungarian trade of 45 percent.[44] On July 28 there was a Brezhnev-Husák summit meeting;[45] then on July 31, Gierek arrived for a meeting with Brezhnev "in an atmosphere of cordiality and mutual understanding."[46] On August 4, it was Ceauşescu's turn,[47] followed on July 7 by Zhivkov,[48] and finally on July 11 by Honecker.[49] The following year in 1981 the same ceremony was repeated with only the order of appearances changed. The Brezhnev-Husák conversations opened the series on July 22, followed by Brezhnev-Kádár on July 28, Brezhnev-Ceauşescu on July 31, Brezhnev-Honecker on August 3, Brezhnev-Zhivkov, who seemed to like the date of August 7, and concluded with the stormy Brezhnev-Kania meeting on August 11 at which, exceptionally, Kania was accompanied by General Jaruzelski who was about to succeed him.[50] With the exception of the last of these summit meetings, called "working conversations," they were all described by communiqués giving the impression of vacation meetings hospitable to the progress of links of friendship and cooperation.

Although Yugoslavia was not a participant in this tradition, contacts between party leaders of the USSR and Yugoslavia have nevertheless also taken on some regularity. Brezhnev came to Belgrade on an "unofficial" visit in 1971 accompanied by a large party delegation;[51] Tito went to Moscow in 1972 to receive the Order of Lenin;[52] and he made an official visit in November 1973.[53] All these occasions permitted the creation of a network of Brezhnev-Tito summit meetings that, although they were less official and solemn than the summer meetings, nevertheless established certain habits. Later years confirmed this impression. In 1977 during Tito's visit to the USSR, the final communiqué, repeating that "the principles of sovereignty and non-intervention" governed relations between the two countries, clearly explained that many-sided cooperation involved the parties as well as the states.[54] The trajectory covered after 1955 when Tito had rejected the idea of privileged links between the parties was far from negligible, and the continuity of these links was confirmed during his visit to the USSR in 1979,[55] and again on Brezhnev's visit to Belgrade in May 1980.[56] On that occasion, Tito's funeral, Brezhnev seized the opportunity to point out how relations between the two states and the two parties had developed in positive ways in a few years. These relations in the "post-Tito" and "post-Brezhnev" context were debated in Moscow in early 1981,[57] in Belgrade in April 1982,[58] and again in Moscow after Brezhnev's death when the Brezhnev-Tito conversations had been replaced by those between Andropov and Ribicić.[59] It is undeniable that a habit of holding summit meetings was established between these two countries that had been so opposed in the past; and it is clear that the changes in leadership, the death of the "historic leaders," helped to simplify relations at the top, not weaken them.

At the summits, a general political line was developed, or rather the politics defined by the "big brother" were communicated, while at lower levels in many specialized meetings the political integration of leaders and programs was carried out. There was an impressive movement of people constantly flowing from Moscow to the East European capitals and from those capitals to Moscow or the major centers of the USSR, countless party delegations discussing in common the great problems: ideological work,[60] political cooperation in the army,[61] political education of young people, propaganda,[62] evaluation of international life,[63] and so on. In addition to debates on major themes by leaders of relatively high rank in the national communist parties, there were bilateral meetings of specific groups: young people, country-to-country friendship groups,[64] unions,[65] journalists,[66] and so on. All these meetings emanated from the communist parties and assured ideological supervision and integration of particular areas of activity. These are only examples designed to illustrate a many-sided program and it would take an entire book to catalogue a year of meetings of this kind.

This network of bilateral links was strengthened by periodic multilateral meetings that brought together according to the same pattern either the communist parties of Warsaw Pact member countries or particular sections of those parties to develop at any given moment principles of common action in a particular area, like ideology,[67] or to work out a common critique of one party or all of them and thereby to accelerate the process of integration.[68]

Bilateral and multilateral party relations—the former were clearly more numerous and greater in scope—had the function of forging the content of political power in each country and of encouraging or accelerating its increasing integration into the community. Bilateral contacts among the states transposed this integration into the internal functioning of the states themselves. Even a very superficial observation of the meetings reported in the Soviet press reveals a continuous and growing movement from the beginning of the last decade at all levels and in all sectors of the state. There were constant meetings of ministers, vice-ministers, working groups, and specialized commissions to discuss concrete problems, to foster one form of cooperation or another, or to sign agreements.[69] Even a quick enumeration of such contacts would be unduly tedious. But it is important to understand that these contacts established in the daily lives of the citizens of these states common habits and common activities that gradually supplanted specifically national habits. One of these common activities deserves particular attention, the education of the young.[70] The number of bilateral meetings devoted to discussing programs and methods of education was very high. And their purpose was clear: gradually to replace particular educational systems, fostered by the local traditions of each country, with an educational system whose principles and content would be decided in common and in which the only survival of particularism would be the vehicle of education, the language of each country.

No doubt on this point the process of integration is still in the early stages. But the intention to work toward training new generations adapted to a more integrated socialist environment has been frequently expressed in the USSR during the last several years. Here too the Soviet model has served as a reference point. All the immediate measures of integration, like the political and economic surveys, only make sense if there will one day be a different intersocialist society, structured in a uniform manner, differentiated only by the use of a variety of languages. This is another version of the old Stalinist dream of a compromise between "national form" (language) and "socialist content" (ways of thinking and acting). The crises of the socialist community and the rise of nationalist aspirations should not conceal the existence of this program, nor that it is the principal focus of the Soviet system and that it is progressing in certain sectors. Economic integration through Comecon is in fact one effective means of gradually creating felt needs for common training, and common elites have already begun to appear.

Economic Integration at the Service of the Political Program

It goes without saying that we will not consider here economic integration in itself. It has been the subject of some remarkable works, it is relatively well known, and it requires specialist training in economics.[71] What is important here is to see its political implications, its contribution to the program of transforming the still diverse Eastern Europe into a well-integrated new entity. In this connection the function of economic integration is clear and the effects it has already achieved are unchallengeable. The instrument of this integration is Comecon, created in 1949, which for a long time seemed to be a structure devoid of effectiveness. It is true that when it was created economic autarky was dominant in the USSR and in Eastern Europe; and being determined to reconstruct its economy, the USSR limited its economic relations with the states of the bloc to periodic confiscations of resources. But gradually, once reconstruction was accomplished and the organizing principles of the camp were developed, new conceptions of economic life based on Comecon replaced autarky and pure and simple exploitation of the weaker countries. Autarky gave way to the "socialist division of labor," and to "socialist economic integration."[72] This development accelerated in the mid-sixties and in 1971 a complex plan of economic integration, designed for a twenty-year period, was the signal for the real beginning of the integrating process that had until then been dormant.

From the beginning, despite the long phase of almost no activity, three factors dominated Comecon: the inherent imbalance created by joining in one institution a superpower and much smaller states that moreover were politically dependent on their larger partner; the Soviet initiative behind its creation and the development of various later programs; and finally, the constant objective to create a homogeneous and later an integrated economic bloc, even if the means for achieving this were not always precise and they changed over time. A corollary difficulty that characterized the system was that the plan of integration, dominated by a large state, coexisted with the juridical sovereignty of the member states and was constantly reaffirmed.[73]

In the course of the last decade, cooperation—that is, integration—has grown considerably both in the number of agreements reached and in the proliferation of common institutions. In 1975 there were forty-six bilateral and multilateral agreements within Comecon designed to promote common enterprises.[74] Marie Lavigne, whose works on socialist integration are authoritative, emphasizes that:

in the last decade, new forms of integration have appeared in the Comecon system. First of all, a plan setting forth multilateral measures of integration for the years 1976 to 1980 was adopted at the 1975 Comecon session, and then long term cooperation programs in 1978 and 1979 for the ten to fifteen following years.[75]

These were vast programs of joint investments, a large number of which were located on Soviet territory. The realization of these programs implied that the East European countries would adapt their economic plans to them and incorporate the programs in their plans. Their realization also required the signing of 232 multilateral agreements, two hundred of which had been signed by early 1982. And each agreement was supplemented by a series of bilateral agreements between the USSR and its partners specifying the contents and methods of cooperation in both directions.[76] This development fostered economic interdependence in a particular direction, strengthening Soviet ascendancy over its allies.[77]

This recent evolution of Comecon explains the proliferation in the course of the last decade of community institutions—"international economic organizations"—established in the various Comecon capitals; their purpose is to organize cooperation in and the coordination of industrial production at the level of individual firms, bypassing the geographical and political framework of the states. Such for example, are *Interelektro* in Moscow, *Interatominstru-*

ment in Warsaw, *Intershimvolokno* in Bucharest, and *Mongolsovtsvetmet* in Ulan Bator, showing that Comecon is a more open institution than the Warsaw Pact. Many similar institutions exist and they have a tendency to prolife-rate.[78] Moreover the system has two specialized banks: the International Bank for Economic Cooperation created in 1964 to facilitate exchanges within Comecon, and the International Bank for Investment created in 1970 and designed to provide long-term loans for Comecon projects, loans in ex-changeable rubles and in hard currencies. Of little importance in the begin-ning, these banks have developed very quickly both as financial instruments for economic relations within the system and for relations between Comecon, its members, and the external world. They thereby also helped to weld together the socialist economic community by multiplying its ties of depen-dency.

Two elements helped to foster the economic authority of the USSR over its allies: the growing indebtedness of the Eastern European states toward the Western world and the economic crisis. In both cases, the USSR has been in a better position than its allies. The indebtedness of the latter was such that new solutions had to be invented. The USSR was better armed to confront the situation than the states whose economies were weak, whose resources in energy and raw materials were limited, and whose reserves of gold and currency were hardly significant.[79] For Western lenders, the USSR was in the end the principal guarantor for its faltering partners, and that placed them in a position of increased dependence on the socialist community and hence on Moscow. The effects of the economic crisis moved in the same direction.[80]

One of the most interesting and profound consequences of this general evolution was the development, beyond contractual ties and economic inter-dependence, of a powerful Comecon bureaucracy, transcending borders and national differences. The situation has been remarkably explained by an American writer, A. J. Smith.[81] He shows how Comecon has proliferated into a series of administrations—a secretariat of Comecon in Moscow, the two banks, many intergovermental organizations, countless associations and joint programs, "permanent commissions," and so on. According to his estimate the Comecon bureaucracy has probably tripled in the course of its existence and has spread to all the countries concerned, and this dispersal has brought about a certain bureaucratic "doubling," since the principal institutions—the two banks located in Moscow, *Intermetal* in Budapest, *Interchim* in Halle in the GDR, and so on—logically enough had corresponding national depart-ments in each member country. As Smith says:

This complex international bureaucracy is like Topsy, it just keeps growing, becoming a proliferating empire reaching from the Caribbean in the Western Hemisphere to the Gobi Desert in central Asia. And, following Parkinson's law, its growth inevitably brought about still more growth, more experts, more meetings, more study groups, more agendas, more commissions, secretariats, travel vouchers, protocols, and regulations.[82]

This portrait, which leads the author to conclude that a proliferating bureaucracy generally leads to a lack of effectiveness, can also lead to a different conclusion not necessarily in contradiction to the notion of ineffectiveness, but seriously modifying that conclusion.

No doubt these countless functionaries and commissions were often ineffective, simply concerned with justifying their existence and their privileges. But at the same time—and this is the most important thing—this bureaucracy, this large and constantly growing body of "international communist functionaries," was creating a new society. It was the crucible of an already denationalized society embodying the objectives and interests of integration and more concerned with the integrated world that allowed it to live than with national interests. Like the Warsaw pact armies, like the serried ranks of delegates of all kinds—from parties, from governments—who constantly circulate from one capital to another to multiply contacts and procedures for integration, these international bureaucrats already represented the "community social space." On the margin of all the national societies that are attached to their own histories and their own nations sharing social and moral values developed in the course of centuries, a "second society" developed throughout the Soviet empire whose values and interests transcended particular borders and particular cultures. The system relied on this second society, if not to transform the societies in their totality, at least to limit and neutralize their aspirations.

It is clear, then, that economic integration is a program going beyond the economy and connected in its political effects to all other forms of integration promoted in order to change the human and moral landscape of the societies that the USSR included within its sphere of control in 1945. It is not surprising that some of these countries, determined to preserve their national existences, have fought economic integration at every step. This was the path followed by Rumania, the perpetual rebel against this subtle enterprise of alignment and integration. From the early sixties on it has challenged all Soviet programs: the socialist division of labor, the complex plan of integration, the international investment bank, and various joint institutions like *Interchim*. Rumania also questioned the capacity of the Secretariat of Comecon to speak in the name of the members of the socialist community in the negotiations with the Common Market that took place in the mid-sixties. In all these circumstances, Bucharest opposed to the community principle the principle of the national interest. But if we look at the course of events closely, we must recognize that Rumanian resistance was a rearguard action, ending up every time with a capitulation. After a period of vehement opposition,

Rumania ended up joining the investment bank in 1972 and *Interchim* in 1970 and signing the protocol for technical standardization in 1975. "The Rumanian attitude, one step back, then one or two steps forward to make up for lost time, seems to have become a classic procedure for the new organizations of Comecon."[83]

To conclude from this that Comecon, whatever the determination and national feeling of its member states, is an inevitable means of integration requires only one step, one that most specialists have taken. If we consider the political element—the formation of new elites—it seems impossible not to conclude that this institution is of decisive importance, is deeply effective, and has no possible counterweight.

*   *   *

The socialist "family" has as we have seen a real existence developed through countless links. Like many families, it is based on juridical realities and on the realities of everyday life. Its institutions—treaties and constitutions—serve as support mechanisms for the whole network of contacts and interdependences that the constant efforts of the USSR over the years have made so numerous. And their effectiveness—even though failures were widespread—comes from the extreme variety of procedures that have proliferated, some of which are barely visible and therefore particularly effective. Like many families, this one is not based on a love match nor even on a *mariage de raison*, but on a forced marriage. Soviet policy has been directed toward providing the means for transforming this forced marriage into a durable union based on reason. And to attain this goal, in addition to the extensive resources it has put into operation it relies on two decisive factors: the prohibition against divorce and the formation of new generations, products of this stormy, often troubled marriage, which it hopes will be able to ignore the past and forget their parents' quarrels, as rising generations often do. This wager on the future has all the more scope because of the lurking presence of military force in the background.

NOTES

1. Speech delivered at the meeting of the Bauman electoral district in Moscow on February 23, 1980, *Pravda*, February 23, 1980.

2. Iu. S. Novopashin, *Mezhdunarodnye otnosheniia novogo tipa*, 38.

3. This is Léo Hamon's thesis, an interpretation we respectfully decline to follow.

4. Law of July 6, 1978. See the commentary (from which the quotation is taken) by G. I. Tunkin and R. A. Mullerson, "Zakon o mezhdunarodnyh dogovoroh SSSR" (Law on the international agreements of the USSR), *Sovetskoe Godudarstvo i Pravo* 2 (Feburary 1979): 22–32; quotation from 24.

5. The source for all the treaties is *Sbornik deistvuiushchih dogovorov, soglashenii i konventsii zakliuchenyh SSSR s inostrannymi gosudarstvami* (Collection of treaties, agreements, and conventions signed by the USSR with foreign states), cited as *Sbornik*. These texts were first published in *Vedomosti Verkhnogo Soveta SSSR*, but the use of collections is more convenient.

6. *Sbornik*, 17–18: 17.

7. *Sbornik*, 31: 47, article 12 of the treaty.

8. *Sbornik*, 17–18: 18–19.

9. This example is taken from the preamble to the Soviet-Hungarian treaty of 1967, *Sbornik*, 25: 38; on the Soviet-Bulgarian treaty of 1967, see ibid., 35.

10. Ibid., preambles to the same treaties.

11. Article 8 of the Soviet-Rumanian treaty of 1970, *Sbornik*, 26: 39.

12. April 6, 1948, *Sbornik*, 13: 22-24; renewed by a protocol on September 19, 1955, ibid., 17–18: 25–26; renewed again on July 20, 1970, ibid., 26: 40.

13. Treaty of April 6, 1948, ibid., 13: 22.

14. Article 1, ibid., 24: 40.

15. Article 8, ibid., 24: 41.

16. Article 8 of the 1967 treaty, ibid., 25: 35–37.

17. Article 7 of the 1967 treaty, ibid., 25: 38–40.

18. Preamble of the 1970 treaty, ibid., 26: 42.

19. Ibid., 43.

20. Article 11, ibid., 44.

21. Ibid., 31: 45–46. This clause appears in the preamble and in Article 4, 45 and 46.

22. Ibid., 46. The language of Article 6 is rather curious. First it says that unchangeability (*nerushimost'*) is a principal condition of European security; later, that the signatories must, in agreement with the Warsaw Pact states, "guarantee the inviolability (*neprikosnovennost'*) of the pact members' borders as they were established at the end of the Second World War and by postwar development by including the border between the GDR and the FRG." 46.

23. G. H. Shahnazarov, "Harakternye cherty protsessa sblizheniia sotsialisticheskih natsii" (The characteristic traits of the process of rapprochement of the socialist states), *Obshchestvennye nauki* (March 1977): 27.

24. "Mezhdunarodnoe soveshchanie kommunisticheskih i rabochih partii, i problemy iuridicheskoi nauki" (The world conference of communist and workers' parties and the problems of juridical science), *Sovetskoe Gosudarstvo i Pravo* 10 (October 1969): 3–10, especially 3–4.

25. All the texts mentioned here except for the Soviet Constitution were consulted in English translation.

26. R. H. Vil'danov, "Mezhdunarodnoe znachenie sovetskoi konstitutsii" (The international significance of the Soviet Constitution), *Sovetskoe Gosudarstvo i Pravo* 10 (October 1977): 36.

27. Ibid., 37; V. Vadimov, *Mezhdunarodnoe znachenie konstitutsii SSSR* (The international significance of the Soviet Constitution) (Moscow, 1977), p. 14.

28. G. H. Shahnazarov, "O nekotoryh tendentsiah razvitiia politicheskoi sistemy sotsializma" (On some tendencies in the development of the socialist political system), *Sovetskoe Gosudarstvo i Pravo* 11 (January 1978): 5.

29. Ibid., 5–6.

30. The text of the Constitution of the GDR was published in *Gesetzbatt der DDR 1974*, vol. 1, no. 47.

31. The text of the Bulgarian Constitution was published in *Derzhaven Vestnik*, 1971, no. 39.

32. Leonid Brezhnev referred to them in his presentation of the Soviet plan, *Pravda*, January 5, 1977; see also the article by V. Vaikelt, "Pervaia sotsialisticheskaia germanskaia konstitutsia" (The first German socialist constitution), *Sovetskoe Gosudarstvo i Pravo* 10 (October 1968): 112, which points out that by 1968 the GDR had set forth as part of its fundamental law its loyalty to socialist internationalism.

33. *Shirka Zákonů Československé Socialistické Republiky*, 1978, no. 62.

34. I. Kovach, "Teoreticheskie voprosy razvitiia vengerskoi konstitutsii" (Theoretical problems of the development of the Hungarian Constitution), *Sovetskoe Gosudarstvo i Pravo* 6 (June 1978): 85–94.

35. On the Polish Constitution, see the excellent study by G. Mond, "Les nouvelles constitutions de l'U.R.S.S. et de la Chine, comparées aux lois fondamentales de la Pologne et de l'Albanie," *Revue d'études comparatives Est-Ouest* 9, 3 (1978): 169–97; A. Lopatka, "Izmeneniia v konstitutsii P.N.R." (The changes in the Constitution of the People's Republic of Poland), *Sovetskoe Gosudarstvo i Pravo* 7 (1977): 108–17.

36. A. Lopatka, op. cit., 112; G. Mond. op. cit., 173, makes the same comment.

37. Identical clauses can be found in the Constitutions of the GDR (Article 3, §§1 and 2) and Bulgaria (Article 1, §3).

38. G. Mond, op. cit., 179.

39. A. Lopatka, op. cit., 109.

40. I. Kovach, op. cit., 89.

41. J. Zakrzewska, "Les révisions de la Constitution de la République socialiste de Roumanie," *Revue d'études comparatives Est-Ouest* 9, 2 (1978): 151–73; O. Bihari, *The Constitutional Models of Socialist State Organization* (Budapest, 1979).

42. M. Suslov, "Delo vsei Partii" (The business of the whole Party), *Pravda*, October 17, 1979.

43. Th. Takowska-Harmstone, comment on H. Carrère d'Encausse, "Les conflits à l'intérieur de la pacte de Varsovie," *Les Superpuissances et leurs alliances militaires* (Quebec, 1982), 84.

44. *Pravda*, July 25, 1980.

45. *Pravda*, July 29, 1980.

46. *Sovetskaia Rossia*, August 1, 1980.

47. *Izvestia*, August 6, 1980.

48. *Pravda*, August 8, 1980.

49. *Pravda*, August 12, 1980.

50. *Pravda*, July 23, 1981; *Pravda*, July 28, 1981; *Pravda*, August 8, 1981; *Pravda*, August 15 and 16, 1981.

51. *Pravda*, September 26, 1971.

52. Decree of the Presidium of the Supreme Soviet granting him the medal, *Pravda*, May 25, 1972; Tito's visit from June 5 to June 10, 1972, *Pravda*, June 5, 6, and 11, 1972.

53. Visit of November 12–15, 1973, *Pravda*, November 16, 1973.

54. *Pravda*, August 19, 20, and 25, 1977.

55.   Visit from May 16 to May 21, 1979, *Pravda*, May 22, 1979.

56.   *Pravda*, May 8, 1980; *Izvestia*, May 9 and 10, 1980.

57.   Conversations of Ponomarev and Rusakov with V. Janzić, executive secretary of the Presidium of the Central Committee of the League of Yugoslav Communists from January 28 to January 31, 1981, *Pravda*, February 4, 1981.

58.   Gromyko's visit to Belgrade, *Pravda*, April 7, 1982.

59.   *Pravda*, November 17, 1982.

60.   For example, *Pravda*, November 1, 1980, on the meeting between the Soviet Communist Party and the SED. on these problems.

61.   For example, the visit to the USSR by officials in charge of political instruction in the GDR army, *Krasnaia Zvezda*, September 16, 1979; *Izvestia*, January 21, 1980 (visit of Marshal Kulikov to Berlin).

62.   For example, the Sofia meeting on "ideological and international" questions, *Pravda*, March 4, 1977; *Sovetskaia Rossia*, April 5, 1980.

63.   For example, *Pravda*, April 30, 1977 and May 9, 1977 reported on the Prague meeting of the editorial committee of the journal, *Problems of Peace and Socialism*.

64.   For example, *Pravda*, January 29, 1972, reported the visit to Moscow by the society for Soviet-Bulgarian friendship; *Pravda*, February 12, 1974, the same; the event occurred at least once a year.

65.   For example, *Trud*, October 3 and 7, 1980; *Pravda*, October 2, 1980, on the Thirty-First Session of the General Committee of the World Federation of Trade Unions; *Pravda*, January 18, 1972, Soviet union delegation in Prague.

66.   For example, on July 3, 1979, the meeting in Moscow of the sixteenth international seminar for journalists, reported in *Izvestia*, July 7, 1980.

67.   For example, *Pravda*, June 3 and 6, 1980, conference of party secretaries in Berlin.

68.   For example, *Pravda*, October 2, 1980, critique by the World Federation of Trade Unions of the Poles for neglecting their union duties.

69.   For example, *Izvestia*, January 24, 1981, economic, scientific, and technical cooperation between the USSR and Rumania.

70.   *Pravda*, December 29, 1971, Soviet-Bulgarian meeting on education; *Pravda*, January 29, 1972, Soviet-Bulgarian meeting on coordination of higher education; *Pravda*, November 25, 1972, Soviet-Bulgarian protocol on cooperation in education; *Pravda*, February 19, 1977, conference of socialist countries in Moscow on cooperation in research.

71.   The most useful works in French are: M. Lavigne, *Les Economies socialistes soviétiques et européennes*, 3rd ed. (Paris, 1979); Lavigne, *Le Comecon* (Paris, 1973). In English: Lavigne, "The Soviet Union inside Comecon," *Soviet Studies* 2 (April 1983): 135–153, and the annual publications of the Joint Economic Committee of the U.S. Congress, which always include a long study of Comecon; notably A. J. Smith, "The Council of Mutual Economic Assistance in 1977; New Economic Power and Some Old and New Problems," Joint Economic Committee, August 25, 1977; P. Marer and J. M. Montias, "C.M.E.A. Integration: Theory and Practice," *East European Economic Assessment*, part 2, Joint Economic Committee, July 10, 1981.

72.   *Pravda*, September 28, 1977.

73.   E. T. Usenko, "Sushtnost' i printsipy sotsialisticheskoi ekonomicheskoi integratsii" (The essence and the principles of socialist economic integration), *Sovetskoe*

Gosudarstvo i Pravo 11 (November 1971): 53–54; see also *Pravda*, September 28, 1977, on the international conference organized in Moscow on "the October Revolution and a new kind of international relations."

74.   Smith, op. cit., 162.

75.   Lavigne, op. cit., 143.

76.   Ibid., 144.

77.   In 1981 at the Twenty-Sixth Congress, Leonid Brezhnev suggested that in order to develop cooperation among socialist states in the course of the next two five-year periods, in addition to common programs there should be common enterprises (Sovmestnye fermy), *Pravda*, February 24, 1981, 2.

78.   P. A. Tokareva, "Novye mezhdunarodnye organizatsii stran sotsializma" (The new international organizations of the socialist countries), *Sovetskoe Gosudarstvo i Pravo* 7 (July 1970).

79.   Smith, op. cit., p. 162.

80.   Lavigne, op. cit., p. 135.

81.   Smith, op. cit., p. 169.

82.   Ibid.

83.   Ibid., 170.

9

THE "SHADOW OF THE KREMLIN"

At first sight, the Warsaw Pact, the military alliance of the communist world, and NATO, the military alliance of the Western world, are the two sides of a single problem: the confrontation between East and West. And the offer periodically made by the USSR to dissolve the two pacts simultaneously merely strengthens this hasty conclusion; a conclusion both hasty and dangerously false. The Warsaw Pact is something entirely different from NATO because of the links it has established among its members, its program, and the actions it has carried out.

The Warsaw Pact: For What Purpose?

The Warsaw Pact was created on May 14, 1955.[1] In principle, it was the Soviet response to the entry of the German Federal Republic into NATO and to the new danger the USSR detected in the Paris agreements that had decided on this expansion of NATO late in 1954, which was carried out on May 9, 1955.[2] But other events surrounding the creation of the Warsaw Pact should also be taken into account and they shed more light on its meaning. On May 15, 1955, the USSR signed the state treaty with Austria, which liberated that country from Soviet troops in exchange for its neutrality.[3] And on the day the Warsaw Pact was born, the Kremlin announced that a Soviet delegation was going to Yugoslavia. It is this cluster of events, all remarkable in the contemporary context, that must be considered in order to grasp the logic of the Warsaw Pact. From the point of view of military forces and alliances, it added nothing to the USSR, since it was superimposed over the dense network of bilateral treaties that organized cooperation among the socialist states. But the situation bequeathed by Stalin to his successors had greatly changed. Despite the campaigns carried out in the West through the intermediary of communist parties, despite frenetic propaganda against "German revanchism," the USSR had been unable to prevent what had seemed unthinkable in 1945: the calming of Europe and the reintegration of Germany into the concert of nations. The USSR feared that this Europe in the process of reconstitution would one day include Austria and thus come dangerously close to the borders of the empire constructed by Stalin after 1945. Moreover the USSR recognized that this formerly monolithic empire had to be adapted to a changing world. Yugoslav rebelliousness after 1948, the Berlin riots of 1953, and also the changes taking place in the USSR all indicated that a new consensus had to be found. To avoid having Austria one day reinforce the Western camp, to strengthen the barriers of 1945 with a second barrier of neutrality, Stalin's successors signed the treaty with Austria. Between an expanded NATO and the socialist world they set up an intermediate zone that they hoped to see one day transformed into a central Europe won over to neutrality. But this central Europe was to be constructed at the expense of NATO alone, not the USSR. The Austrian example was not intended to create any illusions for the West or for the Eastern European states; it would not be extended to the allies of the USSR.[4] And the Warsaw Pact, signed at this difficult moment when the USSR had to confront the cohesion of its adversaries and the dissensions it sensed among its allies, was a global response to these new phenomena. The pact thus had as its primary function to demonstrate that the socialist camp existed and that it could not be changed. At the moment when difficult negotiations with Tito were getting under way, the pact was also in the minds of the Soviet leaders a convenient framework for organizing new relations between the two countries. It was all the more convenient because it was at the outset not very constraining. The bilateral treaties were much more so, and the stationing of Soviet troops in the region guaranteed the effectiveness of those treaties. The clauses of the pact were rather vague. It provided for consultations, mutual defense (Article 4) "in case of armed attack on one or more of the signatory parties," and military cooperation, the institutions for which were defined in Articles 5 and 6 of the treaty. Signed for a period of twenty years with an automatic renewal clause for ten years, this document unquestionably tended by its resemblance to the North Atlantic Treaty to give relations among Eastern European states a contractual aspect, concealing the constraints inherent in the agreements imposed at the end of the war.

Tito never wanted to hear the propositions inviting him to join the organization founded in 1955, and the usefulness of the pact seemed limited because of his absence in the early years. Indeed until the early sixties, no one in the socialist camp was really concerned with its usefulness. This is confirmed by a summary of the activities of the pact during this period. In the five years from 1955 to 1960 the political organs of the pact held four meetings (including the founding meeting), and military cooperation found expression in a single joint military exercise in 1958.[5]

There are explanations for this general indifference to an alliance that had been created with great fanfare. The years from 1956 to 1960 were for the USSR years of renewal in all areas.

Peaceful coexistence, the possibility of which had been proclaimed at the Twentieth Congress, led the USSR to emphasize the elements of détente in international relations, not those of confrontation, like military alliances. In this peaceful phase, the USSR was more concerned with its internal development than with problems of defense and it reduced its military forces. It also attempted—after the Budapest and Warsaw crises—to establish relations with its allies on a different basis. And the "national paths" that were being opened up to them fit in poorly with military integration. Hadn't the Poles demanded of Khrushchev that they be freed from Marshal Rokossowski and the too numerous and indiscreet Soviet advisers? Everything that might recall the military control exercised since 1945 would have gone against the "new order" that the USSR was attempting to establish in Eastern Europe. In these years of change, everything demanded that efforts should be concentrated on the development of the civilian economies.

In the early sixties on the contrary the situation changed very quickly and the Warsaw Pact came to life. In this second phase of its existence, which ran from 1961 to 1968, the pact's activities, so infrequent until then, proliferated, particularly in the military sphere. In the spring of 1961, the Consultative Political Council took note of the insufficiency of military cooperation and of the minor influence of the pact on the defense capabilities of the socialist camp.[6] From that point on the system went into action, and in a few years real joint military activities were organized. Joint maneuvers that had been almost nonexistent in the previous period proliferated to the point that there were nineteen between 1961 and 1968.[7] The equipment of the pact's armed forces was modernized—in those years the pact received the T-54 tank and its air forces were equipped with MIG-21s and SU7s—and systematic training of officers to prepare them for joint tasks was begun. The unification of officer training, notably through intensive instruction in a single language, Russian, and in common techniques, and the uniformity of equipment were then the principal preoccupations of the pact's leaders.

Although the pact's political activities were slower to develop, they nevertheless followed the same rising curve. The 1955 treaty expressly provided that the Consultative Political Committee was to meet twice a year. Although it did not reach this frequency between 1961 and 1968, it did meet ten times during the period, which represented considerable progress over the past. More important, its activity was adapted to events. It is significant that it held two meetings a year at exceptional moments—1961, 1963, 1968—that is, when the pact was revived and when it had to confront crisis situations. If we remember the large number of institutions through which political cooperation between the USSR and its allies has been organized, we can only wonder at the supplementation of political cooperation undertaken by the pact in a system in which political cooperation penetrated everywhere. Up to 1965 political meetings of the pact dealt above all with internal problems of the socialist world and only rarely did the organization issue statements on international problems. There was one notable exception, when the meeting of the Political Council in March 1961 dealt at length with the problem of Berlin. But in 1965 Leonid Brezhnev observed that the pact was not acting adequately as an organ for the definition of common foreign policies.[8] As a consequence the field of its concerns was broadened.[9] At the Bucharest meeting in 1966 and the meeting in Sofia in 1968 the Political Council placed on its agenda a discussion of "American aggression in Vietnam."[10]

The new interest the USSR showed in the pact in the sixties can also be explained by taking into account international relations in general and the effects of these relations on the community of states led by the USSR. In the mid-sixties, the USSR realized that there was a price to be paid for peaceful coexistence and for the sometimes disordered activities of Nikita Khrushchev in the world. The Cuban crisis of 1962 and the conflicts with the West over Berlin demonstrated Western determination not to allow the USSR to use coexistence as a Trojan horse. The "opening to the West" by the USSR had as a counterpart an "opening to the East" by the West, addressing the Eastern European states one by one and attempting to restore a certain European unity without the USSR. In this context, when national feeling in the Eastern European states was growing stronger, when their desire to shape their own fates was being developed by the idea of "national paths," the USSR had at its disposal only one means to tighten the loosening bonds: the Warsaw Pact. The USSR could invoke no prohibition against the states that were undertaking to follow "national paths." Where would it find such a prohibition? On the other hand, the Warsaw Pact offered it a pretext for the strengthening of military links—to stand up to NATO—and for joint political discussions. This was all the more important because decisions taken in the pact did not yet appear to be very constraining.

The decisive turning point was provoked by the Czechoslovak affair, or more probably that was the pretext for it. The Prague Spring led the USSR to organize a systematic mobilization of its allies; a political mobilization, since this was the framework within which pressure could be brought to bear on Prague; and a military mobilization strictly speaking by means of the army maneuvers of the summer of 1968 on Czech territory, and then the invasion of August 21. For the first time in its history, the Warsaw Pact was put forward by the USSR as the framework for the solution to a crisis in the communist world. From that point on, developments moved rapidly. The meeting of the Consultative Political Council held in Budapest on March 17, 1969, profoundly reformed the structures of the pact by adding new institutions designed to give it new effectiveness for which it had until then lacked the means. Three organs were created: the Council of Defense Ministers, the

Military Council, and a technical committee. A first consequence of the creation of these organizations was that the pact members would meet more and more frequently, since there were constantly more grounds for meeting.[11] The Council of Defense Ministers met once a year, the Military Council a minimum of twice a year, and there is no precise information on the activities of the third committee, created in 1969. Nevertheless, it is easy to recognize the progress that was accomplished in the realm of military consultations in comparison with the initial period of the pact's existence. The meetings of the military organs were paralleled by meetings of their political counterparts. Up to 1968 the Ministers of Foreign Affairs were supposed to meet as the need arose, but there was no institutional obligation to do so. The infrequency of these meetings corresponded to the still prevailing lack of organization. There were only three meetings of the Ministers of Foreign Affairs before the Czechoslovak crisis: in April 1959, in June 1966, and in February 1967. The Prague Spring also brought out the urgency of needed change in this area. From 1969 to 1976 the ministers developed the habit of meeting almost annually. This regularity was formalized by the reform decided on in Bucharest in 1976 that created a Council of Ministers of Foreign Affairs assisted by a secretariat, which would meet every year and would become the normal framework for defining a common foreign policy.[12] If we add that military maneuvers, whether joint or national (and national maneuvers were integrated into an overall plan by the existence of the pact), also increased impressively, we can recognize that the slowdown in intersocialist relations of the fifties had been succeeded by a new intensity of intersocialist life.

The Warsaw Pact: what was its purpose? The last quarter-century of its history provides a preliminary answer with no ambiguity. The pact allowed the USSR to put together the universe that was disintegrating in 1955. And precisely those crises that have so strongly shaken the socialist community allowed Moscow to react with additional measures, tightening links and increasing obligations within the pact. Ever more numerous institutions and increasingly frequent contacts have since 1955 served to weld Eastern Europe together; they never have served as operations of defense against the Western world. The function of the pact was thus first of all to replace Stalin's system of violent domination, which the end of the war situation made impossible to perpetuate, with a modern system, acceptable because it was apparently modeled on NATO, a system that enfolded the countries of Eastern Europe in a multitude of bonds all of which emanated from the Kremlin.

Soviet Authority in the Warsaw Pact

If the pact had been nothing but the occasion for increased meetings and the reestablishment of common ties, it would probably have had little usefulness, for both the ties and the meetings were more and more violently challenged by the allies of the USSR from one crisis to the next. But the communist alliance allowed the USSR to impose total authority on its allies and to create within the contested terrain of Eastern Europe a privileged area in which conflicts had already been overcome. From this point of view the structures of the pact and the individuals who participated in its activities provided the USSR with extraordinary means for renewing its domination.[13] The structures of the pact, which in principle ensured the equal participation of all members in the functioning of the institution, were distorted from the beginning by the USSR so that it could occupy the dominant position. This was true of the Soviet position in the joint institutions of the pact and also in the military institutions of each member state.

The makeup of the ruling organs of the pact shows how the entire sytem functioned. The Council of Defense Ministers, which is the supreme military organ of the pact and is in principle its true collective minister of defense, is statutorily made up of seven ministers of the allied states, all of whom have equal rights. The presidency rotates following alphabetical order, which assures that each state will preside over the council at one point or another. But this perfect organization of an egalitarian system conceals an inegalitarian reality. The council in fact has great weaknesses. It is not a permanent organ and an annual session of two days obviously does not give it genuine authority. More seriously, it has no permanent personnel of its own nor does its president have any permanent staff. In administrative matters, he must rely on the central administration of the pact, which is under the control of the commander-in-chief of the pact and under the direct authority of the chief of staff. In other words, the permanent military life of the pact is the domain of two high-ranking military figures who dominate the entire apparatus and have at their disposal a solid infrastructure. And who are these two dominant personalities? The commander-in-chief has been from the beginning a Soviet marshal: Koniev from 1955 to 1960; Grechko from 1960 to 1967; Yakubovsky from 1967 to 1977; Kulikov, since 1977. The documents shed little light on the conditions under which the chief personage of the pact is chosen;[14] on the other hand, it is well known that the partners of the USSR have several times deplored the fact that the high command has always been reserved to the Soviets. The same holds true for the chief of staff, chosen by agreement among all pact members, and this agreement has miraculously until now always settled on Soviet military leaders. The most recent holder of the post is General Gribkov. He was preceded by General Antonov from 1955 to 1962; General Batov from 1962 to 1965; General Kazakov from 1965 to 1968; and General Shtemenko from 1968 to 1976. Aside from the permanence of their functions in contrast to the temporary character of the joint institutions and aside from their authority over the entire administrative apparatus of the pact, these two highest military members enjoy the privilege of sitting on the

Council of Defense Ministers. In this seven-member institution representing the seven states of the pact the addition of the two highest representatives of the system has had the effect of increasing Soviet representation to one third of the membership. The USSR, indeed, includes its own defense minister in the council like each of its partners, as well as Marshall Kulikov and General Gribkov. Decisions must be made unanimously;[15] since unanimity is difficult to reach for ministers who meet infrequently, it is clear that the presence of a weighty Soviet group including two "permanent" members of the pact can be decisive.

The Military Council has a rather similar composition since it includes within its ranks the commander-in-chief, the president, and the chief of staff of the pact as well as a representative from each member state. Like the Council of Defense Ministers, the Military Council has no administrative organization of its own. Meeting twice a year, it depends on the administration and the permanent authorities of the pact. This means that once again the role of the Soviet ally is determinative. The distribution of tasks between the two organs is difficult to determine. The former is probably more oriented toward the definition of a common policy and tends to trespass on the functions of the Political Council. The latter plans maneuvers and training for the armies of the pact. As for the Technical Council, the least known, its members and functions have not been well identified.

In concrete terms this organization operates through a unified command under the direction of the pact's commander-in-chief, the chief of staff, an adjutant-major for each country, and the chief of the pact's antiaircraft forces. In this case too the USSR has at least three representatives, and sometimes four when the chief of antiaircraft forces is a Soviet officer.

Dominating the pact from within thanks to this apparatus, the USSR has the means to penetrate the defense systems of member states. The pact's commander-in-chief is, in fact, supported in each country by a liaison mission established at the Defense Ministry whose function is to ensure permanent contact between the national defense and the unified command.

The joint structures—so dominated by the Soviet Army—have as their primary function the rapid development of military integration. The military leaders of the national armies by reason of their very participation in the joint structures necessarily all have the same training. Soviet military establishments can give this training at all levels. Superior officers in Eastern Europe have attended the major military academies of the USSR, particularly the prestigious Frunze Academy. Officers of lower rank are trained either in the USSR or in their own military schools. The first alternative obviously leads to more brilliant careers. Marshal Yakubovsky has pointed out that the "thousands of officers" trained in the USSR "form the central kernel of the national military officer corps and play a considerable role in the development of their national armed forces."[16] The number of officers trained in this way in every country is high, and this is confirmed by many pieces of information. But more important is the fact that these officers, who have generally spent several years in Soviet schools and have acquired an adequate mastery of the Russian language and a solid acquaintance with the strategic techniques and principles of the pact, are all in positions of authority in their countries. They are thus within the national armies an already denationalized element in agreement with the common ideology, the fundamental principles of the pact, and its unifying vocation. For them, the national armies have already in part ceased being tools of sovereignty and have come to embody the community of a new kind in the process of being constructed.

The unification of weapons and defense techniques is another path toward integration. The USSR is the community's principal arms manufacturer. It has the monopoly on certain weapons and the degree of uniformity in the armaments produced by its partners is very high. Training, weapons, and techniques are all constantly being put together in such a way as to increase the feeling of a brotherhood in arms that is the official objective of the system, as well as the development of the means of defense.[17] To create this fraternity, to bring men together, the USSR uses meetings and maneuvers. Meetings of the officers of the various pact countries on themes of political education and better understanding of the community are among the major activities of the pact.[18] But it is worth nothing that these meetings are generally bilateral and that their function is to make the USSR known to the officers or units of the fraternal armies. This kind of meeting generally takes place in the USSR, and it is not surprising that one of the principle organizers of them has been General Epishev, chief of political administration for the Soviet Army. These meetings often take place in border military regions (the Baltic district, Byelorussia, the Carpathians), and the country most surrounded by them is naturally Poland, because with the exception of Rumania, it has the longest borders with the USSR.

Major military maneuvers are another means for integrating armies and it is easy to understand why these maneuvers have increased with the rise in difficulties within the socialist camp.[19]

From the perspective of the Soviet program of integration, these maneuvers are of interest because they reproduce on the scale of the socialist camp the techniques of military integration that the USSR has applied to its own nationalities. Just as the Soviet Army from a certain level upward and in every case at the top is commanded by Russian officers, so the maneuvers are led or supervised, if not always (this might be demonstrated, but available information does not permit a clear determination on the point), at least very frequently, by Soviet superior officers. Maneuvers are accompanied by a political dimension in which the participation of General Epishev's organization is all the more significant because the Warsaw Pact has no institution specializing in political activity.[20] But what above all characterizes the organization of the Soviet Army as an army integrating a multinational state is the use of the principle of individual recruitment *(Kadrovyi printsip).*[21] As in the Soviet army, the *kadrovyi printsip* applies to the composition of troops involved in joint maneuvers; but in this case the small units play the role played by individuals in the Soviet Army. The troops are also very thoroughly mixed, nationally, culturally, and linguistically. As in the USSR, this determination to blend together men of different origins favors the usefulness of the Russian language, even if multilingualism is a rule in the pact. Information bulletins, orders, and so on are distributed in the languages of all participants. But in practice efficiency ensures a certain superiority for the language that all the military leaders know, Russian. Multilingualism preserves the theory of the equality of all members of the pact. But emergency conditions, and the defense sector is clearly one sector where the term applies, can and must make recourse to the common language overcome that equality. The fact that all the countries of the pact have their own totally sovereign national forces, with the exception of the GDR whose links with the pact are closer,[22] does not prevent these armies from being penetrated from within by a Sovietized officer corps through procedures that unify all the armies (their principles of organization, strategy, and equipment),[23] and finally by the various military advisers that the USSR maintains in each country. All of this makes up a network of obligations and dependencies that weighs on and shapes the national armies and should gradually transform them into national sections of a large integrated army, even if in formal terms the names are not changed.

Forced Integration

The Warsaw Pact has developed differently in different periods, which has strongly helped to conceal its essential function. It is in fact the privileged instrument for the political and not merely military integration of the socialist camp. Because the pact is officially a military institution and because the crises of the socialist camp have tended to be expressed in political terms even though they have been resolved in military terms, there is a tendency to dissociate the Warsaw Pact from the political future of the community of states led by the USSR.

However, the basic documents and Soviet publications dealing with the pact make it impossible to ignore the reality that the function of this institution is to ensure, in the political realm, the security of socialism, the cohesion of the bloc, and the homogeneity of the behavior of its component parts toward the external world. This group of objectives is labeled "socialist internationalism." It is no accident that the pact's political insrument, the Council of Foreign Ministers, established in 1976, was given a permanent secretariat whose headquarters is in Moscow not Warsaw.[24]

The pact is in the first place the guarantor of socialist conquests.[25]

Although the principle was established at the very moment of the pact's creation, it was not until 1968 that the pact really claimed that function. But in placing the entire Czech crisis under the aegis of the pact and mobilizing all of its institutions, the USSR was clearly indicating that it intended to use this framework of action and the means of applying presure it provided to impose on the Eastern European states the perpetuation of the political systems established in 1945. Since 1968 this function of the pact as the "guarantor of socialism" has been repeatedly exercised, both with reference to the military operation in Prague and in totally different contexts. Used for the first time in 1968 for this purpose, the pact performed well enough so that in the late seventies the USSR could appeal to it to legitimize its demands, this time on Poland.

This link between the "threatened conquests of socialism" and the role of the pact has the further advantage, because of the dangers threatening the system, of justifying the permanent stationing of Soviet troops in countries that in principle challenge the right of the Soviet Union to do so. Thus in October 1968 the USSR could force its troops on Czechoslovakia. As two Soviet authors noted with a touch of humor: "The Soviet government has reached agreement with the governments of the four allied states and of Czechoslovakia" so that "the troops necessary for the protection of socialism" would remain where they were as of August 21, without "encroaching on the sovereignty of Czechoslovakia."[26]

The "duty of internationalism" thus justified extended periods of military occupation, insupportable in any other way in the context of European peace. It also justified the very temporary stationing of troops in the course of large-scale maneuvers that might or might not be stages in a process of armed intervention. The essential point was that the USSR could conceal its *coups de force* behind the joint decisions of an institution it dominated without being totally identified with it. And this principle of intervention for a common cause—*vzaimodeistvie*—was in the end a convenient smoke screen for permanently controlling the political orientations of Eastern Europe.

This essentially internal function, as a tool of integration and police force, of the Warsaw Pact comes out clearly if we examine even superficially the state of its weapons. Although the USSR has in fact paid considerable attention to the training, the military exercises, and the political education of the pact armies, it has on the other hand demonstrated a certain negligence in the area of equipment. Its efforts have been essentially concentrated on standardization, which has reinforced dependency, and much less on modernization. If some progress has been accomplished in this area, it remains true that the national armies participating in the pact have much less modern equipment than the Soviet Army. In fact in a hypothetical confrontation with the West the USSR would count on its own forces. The pact is turned inward. It is no doubt a means of defense, but primarily a defense against the inclinations toward change and emancipation on the part of the Eastern European allies, inclinations that have constantly been called "threats challenging the conquests of socialism."

The defense of socialist conquests has two aspects. One is linked to the Soviet style of political system. In this connection, since 1956 as we have seen the USSR has made no concessions. The other is linked to the desire of the member states for international sovereignty. Because they have been aware of the fact that the Warsaw Pact represents a privileged way for the USSR to limit their sovereignty and to impose constant constraint on them, the states of the pact have almost all revolted against it at one point or another. And some have managed to establish a certain distance from it. While Hungary was invaded in 1956 as was Czechoslovakia in 1968, and Poland was normalized from within, Albania left the pact, Rumania has at times maintained a surprising distance from it, and Yugoslavia never joined. These differences in attitude and treatment should be considered carefully because they suggest that within this constrictive pact there is room for a certain heterogeneity. The three normalized countries, each in turn, have attempted to change their ties with the Warsaw Pact. Hungary did it openly by announcing its withdrawal, and it was immediately punished. Poland, which was prudent in October 1956, in the course of an acceleratd march toward autonomy in the succeeding period of optimism tried to reduce its ties with an institution that was not yet very oppressive but which did not include the right to leave. The Hungarian case compared to that of Yugoslavia suggested that sovereignty, the possibility of moving toward an independent national path, required distancing from the pact. The Rapacki plan, proposed in 1957 by the Polish foreign minister, was an important step in this direction.[27] It proposed that a denuclearized zone be established in central Europe covering both certain countries in the Soviet sphere, Poland, Czechoslovakia, and the GDR, and the Federal Republic of Germany. This plan, presented at the Twelfth Session of the United Nations General Assembly, had no more success than the suggestion also made by Rapacki of limited troop withdrawals from the same territory. In 1960 at the Fifteenth Session of the General Assembly, Gomułka reiterated Rapacki's proposals, still with no favorable response. If the USSR was not opposed to the proposals, this was because it hoped to weaken the German defenses; but it never accepted the implicit content of the Rapacki plan, which was to grant Poland a certain degree of neutrality. In that period, despite the Soviet concessions of October 1956, Poland was not a sure ally. At the UN vote on November 21, 1956, it had not come to the support of the USSR, which was being condemned for its intervention in Hungary. This attitude of independence rather than solidarity did not encourage Soviet confidence. Far from acceding to Polish leaders' dreams of neutrality or independence, the USSR in the agreement of December 1956 imposed on them the stationing of a garrison in Silesia.

Czechoslovakia experienced a similar temptation in July 1968 when a group of officers from the Gottwald Political Military Academy developed a program of alternative strategies for Czechoslovakia. Although this document known as the Gottwald Memorandum[28] said that the Warsaw Pact could be maintained for some years, it also suggested the exploration of alternative solutions: neutrality, the organization of a system of regional security without the USSR, or total military sovereignty. The resurgence of the neutralist argument could not fail to impress the USSR much more than protestations of loyalty to the pact. After the invasion, this theme appeared on the list of reasons provided to explain that the pact had to react to preserve "the instrument of international defense."[29] And it is true that the intervention also eliminated the risk of seeing a major country in the pact rejecting it and thereby nourishing the dreams of independence or neutrality harbored by other countries.

There were moreover some reasons for the development of these dreams, since three European communist countries had shown that they could "preserve the conquests of socialism" and not belong to the pact or belong to it only distantly. The case of Yugoslavia was relatively simple. Being on bad terms with the USSR when the Warsaw Pact was established, two weeks later when Khrushchev made his conciliatory journey Yugoslavia clearly stated that it would accept no integration into an organization with supranational tendencies. Endowed with a powerful army at the liberation, Yugoslavia in order to deter a Stalinist coup had subsequently developed extraordinary defense capabilities that included the entire nation.[30]

This strategy of popular defense allowed Yugoslavia to confront the USSR with the fact that it had enough forces to guarantee its own security and had no need for another system of protection. Moreover, socialism, which Soviet leaders in 1955 had recognized as the political system of Yugoslavia, had never been shaken; and until his death Tito maintained a form of socialism that may have been unusual, but it was one over which he had full control.

Albania, a member of the Warsaw Pact in 1955, moved away from it in the early sixties when it came under Chinese influence and it left the pact in 1968. Since this country had always been marginal to Soviet concerns, few efforts were made to hold it back. Quite the contrary, by attacking Albania in 1961, aiming indirectly at China, Soviet leaders merely brushed it out of their path.

Rumania was an entirely different matter; it had carried out the remarkable feat of refusing to cooperate with the pact like the other members without either breaking with it or calling down punishment from the USSR. This state, apparently very secure until the late fifties, obtained from the USSR or forced from it a series of adjustments to its status as an ally, moving it from being a satellite into the category of an independent state.

In 1958 Soviet troops left Rumanian soil even though it had been a conquered country, and Ceauşescu became more outspoken. The 1963 military maneuvers on its territory demonstrated to Rumania the risks of encroachment on its sovereignty that they presented. From that point on Rumania set forth as a principle that it would not be a field for pact maneuvers and would no longer allow foreign troops to cross through its territory. All that it would allow its allies were meetings of ranking officers for indoor strategy sessions. It also agreed to send observers to maneuvers in other countries, whom press reports called, inaccurately, "participants."

The pact's intervention in Prague in 1968 led Rumania to take a further step on the road to disengagement. On the very day of the invasion, Ceauşescu announced the broad principles of Rumanian strategy and the creation of the Patriotic Guard, which would be the instrument of that strategy along with the army. Ceaşescu's strategic position was that Rumania had the responsibility for its own defense and that this defense applied against any invader, no matter who it might be or what motive might be invoked. To guard against a violation of Rumanian sovereignty, which was unlimited, the army was reinforced by a Patriotic Guard that made defense of the country everyone's business. Later, the defense law of 1972 codified these principles, which placed Rumania on the edges of the pact and placed it in contradiction with the theories that had been developed in the alliance after 1968.[31] Ceauşescu constantly repeated that Rumanian military policy was based on a total capacity for self-defense, but that as a "socialist state, in case of a war unleashed by the imperialist states, Rumania would fight beside the other socialist states, whether the Warsaw Pact exists or not."[32] These remarks were at the very least casual toward the pact that the USSR had worked so very hard to develop since 1968—they constituted a theory of defense that placed Rumania within the sphere of the principles developed by Tito against the USSR. All of this appeared at first hardly acceptable to Moscow. However, Rumanian autonomy was never punished. Why did the USSR make this distinction between "good" and "bad" rebels? Had its ideas about the pact become attenuated after 1968?

If we look closely at the arguments presented by Moscow, we can see that on the contrary nothing had been conceded with respect to the fundamental principles of the alliance. Rather the sixties, which witnessed the withdrawal of Albania and Rumania and the development of heterodox ideas in all member countries, were the very years in which the Soviet leaders refined their conceptions of international life and of defense. At the heart of Soviet ideas on the defense of socialist Europe was a reflection on war in the nuclear age.

According to the Soviets, there are no limits to future conflicts in Europe because they will not be conflicts between one state and another but conflicts engendered by imperialism to call into question the conquests of socialism.[33]

This implies the need for a common defense of the socialist states. Against the theories of a separate defense by each nation proposed by the Yugoslavs and their imitators, the Soviet theory repeatedly argued that the other theories corresponded to the prenuclear age; that nuclear weapons made it impossible to think in terms of local conflicts because every conflict would inevitably develop because of nuclear technology into a world nuclear conflict. The theory of total war and nuclear escalation justified Moscow in increasing the integration of the Eastern European armies, and beyond that, of the states.[34] Reasoning always in terms of antagonistic political systems and the imperialist threat weighing on the socialist system, the USSR established on this reasoning the authority of the pact over the member states and rejected all aspirations by these states to follow their own international paths—neutralist paths or ones based on an independent system of defense—asserting that such a choice would bring about the collapse of the whole system. The link between defense of the system and international life was thus presented as an absolute maxim closing off all possibilities of modifying the system on the part of the members of the pact.

Then why were the challenges launched against this theory by Yugoslavia, Albania, and Rumania tolerated? The explanation is not simple; it lies in the dual context of geostrategy and the political systems. The socialist Europe born in 1945 was not, despite Moscow's desire for unification, a homogeneous geopolitical reality. It included two distinct blocs that could be discerned even before Yugoslavia seceded. There was the northern flank or "Iron Triangle" made up of Poland, the GDR, and Czechoslovakia. It controlled the system's access to Western Europe and NATO under the leadership of the United States. By its control over this Iron Triangle, the USSR had access to West Germany and could hold Europe hostage if it wished. The southern flank, the Balkan zone where the three rebel states were located, was in the immediate period less decisive for the security of the system. It controlled access to the eastern Mediterranean, which remained for the moment divided by old historic antagonisms, and Soviet ambitions in that region were at the time secondary. What had been won in 1945 were the northern and central regions and the entire military policy of the Warsaw Pact was to consolidate and extend that control. The southern region was not or at least not totally part of the zone of influence conquered by force of arms during the war, and the Balkan countries had the function of being an avant-garde for other enterprises of expansion, dependent upon other events. This general conception of Soviet interests and spheres of influence explains why the USSR was implacably opposed to any program in the Iron Triangle that would attenuate its control but allowed the countries of the southern flank to move away. This was all the more so because two of these countries, Yugoslavia and Albania, had no common border with the Soviet Union, which made them more difficult to control. The Soviet perception of imperial control had always been based on contiguity (Poland, Czechoslovakia, Hungary, Rumania) or very close proximity (Bulgaria). The only states of the system outside this rule were the GDR and the two independent states on the Adriatic, Yugoslavia and Albania. It is thus easy to see why all movements within the Iron Triangle were held by the USSR to be decisive threats against the system. Any weakening of the cohesion of the system in Poland, the path to communication with Germany and whose very size increased security problems, would undermine the whole alliance. Stalin's vigilance was followed without changes by all his successors because all the conquests of 1945 were linked to control over this pivotal state. And the more that conflicts arose in the system, the more vigilant the USSR felt compelled to be. It was not only because Khrushchev was in power in 1956 that the Polish path was accepted; and it was not only because Brezhnev and Andropov were in charge of the Polish problem in 1980 that they destroyed Polish aspirations. It was above all because leader after leader when confronted with prolonged conflicts invoked a single system of prevention, the Warsaw Pact, which in 1980 could exercise its abilities more effectively than in 1956.

To these different geostrategic conditions, which gave the Iron Triangle more immediate importance than the states of the southern flank, should be added domestic political factors that cannot be ignored. The three states of the southern flank had proved their capacity to preserve themselves as conquests of socialism. While the Soviet model was weakening everywhere, Enver Hoxha asserted that the leading role of the party was unchallenged in his country and, celebrating the thirty-first anniversary of the Albanian Army, he said: "The army has won . . . because its strength is the strength of the party, because the glorious party of labor has always been the organizer and guide of the army."[35]

While a touchy nationalism and the total authority of Enver Hoxha were enough to maintain the vitality of the Soviet model in Albania, the two other rebels of the southern flank found in their domestic situations reasons for strengthening rather than weakening communism. Yugoslavia, and Rumania to a lesser degree, were multiethnic states in which the internationalist ideology of the communist parties offered a convenient and effective argument for the maintenance of unity in societies troubled by particularism. The USSR, which had so constantly used communism by incorporating national aspirations within it and by going beyond those aspirations of "ideological nationalism," felt particularly reassured by this importation of its model into two states that were otherwise so strongly challenging its claims to rule over them. Haunted by the difficulties of interethnic relations, the Soviet leaders knew that they represented an element of weakness in Yugoslavia, because of the large number of groups living together there and their cultural and economic diversity. The same thing was true in Rumania where despite the preponderance of the Rumanian group, which represented seven-eighths of the total population, scattered groups with vigorous nationalist feelings rejected any kind of assimilation.[36] The vulnerability of these states on the national level has until now ensured their loyalty to the "conquests of socialism." And the USSR thinks that this internal vulnerability prevents the states on the southern flank from becoming total dissidents. The case is entirely different for Polish nationalism, which tends to replace communism and to exclude it as a system of common values shaping the collective consciousness. The erosion of the communist system in Poland and the democratic revolutions of Hungary, Poland, and Czechoslovakia threatened to destroy the entire system of 1945, whose foundation was the community of political systems. One can understand why in regard to the northern flank, strategically decisive and so precarious ideologically, the USSR accepted no compromises and based the preservation of the system on the power of the Warsaw Pact.

Invisible Integration

An alliance directed more against its allies than against enemies, the Warsaw Pact does not exist only to contain centrifugal tendencies but also to change gradually the unruly empire. Since 1967 it has accomplished a significant mission in preventing at every attempt the states loyal to the alliance from following the example of the rebels. But its task has also been to strengthen the ties among the better allies, to increase their tendency toward integration, and finally to maintain links with the others in order to prepare for rapprochement. If Czechoslovakia in 1968 was a test providing an answer to the question: "What is the Warsaw Pact good for?" Poland in 1980 was a test illustrating the underground mission of the pact, the barely visible effects of its actions, and the integration in depth accomplished by the institution in the strategic sectors of society. Estimating the chances of intervention by the Warsaw Pact in the Polish crisis in 1980, Polish leaders tended to think that the USSR would not dare to intervene for fear of pitting troops of the pact against the Polish Army. And in fact in 1956 during the Poznań riots, the army's refusal to fire on the workers had required the resort to internal security forces. This necessity was all the more remarkable because the Polish Defense Ministry was then headed by Marshal Rokossowski and at the time the number and influence of Soviet advisers in the Polish Army were impressive. It was perhaps this very open control by the USSR over the Polish Army that explained the army's solidarity with the workers. In 1980 it was the Polish Army that from within carried out the task of the restoration of order that the Warsaw Pact had carried out in Prague twelve years earlier. And it was the Polish Army that resolved the crisis by occupying its own country. This was a totally unprecedented situation that had been foreseen by no one, but it was a natural result of the Warsaw Pact's policy of invisible integration and an indication of its effects.

If in 1980 the Polish Army carried out this mission of the preservation of order in its own country, this was because it was no longer quite the same as the former Polish Army but was rather a detachment of the Warsaw Pact. No doubt each country maintained its own national army in this system. But the national army was commanded by officers whose training followed common principles, common values, and a common strategy developed in the USSR and conveyed by the Warsaw Pact. Many officers had gone through Soviet military schools and particularly through the whole network of meetings and ideological training courses that had helped to shape them. Promotion in the army was tied to adhesion to these common values, to the slow transformation of thinking and behavior that meant that an officer in Prague, Warsaw, or Budapest had more links with his counterparts in the socialist military world than with the society from which he came. Within the national societies there was slowly forming an integrated military elite that superimposed over the national space a new space, the pact and the socialist community.

Maneuvers, so prized in the pact, contributed to this hidden transformation of the national armed forces. Even though they were under the control of the defense authorities of the country in which they took place, these maneuvers in fact largely escaped from that control and pointed up the weakness of individual military systems.

Maneuvers were in fact an opportunity to mix the armies of the various pact countries and to have them enter the national territory of one particular country. Each army was divided, scattered among joint formations, subjected to the authority of foreign leaders, and the role of Soviet higher officers was often decisive. The authority of national high commands and officer corps over their troops was gradually diluted in a system of joint authority, and the armies themselves gradually lost the consciousness of their specificity through these repeated contacts and joint actions with other armies. It is of little importance that General Jaruzelski's actions relied above all on the security forces. What counted in the assumption of control over the Polish crisis by a Polish general supported by national forces was precisely that it illustrated this evolution of training and thinking. General Jaruzelski and the forces on which he relied acted in the name of ideas that long association with the Warsaw Pact had spread through military circles: that the armies were guarantors of the political system and that they had to preserve their country from anarchy. The theory of the "lesser evil"—it is better to take care of the problem oneself than to draw Warsaw Pact troops onto Polish territory—was precisely the theory that Stalin had used to justify the whole system of domination by the Russian Empire and then his own. This was the theory that led the dominated to act as representatives of the dominator on their territory and to accept domination rather than having it forced on them. The Soviet system had almost always sought to avoid domination by violence. When it used violence, this was in the absence of more appropriate means to carry out its plans. But—and the domestic system of the USSR showed this—the patiently pursued objective was to attain imperial cohesion through the cooperation of the subjects. The Soviet model was the Ottoman Empire and the Janissaries that served it. The pact was the most appropriate place for the training of the Janissaries.

But although this extreme and unrecognized form of integration was suitable for countries loyal to the alliance, it was difficult to apply to those that had rebelled and which, because their rebellions had emanated from and strengthened the party, were unattackable.

But the pact still had some usefulness with regard to those countries. The joint maneuvers organized in Bulgaria illustrated this unflagging determination to consider integration into the pact as definitive and to permit no loosening of ties with it. In the last week of September 1982, major pact maneuvers—"Shield 82"—took place in Bulgaria. Several facts are noteworthy, first of all the frequency of maneuvers. In the eighteen months from March 1981 to September 1982 the pact had organized three large joint exercises, two of which—"Soiuz 81" and "Druzhba 82"[38]—took place wholly or partly in Poland. The second noteworthy fact is that the maneuvers of September 1982 took place in the southern part of the alliance where general maneuvers of the pact were an exception. Rumanian opposition to the presence of pact troops on its territory had until 1982 paralyzed the organization of maneuvers in the southern flank. In fact, Rumania's refusal to grant passage to troops through its territory blocked their movement to the loyal ally, Bulgaria. Moreover, Ceauşescu had constantly emphasized in a more general way that he did not wish significant movements of pact troops to take place on his borders. This distrust of the pact had for a long time been effective, and the only general maneuvers that had taken place in the region were those of September 1964 that had brought together Bulgarian, Soviet, and Rumanian troops in southern Bulgaria. Aside from this unique demonstration that had excluded all the states of the northern flank of the pact and had emphasized the particularity of the southern region, the only pact activities had been high command exercises in Bulgaria with Soviet and Rumanian participation in 1972 and exercises in Rumania in 1973 and 1978 with the participation of the Soviets, Bulgarians, and Rumanians alone.[39] The large-scale maneuvers of 1982, "Shield 82"—and this is their point of interest—were the first in this kind of exercise in the southern flank involving all the states of the pact.[40] This very broad participation of alliance troops was reinforced by another noteworthy element, the size of the forces involved and the publicity given to the exercise. Placed under the authority of the Bulgarian Defense Minister, General Dzhurov, the maneuvers brought together

600,000 men and, it seems, were witnessed by Rumanian observers. On the other hand, there were no Western observers. In relation to maneuvers on the borders of countries outside the pact, indeed countries in other alliance systems, this casual attitude toward the Helsinki conventions is extraordinary.[41]

Should we conclude from these maneuvers that the USSR intended to weigh more heavily on Rumania than it had in the preceding years? The answer must be a qualified one. No doubt the USSR respected the Rumanian refusal to allow foreign troops on its territory. The transportation of these numerous troops by air and sea was not simple. But at the same time this impressive deployment of forces in the eastern Mediterranean on the borders of Rumania and Yugoslavia as a demonstration of the pact's ability to transport massive numbers of troops were so many signals addressed to the rebels and more generally to all the states bordering on Bulgaria. In the face of this capacity for rapid intervention by Warsaw Pact troops in southern Europe, the "people's defenses" proclaimed by Yugoslavia and Rumania seemed of little value. Without being directly threatening, the "Shield 82" exercises brutally demonstrated that the Warsaw Pact also existed in the southern Balkans; that no segment of the communist Europe of 1945 was outside its jurisdiction; that at any moment the forces of the pact had the capacity to deploy beyond their usual zones of action. In a period marked by a general tightening of links between the USSR and its allies, such a demonstration in the area of states that were the most reticent toward the pact and the USSR was certainly designed to accelerate a process of reconciliation.

In observing the life of all the institutions of the Warsaw Pact in the course of the last few years—the years of the Polish crisis—we are led to note that the pact was particularly active in all areas. From 1980 to 1983 the meetings of different organizations—the Consultative Political Council, Council of Defense Ministers, Military Council, Council of Foreign Ministers—occurred with great regularity. Although the Political Council, whose role as the central body has been taken over by the Council of Foreign Ministers, only met twice, in May 1980 and January 1983, it nevertheless derived a renewed importance from the exceptional character of these meetings. Because the delegations from each member state at the two meetings of the Political Council included the highest political and military leaders, the meetings appeared as summits of the pact in which the major themes of joint foreign policy were discussed. The 1980 summit, dominated by Leonid Brezhnev, commemorated a quarter century of the pact's existence.[42] It was the occasion for pointing to everything that constituted the cohesion and the necessity of the alliance.

The tone and the theme of the January 1983 summit held in Prague and dominated by Andropov were entirely different.[43] If the pact had been intent on defining internal progress in 1980, in 1983 its attention was directed toward the external world, the confrontation with the West, and the strategic problems of Europe. The proposals put forth at this summit to enter into a treaty of nonagression with NATO and to reestablish détente, although they were coolly received by the West, clearly defined the principal foreign policy line of the USSR to which it intended to commit its allies: the determination to reach a strategic agreement in Europe, and the development of a psychosis of the nuclear danger and its tension.[44]

In addition to these summits, what was most striking during these years was the growth of the role played by the Council of Foreign Ministers. From its creation this organization always met in autumn or winter (October 1980 in Warsaw, December 1981 in Bucharest, October 1982 in Moscow);[45] in January 1981 a meeting of a new kind was added to the activities of the pact, which had been provided for in its organization but had not yet functioned. The vice-ministers of foreign affairs met for two days and debated the pact's most urgent problem of the time: the Polish crisis.[46]

Thus the pact's structure and activities responded to particular situations. In periods when threats were posed to the political system of a socialist country, like 1968 or 1980–81, the pact's level of activity was intense; meetings of all organs and various maneuvers proliferated. One could prepare a chart of the political temperature of the member states by observing the general activities of the organization. On the other hand, when conflicts were calmed, the level of activity followed a more regular pattern. But this general observation should be qualified by another that has less to do with a comparison of particular moments in the history of the pact than with the twenty-five years of its existence. In this perspective the graph of activities follows a different logic. Those activities developed constantly, particularly, and in a lasting way after crises. It was as though the frenetic activity of crisis periods was followed by a period of consolidation, which the entire pact used as a means of self-affirmation.

*   *   *

There is no question that the Warsaw Pact has been an indispensable instrument for Soviet policy in Eastern Europe. It has been used both to justify a military order that prevents or crushes dissidence and to impose on the Eastern European states common directions in domestic and foreign policy; it has trained armies and military officers who have been placed at the juncture of the national states and the international space of socialism.

But to the extent that the system has been coherent, it has also been a remarkable tool for Soviet power in Europe. The pact has allowed the USSR to occupy advanced positions on the European continent well beyond its borders, and thus to exert pressure on the continent as a whole. The internal needs of the pact and its external strategic objectives have led the USSR to increase the number of troops stationed in Eastern Europe and to deploy

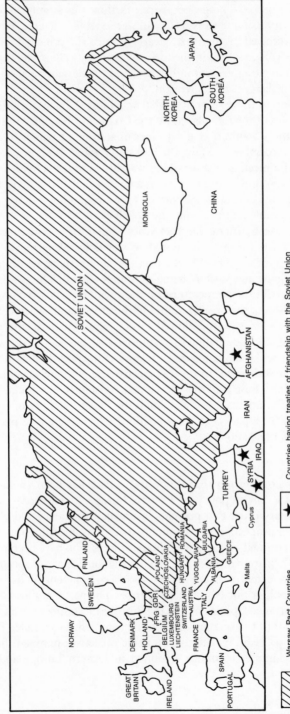

STRUCTURE OF THE WARSAW PACT

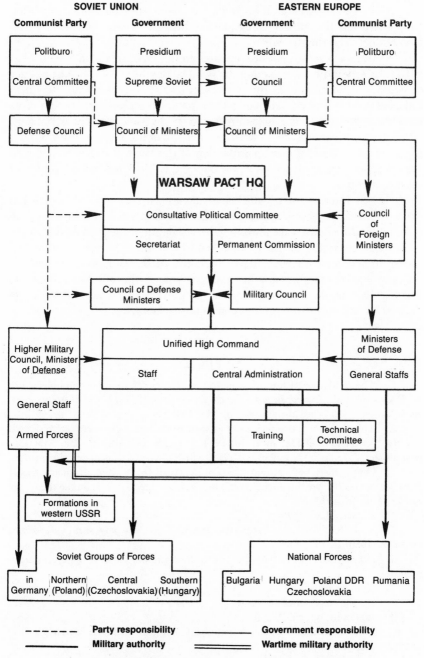

	SOVIET UNION		EASTERN EUROPE	
Communist Party	Government	Government	Communist Party

- - - - - -   **Party responsibility**   ————   **Government responsibility**

————   **Military authority**   ═══   **Wartime military authority**

Source: The Military Balance 1981–1982. London: Institute of Strategic Studies, 1982.

forces that when combined with those of the USSR itself are clearly more significant than those that have been set up by NATO. The defensive instrument can thus take on an offensive character. And such a mutation would have all the greater consequences because of the considerable differences between the two alliances.

The Warsaw Pact cannot be compared to the Western alliance, which has been relatively indifferent to domestic political developments (as the presence of communist ministers in the government of a NATO member country indicates) and has never sent tanks in response to a challenge by one of its members. The difference in nature between the two alliances is obvious: NATO is genuinely directed toward the defense of the Western realm against the external world; the principal function of the Warsaw Pact is to defend a system against those on whom it was imposed in 1945 and has subsequently been reimposed.

It is this internal logic, which has never been contradicted, which has made the pact the privileged but not the only instrument of the European policy of Stalin's heirs. Like him, they have thought of the preservation of the communist system in terms of power, and like him, they have thought that power should serve their political programs. In the end, this synthesis of political and military approaches has guaranteed the effectiveness of the Warsaw Pact in the system conceived by the USSR. It also allows us to understand the real nature of intercommunist relations.

NOTES

1. The fundamental texts relating to the Warsaw Pact have been published in N. Rodionov et al., *Organizatsiia Varshavskogo dogovora—1955–1975: dokumenty i materialy* (Moscow, 1975); see also *Pravda*, May 15, 1955.

2. This theme was bandied about as soon as the Paris agreements were signed. See the "Soviet note of December 10, 1954, to the French, British, and American governments," *Pravda*, December 10, 1954, which opened a violent press campaign.

3. On the merits of neutrality, see *Pravda*, April 16, 1955; on the guarantees of Austrian neutrality, see the Soviet proposals, *Pravda*, May 15, 1955; on the treaty, see *Pravda*, May 16, 1955.

4. *Pravda*, May 22, 1955.

5. V. J. Kulikov, ed., *Varshavskii dogovor—soiuz vo imia mira i sotsializma* (Moscow, 1980), 272ff.

6. *Izvestia*, March 31, 1961, published the communiqué developing this argument.

7. Kulikov, op. cit., 276ff.

8. *Pravda*, September 16, 1965.

9. Rodionov, op. cit., 97, 102–3.

10. Meeting of the Consultative Political Committee in Sofia, March 6 and 7, 1968; *Pravda*, March 9, 1968.

11.   Kulikov, op. cit., 272–93.

12.   *Pravda*, November 27 and December 5, 1976.

13.   On the structure of the pact, the most convenient sources are: Y. Y. Yakubovskii, ed., *Boevoe sodruzhestvo bratskih narodov i armii* (Moscow, 1975), 142–45; and A. S. Bakhov, *Organizatsiia Varshavskogo dogovora* (Moscow, 1971), particularly 81ff.

14.   Yakubovskii, op. cit., 143; *Krasnaia Zvezda*, July 8, 1967, says that "the choice is made by the pact's member states."

15.   Ibid., 142.

16.   Ibid., 163.

17.   Many works evoke this objective: P. J. Efimov, *Boevoi soiuz bratskih armii* (The military alliance of fraternal armies) (Moscow, 1974); P. A. Zhilin and E. Zhadzinc, *Bratsvo po Oruzhiiu* (Fraternity through arms) (Moscow, 1975).

18.   In S. K. Il'in et al, ed., *Partiino-politicheskaia rabota v sovetskih vooruzhenyh silab* (Moscow, 1974), a special chapter is devoted to this problem by V. Semin, "Partiino-politicheskaia rabota v armiiah stran varshovskogo dogorova."

19.   C. Jones, "The Warsaw Pact: Military Exercises and Military Interventions," *Armed Forces and Society*, 7, 1 (Fall 1980): 5–30.

20.   Jilin and Zhadziak, op. cit., 355–56.

21.   I owe to Teresa Rakowska-Harmstone of Carleton University my understanding of the importance of this principle for the Soviet Army and the Warsaw Pact.

22.   The People's Army of the GDR is subordinatd to the high command of the pact and its fleet is under the authority of the Soviet Baltic fleet. M. Czimers, *Der Warschauer Pakt* (Berne, 1972), 29.

23.   Yakubovskii, op. cit., 108.

24.   K. Savinov, *Moguchii faktor mira i stabil'nosti v mezhdunarodnyh otnosheniiah* (Moscow, 1980), 17–19.

25.   See, for example, O. Irinin and F. Nikolaev, "Sotsialisticheskii internatsionalizm v deistvii," *Sovetskoe Gosudarstvo i Pravo*, 12 (1968): 4; E. Lukashevich, "Sotsialisticheskii internatsionalizm—osnova sotrudiuchestva stran sotsializma," *Politicheskoe samoobrazovanie*, December 1976, 43–51; Y. V. Yudinskii, "Internatsional'nye i natsional'nye interessy sotsialisticheskih gosudarstv," *Voprosy Filosofii* 10 (October 1973), 74; article by Zhukov, *Pravda*, August 21, 1968.

26.   Irinin and Nikolaev, op. cit., 6.

27.   *Documents on International Affairs, 1957* (London, 1960), 157.

28.   For the history of this document, see G. H. Skilling, *Czechoslovakia's Interrupted Revolution* (Princeton, 1976), 640–42; J. Erikson and W. Kusin, *The Czechoslovak Reform Movement, 1968* (London, 1973), 43–44. I have obtained from Antonín Snejdárek a detailed narrative of the conditions under which this document was developed and an analysis of its consequences.

29.   See the article by V. Kudriovtsev, *Izvestia*, August 25, 1968; Irinin and Nikolaev, op. cit., 4.

30.   On the organization of this defense capability including the entire society, I am indebted to Mikhailo Markovich for many elements that have helped my understanding.

31.   A. Braun, *Rumanian Foreign Policy Since 1965: The Political and Military Limits of Autonomy* (New York, 1978), 176ff.

32. *Scinteia*, August 21, 1971.

33. V. Samoilenko, "Voennoe sodruzhestvo stran sotsializma," in S. Tiushkevich, ed., *Voina i Armiia* (Moscow, 1977), 366ff.

34. V. D. Sokolovskii, ed., *Voennaia Strategiia* (Moscow, 1963), 207.

35. *Zeri i populit*, July 10, 1974, quoted in G. W. Simmonds, ed., *Nationalism in the U.S.S.R. and Eastern Europe in the Era of Brezhnev and Kossygin* (Detroit, n.d.), 502.

36. M. E. Fischer, "Nation and Nationality in Rumania," in Simmonds, op. cit., 504–24, is an excellent discussion of the subject.

37. *Pravda*, April 8, 1981.

38. *Pravda*, March 5, 1982.

39. For the high command maneuvers in 1973 in Rumania, see *Pravda*, February 22, 1973; we should note that they were led by Marshall Yakubovsky.

40. *Krasnaia Zvezda*, October 2, 1982.

41. The foreign observers came from socialist countries: Cuba, Mongolia, and Vietnam.

42. *Pravda*, May 15 and 16, 1980.

43. *Pravda*, January 4–7, 1983.

44. This theme can also be found in the meeting of the Council of Foreign Ministers in Moscow in October 1982; *Izvestia*, October 22 and 23, 1982.

45. *Pravda*, October 20, 1980; *Izvestia*, October 21, 1980; *Pravda*, December 3, 1981; *Izvestia* December 2 and 3, 1981; *Izvestia*, October 22 and 23, 1982.

46. *Pravda*, January 21, 1981; the Soviet delegation was led by L. F. Ilichev.

CONCLUSION TO PART THREE

"THE HABIT OF LIVING TOGETHER"

The "socialist community"—strictly speaking made up of the USSR and the Eastern European states loyal to the Warsaw Pact—has developed in the course of thirty years both in a centrifugal way, marked by repeated conflicts, and centripetally, moving toward unquestionable integration. In this progress toward integration, toward the establishment of a group of states of a new kind, several important elements are discernible that may help to evaluate its real effects. In the first place, it should be noted that all the moments at which "integrationist" choices were made were in reaction to crisis situations that threatened to undermine the system. The Stalinist rigidity of the early fifties—a closed, monolithic, and uniformly terrorist bloc—was in part a reaction to Tito's insubordination. The development of the Warsaw Pact and of its activities and institutions was in reaction to Rumanian disaffection. Although this disaffection was tolerated for reasons of domestic orthodoxy and out of concern for the preservation of a peaceful international context, the USSR nevertheless increased measures to prevent other countries of the camp from following the same path. The Prague Spring was followed by "multidirectional" integration, combining ideology, bilateral relations, economics, and above all military force. The period after August 1968 was also the period in which the USSR undertook an extraordinary effort to establish itself as a major power in the world. Although the consolidation of "socialist conquests" was not the only function of this power, this concern was nevertheless one of the reasons for the drive to power.

After the Polish crisis, what forms will the movement toward integration assume? Although an answer to this question would require a crystal ball rather than careful analysis, it is nevertheless possible to advance one certainty. The Polish crisis of 1980–1981 will certainly not have the effect of increasing the flexibility of the system as a whole nor of slackening the pressure for integration in the socialist community, but will on the contrary bring about a further degree of integration. History, although it does not provide for predictions, allows at least in the light of past events an understanding of current events, and it demonstrates that the reaction to the Polish crisis will move in the direction of integration.

A second observation has to do with the remarkable variety of means that have been adopted to ensure the success of integration. Everything has contributed to this objective, the development of the states, of the communist parties, and of the ideology legitimizing that development. The Soviet system has countless means at its disposal to establish links among the states and peoples of the socialist community. And by the use of various methods it has scattered attention and distracted suspicion. If we calculate the number of delegations of every kind meeting at every level; if we look closely at the existing contacts in all areas—state, party, various social groups, the army—it is clear that, beyond conflicts, so many bonds have been woven within the community, so many men have met and talked together, that despite everything else there have arisen habits of behavior and a world view that necessarily have long-term consequences. The Soviet program for integration can best be understood in those terms. In the short run, the existing system has to be maintained at any cost. In the long run, these countless contacts should have the effect of creating, if not a "desire to live together," at least "the habit of living together." This is the Soviet wager on the future, transcending pragmatic reactions to each momentary difficulty.

Within this conception of a complex and dense network of tools and processes of integration, the Warsaw Pact occupies a special position. It is the principal tool for integration for many reasons. Because of its control over military force, as experience has shown it has sometimes provided the only solution to a crisis. But this aspect is the least important of all, because if the USSR wished or thought it necessary to intervene with its own armies, it would do so, as it did in 1956. In the area of the internal defense of the "conquests of socialism," the pact is a convenience, sparing the USSR from having to take sole responsibility for unpopular tasks; but it is not indispensable.

It is, on the other hand, indispensable in two other areas; first of all for the legitimation of any program for integration. The theory of socialist internationalism, which makes it a duty of the community to maintain intact a system all of whose elements have been defined, has as a consequence the need for the community to have a means for practicing that internationalism. In this case, the use of a national army (Soviet or not) would be in complete contradiction with that ideology. The Warsaw Pact is the secular arm of the internationalist idea and of the community it supports. It gives a concrete content to those principles.

But seen in this light, the Warsaw Pact is a political tool endowed with military means that allow it to fulfill its function within the system, which is to maintain the system. Developments in the years from 1968 to 1980 thus to a certain extent reconciled the definition of the pact and its real function. Before becoming a military alliance directed against the external world—once again, the military power of the USSR was sufficient for this purpose—it was the privileged instrument for the preservation of the system forged in Europe by Stalin. This is the very heart of communist logic, with military force as a tool for the political program.

The usefulness of the Warsaw Pact for integration has also been more immediate, linked to the exceptional resources it provided for the Soviet program: the justification for the stationing or movement of Soviet troops; but even more the creation of a military milieu of a new kind, adhering to a common system of values, endowed with a common body of knowledge, and already embodying a model of the human community of the future. The importance of the army as an integrating force was understood by the Soviets as well as by their adversaries. All Soviet leaders—from Lenin to Andropov—have been aware that the national army was the privileged location for the development of national consciousness and that integrated armies were the most propitious instruments for breaking down national feeling and developing new value systems. In the opposite direction, Ceauşescu was fully aware that he had to fight in this area in order to disengage his country from Soviet control. He did not disengage it from communist control, because this was not his objective; but that does not affect the pertinence of his judgment.

A final observation has to do with the evolution of the techniques of integration. The USSR, the heir to a great empire that rivaled the Ottoman Empire, an empire reestablished after 1917, has a long tradition of techniques of domination and integration. For a long time, the Soviet regime hesitated among various techniques, but Stalin who so profoundly shaped the system had already been tempted by a system whose effectiveness had been demonstrated by the Ottoman Empire, the system of Janissaries. The Stalinist system was a compromise betwen centralism and the use of those national instruments of power that had been so cleverly manipulated by the Ottoman Empire. If such a system was never really able to function in the USSR, this can be attributed to Stalin's hesitations, to excessive centralism, and to a well-established historical tradition. But in the effort toward integration of the socialist community of the last several years, there are signs of a return toward this system. The high-ranking officers of the pact armies and the states' political leaders, while not slaves impressed into service by force, are nevertheless like the Janissaries in Constantinople trained in the USSR, educated in common values established by "big brother," and returned to their countries of origin as his representative. General Jaruzelski and the military and police forces on which he relies resemble the Janissaries who operated in the Balkans in the past and preserved the order of the Sultan, while the Sultan himself had no need to exercise his military power.

CONCLUSION

The USSR has set up camp in half of Europe and has for forty years spread its protective and dominating umbrella over the region. The situation is paradoxical. The USSR is an empire in crisis. Half made up of populations distinct from the Russian "big brother," the country in its inner circle is subject to tensions and pressures arising from the nationalistic inclinations of its subjects. In Eastern Europe, the second circle of the empire, the situation is no better. Crises have erupted one after another, all for the same reason, the fierce determination to reconquer lost independence. On the European continent, which has experienced for the first time in its history complete peace for forty years, the only place where weapons are fired and tanks and rifles periodically enter into action is the Soviet empire: Berlin, Budapest, Prague, Gdańsk, and Kingir as well as in Soviet territory, so many places where the will of the people has been crushed by military force. The state of war that has been established in Poland for the last several years is an ironic symbol for a Europe at peace.

Confronted with the crisis of the imperial system, the USSR at first sight seems to have adopted a classic reaction, that of Czar Nicholas I, "the policeman of Europe," who had taken on the mission of preserving European balance and suppressing revolutions. Is the USSR of the eighties nothing but a variant of this rigid determination to preserve an archaic order at any cost? Is it nothing but a product of the dream of all emperors "to open a window to the west and gain access to the open sea"?

If this were the meaning of the empire, if it were nothing but an anachronism as the repeated and frequent crises suggest and as those who have rebelled hope, then its end would be near. That end would be all the more foreseeable and unavoidable because the Soviet empire, while legitimizing its domination by the ideology of internationalism, has quite obviously been incapable, as the whole history of crises in Eastern Europe shows, of inventing an alternative system of relations among the nations. And those nations have risen up against the most powerful among them.

But one must guard against such hasty judgments by referring to the past, to known situations. The Soviet empire, as Solzhenitsyn has correctly pointed out, is not traditional Russia. It is the heart of a new system, the world communist system.

This system and the Soviet empire that is a part of it are historically new, original, and diverse configurations, difficult to understand because of their diversity and mobility. In fact the system resembles Russian dolls. At first there is only one figure and everything seems simple. But when you open the doll, others emerge; they are numerous and they all copy the original doll in the minutest detail. Their number is theoretically infinite; the only defining condition for this Russian doll is that except for the differences in size the copy is always perfect.

This is what has happened in the socialist community, grouping the nations of the USSR in a first circle and the states of Eastern Europe in a second one.

But what gives the system its strength and what periodically allows the largest doll to reconstruct the pyramid is the fact that around it, to strengthen it, by a logic in which defense and attack, conservatism and expansionism, are indissolubly linked, there has been established a protective environment that has gradually added new dolls to the already existing number.

For the moment, the system has three levels, analysis of which will provide a measure of the progress the USSR has accomplished in the world since 1945.

The first level is the Warsaw Pact. In 1945 the USSR negotiated a sphere of influence in which "friendly governments" would guarantee the security of its borders. Today this sphere of influence has become the powerful socialist community held together in a political and military system from which no nation has yet been able to escape. In this circle, made up of the seven "major" communist states—USSR, Poland, Czechoslovakia, Bulgaria, Hungary, Rumania, and the GDR—the progress of the USSR has had to do not only with the nature of the alliances that were established but also with a geographical "modification" of the 1945 agreement. Occupied Germany was not a part of this group. Its fate remained open. The USSR alone decided in 1949 to add part of Germany to its system. The socialist family that exists today is thus not the one imposed by the war, but the product of later adjustments ratified by the rest of the world in Helsinki in 1975.

The second level is that of Comecon. Like the Warsaw Pact, which conceals behind its military pretext a remarkable instrument for political integration, Comecon is much more than an instrument for the socialist division of labor or for economic integration. It certainly pursues these aims.

But also, because it is a more open assembly than the Warsaw Pact, Comecon is a welcoming structure for states that the system cannot assimilate or that do not wish to enter the system. Yugoslavia, independent of the socialist family, has been an associated member of Comecon since 1964. This is a pretext for multiplying contacts and links, for preparing for a rapprochement. Mongolia, Vietnam, Cuba, non-European states that could not possibly be included in a military alliance with a European focus, have found in Comecon an appropriate framework for affirming their adherence to the socialist community. Finally, when the USSR places within its sphere of influence states that are still hesitant about their domestic political choices, it helps to direct those choices. Laos and Syria, for example, have started down this road, which tends to distance them more and more from the rest of international society and to a certain extent has helped give an irreversible character to their choices. The permanent expansion of Comecon, despite differences in status among member states, associates, and observers, has a dual advantage. It provides an extended international environment for the recalcitrant members of the socialist family, making the vise of the Warsaw Pact less stifling. It provides them with contacts and possibilities of exchange with a constantly growing group of countries while preserving this opening under the control of the USSR, pillar and architect of this organization.

The third level is comprised of the allies that the USSR has found in the world, chiefly in the third world. The friendship treaties that have proliferated in the last decade (with India, Afghanistan, Iraq, Yemen, Ethiopia, and so on) have added to the hierarchy of communist states and close friends associatd with Comecon a group of more distant allies that have changed the international landscape and opened up possibilities for action by the Eastern European states that have strengthened the community.

The modification of the world political landscape is not a negligible element in the future of Eastern Europe. In the early eighties, when the USSR was advancing toward Africa and its immense resources, the problem posed to the West was how to stop it on this path, not how to make it retreat in Europe, where it was solidly established. The socialist family had already entered into historical reality. The Western world had accepted the logic of the USSR, which consisted in moving forward in order to avoid placing too much weight on the difficulties it encountered where it was established and also to avoid making these difficulties a focus of attention. To preserve itself, this precarious system had to progress. This progress made important failures relative and gave legitimacy to their suppression.

But it would be a mistake to reduce the proliferation of the circles of Soviet influence merely to the desire to preserve an empire. By extending itself the USSR has also been giving itself the means to modify the political situation within its empire. This was true because it could associate its Eastern European allies with its policies and give them an active role in its imperial policy. This strategy of transforming subject states into full-fledged allies was not new, but it took on increased scope here. In the fifties, the USSR used the Eastern European states as a means of carrying out policies it did not wish to conduct openly. It was Czechoslovakia that supplied arms to Egypt in 1955. During the same period, when the USSR was shifting toward the Arabs, Bulgaria and Rumania were the sources of anti-Israeli and anti-Zionist propaganda that came close to being anti-Semitic, and which presented the conflict among Semitic peoples as though it were a racial conflict. Since that time the division of labor in matters of foreign policy has been considerably perfected. Certain Eastern European countries—this was long true for Czechoslovakia—have been preferred centers for harboring international organizations under communist control, like the World Federation of Trade Unions, and for the training of future leaders in Africa. Others, like the GDR, have specialized in "military aid" to third world countries; still others in economic aid or technical cooperation. And others have chosen more hidden activities. Bulgaria, resuming an old tradition, has become a center for both terrorist activities and arms sales.

The existence of this international environment in the socialist camp and the association of Warsaw Pact states with the life of this particular international society, which gravitates around the USSR and which divides the world much more effectively than what has been falsely labeled the Yalta split, has two advantages for the USSR. First of all, it has given substance to the "central core," the Warsaw Pact. Despite resistances and rebellions that have periodically been demonstrated, the pact as a whole exists as part of a larger entity with countless internal forces, and this has been enough to give it cohesion and to confirm the fact that the situation of the early eighties was not that of 1945 or 1956.

But this environment also has allowed the USSR gradually to change the nature of its relations with the states that it has drawn within its sphere of influence, if not with the populations of those states, by using the method it had applied within each state, that of the Janissaries. Just as it uses domestic elites to preserve the system in its name—the example of Poland in 1980 showed that time favored this strategy—so the USSR uses states in the international realm to carry out its policies, and by giving them a particular role, an "imperial function," it has made them into real allies. The troops of the GDR that have been fighting in Ethiopia to "consolidate the revolution" and those who were ready to attack Poland provide evidence that the GDR was ready to assume the role offered to it and to act as a partner of big brother in eastern Africa and even in Europe. Cuba has done the same thing elsewhere. It is normal that some countries have refused to assume this role. The USSR has been counting on time and on the progress it will accomplish in the world to encourage the vocations of Janissary states.

This European empire preserved for decades has evolved over time. In

1945 Stalin imagined it at first as a rampart designed to protect the USSR permanently against any attack from the West. At the same time, he knew that other kinds of attacks would conveniently be prepared behind the ramparts. To what extent does the situation of the eighties justify this second proposition?

Set in the heart of Europe, the USSR has not progressed toward Western Europe since 1945. But the imposing mass of the Warsaw Pact has played a serious role in Europe. Rigorous control over the Iron Triangle to which Moscow has given absolute priority over the last quarter century has placed the most economically prosperous, the most militarily powerful, and the most technologically developed part of Europe within reach of Soviet ambitions. This proximity is enough to make Europe vulnerable. It is all the more vulnerable because, while the USSR has a solid conviction of the virtue (political if not economic) of its system and is inspired by an ideology that legitimizes its expansionist plans, making them a duty, on the other hand, democratic Europe is characterized by its own uncertainties and a lack of conviction in relation to its own defense. As Jean-François Revel has written so pertinently: "Democracy is fundamentally not established to defend itself against external enemies dedicated to its destruction. . . . Democracy is, by design, turned inward. . . . Communism, on the contrary, is necessarily turned outward."[1]

In this respect, the alliance has thus perfectly fulfilled its function. It is a constant implicit threat against Europe and the crises that have ravaged the alliance have in no way attenuated that threat. These crises have no doubt provoked European intellectual circles to awareness of the "communist reality"; they have killed some myths, notably that of communism as an emancipator of peoples; but these truths have gradually become banal and have thereby lost their force and have in no way helped to awaken and mobilize feelings around a common democratic ideal.

But we also have to look at the other side of the alliance, the southern flank, for long somnolent and apparently put in danger by Rumanian dissidence. Here too time has accomplished its work, which has in the end served the interests of the socialist family. With Tito gone, Yugoslavia has no doubt maintained its independence but it is more sensitive than in the past to pressures from neighboring communist states. And becaus he foresaw these coming tendencies before he died, Tito himself had taken some steps toward Moscow, hoping that the restoration of some degree of friendship would protect his country from a forced march to fraternity. Although Rumania, a member of the alliance, continues to speak directly, it has had to accept many accommodations and is still subject to pressures of which the 1982 maneuvers in Bulgaria are probably a foretaste. Regional circumstances have changed and this might give new interest to the southern flank of the alliance. The eastern Mediterranean, long closed to the USSR by a solid American blockade, is slowly but surely developing toward an instability favorable to Soviet plans. Greece is negotiating for the withdrawal of NATO bases. Turkey, internationally isolated and subject throughout the world to terrorism inspired by the Armenian tragedy of 1915, a terrorism that has immediately destabilizing effects, might one day be tempted to slide toward the socialist camp. In this fluid situation, Bulgaria—loyal ally and center of terrorism—can play a decisive role; and the growing unity of the southern flank has become a primary objective. To understand the importance of what is under way in the eastern Mediterranean and the place that the southern flank of the alliance occupies in this strategy, two things have to be borne in mind. First of all, Soviet actions in the world always take place at two levels. Large-scale undertakings, launched wherever the opportunity presents itself (in Angola, for example), are no doubt expressions of an overall expansionist strategy, but they have little scope. If circumstances are very favorable the USSR takes advantage of them, and is ready to withdraw quietly if things turn out badly. These distant conquests are of only moderate interest to it because they would be too costly, if they were not impossible, to preserve. On the other hand, the USSR has always remained faithful to the concept inherited from the empire of conquests through contiguity. Whenever it can extend the territory under its control and establish a coherent whole, it is determined to transform and consolidate by covering this territory with revolutionary legitimacy and the duty of socialist internationalism. Expansion through contiguity is in the realm of the irreversible, because, if a conquest were challenged, the entire system could collapse like a house of cards. In relation to this development of Soviet territory through contiguity, the eastern Mediterranean is a choice objective that circumstances have opened to Soviet ambitions.

The second thing that has to be remembered is that the USSR has not developed its empire at random. It has acted prudently from period to period when circumstances have reduced the risks of expansion. The myth of Yalta has helped to conceal the logic of these conquests by giving credence to the idea that only wars have allowed the USSR to make this kind of progress. However on three occasions it gained ground without war. In 1921 in peacetime the Red Army invaded an independent state on its borders, led moreover by socialists, the state of Georgia. In 1949, recognizing the GDR as an independent state, it annexed it to the European socialist family. Finally, in 1979, again in peacetime, its troops invaded another independent state, Afghanistan. In 1921 and 1979, the pretext for the invasions was the same: it was the duty of "proletarian" internationalism (not "socialist" internationalism, the former referring to communist parties not in power, the latter to those in power), that led the Soviet armies "to the assistance" of communists who "called for their help," both from Tbilisi and from Kabul. But the advances carried out on the eastern borders of the USSR are less important than those accomplished in Europe, first of all because the vocation of the USSR is to be European, even though its ambitions are worldwide. And the eastern European empire is precisely what allows it to reconcile a European vocation with worldwide ambitions. There is no better way to sum up the situation than by recalling the judgment of a writer who has been unjustly forgotten, Mackinder, for whom "whoever rules eastern Europe dominates the continent; whoever rules the continent dominates the world."[2]

"Big brother" is aware of this logic, and although it does not dominate the continent and the world, it dominates eastern Europe and cannot allow any retreat there. And in order not to retreat, it has to take root, to anchor itself in this family that it has established, evidence of its power today and its expansion tomorrow.

NOTES

1. Jean-François Revel, *Comment les démocraties finissent* (Paris, 1953), 11.
2. Sir Halford Mackinder, *Democratic Ideas and Reality* (New York, 1942), 150.

AFTERWORD

International life in the 1970s was noteworthy for the continued development of Soviet power. Big Brother, strengthened by his ruling position in half of Europe, by the progress of communism in the world, and by extraordinary strategic efforts, attained the status of superpower equal to the United States. The USSR expressed this status in the vague but constantly reiterated concept of the correlation of forces; and during the 1970s the balance of power seemed to lean continuously in its favor.

With the beginning of the following decade, this brilliant picture grew dim. Moscow accused the United States, partner and adversary, of wanting to reverse the correlation of forces in its favor and asserted that this intention was illegitimate because it was contrary to the direction of historical development. At the time, the essential elements of the new international landscape were: the end of détente, the return of the United States to the forefront of the world stage, the return to strategic balance in Europe by means of NATO's decision in 1979 to deploy Euromissiles, in order to counter the SS-20s that the USSR had deployed during the preceding decade, and the implementation of that decision by the major European countries in 1983. To deal with those changes over which it had no control (stemming from the dynamic policies of President Reagan), or those it was unable to prevent (the deployment of Euromissiles), the USSR had to count more than ever on the cohesion of its own camp. But this cohesion had been deeply shaken, first by the Polish crisis; then by the end of détente, which provoked anxiety in the states of Eastern Europe whose political and economic links with Western Europe had grown, especially the GDR and Hungary; and by increasing economic difficulties, related to the international crisis but also to efforts that the USSR imposed on its allies (the increase in the price of Soviet oil, aid to Vietnam, and so on.) Although the Soviet leaders were able to restore "order" in Warsaw in 1981, their policy was essentially conservative. It no doubt succeeded, from one crisis to another, in maintaining Eastern Europe within

Big Brother's sphere of influence, but it did not resolve any of the problems that were subtly undermining the socialist family. This semiparalysis is easy to understand. For several years, all Soviet policies were affected by the aging of the ruling group, by a political succession that was constantly being put off, and then with Brezhnev's death in 1983, by a succession that did not lead to a stable solution.

In March 1985 the perspectives changed once again, and in a radical way. The election of Mikhail Gorbachev as general secretary of the Soviet Communist Party took place at a decisive moment—he called it that himself (*perelomnyi punkt*)— and under particularly favorable circumstances. It was a decisive moment because so many problems had accumulated in the USSR, in Eastern Europe, and on the world stage, that it seemed that Gorbachev could only undertake large-scale initiatives. Past sclerosis made dynamism necessary. More than his "skill as a communicator," more than his open manner of speaking, it was the situation itself and the expectations aroused by his rise to power that created a prejudice in his favor. In March 1985, because a change in Soviet policy was necessary, the world was convinced that it would take place. The circumstances also favored a change. The extreme old age of those who had been in power until then made the rise of new men, a new generation, inevitable, and therefore easy. In control of the choice of his colleagues, Gorbachev also seemed to be in control of his political choices. Even the political calendar seemed to operate in his favor. Gorbachev came to power less than a year before the date of the regularly scheduled Congress of the Soviet Communist Party (February 1986), the privileged framework for political adjustments or innovations. All of this ought to have allowed the introduction of a dynamism and a capacity for imagination that had been missing for many years in the relations of Moscow with the socialist family and in the orientations proposed to the fraternal states.

Has Gorbachev met the challenge? Has he found new directions for a community whose centrifugal tendencies have always produced a single reaction in Moscow as a source of tension and crisis: increased alignment and integration?

From the outset, Mikhail Gorbachev presented himself as a leader of Eastern Europe as well as of the USSR; from the outset he set forth the broad outlines of his future policies: firmness on essential principles and flexibility in particular applications.

On principles, Gorbachev had many opportunities to repeat what had always been and remained the Soviet conception of the development of Eastern Europe: the need for cohesion, for increased integration through the development of economic links, the rejection of any deviation. Mikhail Gorbachev set out these principles at the very moment that he came to power (his speech at Chernenko's funeral on March 13, 1985); he repeated them throughout the year between his election and the Twenty-Seventh Congress of the Soviet Communist Party; and he presented the methods of their application in his report to the congress. Economic integration, concerted action by the communist parties, exchanges of experiences, these are the roles Gorbachev assigned to his allies in order to restore dynamism to a community that had been shaken by crises and to give it the means to resolve the internal problems of each member state. Although the speech was hardly original, several aspects of the policies, rather than the statements, of Mikhail Gorbachev are noteworthy, principally the policy of integration, which contrasts with Soviet hesitation during the transitional years of the beginning of the decade.

Hardly had Gorbachev come to power when an opportunity arose to emphasize the continuity of the program of integration: the renewal of the Warsaw Pact in April 1985. After the initial period of thirty years, the conditions of renewal could be opened to debate. Eastern Europe had sufficiently evolved and its states had chosen different paths; should these changes not be reflected in the basic clauses of the alliance, particularly in the length of time for which it was to be renewed? Rumania had frequently expressed the wish that the new period of validity of the treaty be brief—ten years—in anticipation of a simultaneous dissolution of NATO and the Warsaw Pact. But on April 26, 1985, the Kremlin's argument carried the day again and the treaty was renewed for twenty years, with an additional period of automatic extension for ten years. The system put in place in 1955 and its founding text were left unchanged. Since then, there have been numerous meetings of the Pact, and they have all put forward the Soviet desire to present the Warsaw Pact as the expression of a common policy. There were meetings in Sofia (October 21–23, 1985) and Prague (November 21, 1985) bracketing the Reagan-Gorbachev Geneva summit at which Mikhail Gorbachev clearly indicated that he was negotiating with the United States in the name of the whole socialist community, not only the USSR. The defense ministers of the Pact met in East Berlin on December 4, 1985, to define a common response to the American military program. The foreign ministers met in Warsaw on March 19 and 20, 1986, to discuss international problems, principally inter-European relations; heads of state and party leaders met in Budapest in June 1986 and launched an appeal to NATO for a program of mutual reduction of forces in Europe, echoing the proposal put forward by Gorbachev in Berlin on April 18, 1986. From these various summits—there were other less significant ones during the period—several themes can be distinguished that indicate that a "Gorbachev line" does indeed exist. Above all, there is the increasing assertion that communist Europe—Big Brother and the little brothers—speaks to the world with a single voice, through common channels of communication, with the Warsaw Pact at the center.

Although the military usefulness of the Warsaw Pact is highly questionable—since the USSR has full authority over the armed forces of its allies, which can outlast the Pact—its political function as an integrating force has been reaffirmed by Gorbachev and developed from one summit to the next. Moreover, by systematically raising all the international problems dealt with by the USSR in meetings of the Pact—Strategic Defense Initiative, disarmament, relations with the United States—the USSR has strengthened both its position as the leader of Eastern Europe as a whole and its own position in the dialogue that has been opened with the western states, since in that context Gorbachev can rely on the support of his allies. Furthermore, these meetings favored the idea of a common foreign policy at the expense of the argument supported by many East European countries that medium-sized states should have a specific role, an argument that the USSR had encouraged at the time of détente. With Mikhail Gorbachev, this international flexibility seems to have lost ground. The Twenty-Seventh Congress insisted on cohesion and unity, not on political dialogue carried on by each state.

Political and military integration is to be completed by accelerated economic integration. The general secretary of the Soviet Communist Party has not missed a single opportunity for repeating how Comecon should progress through precise methods: the coordination of five-year plans, the conclusion of long-term cooperation agreements, a single common plan to develop scientific and technical activities, the development of exchanges within Comecon and their limitation outside it. These principles, affirmed at the Comecon session in June 1985 and at the Twenty-Seventh Congress reveal Gorbachev's preoccupations. He has a particular interest in cooperation in the scientific and technical realms where the USSR has been suffering from increasing backwardness, and at the party congress he openly expressed the determination to extract the consumer goods the USSR lacks from Eastern Europe. Gorbachev went directly to the point: the USSR had for a long time helped its allies; it was time for efforts to move in the opposite direction and for the Soviet Union to reap the benefits of the investments it had made in Eastern Europe. This is the meaning of the complex program of scientific and technical cooperation adopted by Comecon in December 1985, which defined a concerted policy in five principal areas: computers, robotics, nuclear energy, complex materials, and biotechnology. This program, which covers the period from 1985 to 2000, does not call into question the complex program of 1971, but it clearly demonstrates Soviet determination to give economic integration the force of an irreversible structure, leading eventually to a global common economic policy. In 1971, the national plan of each state had priority over the complex program, but the system set in place under Gorbachev has placed those plans within a common program and a set of common interests. Gorbachev's vision is no doubt more integrative and Soviet-centered than that of Leonid Brezhnev.

Finally, he is determined to reestablish economic exchanges with Western Europe, while not allowing the Eastern European countries to join in such exchanges separately, thereby attaining a certain degree of autonomy. At its June 1985 session, Comecon called for bilateral cooperation with the EEC. This was not a mere formality; it corresponded to a desire to strengthen ties in Europe while fostering further integration of the countries of the East through the mechanism of relations between blocs. The call for cooperation on common projects is not futile either, as the example of Rumania demonstrates, although that country has always been seen as an example of political independence from the USSR. But beyond the political independence displayed by Rumania, the bonds of Soviet-Rumanian cooperation have been strengthened within the framework of Comecon (Rumania is participating in the construction of the "Progress" pipeline that will transport natural gas from Yamburg in Siberia to all the Eastern European countries from 1989 on, and it is contributing to the development of gas production in Turkmenistan and Kazhakstan), and by bilateral projects; in every case, Bucharest is obliged to supply manpower and financial support. These joint projects, which will mobilize substantial resources of the country for the benefit of the USSR because they will be carried out on Soviet territory, clearly reflect Moscow's openly expressed determination to make use of its allies' capabilities, while maintaining complete authority over joint projects. Rumania, which was able for a long time to resist the pressures of Gorbachev's predecessors, has now given in and has probably placed itself in a situation of greater dependence on the Soviet Union than any other country of the socialist community. This development is no doubt the result of internal difficulties, but also of the dynamic politics of the new Soviet leader. If Gorbachev's choices in many areas, particularly internal ones, are still obscure, his attitudes toward Eastern Europe are clear. Integration is an absolute priority, and he has already shown that he can foster its growth.

Nevertheless, the problems that involves have not been solved. What role does the USSR grant to the national experiences of its allies? To what extent will Poland be normalized? Will the GDR continue to serve as a bridge between East and West, as it wishes to do? Gorbachev's approach to all these questions can be glimpsed. It can be characterized as being based on a flexibility of particular policies within the context of constant development of the means of integration. With respect to flexibility, it should be noted first of all that, in contrast to what happened in the USSR after the Twenty-Seventh Congress, Gorbachev did not seek to replace the ruling groups of the Eastern European countries, thereby indicating that those problems were the sovereign prerogative of each state. This was the case even though almost everywhere the leaders had been in power for many years, as they had been in the USSR.

What room is there for individual national paths? For national experiments, of which Hungary and Bulgaria are the most representative for the mid-1980s? Gorbachev dealt at length with the problem of national paths and internationalism at the Twenty-Seventh Congress, where he affirmed the need for every state of the socialist bloc to "combine and compare their particular experiences" on which, in the last analysis, the common interest is based. One of Gorbachev's favorite postulates is that this common interest can be harmoniously combined with individual interests. His reaction to the Hungarian experiment is evidence of this. What was important in that case was that a Hungarian "national path" was developed without conflict in two distinct areas: the economy, as is well known, and in politics, which is less known. Two summit meetings—in September 1985 in Moscow, and in June 1986 in Budapest—gave the USSR the opportunity to define its position with respect to the claim of particularity expressed by the regime of János Kádár. The Thirteenth Congress of the Hungarian Communist Party in March 1985 had strongly affirmed its commitment to the economic reforms under way (workplace councils, elected managers, the development of new forms of private enterprise). In a speech to workers at a Budapest factory in June 1986 Gorbachev expressed the interest of the Soviet Union in their experiment, not only for its effects on the Hungarian economy, but also for the lessons that Moscow could derive from it for its own use. At the same time, he issued a precise warning. According to him, the only measure of success of economic reforms is the "strengthening of socialism in all areas, political, economic, spiritual." In other words, the resurrection of a market economy is acceptable insofar as it remains controlled and the political system is thereby reinforced. This was a clear warning to Hungary and to other states that might attempt to experiment, and to the supporters of radical economic reform in the USSR as well. The logic of the socialist system was to remain unchanged, that is, the progress of socialism, of which the economy is only one element. Under no circumstances would political interests be sacrificed to economic progress. This was a clear indication of the limits of Gorbachev's reformism. The warning was all the more appropriate for Hungary because the "Hungarian path" contains a political component. The electoral law of 1983 provided for contested elections, even for multiple candidates. The system was tested, and its limits demonstrated, in the national elections of June 1985. There were few differences between candidates, no genuine opposition, and no new powers were granted to the parliament. But possibilities were also revealed: there was a hint of an opposition or dissident vote and a proliferation of committees in parliament that might invigorate the body as a whole. It is thus easy to understand the meaning of Gorbachev's veiled warnings in Budapest. Hungary is no doubt an experimental laboratory in which the USSR can test the results of a reform that constantly expands the scope of the market economy and translates economic changes into political terms. The Soviet Union can also test in Hungary the capacity of the political system to control the whole of current developments. Gorbachev, like his predecessors, has demonstrated so much curiosity and indulgence toward the Hungarian model because the problem of reform is now one for the USSR; but the USSR cannot follow that path unless it is permanently established that economic reform will not become a political Pandora's box. Indeed, no "Big Brother" would be able to restore the socialist order in the USSR if it were threatened. It is this ambiguous attitude toward the Hungarian model that explains the sympathy of the new Soviet leadership for another experimental laboratory, Bulgaria. There, the principal concern is not the market but economic intensification. The NEM (New Economic Mechanism), or planned reform, has produced undoubted results, since the rate of economic growth in Bulgaria in 1984 was 4.5 percent which placed it far above the rates of other Eastern European countries and of the Soviet Union, just behind the GDR. It is not surprising in these circumstances that Soviet satisfaction has been expressed in the creation of a long-term program of economic, scientific, and technical cooperation linking the two countries until the end of the century. A careful reading of this program demonstrates that the USSR intends to apply to Bulgaria the principles of economic integration defined by Gorbachev, that is, integration by which the USSR would profit from the progress achieved by its partners. Indeed, the program suggests that in the future Bulgaria will no longer be treated in a privileged manner as a recipient of energy, but will have to submit to Soviet demands. (Until now, it has had the greatest trade deficit with the USSR except for Poland.) And it will have to supply the USSR with industrial exports very broadly covering the sectors of the Soviet economy that are in deficit.

If we consider Gorbachev's prudent approach to Hungary and his demands on Bulgaria, it is easy to see that these two countries with relatively dynamic economies are less a source of inspiration for radical economic reform in the Soviet Union than they are useful tools to palliate, by means of exports, the economic weaknesses of the USSR and perhaps they are an excuse for the delay of reforms.

The Polish normalization is another chapter in the activities of the new Soviet leadership. The state of siege declared in December 1981 did not succeed in establishing a permanent normalization, either in Poland where social discontent and expressions of dissent remain very powerful, or in the international community, whose disapproval has remained constant. However, in the international sphere, recent developments have led to a gradual removal of the Polish program from the field of international relations. The state of siege was abrogated in July 1983. As an immediate consequence, on August 25, 1983, the United States and the Soviet Union signed a five-year grain delivery agreement in Moscow. No doubt this was more a concession by President Reagan to the demands of American farmers than a sign of real normalization; but this agreement nevertheless opened the way to an international thaw on the Polish question. In June 1984, President Mitterrand, who had made Poland and Afghanistan obstacles to any normalization of Franco-Soviet relations (the resumption of more or less regular summits), went to Moscow and thereby opened a new phase of relations with the USSR, marked by Gorbachev's visit to Paris in October 1985 and Mitterrand's visit to Moscow in July 1986. It is noteworthy that in his Kremlin speech of July 7, 1986, President Mitterrand no longer referred to Poland in the list of current international problems. Polish normalization was treated as an accomplished fact in international relations, made evident by the Gorbachev-Reagan summit in Geneva in 1985 and by the fact that the discussions about holding a summit in 1986 or 1987 focused entirely on strategic questions. For international society, five years after the state of siege, Poland had once again become a problem of the socialist community. But the attitude of the new Soviet leadership toward and their judgment of Polish normalization and the policies of General Jaruzelski remained to be clearly defined. When Gorbachev came to power, the situation in Poland seemed blocked from two contrary directions. The Polish authorities maintained that the conflict between government and opposition had practically disappeared and that stability reigned. They were already considering the possibility of calling a party congress to adopt a new program for the party, that is, to restore full life to the normal institutions of a socialist state. This was the logic of developments after the end of the state of siege. To this assertion of complete normalization, the opposition replied that the authorities were confusing a *petitio principii* and the real state of affairs. Even though it was difficult to continue effective opposition under the pressure of increased controls, it was clear according to the opposition that a gulf continued to separate the society which had not accepted the dissolution of Solidarity, from the authorities, which it did not consider representative. The Polish parliamentary elections held on October 13, 1985, confirmed the accuracy of both opposing arguments. The fact that elections could take place (they had been planned for March 1984 but had been delayed because the authorities feared a widespread boycott) showed the capacity the regime had to impose its will on society and to ignore continuing protests. For General Jaruzelski, the growth of popular participation between the local elections of 1984 and the general elections of 1985 (5 percent more participants recognized in both official and opposition figures) clearly indicated the tendency toward normalization. But the significant level of abstention (25 percent in 1984, more than 20 percent in 1985), which showed the impact of the call for a boycott launched by the opposition, demonstrated that it was still being heard by society. Perhaps it was this victory, which he proclaimed, that led General Jaruzelski to give up the post of prime minister to his associate Zbigniew Messner in order to join the great cohort of socialist leaders of state: Honecker, Ceauşescu, Husák, and Zhivkov. This movement indicated increased authority. Since then, Polish normalization has continued along two lines: continued pressure on all possible centers of opposition, and the search for a return to the normal institutions of the socialist state, that is the party. There were increased pressures on the activities of Solidarity and of other movements (notably the arrests of Bogdan Lis, Adam Michnik, and Władisław Frasyniuk in February 1985). At the end of 1985, more than three hundred "non-criminals," that is, political prisoners were held in Polish jails. In July 1985 the adoption of measures dealing with periodic verifications of the political loyalty of members of the educational system led to an extensive purge of the universities and research institutes. A new police law simultaneously allowed for the completion of the system of social control. On November 23, 1985, the weekly *Polityka* violently attacked the program of construction of religious buildings in Poland and suggested that the authorities should adopt a stricter attitude toward the Polish church, accused of seeking to extend its grip on the population.

The other side of the policy of normalization involved the restoration of the party to its central position in society. In November 1985, a conference with five hundred participants—members of the Central Committee, intellectuals, experts—met in Warsaw to prepare a proposed party program, which was adopted at the Polish Party Congress in June 1986. At the center of the program was the clear affirmation of the exclusive role of the party in the leadership of society and an affirmation of Marxist-Leninist ideology. Social forces outside the party (notably the church) and voluntaristic programs found no place in this political conception.

This return to a rigid socialism definitely corresponded to the Soviet conception of Polish normalization; and the Gorbachev group has unambiguously demonstrated that the Polish leadership has its support and approval. General Jaruzelski had already been honored at the Twenty-Eighth Congress of the Soviet Communist Party, and Gorbachev had emphasized the depth of their "camaraderie." On March 17, 1986, immediately after the Twenty-Eighth Congress of the Soviet Communist Party, Soviet Foreign Minister Shevardnadze met General Jaruzelski in Warsaw during an official visit that, Moscow emphasized, "had a special meaning" and "evidenced the deep cooperation between the two greatest European socialist states." Shevardnadze returned several times to the theme of cooperation and asserted that the restoration of order had succeeded thanks to General Jaruzelski's team. This mark of approval went beyond the problem of normalization. Shevardnadze pointed to the general correctness of Polish positions. The same approval of policies followed in Poland since 1981 was indicated by Gorbachev himself when he attended the Tenth Congress of the Polish Communist Party. In his speech on June 30, 1986, he clearly stated that General Jaruzelski's policies had brought about victory in a "struggle for the very existence of socialism in Poland." The general secretary of the Soviet Communist Party added that there had existed no other solution to the recent crisis, since the "achievements of socialism are irreversible," and since "challenging the organization of Europe that had come out of the war amounted to a threat to peace." Gorbachev's speech at the Polish Party Congress essentially repeated without variation the Soviet speech made after the normalization of Czechoslovakia. The identity of views on the future of the socialist system between Brezhnev and Gorbachev is obvious in this case. It is clear that for Moscow the story of Solidarity is at an end and the Polish leaders have succeeded well enough to deserve unstinting Soviet support.

During this period of change, the GDR has posed a familiar problem, how to find a balance between a political and economic system that Moscow cannot but approve and the desire to maintain a certain freedom of action in relations with Western Europe. Erich Honecker's authority in the country and his rigorous economic policies have made the GDR an irreproachable model. It is the economic leader of the socialist bloc, with a growth rate of more than 5 percent in 1985. In a speech delivered in Leningrad in May 1985, Gorbachev paid tribute to the effectiveness and the quality of the GDR's industrial production, presenting it as a model to the sister states. On the other hand, political clouds have not been lacking, all provoked by the question of relations with Western Europe. Forced by Moscow to cancel his trip to the Federal Republic of Germany in the fall of 1984, when Moscow froze its relations with Bonn because of West German support for the deployment of Pershing missiles, Honecker concluded an implicit alliance with Hungary to promote his argument for a continued opening to the West and to preserve his freedom of action in the international sphere. Hungarians and Germans have thus been arguing together that the medium-sized states of Europe should have a particular role, and that internationalism should not be carried on at the expense of national interests.

Honecker's initiatives have been numerous (a joint plan with the West German Social Democrats for a chemical-weapon-free zone in central Europe; trips to East Berlin by British Foreign Secretary Sir Geoffrey Howe in April 1985 and French Prime Minister Laurent Fabius the following June; Honecker's trip to two NATO countries, Italy and Greece; an audience at the Vatican; and the maintenance of links with the Federal Republic, despite Soviet reticence, and even though crises like the blockade of entry into Berlin in the spring of 1986 sometimes darken inter-German relations). This international activity has given Honecker unquestioned authority and a freedom of movement that Gorbachev apparently does not intend to rein in brutally. Effective economic policies that have avoided recourse to dangerous reforms clearly justify granting the GDR the right, up to a certain point, to preserve its interests and possibly to play the role of an intermediary in Europe. One may perhaps notice a nuance of Gorbachev's attitude toward this problem; the USSR clearly wants the initiative for relations with Bonn to be left to it, and for Honecker to subordinate inter-German relations to Soviet decisions, not to conduct them independently, as he has a tendency to do. In return for this acceptance of the privileged role of the USSR in defining the nature of relations with the Federal Republic, Honecker no doubt has considerable latitude to promote his own policies toward the West.

Besides the question of Gorbachev's intentions and policies for the socialist community as a whole, there is also the question of the effects of the Gorbachev program on the fraternal countries individually, and even more its long-term significance for them. *Glasnost'*, the slogan around which the whole debate in the USSR has been concentrated; *perestroika*, the appeal for total restructuring; *uskorenie*, the theme of acceleration which has been more and more strongly developed during the third year of Gorbachevism: how are these perceived and put into practice in a non-Soviet context?

Gorbachev's long speech in the plenum of the Central Committee of the Communist Party of the Soviet Union on 27 January 1987 relaunched the debate on change in the USSR in fairly radical terms. More clearly than before, the secretary-general stated how indispensable it was to introduce changes—and he made this analysis yet again, in the context of a situation characterized by spectacular setbacks—explaining how slowly change was taking place, and how much it was threatened by inertia and obstruction. The frankness of the speech, the more dramatic tone than previously—these were themselves examples of what *glasnost'* is supposed to be. Gorbachev defined the content of *perestroika* yet again, and more clearly than before, in six points which he summarized as follows:

It is clear that the ultimate aim of restructuring is a profound renewal of all aspects of the life of our country, the equipping of socialism with the most up-to-date forms of social organization, the complete development of the humanist character of our system in all its aspects—economic, sociopolitical, and moral. . . .[1]

The wide-ranging criticism of the past, of the adversaries of reform and of the factors that hold it up, the appeal for effort ("restructuring is not a stroll along an easy road, it is a hard climb on paths that are often unexplored") and the insistence on the immensity of the task to be accomplished ("we are only at the beginning of the road"):[2] all this struck a note that in the USSR was fairly new. Is this the case for Eastern Europe as well? The facts oblige one to conclude that as regards open analysis of the faults and even the failures of the system, and also with respect to reform the general, what seems a novelty in the USSR, at least in comparison with the last two decades, is far less so in many fraternal states. At the same time, the situation in the various countries is far from being identical, and by the same token, the great Muscovite house-cleaning provokes varying responses among them.

Hungary and Poland can be justifiably skeptical of the need to copy slavishly the model of frankness proposed by Gorbachev. In these two countries, *glasnost'* has long been in operation, for recurrent crises have dictated its necessity. But in each country, the use to which it is put and the ultimate aims that it serves are different, and there is no reason to abandon these in favor of the Kremlini's variant. In Hungary as in the USSR, *glasnost'* has been linked with the idea of reforming the way in which the system functions, and it has been the more wide-ranging because the exposure of failings serves to stimulate measures intended to ensure that the system functions more effectively. Just as in the USSR, therefore, *glasnost'* (even if in Hungary it does not bear this name) has the double function of bearing witness to the authorities' will to reform, and of permitting them to eliminate individual and systemic faults, to the extent that their exposure brings about countermeasures and correction.

All the same, between Moscow and Budapest there are great differences in the processes behind the employment of *glasnost'*. These differences can be explained, for the most part, by differences of political culture. In Hungary, *glasnost'* has been the product of a situation and a movement that have developed from below. The Hungarian reforms have been under way for a long time, they have produced a multiplicity of debates on the paths to be followed and the progress to be accomplished, and they have also brought in their wake, indeed one might say that they have themselves given birth to, a more open style of communication that ensures for reform a continuing dynamism. In the USSR, the situation is quite the reverse: *glasnost'* is a manifestation of a willed decision to create the conditions for reform. Here it is the authorities that, confronted with the disastrous economic and social situation so often described by Gorbachev, have decided to introduce *glasnost'* into the practice of politics, so as to use it first of all as an instrument of their will to change, and secondly of change itself, realized through reforms. *Glasnost'*, as a style of communication that precedes reform and proclaims its necessity, tends to break up the existing state of things. In Russian and Soviet tradition, such a style is a manifestation of "reform from above." *Glasnost'* is a way of decreeing the necessity of reform, and asserting that the authorities that initiate and control the process are the best equipped to carry it out. No doubt the Soviet talk of openness is pleasant for the Hungarian leaders to hear, since it confirms them in the path that they long ago chose. But it does not imply that they should abandon their own perception of the balanced relationship between reform and *glasnost'*, to the benefit of Gorbachev's willed-from-above variant. In Budapest, openness of communication causes few tremors, for it is organically linked to ongoing reforms. In Gorbachev's variant, *glasnost'* provokes resistance on the part of those who wish to preserve established ways and privileges, and this resistance is all the fiercer because they perceive the transforming function of *glasnost'*.

What is true of Hungary is true also of Poland. As a result of repeated crises since 1956, Poland has become accustomed to a double practice of *glasnost'*, far more radical than that which appears in present-day Soviet utterances. First of all there is the *glasnost'* of the authorities. Gomułka in

1956, then Gierek, then for a short period Kania, and finally Jaruzelski have all, at particular moments when they wanted to criticize the situation inherited from their predecessors or to find support from society, made use of *glasnost'*, and they have called upon the media and society to express themselves freely. These repeated bouts of sincerity have been more or less lasting, depending on what the authorities deemed appropriate to provide an outlet for the major social tensions that have caused or resulted from each crisis. But in addition, what has made a decisive difference in Poland is the fact that this intermittent sincerity on the part of the authorities has been accompanied by a parallel forum of public discussion, an alternative *glasnost'*, which in spite of repression, the authorities have never been able to destroy. The religious authorities (Cardinal Wyszinski during his lifetime, Father Popieluszko, and many others), underground publications with a national circulation, Solidarity, unreconciled intellectuals, and the like—together or separately, all these articulators of opinion and channels of expression form a second arena of Polish political life that the authorities must always take into account. Because this parallel forum of public discussion exists on such a large scale, the authorities, for their part, are obliged to admit a certain amount of *glasnost'*, the effect of which is at once to nourish the distrust of the nation towards them, and to encourage the *glasnost'* that they do not control. Compared with Poland's double *glasnost'*, Gorbachev's open speaking is quite timid. In Poland, it can only serve to confirm the idea that the Polish road is a good one, since it is being followed in the USSR too.

In contrast to these two countries that could not be taken aback by Gorbachevism, two other countries are meeting it with disguised resistance. It is not among the least of the paradoxes of the present period to find encamped on the same line of opposition to the USSR, both the GDR which was always a model of conformity, and Rumania, which has been so lastingly hostile to Moscow. The political leaders of the GDR, headed by Honecker, consider the success of their system sufficiently evident that there is no need for a change of orientation. Why unsettle the authority of the party and the relationship between the party and society by introducing *glasnost'* into the life of the republic? Not only has Honecker judged this to be needless, but in addition he has found it wise to reduce to a minimum his people's knowledge of the new language of the Soviets. Perhaps for the first time in their relations with "big brother," the East German authorities have kept aloof from, and have been literally censoring, both the new style of the Soviets and the actual content of their utterances. It can be no surprise that Rumania has adopted the same attitude of reserve toward *glasnost'*. Ceauşescu has remained faithful to his totalitarian conception of authority, and to the idea that the Soviet model is of no concern to Rumania.

Between these two extremes, the Czechs and the Bulgarians are cautiously searching for an attitude that will conform to their long-term interests. In

Prague, *glasnost'* undoubtedly evokes a past that has never been totally forgotten, but which the continuing presence in office of Gustav Husák has condemned to lasting disavowal. What, actually, would the adoption of *glasnost'* in Czechoslovakia amount to? A revival of the Prague Spring? Or rather the pure and simple adoption of the Soviet model? The two things are far from resembling each other. The *glasnost'* at the heart of Czechoslovak developments in 1968 was the product of the will of society. Returning to their pro-working-class origins, the Czechoslovak authorities took the mood of society as an inspiration, and followed it. The Prague Spring was condemned by Moscow precisely on the grounds that it was not a movement coming from above. Hence the hesitation over the path to be followed that prevails today in Czechoslovakia, and the evident reservations on the part of authorities that came to power in the name of the normalization that annihilated the total *glasnost'* of 1968.

Reservations and caution also characterize the attitude of Bulgaria. Accustomed to follow every turn of Soviet policy, the Sofia authorities have in appearance followed Gorbachev's line. They have appealed to society, and to their own spokesmen, to give proof of the spirit of openness that has triumphed in Moscow. But on close inspection, it is easy to observe that here, *glasnost'* has been invested only with limited significance. It is to bring to light a few abuses, and to underline the good will of the leaders in admitting innovations, but as a whole the movement has remained strictly under the control of the authorities. The party is vigilant lest the grievances appearing in the press involve the system as a whole, or open a debate on central issues of principle. Moreover, this version of *glasnost'* seems in no way favorable to a reforming vision in any field whatever.

These reservations about the Soviet renewal, or rather about transferring it to Eastern Europe, are the result of various factors and are often reinforced by the attitude of the USSR, whose interests in this area are contradictory. Quite obviously, the first of these factors is the personal threat that the East European leaders rightly sense is hanging over them. With the exception of General Jaruzelski, who came to power at the time of the suppression of Solidarity, all the men in office in the fraternal states of the Warsaw Pact, and all the cadres on which they rely, are men of the past—of Brezhnev's time, or even Khrushchev's. Gorbachevism involves, in the first place, the elimination of a whole political generation. This process, which has been largely carried out in Moscow since 1985, has after two years had no counterpart in Eastern Europe. But this only makes the men in power feel all the more threatened. They are threatened by their age. They are threatened by their very long tenure of power, which brings with it, as Gorbachev never ceases to proclaim, inertia and corruption. They are threatened by the impatience of rising generations, excluded from the centers of power by the immovable presence of veterans who do not reflect the image of the societies they lead. They are threatened by Gorbachev's undoubted desire to assure himself of leaders in the fraternal states whose views are close to his own, whose destinies are linked to his, and who by this very fact are compelled to support him. No doubt this fear of being eliminated for the benefit of new ruling groups is everywhere moderated by the awareness that the Soviet interest does not automatically lie in a radical turnover of all the men in office. The terrible results for the USSR of the personnel changes imposed by Khrushchev on Hungary between 1953 and 1955, or of the spontaneous personnel changes that took place in Poland, are well remembered, for out of these came the Hungarian revolution and the Polish October. How can Gorbachev risk bringing about such fateful disturbances of the system? Moreover, by pushing for changes in personnel in the neighboring states, Gorbachev would be going against his own ideas. Has he not continiually affirmed his preoccupation with the internal problems of the USSR, and his desire to break with the interventionist practices of his predecessors, above all in the Communist world? In spite of all this, every East European leader knows that in Gorbachev's eyes, he is under stay of execution. Restructuring and reform demand new men.

It is precisely in connection with reform that the contradictions are sharpest. A priori, the notion of reform, whether economic or even political, is far from alien to the countries of the bloc as a whole. To repeat, in Hungary, in Czechoslovakia, and in Poland, Gorbachev's ideas evoke, respectively, what is now being done, what has been done in the past, and what is wished for in the future. For the Hungarians, who have long been attached to the idea of reforming their economy, who have adopted the principle of multiple-candidacy elections, and whose frontiers are relatively open on account of the undoubted support within society for the system, Gorbachev is not a forerunner but an imitator. Yegor Ligachev, at the conclusion of a visit to Hungary in April 1987, came out as the champion of the Hungarian model, stressing its fundamentally Socialist character and its ability to serve as a model for all experiments with innovation. This eulogy of the Hungarian reforms and their exemplary character, on the part of one who is too easily taken as a Politburo opponent of Gorbachev's reformism, is a good indication of consensus within the USSR on the subject of reform. It also testifies to Moscow's anxiety to reassure its East European allies that the experiment under way in the USSR is strongly based, and in consequence, that the allies of the bloc can support and follow Gorbachev. This legitimation of the Hungarian experiment can only encourage its promoters to advance further down their road. To do so is all the more necessary since the Hungarian economy is in difficulties and the only way out is generally agreed to be that of advancing toward even more liberal solutions, where the market will occupy the central role in the economy. The Gorbachev experiment in the USSR, coming long after the Hungarian experiment, has nothing to teach the

Hungarians, except that they can be bolder in opening their economy to the influence of the market.

The restructuring of the economy is an idea that also finds favor in Poland, such is the scale of the economic disaster there. But as much as he desires economic reforms, General Jaruzelski seems correspondingly unwilling to accompany them with more liberal political measures, for the basis of his power would be thereby reduced. In spite of prohibitions, Solidarity has not vanished from people's awareness. Over against the political authorities, the Polish church holds to the claim that in the absence of other legal structures, it represents the voice and aspirations of society. Here, liberalization would signify a return to the dichotomy desired by Solidarity: the authorities holding political power, and civil society expressing itself through its own channels (labor unions, churches, and so on) and managing its own interests. This latent dichotomy, which martial law could disguise for a time but in no way suppress, is reinforced by the support that Polish society receives from outside, above all from the Vatican. John Paul II's visit to Poland in June 1987 has removed all doubts in this respect. If John Paul II has agreed to acknowledge the legitimacy of those whom the proclamation of martial law put at the head of the Polish state, this has been within the limits of a system where the authorities are obliged to recognize the existence of civil society. For General Jaruzelski, any political reform would be dangerous, since it would legalize the de facto situation defined by the pope, and recreate the duality of power for which Solidarity struggled. Thus, the interests of the men in power in Warsaw can be defined in opposing terms. They agree to a restructuring of the economy, and they refuse any political changes, over which they would be less able than Gorbachev in the USSR to maintain control.

Why should we reform our economy, seeing that it has constantly been operated in a spirit of reform to which its performance testifies? This is the question that the leaders of the German Democratic Republic put quite plainly, thereby making clear, moreover, that the experiment advocated by Gorbachev in no way concerns them. In the economic area, it would seem difficult for the secretary-general of the Communist Party of the Soviet Union to dispute this position; in fact this was what the Soviet minister of foreign affairs, Edvard Shevardnadze, said in the course of his visit to East Berlin on 4 February 1987. After applauding the economic success of East Germany and expounding the electoral reform proposed by the secretary-general for the USSR, Shevardnadze carefully refrained from suggesting a possible extension to the GDR. True, the Soviet ambassador to the Federal Republic of Germany, L. Kvistinsky, said that one of the reasons for the reforms was to make "Socialism more attractive," and that this was a necessary goal throughout Eastern Europe, whether in the GDR or in Poland. But apart from this general remark, the relations between Moscow and its German ally seem to be dominated by caution.

It is in Czechoslovakia, however, that the debate over reforms is the most ambiguous. At the Fifth Plenum of the Central Committee of the Communist Party of Czechoslovakia in March 1987, announcing Gorbachev's coming visit to Prague, Gustav Husák expressed himself on the necessity of his country's taking Soviet developments as an example. The speech was remarkable, first of all, for its revelation of a new Husák. The man who had embodied rejection of the reformism of 1968 had suddenly changed into a reformer. Having affirmed that the projected reconstruction owed nothing to the spirit of 1968, Husák clearly stated that his country would unhesitatingly undertake a radical reform, comprising a law on enterprises in preparation, electoral reform, and general democratization. All the same Husák does not seem to be the man to lead a return to 1968. All his proposals revolve around the central role of the party, especially as regards control of appointments to all government and managerial positions. But in spite of his reservations, Husák seems to be moving away from the conservatism that for nearly twenty years has dominated the life of Czechoslovakia.

Elsewhere, the best ally, Bulgaria, and the least docile, Rumania, again find themselves following the same line, each applauding Gorbachev for what he is doing in the USSR, and asserting that it is doing the same, in its own way. In the case of Rumania one may doubt the truth of this assertion, but the Bulgarian Todor Zhivkov is not incorrect in calling himself a reformer *avant la lettre*. Since the middle of the 1960s he has been listening to liberal economists and pragmatic party cadres who have been calling upon him to reform the management system and to decentralize. The tendency for which he claims to stand dates back to the "League of April," defined by the Congress of the Bulgarian Plenum in April 1956: in other words, Bulgaria has never ceased to attempt reforms within the framework of its specific conditions. This is what Zhivkov stresses, discreetly contrasting the continuity of Bulgarian policy over three decades with the constant Soviet changes of direction.

This brings us to two important problems of Moscow's relations with the fraternal parties. The first is that however much or little they sympathize with Gorbachev's innovations, the East European leaders cannot fail to ask themselves how long the experiment will last. Past experience has taught them the weight of conservative tendencies within the USSR, a fact that is underlined by the most liberal Soviet economists, such as Academician T. Zaslavskaya. Experience has shown them that every effort toward change, notably the reforms of Khrushchev or Kosygin, has in the end bogged down, and given place to a spirit of immobility, for which the USSR is paying today with many years' accumulated interest. They also know that these foward sallies on the part of the Soviets, when reproduced in Eastern Europe, have transformed themselves into violent crises, followed by resumptions of control by a Soviet leadership intent on enforcing alignment with the Soviet model, as much in the abandonment of reform as in reform itself. Everywhere, therefore, there is doubt whether this is a good moment to follow Gorbachev by pledging fidelity to his policy choices. No one in Eastern Europe wants to be associated with the possible failure of Gorbachev, should hope in fact be followed by failure. The bitter memory of past experiments clearly explains the caution and reserve that are everywhere displayed.

A second problem is connected with that of relations within the bloc. Every country of Eastern Europe faces two questions: What is the concrete significance for each of us of the new policy of the USSR? And what, in terms of this innovating vision, will the Socialist community look like? The renewal of East-West relations that Gorbachev desires, and his strategic proposals, do not have the same advantages for everyone. Hungary, Poland, and even Czechoslovakia may unreservedly applaud the idea of a non-nuclear Europe which would thereby achieve the conditions for dialogue and contact between its two halves; but the GDR is anxious about the price that will have to be paid. Gorbachev was acclaimed by the people of Prague in April 1987, and in June by the youth of East Berlin. The meaning of these acclamations, however, was not identical in both cities. In Prague, it was the opening towards Western Europe—"Europe is our common dwelling," said Gorbachev in Prague—and some kind of return to the reformism of 1968, that the crowds were applauding with their constant repetition of the name of Gorbachev. In East Berlin, the cries of "Long live Gorbachev!" signified the revolt of youth against an authoritarian system that is remote from the cultural and economic values of the western world. What East German youth was calling for was freedom of movement, rock culture, leisure civilization, and the consumer society, of which the other Germany is for them the symbol. True, Gorbachev's foreign-policy pronouncements, from his exposition of his "new political thinking" to his Prague speech, can only give pleasure to his allies. But in Prague, there are questions about the precise meaning of his speech, over and above the generalities. Does the reduction of tensions imply that the Soviet troops, stationed in Czechoslovakia since the summer of 1968, will at last leave the country?

Even more serious is the question of the nature of the relations between Socialist states. Does Gorbachev intend to call into question the most decisive and weighty aspect of his relationship, Socialist internationalism, with the consequence that results from it in fact if not in law: limited sovereignty? In this area, Soviet utterances during the "Gorbachev era" have been particularly ambiguous. Soviet authorities—Yuri Shahnazarov, president of the Soviet Political Science Association, or Yuri Novopachin, department chairman at the Institute for Economics of the World Socialist System—have been insisting since 1985 that it would be an error to ignore the aspect of national interest in the international relations of the Socialist states, and to build the relations between Socialist states on a hierarchical basis. As between Socialist states, Novopachin assures us, there exists neither hierarchy nor subordination, and democratic centralism has no place in their relations.[3] In Prague, Gorbachev said the same; and in Budapest, Ligachev repeated that "every country must follow its own road. . . . If it was once possible to think that the conductor of this orchestra was to be found in Moscow, that is no longer true."

Should one conclude from these statements that the "new political thinking" places state sovereignty above the common interests of the bloc? Looking at the picture as a whole, at the spurring of reform and the common planning, one must qualify this impression. As Gorbachev becomes aware of the anxieties or skepticism of the men he deals with, Honecker, Zhivkov, Ceaușescu, or Husák (whether on account of the threat to their personal position or because of their doubts about the longevity of Gorbachev's reforms) he knows that he must be cautious. When he says that "no party has a monopoly of truth" it is more to reassure all those who fear that dangerous policy shifts may be imposed on them than to bring into question the bases of the solidarity of the bloc.

For even while Gorbachev affirms the right of each communist party to follow its "own road" in the matter of restructuring, he caps this proposition by indicating what the Socialist community as a whole demands. It requires "greater dynamism" in relations between Socialist countries, and rapid progress in economic integration.[4] As part of the flood of measures concerning foreign trade and joint ventures, the internal relations of the bloc have been reorganized and restructured by the decrees of 19 August 1986 and of January 1987.[5] These two documents are intended to permit a better organization of cooperation between the Socialist countries, which has suffered considerably up to now from the economic disorganization of the bloc. Within this perspective, the reforms that Gorbachev has been preaching to all his allies should give real effectiveness to a better integrated Socialist community. Here, too, the allies of the USSR may feel hesitation. Even if, for most Eastern European leaders, economic reforms are an unarguable necessity, it does not follow that their result must be to accelerate or contribute to integration. This, however, is Gorbachev's driving idea. For Gorbachev, economic integration of the bloc is an essential condition for acceleration (*uskorenie*) of the economic progress of the alliance. But to attain it, even while he calls upon his allies to follow him on the road of change, he must be careful not to awaken in Eastern Europe those hopes of a radical alteration in the political system, or in relations with the USSR, that every change of this kind tends to arouse. If renewal is hard to bring about in the USSR on account of the obstructions that slow it and the possibility of losing control, it is still harder to bring it about in Eastern Europe, where the USSR has too often in the past lost control of situations that it has itself created.

How can the Socialist community be reformed without destroying it? That is Gorbachev's dilemma, and he has no other guidance for resolving it than his own will and the failures of his predecessors.

Paris, 15 June 1987

NOTES

1. *Kommunist*, no. 5 (February 1987): 13.
2. These two quotations are taken from Gorbachev's closing speech to the plenum on 28 January 1987. Ibid., 49.
3. *Rabochii Klass i Sovremenii Mir,* no. 5 (1985): 55, 56.
4. Speech in Prague, 10 April 1987.
5. *Pravda,* 24 September 1986; *Ekonomicheskaia Gazeta* (June 1987): 17–18.

BIBLIOGRAPHY

This bibliography does not cite most of the titles referred to in the notes. It lists only a certain number of basic, or recent, works that could not be integrated into the notes.

I. DOCUMENTS

IN RUSSIAN:

Brezhnev, L. I. *Leninskim kursom, Rechi i stat'i* (On Lenin's course, speeches and articles). Vol. 6, Moscow, 1978.

Diplomaticheskii Slovar'. 2 vols., Moscow, 1964.

Mezhdunarodnye otnoshenia posle vtoroi mirovoi voiny (International relations after the Second World War). 3 vols., Moscow, 1963—1965.

Sbornik deistvuiushchih dogovorov soglashenii i konventsii, zakliuchennyh SSSR s inostrannami stranami (Collection of treaties, agreements, and conventions between the USSR and foreign states). Moscow (vols. 13 to 31 cover the years from 1943 to the present).

Sovetskii Soiuz na mezhdunarodnyh konferentsiah perioda velikoi otechesvennoi voiny—1941– 1945 (The Soviet Union in the international conferences of the period of the great patriotic war). 6 vols. Moscow, 1970, (esp. v. 1: Moscow; v. 2: Teheran; v. 4: Yalta).

Sovetsko-chehoslovatskie otnoshenia: dokumenty i materialy (Soviet-Czechoslovak relations: documents and materials). 4 vols., Moscow 1972–1986.

SSSR i strany narodnoj demokratii: stanovlenie otnoshenii druzhby i sotrudnichestva: 1944– 1949 (The USSR and the countries of People's Democracy: the formation of a relationship of friendship and cooperation). Moscow, 1985.

Tegeran-Yalta-Potsdam—sbornik dokumentov (Teheran-Yalta-Potsdam—collection of documents). Moscow, 1967.

Vneshnaia politika sovetskogo soiuza, dokumenty i materialy (The foreign policy of the Soviet Union—documents and materials). 2 vols., Moscow 1945–1951.

Zakonomernosti razvitija mirovoj sistemy sotsializma: ukazatel' literatury, 1981–1985 g. (The laws of development of the world socialist system: a guide to the literature, 1981–1985). Moscow, 1985.

IN ENGLISH:

Library of Congress, *Soviet Diplomacy and Negotiating Behavior.* Vol. 1, Washington, D.C., 1979.

Triska, J., and Slusser, R., *A Calendar of Soviet Treaties, 1917–1957.* Stanford, Calif., 1959.

United States Department of State. *Foreign Relations of the United States: Diplomatic Papers.* Washington, D.C., 1955.

———. *USSR and Eastern Europe: A List of Current Social Science Research by Private Scholars and Academic Centers.* Washington, D.C., 1968.

United States House of Representatives. Committee on Foreign Affairs. *The Strategy and Tactics of World Communism.* 2 vols., Washington, D.C., 1948–49. (On the Prague coup and East European political leaders).

———. *The Cold War: Origins and Development: Hearings.* Washington, D.C., 1971.

United States Senate. Committee on Foreign Relations. *Czechoslovakia 1968: Report to the Committee.* Washington, D.C., 1968.

II. NEWSPAPERS AND PERIODICALS

Pravda; Izvestia; Krasnaia Zvezda (Red Star); *Literaturnaia Gazeta* (Literary gazette), *Kommunist; Mirovaia Ekonomika i Mirovye Otnoshenia* (World economy and international relations); *Sovetskoe Gosudarstvo i Pravo* (Soviet state and law); *Voprosy Filosofii* (Questions of philosophy); *Voprosy Istorii KPSS* (Questions of the history of the Communist Party of the Soviet Union); *The Military Balance*, annual publication of the International Institute for Strategic Studies (London).

III. BOOKS

IN RUSSIAN:

Angelov, S., ed. *Sotsialisticheskii internatsionalizm: teoriia i praktika mezhdunarodnyh otnoshenii novogo tipa* (Socialist internationalism: Theory and practice of a new kind of international relations). Moscow, 1979.

Diplomatiia sotsializma (The diplomacy of socialism), foreword by A. Gromyko. Moscow, 1975.

Dolgin, V. G. *V edinstve—Sila sodruzhestva sotsialisticheskih stran* (In unity—the strength of the friendship among socialist countries). Moscow, 1977.

Dorotchenkov, A. *Internatsional'noe i natsional'noe v mirovoi sotsialisticheskoi sisteme* (The International and the National in the world socialist system). Moscow, 1975.

Gribkov, A. I., ed. *Varshavskii dogovor: soiuz vo ime mira i sotsializma* (The Warsaw Pact: union for peace and socialism). Moscow, 1980.

Gromyko, Hvostov, Ponomarev, eds. *Istoriia vneshnei politiki SSSR* (History of the foreign policy of the USSR). (3rd ed.), 2 vols., Moscow, 1977.

Inozemstev, N. *Leninskii kurs mezhdunarodnoi politiki KPSS* (The Leninist path of the foreign policy of the Soviet Communist Party). Moscow, 1978.

Iuralev, *Mezhdunarodny sviazi SEV* (The international relations of Comecon). Moscow, 1978.

Kandalov, J. *Ideologicheskoe i kul'turnoe sotrudnichestvo bratskih stran* (Ideological and cultural cooperation of fraternal countries). Moscow, 1979.

Karavaev, V. P. *Integratsiia i investitsii—problemy sotrudnichestva SEV* (Integration and investments: problems of cooperation in Comecon). Moscow, 1979.

Ladygin, B. N. *Istoricheskii opyt sotrudnichestva stran SEV* (The historical experience of cooperation among the Comecon countries). Moscow, 1980.

Mezhdunarodnaia politika KPSS i vneshnie funktsii soveteskogo gosudarstva (The foreign policy of the Soviet Communist Party and the international functions of the Soviet State). Moscow, 1976.

Mihailov, B. I., *Sovremennyi etap sotsialisticheskoi integratsii* (The current stage of socialist integration). Moscow, 1980.

Mikul'ski, K. I. ed. *SEV—mezhdunarodnoe znachenie sotsialisticheskoi integratsii* (Comecon: the international significance of socialist integration). Moscow, 1979.

Narochnitskii, A. L., ed. *Leninskii traditsii vneshnei politiki sovetskogo soiuza* (The Leninist traditions of the foreign policy of the Soviet Communist Party). Moscow, 1977.

Solov'ev, M. *Suverenitet i sotsialisticheskii internationalizm* (Sovereignty and socialist internationalism). Moscow, 1974.

Teplov, L. *Varshavskii dogovor i Nato: dva kursi, dve politiki* (The Warsaw Pact and Nato: Two paths, two policies). Moscow, 1979.

Ukreplenie edinstva sotsialisticheskih stran (Strengthening the unity of the socialist countries). Moscow, 1977.

Velikaia sila internatsional'nogo edinstva (The great strength of international unity). Moscow, 1979.

IN WESTERN LANGUAGES:

Aspaturian, V. *Process and Power in Soviet Foreign Policy.* Boston, 1971.

Beloff, Nora. *Tito's Flawed Legacy.* London, 1985.

Dawisha, K., and P. Hanson, eds. *Soviet-East European Dilemmas: Coercion, Competition and Consent.* London, 1981.

Drachkovitch, Milorad. *East Central Europe: Yesterday, Today, Tomorrow,* Stanford, 1982.

Edmonds, R. *Soviet Foreign Policy.* Oxford, 1976.

Gawanda, J. A. *The Soviet Domination of Eastern Europe in the Light of International Law.* New York, 1974.

Gerner, K. *The Soviet Union and Central Europe in the Post-War Era: A Study in Precarious Security.* Stockholm, 1984.

Goodman, E. *The Soviet Design for a World State,* New York, 1960.

Hoxha, Enver. *Les Titistes: notes historiques.* Tirana, 1982.

Hutchings, R. L. *Soviet-East European Relations: Consolidation and Conflict 1968–1980.* Madison, Wis., 1983.

Johnson, A. Ross, Robert W. Dean, and Alexander Alexeiev. *East European Military Establishments: The Warsaw Pact Northern Tier.* New York, 1982.

Joint Economic Committee. *Eastern European Economics, post Helsinki.* Washington, D.C., 1977.

Jones, C. D. *Soviet Influence in Eastern Europe: Political Autonomy and the Warsaw Pact.* New York, 1981.

Kanet, Roger. *Soviet Foreign Policy and East-West Relations.* New York, 1982.

Kaplan, Stephen S. *Diplomacy of Power: Soviet Armed Forces as a Political Instrument.* Washington, D.C., 1981.

Levesque, J. *L'U.R.S.S. et sa politique internationale, de 1917 à nos jours.* Paris, 1980.

Lewis, W. J. *The Warsaw Pact: Arms, Doctrine, Strategy.* New York, 1982.

Lewytzkyi, Boris, and Juliusz Stroynowski, eds. *Who's Who in the Socialist Countries?* New York, 1978.

Linden, R. L. *Bear and Foxes: The International Relations of the East European States, 1945–1969.* New York, 1979.

McCauley, M., ed. *Communist Power in Europe, 1944–1949.* London, 1972.

Meiklejohn, Terry S., ed. *Soviet Policy in Eastern Europe.* New Haven, 1984.

Nato and the Warsaw Pact: force comparisons. Brussels, 1984.

Nelson, Daniel N., ed. *Soviet Allies: The Warsaw Pact and the Issue of Reliability.* Boulder, Col., 1984.

Nogee, J., and R. Donaldson. *Soviet Foreign Policy since World War II.* New York, 1981.

Oudenaren, John van. *The Soviet Union and Eastern Europe: Options for the 1980's and Beyond.* Santa Monica, Calif., 1984.

Potichny, P., and J. Schapiro, eds. *From the Cold War to Detente.* New York, 1976.

Raina, Peter. *Independent Social Movements in Poland.* London, 1981.

Rakowska-Harmstone, Theresa, et al. *Warsaw Pact: The Question of Cohesion.* 6 vols., Ottawa, 1984–86.

Remington, R. *The Warsaw Pact.* Cambridge, Mass., 1971.

Rice, C. *The Soviet Union and the Czechoslovak Army, 1948–1983: Uncertain Allegiance.* Princeton, 1984.

Rubinstein, Alvin Z. *Soviet Foreign Policy since World War II.* Cambridge, Mass, 1981.

Sik, O. *The Communist Power System.* New York, 1981.

Sodaro, Michael J., and Sharon L. Wolchik, eds. *Foreign and Domestic Policy in Eastern Europe in the 1980's: Trends and Prospects.* New York, 1983.

Staar, Richard I., ed. *Communist Regimes in Eastern Europe.* 4th ed., revised, Stanford, 1982.

———. *The Sovietalisation of a Captive People.* Westport, Conn., 1975.

Staniszkis, Jadwiga. *Poland's Self-Limiting revolution.* Princeton and New York, 1984.

Ulam, Adam. *Dangerous Relations: The Soviet Union in World Politics 1970–1982.* New York, 1983.

———. *Expansion and Coexistence: The History of Soviet Foreign Policy, 1917–1967.* New York, 1968.

Volgyes, Ivan. *The Political Reliability of the Warsaw Pact Armies: The Southern Tier.* Durham, N.C., 1982.

INDEX